Learning to Teach English in the Secondary School
2nd Edition

How do you approach teaching English in the modern classroom?

What is expected of a would-be English teacher?

This best-selling textbook combines theory and practice to present a broad introduction to the opportunities and challenges of teaching English in secondary school classrooms. Each chapter explains the background to current debates about teaching the subject, and provides tasks, teaching ideas and further reading to explore issues and ideas in relation to school experience.

Already a major text for most university teaching courses, this new edition has been thoroughly updated in the light of new legislation and includes fresh chapters on the National Literacy Strategy, Media and ICT. Other chapters suggest a broad range of approaches to teaching such crucial areas as:

- reading and writing, speaking and listening;
- drama, media studies and information technology;
- grammar, poetry, and language study;
- Shakespeare;
- post-16 English language and literature.

Written particularly with the new and student teacher in mind, this book offers principles and practical examples of teaching and learning in a twenty-first-century context as new notions of literacy compete with demands of national assessment. Taking these changing ideologies as a starting point, the text also addresses questions about the nature of teacher education. It raises issues concerning competence-based courses, working with a mentor in school and monitoring the development of a student teacher.

Jon Davison is currently Professor of Education and Head of the School of Education at the London Metropolitan University. **Jane Dowson** is Senior Lecturer in English at De Montfort University.

Related titles

Learning to Teach Subjects in the Secondary School Series

Series Editors
Susan Capel, Canterbury Christ Church College; Marilyn Leask, De Montfort University, Bedford; and Tony Turner, Institute of Education, University of London.

Designed for all students learning to teach in secondary schools, and particularly those on school-based initial teacher training courses, the books in this series complement *Learning to Teach in the Secondary School* and its companion, *Starting to Teach in the Secondary School*. Each book in the series applies underpinning theory and addresses practical issues to support students in school and in the training institution in learning how to teach a particular subject.

Learning to Teach Modern Foreign Languages in the Secondary School
Norbert Pachler and Kit Field

Learning to Teach History in the Secondary School
Terry Haydn, James Arthur and Martin Hunt

Learning to Teach Physical Education in the Secondary School
Susan Capel

Learning to Teach Science in the Secondary School
Tony Turner and Wendy DiMarco

Learning to Teach Mathematics in the Secondary School
Sue Johnston-Wilder, Peter Johnston-Wilder, David Pimm and John Westwell

Learning to Teach Art and Design in the Secondary School
Nicholas Addison and Lesley Burgess

Learning to Teach Geography in the Secondary School
David Lambert and David Balderstone

Learning to Teach Religious Education in the Secondary School
Andrew Wright and Ann-Marie Brandom

Learning to Teach English in the Secondary School
2nd Edition

A companion to school experience

Jon Davison and Jane Dowson

 RoutledgeFalmer
Taylor & Francis Group

LONDON AND NEW YORK

First published 2003 by RoutledgeFalmer
2 Park Square, Milton Park, Abingdon, Oxon, OX14 4RN

Simultaneously published in the USA and Canada
by RoutledgeFalmer
270 Madison Avenue, New York, NY 10016

RoutledgeFalmer is an imprint of the Taylor & Francis Group

© 2003 Jon Davison and Jane Dowson

Reprinted 2004, 2006 (twice)

Typeset in Bembo by Keystroke, Jacaranda Lodge, Wolverhampton
Printed and bound in Great Britain by TJ International Ltd, Padstow, Cornwall

British Library Cataloguing in Publication Data
A catalogue record for this book is available from the British Library

Library of Congress Cataloging in Publication Data
A catalog record for this book has been requested

ISBN 0–415–30676–0

Contents

Illustrations

FIGURES

TABLES

TASKS

Contributors

Elspeth and **Richard Bain** have both been heads of English in comprehensive schools. Elspeth is presently combining work as a freelance education consultant with lecturing on the PGCE course at Newcastle University. Richard is a former English adviser and is now headteacher of Hall Garth School, Middlesbrough. They wrote *The Grammar Book* (NATE, 1996), a revised edition of which is published in 2003.

Gabrielle Cliff Hodges is a lecturer in education at the University of Cambridge Faculty of Education, where she is secondary team leader and co-ordinates the secondary English and drama PGCE course, responsibilities she held previously at Homerton College, Cambridge. She was formerly head of English in a Cambridge-shire comprehensive school. From 1997 to 1998 she was Chair of the National Association for the Teaching of English. She is author of *Two Poems by John Keats* (NATE, 1998) and co-editor of *Tales, Teller and Texts* (Cassell, 2000). She has also published a number of chapters and articles on reading, writing and language in secondary English teaching.

Caroline Daly is a lecturer at the Institute of Education, London University, where she currently teaches on the PGCE secondary English course and has been involved in the initial and continuing education of teachers for seven years. She taught English in secondary schools for eleven years, five of them as a head of department. She has been involved in a range of professional development for new teachers, including training English teachers on Jersey and developing online and outreach distance courses for teachers both internationally and in the UK. Publications include work in the field of contemporary teacher education, gender difference in English and professional development.

Jon Davison is Professor of Education and Fellow of the Royal Society of Arts. Currently, he is head of the Department of Education at London Metropolitan University. Previously, he was Professor of Teacher Education at University College

Northampton and his research interests include sociolinguistics, citizenship education, personal and social education. He taught in London comprehensives for seventeen years. After working at the English and Media Centre, London, he has spent the past ten years working in teacher education. As well as publishing widely on the teaching and learning of English and media education, the other main areas of his research and publication are citizenship education and teacher education. His recent publications include *Subject Mentoring in the Secondary School* (Routledge, 1998), *Social Literacy, Citizenship and the National Curriculum* (RoutledgeFalmer, 2000), *Issues in Teaching English* (Routledge, 2000) and *Professional Values and Practices* (RoutledgeFalmer) 2003.

Jane Dowson is a senior lecturer in English at De Montfort University where she co-ordinated the PGCE and B.Ed. secondary English courses at the Bedford campus. She spent ten years teaching English in an upper school and was a member of the Northamptonshire and East Midlands Flexible Learning working parties. She was a member of the National Shakespeare in Schools Project 1992 to 1993, sponsored by RSA and RSC. She contributed chapters to *The School Curriculum to Learning to Teach in the Secondary School* (Routledge, 1995). Publications on women's poetry include *Women's Poetry of the 1930s: A Critical Anthology* (Routledge, 1995) and *Women, Modernism and British Poetry 1910–39* (Ashgate, 2002).

Peter Gilbert was educated for six years at Hull University and has taught English in an upper school in the East Midlands for twenty-five years. He is an experienced GCSE examiner and qualified verifier for GNVQ. Currently, he is deputy head of Sixth with a responsibility for the delivery of Key Skills, communication studies, ICT in English and general studies.

Rob McInnes is head of Media Studies at Forest Hill School, London. He has been an examiner for GCSE and A level Media Studies and English and is a qualified assessor trainer for GNVQ. He has run INSET in Media Studies and ICT and is a member of the British Film Institute's secondary teachers' advisory group. He has contributed to modules in the MA in Education at Goldsmiths College and his research interests include gender and homophobia, film and media literacy.

John Moss is head of secondary education at Canterbury Christ Church University College where he is responsible for a twelve-subject secondary PGCE programme. A former head of English, drama and Media Studies in a large comprehensive school, he has taught undergraduate English and drama at university level and secondary PGCE courses for ten years. He is co-author of *Subject Mentoring in the Secondary School* (Routledge, 1997), co-editor of *Issues in English Teaching* (Routledge, 2000) and series editor of series of books on citizenship in the secondary curriculum.

Veronica Raybould is currently assistant Head of English at Weavers School, Wellingborough. She has a particular interest in teaching and learning styles, especially with regard to the transition from GCSE to AS.

Elaine Scarratt is an experienced media teacher who has worked in several London schools. Formerly, she was head of media at Christ the King VI Form College. She is a freelance media adviser, teacher-trainer and writer. She delivers INSET for teachers, events for students and writes resources for use in the classroom. She is an associate tutor of the British Film Institute. Recent publications include *The Science Fiction Genre: A Teacher's Guide* (Auteur, 2001), and *The Science Fiction Genre: Classroom Resources* (Auteur, 2001).

Jo Westbrook is a senior lecturer in education at Canterbury Christ Church University College, and currently joint Programme Director of the PGCE Modular Programme. Previously she was a head of English and Media Studies at a London comprehensive, completing an MA on the use of the shared reader in the classroom. She then taught in Uganda for two years as an English teacher-trainer with VSO, undertaking gender and education work with other non-governmental organisations. At Canterbury Jo taught on the full-time English PGCE programme, and carried out research on the underachievement of pupils at Key Stage 3 in English for QCA before developing the new flexible route to PGCE in English. She has written distance learning materials for secondary English in collaboration with three other universities, to be published as *The Complete Guide to Becoming an English Teacher* by Paul Chapman in 2003. Her interests focus on what is read in the classroom, how, and by whom.

Acknowledgements

We would like to thank the series editors of *Learning to Teach Subjects in the Secondary School*, particularly Sue Capel and, at Routledge, Helen Fairlie for their guidance and support.

Permission to use materials has been granted as follows:

'GCSE '98: What's the Difference?' (*English and Media Magazine*, 34, summer 1996, pp. 21–26), by the English and Media Centre.

'GCSE English: The Background to the Current Concerns' (*NATE News*, spring 1994, p. 9), by NATE.

Permission to print 'The Writer', by Sujata Bhatt, from *Jumping Across Worlds* (Bhinda, ed., 1994, NATE), originally published in *Brunizem* (Bloom, Carcanet) has been given by Carcanet Press.

Permission to print 'Don' Go Ova Dere' by Valerie Bloom from *Duppy Jamboree* (Bloom, 1992, Cambridge University Press) has been given by Valerie Bloom and Cambridge University Press.

Permission to print 'Youth and Age' from *Catching the Spider* by John Mole (Mole, 1990, Blackie) has been given by John Mole.

'Skills', by Anne Stevenson, from *Four and a Half Dancing Men* (Stevenson, 1993, Oxford University Press) has been printed by permission of Oxford University Press.

'The Fair' by Vernon Scannell was taken from Vernon Scannell's *Selected Poems* (Allison and Busby) and has been reproduced by permission of the author.

Introduction to the series

The second edition of *Learning to Teach English in the Secondary School* is one of a series of books entitled *Learning to Teach Subjects in the Secondary School* covering most subjects in the secondary-school curriculum. The books in this series support and complement *Learning to Teach in the Secondary School: A Companion to School Experience, 3rd Edition* (Capel, Leask and Turner, 2001), which was first published in 1995. These books are designed for student teachers learning to teach on different types of initial teacher education courses and in different places. However, it is hoped that they will be equally useful to tutors and mentors in their work with student teachers. In 1996 a complementary book was published entitled *Starting to Teach in the Secondary School: A Companion for the Newly Qualified Teacher* (Capel, Leask and Turner, 1996). That second book was designed to support newly qualified teachers in their first post and covered aspects of teaching which are likely to be of concern in the first year of teaching.

The information in the subject books does not repeat that in *Learning to Teach*; rather, the content of that book is adapted and extended to address the needs of student teachers learning to teach a specific subject. In each of the subject books, therefore, reference is made to *Learning to Teach*, where appropriate. It is recommended that you have both books so that you can cross-reference when needed.

The positive feedback on *Learning to Teach*, particularly the way it has supported the learning of student teachers in their development into effective, reflective teachers, has encouraged us to retain the main features of that book in the subject series. Thus, the subject books are designed so that elements of appropriate theory introduce each behaviour or issue. Recent research into teaching and learning is incorporated into this. This material is interwoven with tasks designed to help you identify key features of the behaviour or issue and apply this to your own practice.

Although the basic content of each subject book is similar, each book is designed to address the unique nature of each subject. The second edition of *Learning to Teach English in the Secondary School* is a substantial revision of the first edition with many new or completely rewritten chapters. This edition retains the thrust of the earlier book, such as the centrality of language to learning and pupil development, and engages with the debates relating to culture and correctness.

We, as editors, have been pleased with the reception given to the first edition of this book and to the 'Learning to Teach' series as a whole. We hope that, whatever initial teacher education programme you are following and wherever you may be following that course, you find the second edition of this book supports your development towards becoming an effective, reflective teacher of English.

Susan Capel, Marilyn Leask and Tony Turner
May 2003

Introduction to the Second Edition

Jon Davison and Jane Dowson

The final paragraph of the Introduction to the first edition of this book begins: 'It is a truism that what is most up-to-date is quickly dated.' If a week in politics is a long time, four years in the teaching of English can seem aeons. Since we published the first edition of this book there have been:

- four Secretaries of State for Education;
- two new Circulars governing teacher education;
- the introduction of Skills Tests to achieve Qualified Teacher Status;
- a complete revision of the National Curriculum;
- the introduction of the National Literacy Strategy in primary schools and latterly at Key Stage 3;
- new GCSE requirements;
- the revision of A level into AS and A2 levels;

and as this edition goes to press a new discussion is beginning about complete changes to A level that may mean it becomes more like the baccalaureate. There would seem little point in attempting to justify the decision to publish a second edition.

While there have been many changes in the world of English teaching, the aim of the second edition remains the same as the first edition. Our aim is to promote a coherent approach to school experience that will help you to draw together and investigate what you read, what you have experienced during your own education, and your school experience as an English specialist. All chapters in the second edition of *Learning to Teach English in the Secondary School* have been revised to take account of the changes described above: some have been totally rewritten and we commissioned a completely new chapter on the National Literacy Strategy. You will find that the Introduction to the first edition will support you by offering ways in which this book might be used to help you to develop your knowledge skills and understanding of English teaching during school experience. More general approaches to school experience may be found in the companion volume *Learning to Teach in the Secondary School* (3rd edn) (Capel *et al.*, 2001).

We hope you will enjoy your school experience and that you find the book a helpful source of information and ideas. We welcome comments and feedback from student teachers, tutors and mentors.

Jon Davison and Jane Dowson
April 2003

Introduction to the First Edition

What is expected of a would-be teacher of English and what does the student teacher expect from a teacher education course? DES Circular 9/92 heralded the era of competence-based teacher education with a requirement for substantial elements of Initial Teacher Education (ITE) courses to be based in school. Two-thirds of secondary PGCE courses are spent in school; therefore, during those 120 days, much of the responsibility for the development of student teachers now rests with mentors working in partnership with Higher Education Institutions (HEIs). Therefore, much of the time on your course will be spent working with your mentor and departmental colleagues in school, not only to develop your classroom skills, but also to develop you in the widest sense as a subject specialist. In recent years, the terms 'reflection' and the development of the student teacher as a 'reflective practitioner' (Schön, 1983; Calderhead, 1989; Lucas, 1991; Rudduck, 1991) have become central to ITE programmes run by HEIs. Indeed, it would appear that the reflective practitioner is now 'the dominant model of professional in teacher education' (Whiting et al., 1996). The aim of this book, therefore, is to promote a coherent approach to school experience which will help you to draw together and investigate what you read, what you have experienced during your own education, and your school experience as an English specialist. More general approaches to school experience can be found in the companion volume *Learning to Teach in the Secondary School* (Capel et al. 1995).

Learning to Teach in the Secondary School is a valuable introduction to issues which concern every student and new teacher; *Learning to Teach English in the Secondary School* is complementary in looking at aspects like assessment or being a 'professional' in the context of becoming a subject specialist in English. The chapters introduce issues concerning the teaching of English which particularly relate to current developments such as competence-based and competence-assessed courses; working with a mentor; working with the National Curriculum; using IT in English lessons; understanding GNVQ. In addition, we are introducing aspects of English teaching which sound familiar, such as speaking and listening, reading, writing, and teaching Shakespeare.

How might you use this book? It is intended to be sufficiently flexible to suit different stages of initial teacher education and different contexts. It is assumed that the book can be read in its entirety as a course text and also be used as a reference book, particularly on school experience. For example, you may be teaching a scheme of work on poetry or be involved in assessing speaking and listening for the first time: you would then consult the relevant chapters for principles and ideas which would aid your planning and your evaluation of your lessons. Some tasks are more suited to your university or college sessions, and may be directed by the tutor; others are clearly school-based. It is unlikely that you will undertake all the tasks but you may wish to try some out on your own or with a partner. Above all, the tasks are designed to guide your thinking and enquiry about *why* teachers do what they do and *why* you will make the decisions that you do. What is important, however, is that you consider and apply the principles to your particular context.

In the following chapters, the point is made several times that, just as when you are teaching, aspects of English are integrated, so, although these chapters are separated into activities such as 'Writing', 'Drama' or 'Knowledge about language and grammar' for the purposes of investigation, it is recognised that they are all interdependent and interactive. You will be able to transfer principles raised in one area to their significance in another area; this is particularly true, of course, with media and information technology education.

It is usual for student teachers to begin a course with a fairly clear idea about what 'being an English teacher' is like; their reading and observations in school soon illustrate that there are many models of English teacher and that there are competing ideas about the aims of English teaching; they may be surprised to realise the extent to which English is perceived as 'political' by politicians, journalists and teachers. The lack of clarity and lack of consensus about the nature and aims of English teaching can be unsettling, but also exciting as the English teacher appreciates the significance of their role; because of the relationship between language and power, English teaching, which is based on a notion of literacy, is inherently political. As Burgess puts it, 'the connections between language, education and full participation in a political democracy have lain behind debates round English throughout two centuries' (Burgess, 1996, p. 67).

It is in the context of encouraging new teachers to participate in the debates about language, education and power that the first three chapters outline the 'battles' for English; they examine the changing ideas about the nature of English and their implications for the perceived roles of the English teacher. The background to current legislation demonstrates that a concept of what constitutes 'good practice' in English teaching is not fixed and never has been. English teachers may argue fiercely about whether to set their groups, whether drama should be used by all teachers, whether all pupils should take literature exams or how best to teach a child to spell or recognise a sentence.

Debates about the relative importance of grammar and spelling, language and literature, drama and media studies are long-standing and continuing. If you are coming to this book hoping for 'answers' you may be disappointed. We cannot reduce complicated processes concerning the relationship between language, thinking and identity into simple guidelines; we cannot resolve the questions about the proper nature of language study or how to teach someone to read or spell. These debates, along with 'what constitutes a text', and more precisely what constitutes a 'good text' or 'major author' are the bread and butter of English and cultural studies; these debates keep English as a dynamic subject which interacts with social trends.

The chapters consciously combine the critical issues surrounding each aspect of English teaching with ideas for classroom practice in order to encourage individual critical thinking. Many of the tasks are exploratory in nature and aim to provide opportunities to develop principles by which to make decisions concerning what and how to teach a text or an oral lesson or GCE A level; they are not offering blueprints. There are, however, some common approaches to the discussions and tasks; most significantly, there is a consensus that the job of the English teacher is to enable each child to become more literate. Although there is disagreement about what constitutes literacy, the current thinking is that we should speak of 'literacies' as incorporating the range of texts which people read; this version of literacy is not as radical as it might sound to conservative thinkers. The development of literacy has always been based upon available reading material; available reading material now encompasses all kinds of fiction and non-fiction, media and technological sources.

Many applicants to teacher education declare a love of 'literature', 'reading' or 'books' as their reason for wanting to teach English. Once on the course, they find themselves being asked to question the definition of 'book', the terms of describing a 'text' and the notion of reading. In schools they find that teaching a literary work is a small part of what English teachers do. The skills of critical analysis, however, which they have developed during their degree, are central to all areas of English teaching. *Learning to Teach English in the Secondary School* offers opportunities to work through the transition from previous engagement with English or cultural studies to the school curriculum; with its emphasis on 'critical practice', it suggests that it is not only possible but essential to retain a critical perspective on your reading and school experience, and on your model of initial teacher education. It is intended that, from an understanding of historical changes in the subject from the more remote and recent past, you will develop alternative ways of seeing the present conditions in education. We are also concerned that you will be a participant in setting the agenda for English teaching in the future.

It is a truism that what is most up-to-date is quickly dated. This is particularly applicable to the English curriculum which is subject to frequent changes in statutory requirements. We have had to make reference to current orders, particularly reference to the National Curriculum, but realise that these may change. At all times, it is acknowledged that it is the *principles* of suggested teaching ideas which are important and that these would have to be implemented with reference to current syllabuses and resources.

INTRODUCTION ... ARE YOU COMING FROM?

As you begin your secondary English ITE course, you will bring to it a perception of what English teaching is about which has been formed from a combination of the following: your own school experience of being taught English; your undergraduate studies in English, and perhaps other subjects; information you have gleaned from sources such as the Press, observation visits to schools, and conversations with teachers whom you know; and, in some cases, work experience which is related to your planned career, such as TEFL teaching or running a youth club drama group.

Any analysis you have undertaken of these experiences may have engaged you in thinking about one or more of three different approaches to defining what English is: the identity of English as an academic subject, its scope and limits; the effective teaching and learning of English in schools; and the English curriculum as it is defined by the National Curriculum and its assessment mechanisms.

If you were asked what English is during an undergraduate literature or language seminar, you would probably have concentrated on the first of these matters, and it is also likely that you would feel more confident about it than the others. You will therefore expect your ITE course to require you to explore ideas about the teaching and learning of English and the relationship between these ideas and the statutory curriculum. You may not realise at this point that these explorations are likely to challenge you to re-evaluate your understanding of what English as an academic subject is.

THE DIVERSITY OF ENGLISH

Your re-evaluation of English may well begin as soon as you meet the other members of your ITE English method group. You will find that the ideas of your fellow student teachers have been influenced by a wide range of different academic experiences of

OBJECTIVES

By the end of this chapter you should:

- be aware of the major versions of English available to you and their implications for your work;
- be aware of the complexity of the debates about English;
- be able to place your own past, present and future experiences of English in the context of these debates.

English. You may find, in a single ITE English group, student teachers who have experienced:

- A levels in English which explored English literature, the English language, or both, in varying combinations;
- chronologically structured English literature degrees, whose overarching questions and concerns were with the relationships between literary tradition and originality or issues of canonicity;
- degrees in English language which explored historical and geographical variations in English, and students learned to use sophisticated tools for analysing spoken and written language;
- degrees in English language and literature in which studying the history of the language and stylistics has given students a perception of the significance of language change and writers' language choices to the analysis of literature;
- degrees centred on current debates about the value of different kinds of literary theory and the ways in which they can inform reading practices, which have been explored by reference to a range of literary and non-literary texts;
- joint honours degrees in which the study of philosophy, history or art has given students particular perspectives on ways in which the study of literature can be enriched by a knowledge of one or more types of social, historical or cultural context;
- joint honours degrees in English and drama in which, among other things, students have experienced the value of practical drama methods in interpreting texts;
- joint honours degrees in English and education in which students have explored issues such as language development which have a direct bearing on the teaching they will undertake in school.

You may value highly the approaches to English you have experienced, or you may have developed a critical distance from them. In either case you will expect the school English curriculum to be underpinned by theoretical positions about the subject which you can compare with those which have influenced your own educational experiences to date. However, the variety of ideas about 'what English is' is represented in an ongoing debate about the school English curriculum which is complicated by further debates about how children learn.

The Cox Report views of English

The debates about English are particularly clearly illustrated by the problem that faced Brian Cox's committee when it was appointed to draw up the first National Curriculum for English in the late 1980s. The Cox Report's authors pointed out:

> Throughout our work we were acutely aware of the differing opinions that are held on a number of issues that lie at the heart of the English curriculum and its teaching. Our Report would not be credible if it did not acknowledge these differences and explain our response to them.
>
> (DES, 1989, para. 1.17)

Task 1.1 The educational purposes of English

Write a fifty-word statement defining the educational purposes of English as you understand them from your own educational experience at A level and/or degree level. Exchange your statement with another student teacher and write a fifty-word commentary on his or her statement. In a group discuss the statements and commentaries you have produced, identifying repeated words and ideas and any contradictions. Try to achieve a consensus statement, and consider the reasons for your ability or inability to do this.

The Report went on, famously, to define the different views of English which its writers found in the teaching profession:

> 2.21 A 'personal growth' view focuses on the child: it emphasises the relationship between language and learning in the individual child, and the role of literature in developing children's imaginative and aesthetic lives.

This view is associated with work undertaken in the 1960s on the need for a child-centred approach to learning in English, which permanently changed the subject. John Dixon's *Growth Through English*, first published in 1967, was a particularly influential book, which makes a strong case for the importance of activities such as creative writing, talk and improvised drama. The history of the National Curriculum and public examinations since this time confirms that these activities have become increasingly embedded in English, although other priorities in today's crowded curriculum may hamper teachers' attempts to give their pupils the space for imaginative and aesthetic development which Dixon envisaged.

> 2.22 A 'cross-curricular' view focuses on the school: it emphasises that all teachers (of English and of other subjects) have a responsibility to help

children with the language demands of different subjects on the school curriculum: otherwise areas of the curriculum may be closed to them.

This view is now promoted strongly by the National Literacy Strategy (NLS). As the Introduction to the *Framework for Teaching English: Years 7, 8 and 9* (DfEE, 2001) puts it: 'Language is the prime medium through which pupils learn and express themselves across the curriculum, and all teachers have a stake in effective literacy.' Although there are differences of emphasis and approach, the NLS may be regarded as the first systematic attempt to implement the recommendations on language across the curriculum of Chapter 12 of the Bullock Report, *A Language for Life* (DES, 1975) which was strongly influenced by the work of Barnes, Britton and Rosen (1969) in *Language, the Learner and the School*. In the 1970s many schools devised language across the curriculum policies in response to Bullock, but implementation was patchy.

> 2.23 An 'adult needs' view focuses on communication outside the school: it emphasises the responsibility of English teachers to prepare children for the language demands of adult life, including the workplace, in a fast-changing world. Children need to learn to deal with the day-to-day demands of spoken language and of print; they also need to be able to write clearly, appropriately and effectively.

This view is also promoted by the NLS: 'Effective literacy is the key to . . . equipping pupils with the skills and knowledge they need for life beyond school' (DfEE, 2001, p. 9). Cox's reference to a 'fast-changing world' implies that an adult needs view of English will also place considerable emphasis on ICT and the literacies involved in using new technologies. Another, richer, kind of adult needs view of English has been generated by recognition, in *The National Curriculum for England: Citizenship* (DfEE/QCA, 1999a), of the contribution which skills developed in English can make to a person's capacity for full participation in a democratic society. For example, the Citizenship programme of study includes, under 'Developing skills of participation and responsible action', 'Pupils should be taught to: think about topical political, spiritual, moral, social and cultural issues, problems and events by analysing information and its sources', and links this to reading requirements in the English curriculum.

> 2.24 A 'cultural heritage' view emphasises the responsibility of schools to lead children to an appreciation of those works of literature that have been widely regarded as amongst the finest in the language.

This view is associated with schools of literary criticism, which claim to be able to determine which books are most worth reading. A leading figure in the history of the idea of cultural heritage is F. R. Leavis, who, for example, in his book on the novel, *The Great Tradition* (1948), argued that the great novelists can be identified as those who are 'distinguished by a vital capacity for experience, a kind of reverent openness before life, and a marked moral intensity'. The ongoing influence of the cultural heritage view of English is stated explicitly in the current *National Curriculum for England: English* (DfEE/QCA, 1999b):

English literary heritage
2. Pupils should be taught:
how and why texts have been influential and significant
the characteristics of texts that are considered to be of high quality
the appeal and importance of these texts over time

2.25 A 'cultural analysis' view emphasises the role of English in helping
children towards a critical understanding of the world and cultural
environment in which they live. Children should know about the processes
by which meanings are conveyed, and about the ways in which print and
other media carry values.

This view is associated with forms of criticism which acknowledge that the interactions among writers, readers and texts are influenced by a range of social, cultural
and historical factors. Holders of the cultural analysis view may believe that the
investigation of these interactions in relation to any text – literary or non-literary, print
or non-print, written or spoken – is potentially of equal value, since the value of any
text is not absolute but culturally determined. Without quite taking this position,
public examination criteria for English literature have been modified in recent years
to take more account of the cultural analysis view of English. At GCSE, for example,
'candidates are required to demonstrate their ability to . . . relate texts to their social,
cultural and historical contexts and literary traditions' (QCA, 2001). The ways in
which English can draw on a range of kinds of critical theory are increasingly recognised
and have been explored by many commentators (see e.g. Moss, 2000).
    These views of English have been the subject of much discussion and research, both
by those who have attempted to find out to what extent each view is represented in
the teaching profession (e.g. Goodwyn, 1992), and by those who have questioned the
validity of the categories or their definitions, or suggested other ways of defining
viewpoints in the debate about what English is (e.g. Marshall, 2000). You may be
particularly interested in a contribution to this debate, made shortly after the Cox
Report was published, by a group of student teachers (see Daly *et al.* 1989). The
historical context of the debate among views of English which Cox identified is
explored further in Chapters 2 and 3.

CONSENSUS OR COMPROMISE?

What has become most clear from this debate is that many teachers cannot accept the
position which Cox took, that the different views 'are not sharply distinguishable, and
. . . certainly not mutually exclusive' (para. 2.20). Reading between the lines of the
definitions of the 'cultural heritage' view and the 'cultural analysis' view, for example,
it is not difficult to find a sharp distinction between the 'appreciation of those works
of literature that have been widely regarded as amongst the finest', and 'critical understanding of the . . . cultural environment' (paras 2.24–2.25). The distinction is between
being taught a taste for what a particular group in society, whose identity is hidden by
the passive construction, wishes to have culturally transmitted, and learning to make

an active analytical response to all the signs and sign systems of the cultural products available to that analysis.

You may find this distinction reflected in positions held in your ITE English group, which may include those whose ambition as teachers is 'to pass on' something (e.g. a love of a particular kind of literature), and those who seek 'to change' something, perhaps their pupils' sense of their own power to influence the development of society. Daly *et al.* provide an important statement of one version of the second position: 'we must develop goals, classroom approaches and materials which will transform "English" into the study of how and why our entire culture is produced, sustained, challenged, remade' (1989, p. 16). The distinction between 'cultural heritage' and 'cultural analysis' is both profound and political. Cox produced a compromise rather than a consensus English curriculum, perhaps in an attempt to steer a course between the Scylla and Charybdis of extreme views. However, his report still provides the most comprehensive, relatively recent official rationale for English.

Later in this chapter, you will be asked to consider where the *National Curriculum for England: English* is placed in the 'Which English?' debate. However, it will be useful for you to explore this new curriculum with knowledge of two particularly coherent curriculum documents with clearly identified rationales for the models of English they promote.

Critical literacy in practice

One particularly valuable attempt at achieving a coherent radical vision of English which nevertheless acknowledges the complexity of the arguments about it may be found in West and Dickey's *Redbridge High School English Department Handbook* (1990). This book draws on a range of ideas about language, learning and literacy to formulate a theoretical position which might drive the work of a secondary English department in a typical urban high school: a multifaceted statement of departmental philosophy introduces detailed suggestions for teaching. A key text for the authors is Freire's *Literacy: Reading the Word and the World* (1987) from which they derive a view of English as 'critical literacy': English is concerned with the processes of language and with all aspects of the making of meaning. Its business is the production, reproduction and critical interpretation of texts, both verbal and visual, spoken and written.

> Its aim is to help [pupils] achieve critical literacy. To do this it seeks to:
> * enable [pupils] to make meaning
> * develop their understanding of the processes whereby meanings are made
> * develop [pupils'] understanding of the processes whereby meanings conflict and change.
>
> (West and Dickey, 1990, pp. 10, 23)

The authors note that this definition is intended to encompass 'aspects of Media Education and Drama that are undertaken by the English department'. They state that they see the definition as building on Cox's description of 'cultural analysis' by emphasising the social dimension of literacy: in a democratic society, pupils have the right to *make* and *contest* meanings as well as to understand how they are made. This definition of critical literacy informs the practical details of the schemes of work suggested in the book, and, in doing so, illustrates how the way teachers think about what English is influences their planning models and classroom practice.

Whether or not your vision for English is the same as West and Dickey's, it is vital for your practice to be similarly principled: you need to learn how your conception of what English is can inform all the decisions you make about content, lesson structure and sequence, teaching and learning objectives and assessment strategies.

All of West and Dickey's schemes of work include sections headed: starting point, exploration, reshaping, presentation and opportunities for reflection/evaluation. For example, in a unit of work called 'Introduction to media education' pupils work on a photographic project. Among other things, the pupils are asked to:

- start by discussing the statement: 'The Camera Never Lies . . .' and by creating a display about this idea;
- explore a range of magazine photographs in a sequence of work which draws attention to issues of authorship, intention, technique and representation;
- 'reshape' a collection of photographs of their school which they take themselves into sets of six frame sequences, some negative, some positive, some balanced;
- present a selection of the photographs to an audience either within the class or outside it;
- reflect on the presentations in oral and written responses which may cover issues such as: the way the project has affected their view of the school; their understanding of the relationship between selectivity and representation.

(Selected and adapted from West and Dickey, 1990, pp. 151–152)

This unit of work shows how pupils who are studying the ways in which texts (here, primarily visual texts) are created, can extend their learning in important ways by participating in the processes by which similar texts are shaped and reshaped. Above all, pupils following this unit of work will learn about the power of makers of texts to make meaning consciously, deliberately and persuasively, and to contest meanings constructed by other makers of texts.

For readers who would like to explore the possibilities of critical literacy further, an account of radical critical literacy in practice may be found in *None But our Words: Critical Literacy in Classroom and Community* (Searle, 1998). Lankshear's chapter 'Critical social literacy for the classroom: An approach using conventional texts across the curriculum' (Lankshear, 1997) has a self-explanatory title.

LINC'S FUNCTIONAL MODEL OF LANGUAGE

While learning about and through textual construction is at the heart of the model of critical literacy proposed by West and Dickey, their definition begins by identifying 'the processes of language' as the primary concern of English. The unpublished materials produced by the Language in the National Curriculum (LINC) project offered a model of language which could provide a coherent rationale for the English curriculum, and which complements West and Dickey's work through its comparable emphasis on meaning-making. The authors of the materials see their work as an attempt to form a synthesis of the language theories of Britton and Halliday. Britton's importance is that his work, centred in language in education, 'clearly demonstrated the centrality of context, purpose and audience in language use [and is] grounded in fundamental consideration of the relationship between language and thought'. Halliday's work complemented this by offering 'functional theories of language [which] placed meaning at the centre' (LINC, 1992, p. 2). The authors define the theories of language implicit in the materials as follows:

1   As humans we use language primarily for social reasons, and for a multiplicity of purposes.
2   Language is dynamic. It varies from one context to another and from one set of users to another. Language also changes over time.
3   Language embodies social and cultural values and also carries meanings related to each user's unique identity.
4   Language reveals and conceals much about human relationships. There are intimate connections, for example, between language and social power, language and culture and language and gender.
5   Language is a system and is systematically organised.
6   Meanings created in and through language can constrain us as well as liberate us. Language users must constantly negotiate and renegotiate meanings.

(LINC, 1992, pp. 1–2)

The practical implications of the LINC view of language for teaching are best indicated in *Knowledge about Language and the Curriculum: The LINC Reader* (Carter, 1990). In particular, George Keith, in Chapter 4, outlines a scheme of work for Key Stage 3 which any English department could usefully consider using as the basis of a coherent and systematic approach to language teaching. The integrity of the scheme of work derives from the centrality accorded to work on language and society and the investigation of talk. The following practical suggestions for exploring this topic demonstrate how the LINC theories of language recorded above can be translated into schemes of work:

• using questionnaires and interviews to find out information about people's attitudes, beliefs, opinions: *vox populi* – getting people talking (will involve reflection on method of enquiry as well as on content of data);
• 'they don't speak our language' – enquiries into occupational dialects;
• jargon; officialese; slang; codes; accents; Received Pronunciation; talking 'posh'; talking 'dead common'; regional stereotypes and foreign accent stereotypes – use BBC tapes, *English with an Accent, English Dialects*;
• 'the language of situations' (pragmatics) – having an argument; being questioned or interviewed; threatening, bullying; embarrassing situations;
• euphemisms and taboo subjects in conversation;

Task 1.2 Views of English in the classroom

Observe three English lessons at your placement school with the intention of determining what view of English is being communicated to pupils or constructed by them. Make notes on matters such as: the choice of material; statements made by the teacher about the purpose of the work; the kinds of questions the teacher asks; the sequence of activities pupils engage in. You may find evidence of more than one view of English in a single lesson, or that one teacher teaches lessons which seem to offer very different views of English on the same day. Discuss your findings with the teachers and/or your fellow student teachers.

- ways people talk to each other (gender, age, social class, social power);
- the speech of young children as a source of knowledge about language.

(Carter, 1990, pp. 90–91)

A version of English bringing together the concerns of critical literacy and the LINC project's approach to language teaching could have a coherent rationale encompassing the exploration of meaning-making in texts and language. The LINC project and its materials are discussed further in Chapter 2.

ENGLISH IN THE NATIONAL CURRICULUM (2000)

As Cox points out in his book *Cox on Cox* (1991), it was against his wishes that his Report was published with the chapters (1–14) which detail its rationale *following* those (15–17) which defined what became the statutory English curriculum in *English in the National Curriculum* (DES, 1990). The Orders did not include this rationale at all, but at least teachers could turn to the report to help them understand the thinking behind the requirements placed upon them.

In the next version of the National Curriculum, *English in the National Curriculum* (DFE, 1995), two pages of General Requirements offer the only overview of English, and this is more concerned with stressing the importance of standard English than offering a rationale for the whole English curriculum. Moreover, this curriculum statement was a heavily redrafted revision of earlier documents, in which meaning was lost as the result of unacknowledged battles between various interest groups to control the definition of the curriculum.

There is only scope in this chapter to illustrate this point with one small example, so a statement about a particularly controversial issue, the place of Standard English in the curriculum, has been chosen. According to *English in the National Curriculum* (DFE, 1995):

The richness of dialects and other languages can make an important contribution to pupils' knowledge and understanding of standard English.

(DFE, 1995, p. 2, para. 2)

The first thing to notice about this sentence is that it is ungrammatical. It needs to be prefaced by 'Learning about . . .' or 'Experience of . . .' to make sense. Second, the sentence makes the nonsensical and linguistically imperialistic claim that the main purpose and value of learning about other forms of language is to inform an understanding of standard English. We can expose the battle for control of the curriculum that was taking place by finding the equivalent sentence in *English in the National Curriculum: Draft Proposals, May 1994*, the consultation document produced as a first draft of the 1995 Orders:

> The richness of other languages and dialects can make an important contribution to pupils' knowledge and understanding of language.
> (SCAA, 1994, p. 1, para. 4)

This sentence has nothing to do with standard English, and makes a much more logical statement about the relationship between the study of examples of kinds of language and the development of an understanding of language principles.

In view of the mutilation of the Cox Report in the 1990 Orders and the garbled guidance of the 1995 Orders, it should perhaps not surprise us that the rationale for *The National Curriculum for England: English* (DfEE/QCA, 1999b) is very thin. In a short statement headed 'The importance of English' (p. 14), traces of the debate in Cox can be detected, but in a watered-down and neutralised form, so that the tensions among different views have been dissolved in an apparently seamless consensus, the origins of which cannot be determined.

Curriculum 2000 statement	View of English suggested
English is a vital way of communicating in school	cross-curricular view
in public life and internationally	adult needs view, with a nod to globalisation
Literature in English is rich and influential	cultural heritage view, although 'Literature in English' means something broader than 'English Literature'
reflecting the experience of people from many countries and times	perhaps a cultural analysis view, and also reflecting the Curriculum 2000's concern with inclusion
In studying English pupils develop skills in speaking, listening, reading and writing	perhaps a 'basic skills' adult needs view
It enables them to express themselves creatively and imaginatively	personal growth view
and to communicate with others effectively	adult needs view
Pupils learn to become enthusiastic [readers]	personal growth view, but research evidence might challenge this assertion

and critical readers	cultural heritage or cultural analysis view: it depends what kind of critical reading is meant
of stories, poetry and drama	cultural heritage literary texts prioritised
as well as non-fiction and media texts	cultural analysis view that all texts have value then acknowledged
The study of English helps pupils understand how language works by looking at its patterns, structures and origins	a hint of LINC language learning objectives, although 'looking at' sounds rather distant from meaning-making and not exactly rigorous either
Using this knowledge pupils can choose and adapt what they say and write in different situations	a hint of the empowerment promoted by critical literacy

The brevity of this statement makes a startling contrast with Cox's fourteen chapters, but also with the comparative richness of Curriculum 2000's rationale for the curriculum as a whole, especially its detailed statements about inclusion, and point-by-point analysis of the methodology needed to ensure that the principles of inclusion are represented in practice. Is the implication that the Cox compromise has become so much the orthodoxy that it does not even need to be acknowledged as such?

The answer to this question is that, in the proliferation of official documentation which now underpins the teaching of English in schools, the debate continues. There is only space in this chapter to consider two examples, so NLS documentation, which has a strong influence on the English curriculum at Key Stage 3, and the Qualification and Curriculum Authority's (QCA) national requirements for GCSE examinations, which are equally influential at Key Stage 4, have been chosen.

The NLS *Framework for Teaching English: Years 7, 8 and 9* does have a section entitled 'Rationale' including a statement about literacy:

> The notion of literacy embedded in the objectives is much more than simply the acquisition of 'basic skills' which is sometimes implied by the word: it encompasses the ability to recognise, understand and manipulate the conventions of language, and develop pupils' ability to use language imaginatively and flexibly. The Framework also encompasses speaking and listening to support English teachers in planning to meet the full demands of the National Curriculum, and to tie in the development of oral skills with parallel demands in written text.
>
> (DfEE, 2001, pp. 9–10)

What is striking here includes:

- the clear statement that literacy goes beyond the 'basic skills' which may meet a narrow definition of adult needs, but lack of clarity about what this additional value of literacy is;

- the hint of pupil ownership of language, which might be linked to a view of English based in critical literacy, in the suggestion that pupils should learn to 'manipulate' language and use it 'flexibly';
- the hint of a recognition of personal growth in the word 'imaginatively' – but the lack of any sense of a deep understanding of the connections between speaking and listening, reading and writing in the curiously bolted-on sentence about speaking and listening (it is also interesting that the term 'oracy', which has given speaking and listening more weight in recent years has not been used);
- the distant hint of the LINC project's view of language in the recognition of pupils' needs to recognise and understand the conventions of language as a means of informing their use of them;
- the absence of any sign of the cultural heritage or cultural analysis views of English: no attempt has been made to suggest how the NLS project's vision of literacy informs decisions about what will be read and why. (However, the NLS objectives for reading are more in tune with cultural analysis than cultural heritage.)

Something that has been implied in this chapter to date, but not yet explicitly stated, is that the question 'Which English?' increasingly involves further questions including: 'English and/or literacy?' and 'Which literacy (or literacies)?' The NLS emphasis on a cross-curricular and adult needs view of literacy is prioritising these components of the Cox compromise.

The rationale for English at Key Stage 4 in QCA's 'GCSE criteria for English and English literature' (QCA, 2001) is worthy of note because of its influence on all work at this key stage. For example, the criteria for English literature provide an indication of the current state of the debate between the cultural heritage and cultural analysis views of English. The course specification requirements include the statement that: 'The works studied must be of sufficient substance and quality to merit serious consideration.' Since some adherents of a cultural analysis view would maintain that any text merits serious consideration, the continuing strength of the cultural heritage position seems clear. The requirements also state that a specification must 'require assessment of candidates' understanding of literary tradition, and appreciation of social and historical influences and cultural contexts'. Although 'appreciation' does not suggest the kind of interrogation some cultural analysts would call for, this statement does invite teachers to use approaches to texts derived from cultural analysis more strongly than has been the case previously.

However, neither the NLS rationale nor QCA's criteria has the coherence of the LINC materials or West and Dickey's interpretation of critical literacy. Each new official curriculum document shifts the balance among the components of the Cox compromise. The implications of this situation for you as a student teacher are serious. You need to define a rationale for your teaching, however provisionally, in order to set the learning objectives of any lesson. It will be helpful for you to discover where the tutors responsible for your ITE course and the teachers in your placement schools stand in relation to the various debates which have been identified above. Some of the questions you should ask tutors, heads of English departments and mentors include the following:

- Does your English teaching aim to reflect the complexity of the debates about what English and literacy are, or to reflect a particular view of what English and/or literacy are?
- How are your aims interpreted at the practical levels of planning, teaching, assessment and evaluation?
- Do you expect me to teach as if I share your aims in my teaching?
- How do you reconcile your aims with the demands of national assessment requirements such as those of the SATs and the learning objectives in GCSE and A Level specifications?
- In what ways does the National Curriculum inform your practice and how should it influence mine?
- In what other official curriculum documents are there statements which strongly influence your work?
- How as a student teacher can I experiment to begin to formulate and implement my own views of English?

Task 1.3 Exploring language debates in official documents

Identify a language issue, such as multilingualism, drafting, dialect, discourse structure, grammar, literary English, language variety, spoken standard English. Either on your own or in a group of student teachers, find and compare statements about this issue in *English for Ages 5 to 16* (1989); *Language in the National Curriculum: Materials for Professional Development* (1992), *English in the National Curriculum* (1995), *The National Curriculum for England: English* (1999), the NLS *Framework For teaching English: Years 7, 8 and 9* (2001), and QCA National *GCSE Criteria for English and English Literature* (2001). What similarities and differences, emphases and omissions do you notice in the documents? Where does *The National Curriculum for England: English* stand on this issue in relation to ongoing debates about language represented in the documents collectively?

FUTURES

So far, this chapter has asked you to consider ideas about English which are derived from your own educational experience, from recently formulated but established views of the subject, and from debates which have contributed to the introduction and revision of the National Curriculum. The last part of the chapter will focus on some developments which are currently transforming teachers' perceptions of what school curriculum English is or can be. Three central threads in these developments concern: ideas about the importance of genre and rhetoric; the impact of new technologies on speaking, reading and writing and the relationships between them; and the regionalisation and globalisation of English.

Postmodern textuality: genre and rhetoric

One way in which the 'personal growth' and 'cultural analysis' views of English may form a new synthesis is through an adjustment of the ideas about the self which are associated with the former, in the light of ideas about genre and rhetoric which are associated with the latter. The discussion of 'critical literacy' earlier in this chapter drew attention to the value of examining the ways in which meanings are constructed in texts. Pupils who are to be politically empowered by the English curriculum need to understand both how different genres work and how to select and adapt the genre which is most appropriate to their purpose when they seek to use spoken or written texts to exert influence on society. This understanding must be based partly on consideration of the conventions used in different genres. Some of these conventions are major and structural, but others operate at the level of syntax and vocabulary. For example, science fiction often translates familiar social and ethical problems to unfamiliar narrative contexts, but also makes use of specialised vocabulary to define the technological capabilities of its characters.

The art of rhetoric was concerned historically with using language to exert influence, or to persuade, and in particular with the careful selection of figures of speech, the arrangement of language features in a spoken or written text, and with oratorical delivery. It offers us insights into the constructedness of texts at the level of language detail, and promotes the view that effective oral communication is founded on technique rather than on personality traits. Thinking about rhetoric and genre together can help us to see that the composition of a text in a particular genre and using particular rhetorical devices has something of the nature of a scientific experiment about it, since it involves throwing one of a number of available frameworks over reality. It may even suggest that meaning exists only in the constructs of different generic and rhetorical procedures. Another way of putting this is to say that rhetoric and genre provide the kind of real or imaginary theatrical masks which actors use to establish character and to make the communication of dramatic meaning possible.

This view of textual construction has something in common with postmodern views of the fragmentation and constructedness of the self, which in some versions would suggest that the self is identifiable and definable only in terms of the language or conventions through which it is expressed at particular times. Personal growth may then be about the taking on of new selves *through* the taking on of new rhetorical and generic conventions. Teaching in a way which draws attention to rhetoric and genre may then make an important contribution to the personal growth of those who experience it. In practical terms this may mean placing greater emphasis on allowing pupils to experiment with the conventions of genres, by providing them with opportunities for parody, to transpose texts from one genre to another, and to create new genres or texts which, like a considerable number of postmodern 'literary' texts, make use of a number of different genres.

Literacies and new technologies

New technologies are having an accelerating impact on our understanding of what it is to be literate, and how literacy is achieved. As noted above, *The National Curriculum for England: English* (1999b) includes the statement that 'In English pupils develop skills in speaking, listening, reading and writing'. It is widely recognised that a fifth term 'viewing' needs to be inserted into this list of processes, to reflect the media literacy which plays such an important role in pupils' lives and their language development. However, we must now also acknowledge the relevance to language development of the Internet, CD-ROMs, multimedia texts, hypertext and e-mail, and that these technologies challenge the ways in which we understand both the individual processes of reading, writing, speaking and listening, and the relationships between them.

For example, reading texts on computers, and especially Web pages with hyperlinks, draws attention to the multidimensionality of reading, which has never been so apparent before. We know that we are not obliged just to read in a sequential way across and down a two-dimensional page, but nor are we limited to exploring the two-dimensional architecture of that page as we do when, for example, we look at a footnote. Reading a Website is more like playing three-dimensional chess: one move through a hyperlink can completely redirect our attention, and even if we do choose to return to our earlier preoccupations it may be with an entirely new perspective on them. This experience modifies our understanding of what reading is. Some other experiences of using the Internet challenge our conceptions of the boundaries between the different language processes. For example, chat rooms on which ephemeral comments about a topic can be recorded and responded to, and which are periodically cleared by whoever maintains the site, are redefining the boundaries between speech and writing.

New technologies can also cause us to rethink our positions in relation to the established views of English discussed earlier in this chapter. For example, the Internet may affect the extent to which we tend towards 'cultural heritage' or 'cultural analysis' views. It is making available a wide range of texts which it was previously difficult to access. A substantial number of pre-twentieth-century literary texts by women which are out of print are available on the Internet. This makes it much easier than before to demonstrate that the male white literary canon promoted in the 'cultural heritage' view of English is a construct. For some time, word processing has made texts available to readers in many different states and drafts in a way which shows us that meanings are not fixed.

The discussion of the drafting of the 1995 National Curriculum illustrates how access to such drafts can affect our understanding of the material with which we are presented, and allow us to recognise how the possibility of shifting meaning in particular directions is related to power. The easy links between pages and sites on the Internet make readers very aware of the intertextual context of texts, and draw attention to the ways in which many apparently coherent and complete texts both contain gaps and draw, in different ways, on the work of a multiplicity of authors. Indeed, readers using the Internet have to learn to recognise and accommodate the fact that what they experience as a single reading event consists of texts produced by many different authors. These processes promote modes of reading which are linked with the 'cultural analysis' view of English.

Regionalisation and globalisation

While all versions of the National Curriculum for English have maintained the importance of standard English, students of language are gaining more access to other systematic, rule-governed and dynamic versions of English than has ever been available before. Academic studies have long drawn attention to differences such as those between American standard English and English standard English to explode the myth that there is one standard English which should be developed and used for global communication, and they have also demonstrated the systematic, rule-governed character of all dialects. However, in the past ten years, recognition of the value of regional and international varieties of English in the media, in film and in literature has reoriented the way many readers of visual and printed texts perceive their relationship to speakers and writers who use dialects other than those with which they are most familiar. We place more value on the global diversity of Englishes than on the dominance of one English, and recognise that the high status accorded to particular versions of English has been culturally determined.

In this context, one important word-level shift in the latest version of the National Curriculum is that the category of texts previously described as 'texts from other cultures' has now been properly retitled 'Texts from different cultures and traditions' (p. 34). Statements about the relationship between standard English and other forms of English have also been modified, to acknowledge, for example, that other varieties of English have their own grammar: 'Pupils should be taught about how language varies, including: . . . the vocabulary and grammar of standard English and dialectical variation' (p. 32). However, there is still some distance to travel before it is acknowledged that a rich perception of the language heritage of English may be that our own version of English, whatever that may be, exists as one variety of a language which twenty-first-century communications technology makes globally available alongside many others.

Task 1.4 The textual representation of the diversity of English

What all three sections of the preceding discussion of 'futures' for English have in common is a sense of a need to develop approaches to teaching which promote and celebrate diversity and flexibility in language use, a moving in and out of and between genres, language modes, texts and/or cultural perspectives.

Find a literary or non-literary text or group of texts in which the writer or producer encourages the reader or viewer to experience shifts in meaning or a multiplicity of meanings, and write a commentary in which you either describe your response to the material or suggest ways in which you could use it in the classroom.

SUMMARY AND KEY POINTS

The claims that can be made for the possible effect of centring teaching on the developments in English discussed in the final part of this chapter may be large or small. There is no doubt that developments in each area are giving teachers new insights into literacy and into the ways in which language works. However, it is important to remain cautious about the extent to which any of these developments will transform the educational experience or lives of pupils. Centring the writing curriculum on genre and rhetoric will not in itself give pupils access to the audiences they need to begin to influence society; battles are currently taking place to achieve structural control of the Internet which may limit the access to it of many less privileged groups in global culture; there are questions to ask about the domination of global language culture by particular Englishes and by Englishes collectively.

Many of the formulations of English discussed in this chapter may be interpreted as serving the interests of particular privileged groups rather than as genuinely offering pupils the empowerment which can be stated as at least one justification for even those versions of English which may now strike us as most reactionary. As you begin your development as an English teacher, one question which you should keep firmly at the centre of your thinking, despite the temptation to abandon it which may result from your having to address more immediate issues, concerns your pupils more than English. What futures do you imagine for them, and how can your English teaching contribute to their development towards those futures?

FURTHER READING

Brief discussions of the current directions of English teaching may be found in *English in Education* (2000) 34 (1), a volume of the journal devoted to 'English in the New Millennium'. See also 'Beliefs about English', *English in Education* (1995) 29 (3), by Robin Peel and Sandra Hargreaves, and a collection of short articles by various authors grouped under the heading 'The future of English' (1996) in the *English and Media Magazine*, 34, pp. 4–20.

Writing the Future: English and the Making of a Culture of Innovation (NATE, 1995) by Gunther Kress challenges us to develop a curriculum for English to meet the needs of the social individual in the twenty-first century.

Issues in English Teaching (Routledge, 2000) edited by Jon Davison and John Moss is a collection of essays by various authors which invites further exploration of many of the issues raised in this chapter and elsewhere in this book.

Redesigning English: New Texts, New Identities by S. Goodman and D. Graddol, and *Learning English: Development and Diversity* edited by N. Mercer and J. Swann (both Routledge, 1997) consider respectively what kind of language English is becoming globally, and the issues involved in teaching English. They are part of an excellent series supporting an Open University course on the English language.

2 Battles for English

Jon Davison

> English is a subject suitable for women and the second- and third-rate men who are to become schoolmasters.
>
> (Professor Sanday 1893)

INTRODUCTION

Because of the way in which English literature is often presented as a body of historical texts, there is a notion that English as a subject spreads back into the mists of time. English as a recognisable school subject has existed since only the beginning of the twentieth century and the category of English literature as we know it is little more than a hundred years old (Gossman 1981, p. 341). The Oxford School of English was not established until 1894 in the face of strong opposition from the Classicists as the

---

Task 2.1
Why English?

Before you read any further, answer this question:

> *Why should it be mandatory for every child in this country to study English in school as part of a core of the National Curriculum?*

Either by yourself or with a partner, brainstorm all the reasons you would give for studying English. Then list your reasons in order of importance. If possible, discuss them with another student teacher/pair and be prepared to justify your list and the relative importance of your reasons. Then as you read this chapter, look for the connections between your reasons and the reasons others have given during the last hundred years.

quotation which opens this chapter indicates (Palmer 1965, pp. 104–117). Nevertheless, within the last century the centrality of English to the education of children was recognised and the subject now exists as part of the 'core' of the National Curriculum. However, the progress from new to established subject was not a smooth journey and, at times, the conflicting beliefs about the nature and purpose of English caused fierce debate, not least during the late 1980s when there were two national reports on the teaching of English: Kingman and Cox. The National Curriculum Order for English, produced in 1990, was revised in 1993, 1994 and 1999. This chapter explores the roots of the views about English teaching that underpinned the recent debates.

OBJECTIVES

By the end of this chapter you should:

- have some knowledge of the key reports which determined the shape of English as a subject;
- be aware of philosophies and attitudes to culture and social class which underpinned the establishment of English on the curriculum;
- understand the importance to the subject that has been placed upon the literary 'canon';
- be aware of the reasons why notions of 'correctness' have been seen as central to English;
- begin to understand that different and conflicting paradigms of English teaching have existed;
- become aware of the philosophies which underpinned the ways in which you were taught English;
- have some knowledge of the development of the National Curriculum;
- begin to understand that different and conflicting paradigms of English have influenced the National Curriculum for English.

THE NINETEENTH CENTURY

Before the turn of the last century, English did not exist as a separate school subject (Ball 1985, p. 53). It was not until 1904 that the Board of Education *Regulations* required all elementary and secondary schools to offer courses in English language and literature. The reasons for the subject's inclusion in the curriculum of state schools were not necessarily ones that teachers today might deem educational. Indeed, some commentators (e.g. Eagleton 1983, p. 23ff.) believe that the need for state education and the importance of English was 'advocated in a hard-headed way as a means of social control' (Gossman 1981, p. 82). There is not space in a chapter of this length fully to detail the growth of the subject; however, the main strands of development are worth exploration as many of the earlier beliefs and opinions about the subject can be found to underpin much of what happens in the name of English today. Although the Cox Report notes that 'views about English teaching have changed in the last twenty years and will continue to do so' (DES 1989, para. 2.4), it is possible to trace the differing views of English teaching back to the origins of state education in this England.

With the growth of Victorian technology there was a need for a workforce trained 'in terms of future adult work': a workforce comprising adults who could read simple instructions; understand verbal commands; give and receive information and who exhibited 'habits of regularity, "self discipline", obedience and trained effort' (Williams 1961, p. 62). Broadly, this utilitarian approach to education was dealt with in terms of 'Reading' and 'Writing' lessons. Later the Board of Education *Elementary Code* (1904, p. viii) averred that teachers should give pupils:

> some power over language as an instrument of thought and expression, and while making them conscious of the limitations of their own knowledge, to develop in them [*such*] a taste for good reading and thoughtful study . . . to implant in the children habits of industry, self control and courageous perseverance in the face of difficulties.

For Matthew Arnold, poet and HMI, writing in 1871, English literature was 'the greatest power available in education'. Arnold was much influenced in his thinking by Wordsworth. As a child he spent holidays in the cottage neighbouring the poet's own cottage and, as he grew up, he developed a belief in the power of poetry to act as 'an excellent social cement' (Eagleton 1983, p. 23). In the Preface to his *Lyrical Ballads* (1800), Wordsworth argues:

> Poetry is the first and last of all knowledge – it is as immortal as the heart of man. . . . The Poet binds together by passion and knowledge the vast empire of human society, as it is spread over the whole earth, and over all time.

Elsewhere, in *A Defense of Poetry* (1840) Shelley regards poetry as 'something divine', because 'it is not like reasoning. . . . It is as it were the interpretation of a diviner nature through our own.' To inhabit the realm of literature is to somehow transcend the quotidian; to be at one with a diviner nature; to be at one with the 'vast empire of human society'. That its nature could not be debated, rather its truths could only be 'felt' or 'experienced' is significant, because this view gave rise to the development of poetry 'appreciation' rather than 'criticism' in the school curriculum for much of the first half of the twentieth century. As Palmer (1965, p. 39) puts it: 'The main emphasis in the moral evangelical approach to literature is upon reading, upon the value of making contact with the great imaginations of the past.'

ENGLISH AND THE BOARD OF EDUCATION

> The present is an age of educational reform. The methods of teaching most of the subjects in the curriculum have undergone considerable changes and been vastly improved, during the last decade.
>
> (Roberts and Barter 1908, p. 1)

Good taste vs. slang

The reader might be forgiven for thinking that this quotation from *The Teaching of English* had been written in the 1990s. However, the first twenty years of the twentieth century saw an outpouring of publications from the Board of Education that attempted to define and structure the curriculum in elementary and secondary schools. Board of Education *Circular 753* was instrumental in establishing the nature of English as it came to be in school. It shows clearly the underlying philosophies mentioned earlier:

> instruction in English in the secondary school aims at training the mind to appreciate English Literature and at cultivating the power of using the English Language in speech and writing. . . . Literature supplies the enlarged vocabulary which is the mechanism of enlarged thought, and for want of which people fall helplessly back on slang, the base coin of the language. Pure English is not merely an accomplishment, but an index to and a formative influence over character.
>
> (1910, para. 2)

Clearly, the approach is a high cultural, pure-English-as-civilising-agent approach advocated in the previous century by Matthew Arnold. The *Circular* envisages its own literary canon: a body of great literary works to which pupils need to be introduced. Pupils 'should be taught to understand, not to criticise or judge' the great works (ibid., para. 36). Texts recommended include *Hiawatha, Ancient Mariner, Robinson Crusoe, Stories of Heroes, Patriotic Songs, Gulliver's Travels,* and the poetic works of Milton, Gray, Coleridge, Tennyson and Wordsworth. There is an obvious lack of Dickens, or any other novelist, who might venture into the realms of social realism; but stories of courage distanced in the realms of Romanticism were quite acceptable. Maybin (1996, p. 236) reminds us that canonical texts have always been important not only because they are regarded as the backbone of English literature, but also in relation to the definition of standard English. In compiling his English dictionary, Samuel Johnson based it upon the books he regarded as illustrating 'authoritative uses and meanings in the language'. Similarly, histories of English languages in the nineteenth century focused upon the written works that were believed to be most important rather than the spoken word. The importance of literature in relation to its 'divine' nature; in relation to notions of correctness and Standard English, and the subordinate status of the spoken word, fundamentally determined the nature of English in school throughout the twentieth century.

The unsuitability of novels

Startlingly perhaps for teachers today, the *Circular* has this to say: 'Novels, indeed, though occasionally points for discussion, are rarely suitable for reading in school' (para. 34) and 'Boys and girls will read of their own accord many books – chiefly fiction. These . . . are only of transitory interest, and involve little or no mental effort' (para. 17). How different from the current National Curriculum's 'During Key Stages

3 and 4 pupils read a wide range of texts independently, both for pleasure and for study. They become enthusiastic, discriminating and responsive readers, understanding layers of meaning, and appreciating what they read on a critical level' (DFE/QCA, 1999b, p. 34).

Part of the explanation for the *Circular*'s antipathy to novels lies in the growth of mass production. For at least twenty years, novels had been widely and cheaply available. A further explanation of this hostility to popular culture lies in the view of high culture that underpins *Circular 753*: 'the real teachers of Literature are the great writers themselves . . . the greater the work, the more it speaks for itself' (para. 21). Such an attitude to the difference between literary language and the spoken language of working-class children and the negative effects of popular culture is also in evidence in the Newbolt Report (BoE 1921, par. 59):

> The great difficulty of teachers in elementary schools in many districts is
> that they have to fight against evil habits of speech contracted in home and
> street. The teacher's struggle is thus not with ignorance but with a
> perverted power.

The document displays a clear attitude to children from the working class, who in their culture of 'home and street' are believed to threaten established norms, not through ignorance but by virtue of a 'perverted power'. Part of this power was no doubt located within developing popular culture. Therefore, the best thing an English teacher can do for a pupil is '. . . to keep him from the danger of the catchword and everyday claptrap' (BoE 1921, para. 81); 'to teach all pupils who either speak a definite dialect or whose speech is disfigured by vulgarisms, to speak Standard English' (para. 67) – there is no acknowledgement that standard English is, in itself, a dialect.

Task 2.2 Correctness and character

Look back over this chapter so far. Examine the language of the educational policy makers. Alone, or with a partner answer the following questions:

- What recurring connotations do you notice in the language (e.g. the adjectives) used to describe the working class and children's spoken language? What attitudes does such language display?
- How important do you believe standard English is in written work?
- How important do you believe standard English is in speaking?
- Can great literature be inspirational and an influence over the formation of character?
- Can/should English teaching be used as a form of *social engineering*?

How do the reasons given in these early documents for the importance of studying English compare with your reasons produced in Task 2.1?

THE NEWBOLT REPORT

> The most formidable institution we had to fight in Germany was not the arsenals of the Krupps or the yards in which they turned out submarines, but the schools of Germany. . . . An educated man is a better worker, a more formidable warrior, and a better citizen.
>
> (Lloyd George 1918)

Play up! and play the game!

It is significant that the first major evaluation of education after the First World War was carried out into *The Teaching of English in England* (BoE 1921) by what came to be known as the Newbolt Committee. The constitution of the Committee bears analysis, for its composition undoubtedly shaped the approach to English that underpinned not only the Report, but also the teaching of English for the following thirty years. Sir Henry Newbolt chaired the Committee. Oxford educated and Professor of Poetry from 1911 to 1921, Newbolt is, perhaps, now best remembered for his poem *Vitae Lampada*, which details the virtues of self-sacrifice for one's country and contains the refrain: 'Play up! play up! and play the game!' Other Oxford men on the Committee were John Bailey, F. S. Boas and Professor C. H. Firth, while from Cambridge came Sir Arthur Quiller-Couch and John Dover Wilson (critic and HMI). Other notable members included Professor Caroline Spurgeon, best known for her exhaustive work on Shakespeare's imagery, J. H. Fowler of *English Usage* fame and George Sampson, author of *English for the English*. With such luminaries on a committee of fourteen members, it is not surprising that notions of correctness, cultural heritage and a belief in the humanising nature of literature should hold sway.

The Committee discovered that, in schools, 'English was often regarded as being inferior in importance, hardly worthy of any substantial place in the curriculum' (par. 6); while in boys' schools the study of English was 'almost entirely neglected' (para. 106). More worrying to the Committee was the attitude of the working class,

> especially those belonging to organised labour movements, [who] were antagonistic to, and contemptuous of literature . . . a subject to be despised by really virile men . . . to be classed by a large number of thinking working men with antimacassars, fish-knives and other unintelligible and futile trivialities of 'middle-class culture' and 'to side-track the working movement'.
>
> (para. 233)

Although the Report is lengthy (393 pages) it is 'seldom positive in its proposals' (Palmer 1965, p. 82). Like all reports produced by a committee it is, on occasion, contradictory. English is asserted to be the 'basis of school life' (para. 61) and the Report coins a phrase which still has currency: 'every teacher is a teacher of English, because every teacher is a teacher in English' (para. 64). However, in a contradictory paragraph it notes that good English teaching 'demands skill and resource, [and] is too often thought a task which any teacher can perform' (para. 116).

Changing methodologies

Although the Report's central philosophy mirrors earlier Board of Education publications, its approach to methodology is different. The Report is critical of the approaches advocated in *Circular 753*. It deplores that there was often 'Too much emphasis on grammar and punctuation, spelling' (para. 79). Paragraph 81 lists eleven 'positive methods' for the improvement of English lessons. While most are fairly standard and had been proposed earlier – 'listening'; 'using the dictionary'; 'summarising' – three recommendations appear surprising:

> (g)   proposals from the children about the choice of subjects; class discussions, dramatic work;
> (h)   preparation in advance of the subject matter of composition . . .
> (k)   free and friendly criticism by the scholars of each other's work.
>
> All agree in emphasising the value of oral exercises.
>
> (BoE 1921, para. 81)

Such methodology would not seem out of place in an English department today. However, in the 1920s it is obvious that factors such as class size would have militated against the adoption of these recommendations, in the same way it did against the Report's belief in the value of discussion between small 'groups of children' (para. 74). It is clear that within its short existence as a curriculum subject, what we now believe to be 'traditional' methods were the backbone of English teaching, while the more progressive recommendations would not be adopted for approximately fifty years.

THE 1930s

For the authors of the Spens Report, hope lay in the great tradition and the values and higher moral code espoused by the great writers: 'it involves the submission of the pupil to the influences of the great tradition; it is his endeavour to learn to do fine things in a fine way' (BoE 1938, p. 161). The study of literature was believed to exercise 'a wide influence upon the life and outlook of the adolescent, more general and long lasting in its effects than that normally exercised by any other subject in the curriculum' (p. 218). Teachers 'may yet succeed in making the normal citizen of this country conscious and proud of his unequalled literary heritage' (p. 228). Here again we are presented with a view of culture as complete: a legacy, an heirloom, which, having been cherished, is to be handed down to the next generation. Presumably, any citizen not 'conscious and proud of his unequalled literary heritage' is perforce 'abnormal'.

More worrying for some was the standard of spoken English, which was seen (or heard?) as 'slovenly, ungrammatical, and often incomprehensible to a stranger' (p. 220), but which the 'common habit of English teaching' (p. 222) would cure. The textbook *Good and Bad English* (Whitten and Whittaker 1938, pp. 69–71) mirrors this attitude throughout: for example, 'NEVER – *never* – write "alright". It is all wrong (not alwrong), and it stamps a person who uses it as uneducated.' Similar attitudes may be found in the April 1993 draft proposals for National Curriculum *English 5–16* (DES 1993a) in its regular restatement that, from Key Stage 1 pupils 'should speak clearly using Standard English' and 'should be taught to speak accurately, precisely, and with clear diction'. The draft proposals include a variety of 'Examples': 'We were (not was) late back from the trip'; 'We won (not winned) at cricket'; 'Pass me those (not them) books'; 'Clive and I (not me) are going to Wembley'; 'We haven't seen anybody (not nobody)' (pp. 9–23).

If high culture was to be the saviour of working-class children, the Spens Report, like earlier documents, knew where to lay the blame for their slovenly language:

> Teachers everywhere are tackling this problem [debased forms of English] though they are not to be envied in their struggle against the natural conservatism of childhood allied to the popularisation of the infectious accents of Hollywood. The pervading influences of the hoarding, the cinema, and a large section of the public press, are (in this respect as in others) subtly corrupting the taste and habits of the rising generation.
>
> (BoE 1938, pp. 222–223)

The burgeoning mass media, like some virulent disease ('infectious'), were portrayed as corrupting a whole generation. As in earlier documents, the language of disease, corruption and perversion links the mass media and the working class. Popular culture was seen as a threat because pupils needed no introduction to it – it was the stuff of their lives – whereas they needed to be 'brought into the presence' of great writers who would civilise them.

LEAVIS

> English students in England today are 'Leavisites' whether they know it or not.
>
> (Eagleton 1983, p. 31)

The Great Tradition and *Practical Criticism*

Arguably, the major influence upon the development of teaching English literature in this country was the launch of the critical journal *Scrutiny* in 1932 and the development of the 'Cambridge School' of English. Central to Leavisite critical theory is the notion of 'close reading' or 'practical criticism' (Richards 1929) of texts, whereby the critic deals with 'an individual's work rather than a writer's achievements as a whole' (Daiches 1956, p. 299). Unlike the vagaries of the Romantic appreciation promoted by Arnold and his descendants, which culminated in the Board of Education promoting a love of greatness in literature without judgement, practical criticism is 'unafraid to take the text apart' (Eagleton 1983, p. 43). For F. R. Leavis, texts would be analysed in relation to the literary standards exemplified in the canon of great literature. It is this method which has come to be at the very core of the teaching of English literature in universities and schools. However, while Leavis's methodology may have differed from Newbolt's and Arnold's, his philosophy was strikingly similar. The Leavisite canon included *inter alia* Chaucer, Shakespeare, Jonson, Bunyan, Pope, Blake, Wordsworth, Keats, Austen and George Eliot. To be included in the canon a text had to 'display particular kinds of moral, aesthetic and "English" qualities which would arm readers against the moral, aesthetic and commercial degeneration of the age' (Maybin 1996, p. 245). It is clear that the belief in the humanising effects of great literature, produced in some past golden age, is central to the Leavisite view.

However, the Norwood Report (BoE 1943), *Curriculum and Examinations in Secondary Schools*, not only criticises the notion of close reading but also reaffirms the power of literature proposed by Arnold and Newbolt. Paragraph 93 of the Report argues that 'too much attention has been paid to aspects [of great literature] which are of secondary importance and the higher values have been obscured.' It asserts that these values are 'final and absolute: they cannot be broken down into constituent parts: they are beyond analysis and wait upon the appreciative powers of the pupil.' The paragraph concludes that the teaching of English literature is concerned with that 'which is past analysis or explanation, and values which must be caught rather than taught'.

To sum up, in all educational documentation relating to the study of English which was produced before the Second World War, it is possible to identify a number of recurring themes. First, there is a belief that it is possible to identify a number of works from the past that stand the test of time because they exhibit certain values and qualities which are universal. Second, a conviction that such works have a humanising effect on the lower classes and are therefore an aid to social stability. Third, pupils should be taught to appreciate great literature, not to criticise it. Fourth, the spoken and written language of working-class children is of extremely low quality. Fifth, the exposure of pupils to 'fine writing' will enable them to write and speak standard English. Sixth, popular culture should be seen as a corrupting influence and an enemy to high culture.

ENGLISH TEACHING POSTWAR

If the Oxford and Cambridge Schools were instrumental in shaping the 'English as literature' paradigm of the subject prior to the Second World War, arguably the most influential institution postwar has been the University of London Institute of Education (formerly the London Day Training College). Foremost among those associated with the Institute who helped to shape the teaching of English in the second half of the twentieth century were Britton, Barnes, Rosen and Martin. While the Cambridge School, for the most part, addressed itself to the teaching of the subject in grammar schools, the 'London School' was more associated with the spread of comprehensive education in the 1950s and 1960s. The difference between London and Cambridge in Britton's words was the difference 'between *using* the mother tongue and *studying* it' (Britton 1973, p. 18). Ball (1985, p. 68) characterises the London approach as the 'English as language' paradigm of English teaching. Key texts that have underpinned the development of this paradigm are, among others, *Language and Learning* (Britton 1970); *From Communication to Curriculum* (Barnes 1976); and *Language, the Learner and the School* (Barnes *et al.* 1975). Since the 1950s it is clear that both paradigms of English teaching have held sway, often to be found in the differing approaches of members of the same English department.

If societal influences in Victorian times and in the 1920s and 1930s may be seen in some ways to have shaped the foundations of English teaching, the same may be said of the 1960s and 1970s. These two decades saw not only massive changes technologically in the 1960s and an economic recession in the 1970s, but also radical changes in relation to state education. The Certificate of Secondary Education (CSE) English was introduced. It ran alongside O level courses; but whereas O level English examinations comprised 'Composition', 'Comprehension', 'Précis', 'Grammar/Vocabulary exercises', CSE was much less formal. Similarly, while O level English literature syllabuses focused, in the main, on writers drawn from the canon, CSE texts were more likely to be written by contemporary authors. Furthermore, the introduction of CSE Mode 3 examinations – set and marked by teachers in school – and up to 100 per cent coursework elements were regarded as 'soft options' open to cheating by those who favoured the traditional 'terminal' O level examination. Elsewhere, the restructuring of the teaching profession, changes in teacher education, the spread of comprehensive schooling, the Raising of the School Leaving Age (RoSLA), the work of the Schools Council, all contributed to the conditions for curricular change.

However, the emergence of a language-based model of English teaching that was not necessarily focused upon 'traditional' notions of grammatical correctness; of a model that some characterised as being in direct opposition to the 'traditional' literature-based model, caused genuine tensions – not only within English departments but also in society at large. Subsequently, the publication of the *Black Papers*; concerns over 'falling standards' and 'progressive child-centred' education; the perceived threat to the Eleven-plus and grammar schools through comprehensive schooling, led to the establishment of another enquiry into all aspects of English teaching, chaired by Sir Alan Bullock.

A Language for Life

It is clear that the Bullock Report gathered evidence of a variety of practices in schools which were both 'traditional' and 'progressive'. *A Language for Life* (DES 1975) concludes: 'The time has come to raise language as a high priority in the complex life of the secondary school.' The Report condemns the study of grammar in isolation, but asserts the traditional role of the teacher when it maintains the importance of teacher intervention in pupils' work. Both paradigms of English teaching – 'as language' and 'as literature' – are reinforced positively.

ENGLISH FROM 5 TO 16

Secretary of State Sir Keith Joseph's speech to the North of England Education Conference on 6 January 1984 outlined the government's intention to 'raise standards' through a move towards the establishment of agreed criteria for subjects and their assessment, which would lay the foundations of a national curriculum. His speech was

Task 2.3 How were you taught English

Think back to your own school days. How were you taught English? What emphasis was placed upon the study of English literature? Which texts were studied? How were they chosen? What part did 'appreciation' or 'criticism' play? What room was there for enjoyment? Did the teaching of grammar take place? Was this done in isolation, or in relation to literature, or your own writing? What emphasis was placed upon standard English in writing and speaking? What strategies did your teachers use when correcting your work? What emphasis was placed upon discussion? Which paradigm of English do you feel characterised the way you were taught the subject? Did different teachers exemplify different models of the subject?

If possible, share your experiences with another student teacher. You might wish to discuss with your mentor, or another member of the English department in your placement school, the ways in which he or she was taught English and whether it has affected the beliefs they hold about the subject.

followed swiftly by a series of HMI discussion documents 'intended as a contribution to the process of developing general agreement about curricular aims and objectives' (HMI 1984b, p. 54). Significantly, *The Curriculum from 5 to 16* (HMI 1984b) was the second document in the series, the first being *English from 5 to 16* (HMI 1984a). English as a subject was still considered of special importance to HMI and policy-makers alike.

HMI recognised that *English from 5 to 16* 'was the most controversial publication in an HMI series' (HMI 1986, p. 18). The document listed a number of age-related objectives for pupil development in the areas of Listening, Speaking, Reading, Writing and 'About language' – nomenclature developed, perhaps, to avoid the heated 'grammar' debate. The document contains all the beliefs about the purposes and nature of the subject described previously: 'Speak clearly, audibly and pleasantly, in an accent intelligible to the listener(s)' (HMI 1984a, p. 10). Similarly, the seeds of National Curriculum English are also being sown: 'Have experienced some literature and drama of high quality, not limited to the twentieth century, including Shakespeare' and 'Read newspapers, magazines and advertising material critically . . . apply similar judgments to entertainment in other media – theatre, cinema or video films, television and radio' (p. 11).

Responses to the document were heated, and many respondents expressed themselves in 'matters of belief, principle and practice which were close to their hearts' (HMI 1986, p. 1). Responses were collated and discussed in *English from 5 to 16: The Responses to Curriculum Matters 1* (HMI 1986). This report shows respondents to be 'anxious or angry' (p. 5) about the proposals in the earlier publication. Because the earlier document had been such a mixture of approaches to the subject both 'traditional' and 'progressive' all parties felt dissatisfied (p. 7). Elsewhere, 'There were widespread expressions of support for increased attention to the spoken word (speaking and listening)' (p. 18). Of course, those who responded to *Curriculum Matters 1* were a self-selecting group and may in no way be truly representative of the views of English teachers as a whole. Although many respondents were groups – schools, LEAs, HEIs and representative bodies – only 913 responses were received in total.

Within the paper's 'Conclusions' HMI consider:

> It may be that a concentrated and thorough public discussion of the issues is needed; perhaps even a national enquiry is required to focus opinion and guide policy formation about what should be taught about our language and what needs to be known by teachers and pupils.
>
> (p. 19)

Within six months a Committee of Enquiry into the Teaching of English Language had been announced.

Task 2.4 Principles of English teaching

Obtain copies of *English from 5 to 16* (HMI, 1984) and *English from 5 to 16: The Responses to Curriculum Matters 1* (HMI, 1986).
   First, examine 'Some Principles of English Teaching' (pp 13 – 16) in *Curriculum Matters 1*. You may wish to discuss this section of the document with another student teacher or your mentor/tutor. What reservations or questions would you wish to raise with HMI about the beliefs expressed here? Second, read 'Matters Arising' (pp 10 – 18) in *The Responses* document. How far are your own views represented in this section? Keep any notes you make and use them in any work you undertake on National Curriculum English or which asks you to give an account of your own beliefs about the purposes of teaching English.

THE KINGMAN REPORT

Secretary of State for Education Kenneth Baker announced the formation of the Kingman Committee which was to 'recommend benchmarks for what children should know about how the language works at ages 11 and 16' (*Independent*, 17 January 1987). He lamented the fact that schools no longer taught grammar and that little had been put in its place. Significantly, the first of the terms of reference for the Committee was:

> 1. To recommend a model of the English language, whether spoken or written, which would:
> i) Serve as the basis of how teachers are trained to understand how the English language works.
>
> (DES 1988a, p. 73)

This statement signalled the government's intention to control teacher education more tightly, particularly in the area of English. *The Report of the Committee of Enquiry into the Teaching of English Language* (DES 1988a) was published in March the following year and some readers were not heartened by the fact that its opening line was a quotation from the Newbolt Report (BoE 1921). However, there was equal concern expressed in some quarters that the Report did not recommend a return to the formal teaching of grammar. For the purposes of this chapter it is worth noting that the Report did, indeed, make recommendations for the teaching of knowledge about language in teacher education programmes. Thus it gave birth to the ill-fated Language in the National Curriculum (LINC) project which was set up to develop training materials to improve learning about language.

LANGUAGE IN THE NATIONAL CURRICULUM

The LINC project (1989 to 1992) was just one of three major projects (The National Writing project (1985 to 1989) and the National Oracy project (1987 to 1993)) related to the teaching of English. The LINC project, however, was controlled directly by the DES, because the Kingman Report had 'failed to deliver the two simple, linked nostrums expected of it: that the most important thing teachers need to know about language concerns the grammar of sentences; and that children come to command language by being taught the grammar of sentences in advance' (Richmond 1992, p. 14).

Because the project's teaching package still did not deliver the required approach to grammar, the government not only refused to publish it, but they maintained Crown copyright on the materials – thereby preventing anyone from publishing them. Nevertheless, it is estimated (Richmond 1992, p. 17) that at least 20,000 photocopied packages of the materials were in schools, LEAs and HEIs in 1992. It may be that the department in which you are working has a copy. The ban on the materials provoked certain sections of the Press to new heights of vitriol about progressive teaching methods in English. An ill-informed article, which referred to the LINK project throughout, in the *Daily Telegraph* (28 June 1992), is typical of the reaction:

> And although the DES will not publish the document, it is being distributed to teacher training institutions, where its voodoo theories about the nature of language will appeal to the impressionable mind of the young woman with low A-levels in 'soft' subjects who, statistically speaking, is the typical student in these establishments.

Ouch!

ENGLISH IN THE NATIONAL CURRICULUM

National Curriculum English is a little over a decade old. Since its inception it has gone through three revisions. Chapter 3, 'Working with the National Curriculum', considers the changes to it after 1995 and explores the current English Order. The remainder of this chapter gives an account of the foundations of the National Curriculum English and the tensions that arose from the diametrically opposed versions of English outlined above. (For a full account of the introduction of the National Curriculum, see *Learning to Teach in the Secondary School 3rd Edition* (Capel *et al.* 2001).)

Section B of the Cox Curriculum introduced the concept of Programmes of Study into Practice subdivided into the Attainment Targets of: Speaking and Listening; Reading; Writing; Spelling, handwriting and presentation. It was prefaced, however, with the recognition that although the curriculum had to be divided up for the purposes of assessment, in practice the aspects were integrated:

> The profile components are inter-related. For example, group discussion may precede and follow individual writing; writing may be collaborative; and listening to stories is often a preparation for reading. . . . Because of the inter-relationship between the language modes, in good classroom practice the programmes of study will necessarily and rightly be integrated.
>
> (DES and WO 1989).[1]

Other general guidance points were that teachers should plan to provide opportunities for pupils to use language in increasingly challenging ways, to take account of pupils' interests and maturity, and that the subsequent sections were illustrations of 'breadth and progression'. For example, the 'Requirement for Speaking and Listening' was as follows:

> **KS3 Breadth:** A wider range of contexts requiring individual contributions will be expected. Pupils should have opportunities for taking responsibility, such as making notes, or presenting findings on the group's behalf. In addition to a developing sensitivity to others, children take more formal individual roles such as giving a talk, or leading a group activity. They develop understanding of appropriate uses of varieties of English and of the social implications of inappropriate usage.
>
> **Progression:** Children show increasing confidence and fluency, taking leading and discerning roles in discussion, encouraging others and responding with understanding and appreciation. They show rigour in their use of argument and evidence and take effective account of audience.

The 'Implications for Teacher and Learning' were:

> At KS3 the teacher will need to help children extend their thinking and to reflect on their contribution. Activities will need to be increasingly varied, for example, the devising and production of drama where children make decisions, allocate responsibilities, conduct the rehearsal, present and evaluate it, giving reasons for their choice of setting, characterisation and event. In planning a poetry anthology, the children could discuss possible themes and layout, evaluate their reading and writing together, and use the anthology with their chosen audience to evaluate its success. Listening to different examples of dialect poetry, constructing them and devising and recording their own, will develop understanding of forms.
>
> (NCC 1990, B2, B3)

---

1   Material from the National Curriculum is Crown copyright and is reproduced by permission of the Controller of HMSO.

These examples illustrate the ways in which the English Orders built upon common good practice in English teaching; they gave practical illustrations which teachers found helpful and could adapt to their own contexts. They demonstrated ways in which the attainment targets are interrelated while identifying a specific focus for assessment. They stressed the importance of pupil progression through increasingly challenging tasks and the importance of developing language skills, including standard English where appropriate, while appreciating language differences such as dialect.

The 'Requirements of Reading' were similarly in tune with teacher philosophy and practice of combining cultural heritage with cultural analysis. At Key Stage 3 it required pupils to have the opportunity to read in a variety of ways and a variety of texts; these included 'literature which is more distant in time from the pupils' immediate experience' and 'information texts of a highly specific kind', 'so that pupils could become versed in the interpretation of T.V., radio and the mass media'. At Key Stage 4 it stated that the range of texts 'will be largely determined by the level of difficulty which is appropriate'; the curriculum should include pre-twentieth-century writing, Shakespeare and reference material of all kinds, as well as media texts.

Again, the requirements specified what was meant by 'broad and balanced' while allowing teachers to judge what was appropriate and to choose which pre-twentieth-century, Shakespeare and media texts should be studied. In the 'Implications', a 'wide range of writers' was emphasised in order to extend pupils' awareness of cultural contexts and their language competence. There was a balance between the historical significance of texts and the importance of engaging with contemporary forms of information and reading.

Range and variety were also central to the Programmes of Study for KS3 Writing. The aim was to equip pupils to write in a variety of situations with a variety of purposes. At Key Stage 3 they should be 'using more complex grammatical structures and more varied vocabulary', and at Key Stage 4 they should be able to 'understand stylistic effects' and be involved in evaluating the success of their writing. To this end, reciprocal learning was recommended: 'The development of collaborative writing and of the pupils as critical readers of each other's work will help understanding of layout, spelling and punctuation and grammar and the craft of writing' (B6 and B7).

The 'Requirement for Spelling, Handwriting (levels 1 – 4) and Presentation (levels 1 – 7)' gave constructive guidelines. For example, with spelling, it laid out that 'A variety of techniques help children to master spelling conventions'. These included:

- reading with the teacher and referring to print such as captions and lists in the classroom;
- composing stories and poems and discussing the spelling of words and their patterns;
- grouping words and looking for common letter clusters in books and magazines;
- encouraging the development of visual memory;
- encouraging children to identify a word.

The Cox National Curriculum Order was influential upon the acceptance and implementation of Schemes of Work that correlated to the programmes of Study and clarified assessment objectives. It defined their nature and purpose:

> A scheme of work is a written practical guide to teaching and describes the work planned for pupils in a class or group over a specific period. It is an essential part of the school's responsibility. The scheme of work will include elements unique to English and will show where English work supports and is integrated with other subjects.
>
> (1.1., C.1.)

- Furthermore, it advised that overall planning to implement the National Curriculum in English involves recognising and taking account of: the core and other foundation subjects of the National Curriculum; cross-curricular elements; the school's National Curriculum development plan; and equal opportunities for all pupils.

There was a section on 'Bilingual Children' which gave guidance about building upon and creating opportunities for using their first language while providing access to the curriculum and an enhancement of their learning of English (2.9 – 2.14, C2–3). The first point under 'Organisation and Planning' was that 'Planning will need to be flexible in order to recognise the needs of individual children and to ensure progression, differentiation and relevance' (3.1, C4). There followed example tables of curriculum planning, and more detailed guidelines for preparing a scheme of work and reviewing resources. These guidelines were the framework within which English departments adapted their syllabuses.

There were clear statements about the distinctive values of literature, language, media education, drama, information technology and information retrieval. Each section was prefaced by a quotation, mostly from the Cox Report, which, informed by research and experience, had worked through the issues of cultural change and of value in teaching knowledge about language and texts. The following statements are reproduced because they summarise the position of teachers concerning the respective areas of study.

Literature:

> An active involvement with literature enables pupils to share the experience of others. They will encounter and come to understand a wide range of feelings and relationships by entering vicariously the worlds of others, and in consequence they are likely to understand more of themselves.
>
> (DES and WO 1990, 1.0, D1)

Language:

> Knowledge about Language would be an integral part of work in English, not a separate body of knowledge to be added on to the traditional English curriculum.
>
> (DES and WO 1990, 2.0, D7)

Drama:

> Drama is not simply a subject, but also a method, a learning tool.
> Furthermore, it is one of the key ways in which children can gain
> understanding of themselves and of others. . . . Planning for Drama in the
> classroom requires a clear understanding of its nature and the contribution
> it can make to children's learning. Drama is not simply confined to one
> strand in the Statements of Attainment which ceases after level 6. It is
> central in developing all major aspects of English.
>
> (DES and WO 1990, 3.0, D11)

Media education:

> It aims to develop systematically children's critical and creative powers
> through analysis and production of media artefacts.
>
> (DES and WO 1990, 4.0, D16)

Information technology:

> English teachers have much to contribute to children's familiarity with this
> technology and its uses, alongside the major aim of exploring it to promote
> language knowledge and skills in themselves.
>
> (DES and WO 1990, 5.0, D21)

Information retrieval:

The section on information retrieval suggested ways in which the following statement
could be implemented:

> Good schools foster positive attitudes towards books and literature,
> encouraging pupils to become attentive listeners and reflective readers,
> library members both in and out of school, and book owners.
>
> (DES and WO 1990, 6.0, D22)

Although there was some disagreement about the emphasis on individual development
in terms of personal relationships rather than of cultural identities, teachers were won
over by the tone of the guidelines which respected their professional judgement while
giving a clear rationale and useful examples. Even the guidelines on assessment were
clear and acceptable.

Assessment:

> The assessment process should not determine what is to be taught and
> learned. It should be the servant, not the master of the curriculum. Yet it
> should not simply be a bolt-on addition at the end. Rather it should be an
> integral part of the educational process, providing both 'feedback' and
> 'feedforward'.
>
> (DES 1988b, 1.0, E1)

Section E, 'Gathering Evidence of Achievements', was informed by TGAT's advice that 'assessment should be integral to the curriculum'. It offered guidance about how it could be incorporated into everyday teaching. '*The guidance is by no means definitive, nor is it a requirement.* Teachers will want to adopt approaches to the gathering of evidence about their pupils' attainments which suit their own teaching style and which, at the end of the key stage, enable them to form a sound judgement of the level of each pupil's attainments in relation to the statutory attainment targets' (1.1, E1). The fact that the phrase '*by no means definitive*' was in italics emphasised the respect for a teacher's judgement.

Generally, teachers were in sympathy with the Cox curriculum and were provided with time in order to rewrite their syllabuses in a way which accorded with the guidelines. Many departments found that this exercise was useful to their own professional development and in moderating their own practices. Teachers had to become familiar with the Orders and mark according to a ten-level scale. The ten levels were the most controversial and unsatisfactory aspect of the Orders because they required identification of one skill in a complex situation.

Task 2.5 Assessing writing

In order to understand some of the concerns about assessment of English to levels, read the following extract from the Cox Report (DES and WO, 1989):

> The best writing is vigorous, committed, honest and interesting. We have not included these qualities in our statements of attainment because they cannot be mapped onto levels.
>
> (par. 17.31)

1   What do you think of this statement? Are there other elements of writing which display quality?
2   Do you believe it is possible to assess how 'vigorous, committed, honest and interesting' a piece of pupil's writing is?
3   If you believe it is possible so to do, how would you go about it? What features would you look for?
4   If you believe it is not possible so to do, does this fact tell us more about:
   ● the nature of the writing process;
   ● the difficulties of defining quality in writing objectively;
   ● the deficiency of a hierarchical model of assessment;
   ● the belief that English teachers should assess only the assessible, such as correctness of spelling, grammar and punctuation?

You may wish to discuss your responses with another student teacher or your mentor/tutor. Keep any notes you make and use them in your work on assessment in English.

KEY STAGE 4 AND GCSE

In 1989, the GCSE examination had been introduced in order to simplify and equalise assessment at age 16, by providing one examination (instead of O Level and CSE) using variously numbers and grades. GCSE assessment was flexible between and within subjects, ranging from 100 per cent coursework (which had to include 20 per cent timed exercises under examination conditions) to 100 per cent 'open' or 'closed' book examinations, with differing proportions according to the examination board and there were often options within the single syllabus. Boards developed syllabuses in English language, English literature and English (a combination of language and literature). They also developed possibilities for cross-over work between English language and literature, and with humanities, such as the diary of a soldier in the First World War, but a maximum of two pieces of coursework. The GCSE examination proved to make demands on pupils in terms of workload and the pressure of continual assessment. The existing GCSE syllabuses were perceived as appropriate and successful ways of assessing the Brian Cox curriculum requirements at Key Stage 4; the only issue was over whether to mark and record by levels or grades and to streamline systems of recording. Since it had only just been introduced it was also considered needless to change it.

In 1992, legislation for GCSE was changed, making more examination compulsory and minimising the importance of speaking and listening. It introduced tiered examination papers. In the 1992 examination there was a last-minute decision to award separate marks, worth 5 per cent, for accurate spelling, punctuation and grammar in terminal examination papers. The same requirements were also to be applied to coursework. In 1994, requirements changed again and syllabuses had to come into line.

SUMMARY AND KEY POINTS

English is a relatively young subject. It has existed for a little over a century. Major reforms in the subject appear to take place in times of great social change. English in schools has been regarded as important for a variety of reasons – not least for the belief in the 'humanising' qualities of English literature. A number of works from the past have been identified that are believed to exhibit certain values and qualities which are universal and which will stand the test of time. These texts have formed the literary canon. Authors included in the canon have been the bases for school examination syllabuses. The most fundamental change in relation to the study of literature has been the move from literary appreciation to literary criticism.

Notions of correctness and the importance of standard English have been linked to a 'high culture' view of the subject, which have put it in opposition to popular cultural forms. Since the Second World War, the 'English as language' paradigm has placed greater emphasis upon using the subject rather than studying the subject. Opposing models of English teaching have given rise to tensions within the school and in society at large.

The National Curriculum was born out of an almost unprecedented plethora of educational documentation produced by the government and its agencies. For the first time in the history of state education, a curriculum for secondary schools was centrally imposed. English as a subject continued to be regarded as central to the politics of education. Opposing models of English continued, and continue, to create tensions for educationists and policy-makers. It would appear that for much of the latter half of the 1980s the government sought to 'turn back the clock' in order to produce an English curriculum founded upon notions of correctness, standard English and formal grammar, which culminated in the proposals for the Revised Orders for English (DES and WO 1993). Chapter 3 discusses the development of the National Curriculum from the publication of the 1995 Orders.

FURTHER READING

Eagleton, T. (1983) *Literary Theory*, Oxford: Blackwell. Eagleton's book provides a comprehensive overview of literary theory. Chapter 1, 'The rise of English', charts in detail the development of approaches to English literature that influenced the ways in which the subject has come to be taught in school.

Black, P. *et al.* (1992) *Education: Putting the Record Straight*, Stafford: Network Educational Press. This collection of papers is written by many of the educationists who were at the heart of the development of the National Curriculum. It is a highly critical insider's view of the political machinations which influenced the development of education in this country in the 1980s and 1990s.

Cox, B. (1995) *The Battle for the National Curriculum*, London: Hodder & Stoughton. This book gives an account of the implementation of the 1990 National Curriculum for English and the process by which it was replaced by the 1995 English in the National Curriculum. Although it pulls no punches in describing the political interference and shortcomings of the new Order, it recognises positive aspects in relation to the limits of the 1989 Curriculum. Brian Cox suggests a way forward, rather than simply a nostalgic view of the current situation.

LATE (1996) *The Real Cost of SATs: A Report for the London Association for the Teaching of English*, London: LATE. This report looks at the financial and educational costs of SATs, based on a questionnaire sent to schools after the 1995 tests. It reveals the amount of money and the cost of teaching time, workload and strain, and common objections such as the prevention of providing a broad and balanced English curriculum, inaccurate results, inappropriate means of testing the content of the National Curriculum, teacher morale, and standards of achievement.

National Oracy Project (1991) *Teaching Talking and Learning at Key Stage 3*, London: NCC/NOP.

National Oracy Project (1993) *Teaching Talking and Learning at Key Stage 4*, London: NCC/NOP.
Together with the NOP's reports on Key Stages 1 and 2, these publications contain accounts of good practice within the English classroom, particularly in relation to equal opportunities, gender and bilingualism.

National Writing Project (1993) *Responding to and Assessing Writing*, London: Nelson. This report considers key strategies for developing opportunities for a range of responses to pupil writing in the classroom.

Richmond, J. (1992) 'Unstable materials: the LINC story', *English and Media Magazine*, spring, English and Media Centre/NATE. John Richmond was joint leader of the North London Language Consortium, one of the consortia of LEAs which conducted the work of the LINC project. His article describes in detail the conflict between the government and those working on the project.

3 Working with the National Curriculum

Jane Dowson and Jo Westbrook

INTRODUCTION

This chapter follows on from Chapter 2, 'Battles for English', by an examination of the historical, cultural and political moves from *English in the National Curriculum* (DFE, 1995) to the present *The National Curriculum for England* (DfEE/QCA, 1999), and the implications for English teaching to how it works in practice, and in tandem with the National Literacy Strategy.

The 1995 (Dearing) National Curriculum was literally a 'slimmed-down' version of the earlier model but without the helpful non-statutory guidance, and it did not eliminate testing by examination or tiered papers. It is useful to gain an overview of what the 1995 National Curriculum contained, to understand the rationale, structure and content of the present 'Curriculum 2000'. Each Attainment Target of the 1995 Orders covered range, key skills, and standard English and language study with the content described in short prose paragraphs. Speaking and listening focused on formal contexts and skills for oracy, including the subtler skills of recognising ambiguity and differences in tone. Drama had its own subsection but the skills focused on communication and language rather than on the techniques and conventions specific to drama teaching. The requirement for standard English in informal and formal situations, together with the hotch-potch of language development, 'word coinage' and grammar which comprised language study content narrowed down the promising start for En1 Speaking and listening. En2 Reading emphasised the English literary heritage and 'works of high quality by contemporary writers' (DfE, 1995, p. 20) with prescribed reading lists of 'major authors'. Pupils' reading had to include two Shakespeare plays, drama by major playwrights, two works of fiction and poems by four major poets before and after 1900. It did include two lines on texts from 'other cultures and traditions', and small subsections on non-fiction and media texts, the latter of which should also 'be of high quality'. This noun phrase comes up no less than seven times in the reading section, most directly in the key skills where pupils are to be given opportunities to 'appreciate the characteristics that distinguish literature of high quality' (DfE, 1995, p. 21). En3 Writing focused, interestingly, on two main purposes for writing: its 'aesthetic and imaginative purposes', and 'to develop thinking'. The planning and drafting of narratives, poems, scripts and non-fiction pieces was emphasised. Language study was another mixed bag, but also consisted of four distinct subsections: discourse structure; phrase, clause and sentence structure; words; and punctuation. The expansion of technical terminology for grammar in 1995 may be seen as the forerunner of what became the Conservative government's National Literary Project, and then Labour's National Literary Strategy.

The 1995 Revised Orders was thus a return to the English literary heritage and standard English. Some of the 1989 Cox curriculum's ideas about the writing process, and the need for culturally different texts, media and non-fiction were perhaps reluctantly retained. Achievement was measured by Attainment Targets for each section; progression was identified through eight level descriptions. It is important to remember that the level descriptions were deliberately placed after the programmes of study to endorse the principle that the programmes of study, not assessment, should guide teaching. The more explicit technical terminology covered in writing especially, however, meant that vocabulary, spelling, grammar, punctuation, sentence structure and handwriting were measured easily in teacher assessment, and in the Key Stage 3 tests at the end of Year 9. Assessment began to dominate the Key Stage 3 curriculum in particular; schools stopped teaching the curriculum in January of Year 9 to revise for the tests in May.

This was still an 'entitlement curriculum' and English teachers tried to fulfil this aim by differentiating through difficulty of text rather than by setting groups. 'Differentiation by offering choice, negotiation and intervention at the individual level' (Daw, 1995, p. 12). The slimmed-down Revised Orders did offer the opportunity for teachers to go beyond the narrow focus on skills and the prescribed texts, particularly since 'text' increasingly meant media or information text as well as a written or more narrowly 'literary' text and since the meaning of 'literacy' had broadened to include the ability to read and write in several media.

The Revised Orders, with its uncertain mix of content and skills, could be said to reflect the turning, and churning, state of the nation at the tail-end of eighteen years of Conservative rule. With the election of New Labour in May 1997 and their election mantra of 'education, education, education' it was inevitable that there would be yet another revision of the National Curriculum in 1999.

The current National Curriculum for English (DfEE/QCA, 1999b) presents three major challenges for teachers: one is to plan their syllabuses and schemes of work so that all pupils have the best opportunities to perform to the best of their abilities in terms of the requirements of the programmes of study and of public examinations. The second is to plan for continuity and progression for all pupils. The third challenge is to the teacher's own subject knowledge; student teachers start their training with different experiences of studying English and have different strengths and gaps in terms of the school curriculum requirements. The importance of viewing the development of your own subject knowledge as part of your role as an English teacher is discussed in Chapter 14, 'Critical Practice'.

In this chapter, there is an emphasis on planning for working with the National Curriculum programmes of study. The sample lesson plan and scheme of work are designed to demonstrate ways of meeting the objectives in terms of knowledge, skills and understanding, and breadth of study. At the same time, you will need to understand how the National Curriculum dovetails with the National Literacy Strategy at Key Stage 3 in terms of coverage of content and objectives. At Key Stage 4 the new GCSE specifications will inform your planning for Years 10 and 11. It is envisaged that this chapter will be read in conjunction with all the other chapters so that you will want to include the principles identified there in your planning.

OBJECTIVES

By the end of this chapter you should:

- be able to have a working knowledge of the programmes of study for the National Curriculum and its assessment at Key Stages 3 and 4;
- consider ways of working with both the requirements of the National Curriculum and the National Literacy Strategy;
- consider your own strengths and weaknesses in terms of subject knowledge.

REVISION OF THE NATIONAL CURRICULUM (DFEE/QCA, 1999)

The new Labour government, with David Blunkett as Secretary of State for Education, immediately set about revising the National Curriculum to reflect the new thinking about inclusion and entitlement, under the rigorous umbrella of raising standards for all. Blunkett also wanted a more explicit rationale for the school curriculum that would:

1   Establish an entitlement curriculum for all pupils.
2   Establish standards.
3   Promote continuity and coherence.
4   Promote public understanding.

Revisions to the National Curriculum were in schools by autumn 1999, with the requirement that they should be in place by September 2000. There were only minor modifications to GCSE syllabuses, which started in 2000 for 2002. Crucially the National Curriculum was aligned with the National Literacy Strategy which Labour had pushed out as its first major educational initiative in September 1997 to all primary schools. Primary teachers had to work with two very different documents to inform their planning; the Dearing 1995 curriculum began to look like the reductionist hybrid it was.

NATIONAL CURRICULUM ENGLISH AT KEY STAGES 3 AND 4

Each of the programmes of study for English has two main sections. Within 'Knowledge, skills and understanding' there are subsections, giving a far more detailed breakdown of the skills to be learned than in the previous curriculum, with bullet points to clarify each statement. The Breadth of study section gives the range of activities, contexts and purposes through which knowledge, skills and understanding should be taught – i.e. 'what' pupils should talk about, and listen to, including exemplar and compulsory lists of texts to read, and lists of examples of text types to write/produce. The main features of the programmes of study are:

EN1 Speaking and listening

Knowledge, skills and understanding

1 **Speaking** – structure talk clearly; use illustrations, gestures, visual aids, vary word choices, use spoken standard English, evaluate the effectiveness of their speech.
2 **Listening** – recall main features of a talk, identify explicit and implicit meanings, distinguish tone, recognise ambiguity and 'gloss', ask questions.
3 **Group discussion and interaction** – make different types of contributions and roles, take other views into account, summarise main points, help the group to complete tasks by clarifying and synthesising others' ideas.
4 **Drama** – use a variety of dramatic techniques, use different ways to convey action, character, atmosphere and tension, appreciate dramatic effect, critically evaluate drama performances.
5 **Standard English**
6 **Language variation** – use of standard English, influences of spoken and written language, vocabulary and grammar of standard English and dialectal variation, development of English over time.

En1 gives speaking and listening as two separate but related skills with a third new heading of group discussion and interaction. This is a curriculum aimed at fostering an adult needs use of formal speech, with an emphasis on presentation and active listening skills. The democratisation of speech in the classroom as a crucial part of citizenship education may be seen in the criteria for group discussion and interaction. The fourth section promotes the status of drama as its own discrete subject with particular conventions and strategies, but also as an important tool in the English classroom. Standard English has one line: 'Pupils should be taught to use the vocabulary, structures and grammar of spoken standard English fluently and accurately in informal and formal situations.' The notes in the margin categorically give the most common (and therefore undesirable) 'non-standard usages' in England. The implications here are that teachers are to eliminate these 'usages' in their classrooms, oddly working against New Labour's sense of inclusion and entitlement for all.

En2 Reading

Knowledge, skills and understanding

1   **Understanding texts**
  - **Reading for meaning** – extract meaning beyond the literal, analyse different interpretations, explore ideas, values, identify perspectives, consider how meanings are changed when texts are adapted to different media, read complete texts.
  - **Understanding the author's craft** – how language is used in imaginative ways, writer's presentation of ideas, character, plot, variation in techniques, structure, comparison of texts.
2   **English literary heritage** – how and why texts have been influential and their appeal, characteristics of texts considered to be of high quality.
3   **Texts from different cultures and traditions** – values and assumptions in texts, subject matter, language, distinctive qualities of literature from different traditions, comparisons between texts.
4   **Printed and ICT-based information texts** – select, synthesise, evaluate information, sift relevant from irrelevant, identify characteristic features at word, sentence and text level.
5   **Media and moving image texts** – how meaning is conveyed in texts that include print, images, sound, choice of form, layout, nature and purpose of media products which influence content and meaning, how audiences and readers choose and respond to media.
6   **Language structure and variation** – 'Pupils should be taught to draw on their knowledge of grammar and language variation to develop their understanding of texts and how language works.'

Blunkett responded to calls for the curriculum to reflect contemporary society by enlarging the place of media, ICT, non-fiction and non-literary texts, and by the inclusion of recent and contemporary examples of drama, fiction and poetry. The blossoming of children's literature in the 1990s, culminating in Philip Pullman winning the Whitbread Prize for 1999 with *The Amber Spyglass* may be seen in this enriched sense of texts relevant for teenagers. English literary heritage becomes simply one section in harmony with others. The semantic change from texts from '*other*' to '*different* cultures and traditions' suggests an awareness of the diversity of cultures and literary traditions within our own shores, as well as those from overseas. The range of literature to be read at Key Stages 3 and 4 remains the same as in the 1995 curriculum, but the onset of the First World War in 1914 becomes the watershed for 'pre- and post-' texts, echoing Virginia Woolf's view that the world changed in 1910. Infamously, however, Blunkett caved in to pressures from the more traditional elements of his government and advisers at the last minute before publication by making compulsory the exemplar lists of pre-1914 major writers and poets, which were printed in boldface. Complete texts are to be read, which you may need to remember once in the midst of juggling time in your planning, and in the face of pressure to meet school and class targets. There is also a requirement to compare texts that echoes the criteria. The non-fiction and non-literary texts include, for the first time, personal records and viewpoints on society, travel writing, reportage and the 'natural world'.

En3 Writing

Knowledge, skills and understanding

1   **Composition**
   - **Writing to imagine, explore, entertain** – draw on their experience of good literature, use imaginative vocabulary; exploit choice of language and structure and range of techniques.
   - **Writing to inform, explain, describe** – form sentences and paragraphs that express connections between idea, use form language, consider the reader, present material clearly.
   - **Writing to persuade, argue, advise** – develop logical arguments, use persuasive techniques, use language to gain attention.
   - **Writing to analyse, review, comment** – reflect on the significance of the subject matter, form own view, organise ideas, take account of reader's knowledge.

2   **Planning and drafting**
   Plan, draft, proofread work on paper and on screen, analyse their own and other's writing.

3   **Punctuation** – use the full range of punctuation marks, to help the reader.

4   **Spelling** – word families, stems, prefix, suffixes, inflections, polysyllabic words, check for errors, use of dictionaries and a thesaurus.

5   **Handwriting and presentation** – write neatly and legibly, make full use of different presentational devices.

6   **Standard English** – variations in written standard English, and how they differ from spoken language.

7   **Language structure** – sentence grammar, and whole-text cohesions, word classes, phrases, clauses, paragraph structure, whole text structure, grammatical terminology.

Breadth of study includes a very wide range of texts, including screenplays, information leaflets, editorials, polemical essays and reviews, as well as the requirement that writing is to be taught for thinking and learning, for known and unknown readers.

Non-fiction writing takes up three-quarters of the En3 writing programmes of study, leaving imaginative, creative writing to a quarter of the output required. This is an extraordinary swing away from Britton's expressive and poetic writing of the 1970s, towards 'the information age' production of non-fiction texts. These include texts produced by computers, cameras and videos, and so reflect new technologies, bringing them into the mainstream. It is also a move towards a functional literacy approach to English teaching, an adult needs model which critics argue takes away the creative sparkle in the English classroom. The weightiness of the 'secretarial' aspects of writing, as opposed to the 'composition' side, adds to this view.

En1 speaking and listening and En3 writing are in many ways a more detailed and coherent version of the 1995 curriculum, with the technical terminology unapologetically highlighted. It is at this level that the National Curriculum dovetails into the National Literacy Strategy with its lists of word and sentence-level objectives (see Chapter 4 for more guidance on the relationship between the two documents). The National Curriculum 1999 is a richer definition of 'English' with a wider range of literary and non-literary texts to be read and produced. Conversely, the level of detailed prescription is greater than in the 1995 Revised Orders, especially for language, and the requirement for standard English. A curriculum can never reflect accurately the felt pluralism of contemporary society, nor include what is viewed as cutting-edge technologies and art forms. A curriculum, particularly with such a subjective subject as 'English' and 'literature', will be necessarily conservative and therefore will never satisfy everyone.

NATIONAL CURRICULUM ENGLISH AT KEY STAGES 3 AND 4

The National Curriculum for England (DfE/QCA, 1999) sets out the requirements for pupils aged 5 to 16. It is organised into programmes of study (PoS) which set out the material to be covered and the opportunities which pupils must experience. Although you will be concentrating on the programmes of study for Key Stages 3 and 4, you should remember that there should be a continuum throughout all key stages; just as work at Key Stage 4 will be viewed as a development of Key Stage 3, Key Stage 3 should build upon pupils' learning at Key Stage 2. The NLS makes this continuity explicit with its detailed objectives consolidating learning from each year, and moving pupils on. At secondary level, the Programmes of Study in the National Curriculum for Key Stages 3 and 4 are combined, but specific knowledge and skills are identified for assessment at each stage: at Key Stage 3 through Standard Assessment Tests (SATs) and at Key Stage 4 by GCSE coursework and examination. The Attainment targets for each aspect of English have remained the same as in the 1995 English Order, with eight assessment levels with an 'exceptional performance' level. These levels have been criticised as being out of step with the new content of the 1999 curriculum, and in remaining unhelpful in accurately describing pupil progression. Many departments have rewritten the levels in pupil-friendly language so that the assessment criteria may be shared with pupils, and made explicit. Departments have also attempted to enlarge the descriptions, and adding pluses and minuses so that there is a greater sense of progression for pupils. At the time of writing QCA is rewriting the assessment-level descriptions; you will need to keep a check on changes taking place. The majority of pupils working at Key Stage 3 should be working within levels 4 to 7, and at Key Stage 4 between levels 5 and 8, with the brightest achieving 'exceptional performance'. The requirements state that it should be made possible to select material from earlier or later Key Stages than that identified for the majority of pupils.

The 1999 English curriculum also has nine pages of 'Inclusion: providing effective learning opportunities for all pupils' that are common requirements for all subjects. The three principles for inclusion listed in some detail are:

1   Setting suitable learning challenges.
2   Responding to pupils' diverse learning needs.
3   Overcoming potential barriers to learning and assessment for individuals and
     groups of pupils.

Full recognition is given to the ethnic diversity of pupils, their social and cultural
backgrounds, and their language needs, as well as giving specific strategies to support
pupils with SEN. Teachers will want to follow these guidelines by developing a range
of strategies so that all pupils have opportunities to participate in all activities. There
are two final sections of the English curriculum. 'Use of language across the curriculum'
reflects the literacy across the curriculum arm of the NLS in schools, as does the 'Use
of information and communication technology across the curriculum' section.

WORKING WITH THE NATIONAL CURRICULUM AND THE NATIONAL LITERACY STRATEGY AT KEY STAGE 3

Although the requirements of the National Curriculum are common to all maintained
schools, they have to be 'translated' into a syllabus that is broken down into schemes
of work. The National Curriculum gives an overview of Key Stages 3 and 4, with a
focus on text level, and breadth of study. Since September 2001, the Framework for
teaching English: Years 7, 8 and 9 is the main planning and teaching tool at Key Stage
3 in schools to be referred to alongside the National Curriculum. As a broad
generalisation the National Curriculum remains the 'English' part of English teaching,
while the NLS gives the focus to the 'Literacy' part of English teaching. You will need
to read Chapter 4, 'Speaking and Listening', on further details of working with the
Framework. As an introduction here, however, the Framework gives very detailed
short teaching objectives for each year group at five levels:

- Word level
- Sentence level
- Text level – Reading
- Text level – Writing
- Speaking and listening.

The NLS uses precise terminology, with a focus on the gradual progression of skills and
concepts 'in a widening range of contexts' (The Framework', p. 12). Long-term plans
give an overview of each term for each year group, ensuring that the content of the
National Curriculum and the objectives from the NLS for that year are covered, and
a balance of fiction and non-fiction texts and a range of activities. Medium-term plans
give details of the texts and clusters of objectives to be covered over a half-term or three-
to four-week period. When planning for a half-term's work (medium-term), you will
need to look at the National Curriculum for meeting the literature requirements (e.g.
the breadth of study) and given examples (Major writers from different cultures and
traditions – *Green Days by the River* for Year 9, p. 35), and then the knowledge, skills
and understanding under 'Texts from different cultures and traditions' (p. 34):

- to understand the values and assumptions in the texts;
- the significance of the subject matter and the language;
- the distinctive qualities of literature from different traditions.

The cluster of objectives for that half-term will come from the Framework, with particular objectives placed logically according to progression over the planned time. For example, for the final week's work completing the reading of *Green Days by the River* the objectives might be as follows.

Framework for teaching English: Years 7, 8 and 9

Year 9 text level – Reading

Reading for meaning
6 'Comment on the authorial perspectives offered in texts on individuals, community and society in texts from different cultures.'

Year 9 Speaking and listening

Group discussion and interaction
9 'Discuss and evaluate conflicting evidence to arrive at a considered viewpoint.'

Year 9 Word level

Vocabulary
7 'Recognise layers of meaning in the writer's choice of words (e.g. connotation, implied meaning, different types or multiple meanings).'

Key objectives – 'important markers of progress' (The Framework, p. 12) for each year group – are given in boldface print to provide a clear focus and to inform assessment tasks.

As a subject teacher, you have to follow the syllabus and schemes of work of your department but you are also responsible for designing them to fit the abilities of your particular class and for using the resources available, making your own if necessary. You therefore need to become familiar with the programmes of study and also the syllabus at your school; you should discuss with experienced teachers how they plan their schemes of work and lessons, and which resources are applicable to which units of the department's syllabus. This latter point is important for two reasons: you may find that you are spending time developing worksheets or photocopying texts which already exist in the department or you may be using a text with Year 9 which the department usually reserves for Year 10. The following tables and tasks are designed to help you to get to know *English in the National Curriculum* and to see how it works in practice with reference to a school's syllabus and your lesson planning. Figure 3.1 outlines what has to be included at Key Stage 3.

Knowledge, skills and understanding	Breadth of study
Speaking and listening 1 **Speaking** 2 **Listening** 3 **Group discussion and interaction** 4 **Drama** 5 **Standard English** 6 **Language variation**	• Describe, narrate, explain, argue, contributing in different contexts, and formal and informal presentations • Listen actively to live talks, recordings • Take different roles in groups discussions • Improvise, work in role, script and perform plays, evaluate performances
Reading 1 **Understanding texts** **Reading for meaning, understanding the author's craft** 2 **English literary heritage** 3 **Texts from different cultures and traditions** 4 **Printed and ICT-based information texts** 5 **Media and moving image texts** 6 **Language structure and variation**	The requirements for reading are in terms of two main genres of literature and non-fiction and non-literary texts: **Literature** • One Shakespeare play • Drama by major playwrights • Pre-1914 major poets from list • Post-1914 major poets • Pre-1914 major fiction authors from list • Post-1914 major fiction authors • Recent and contemporary drama, fiction and poetry written for young people • Texts from different cultures and traditions **Non-fiction and non-literary texts** • Literary non-fiction • Print and ICT-based information texts • Media and moving image texts **Language structure and variation** • Draw on knowledge of grammar and language variation to develop understanding of texts

Writing
1   **Composition**
     Writing to imagine, explore, entertain
     Writing to inform, explain, describe
     Writing to persuade, argue, advise
     Writing to analyse, review, comment
2   **Planning and drafting**
3   **Punctuation**
4   **Spelling**
5   **Handwriting and presentation**
6   **Standard English**
7   **Language structure**
	• Write a variety of narrative forms: stories, poems, play scripts, screenplays, diaries
	• Write a variety of non-literary forms: minutes, information leaflets, brochures, adverts, letters, essays, reviews, articles, reports
	• Planning, drafting, redrafting, proof-reading
	• Writing for known and unknown audiences
	• Note-taking, summarising
	• Improve spelling, sophisticated spelling, and presentation
	• Word classes, use of complex sentences, paragraph and text structure, grammatical terminology

continued

Knowledge, skills and understanding	Breadth of study
Assessment objectives **– SAT** **Paper 1** **Paper 2**	• Reading comprehension • Comparison of two scenes from a Shakespeare play • Writing tasks for different audiences (e.g.letters, diaries, reports, reviews) • Creative writing

Figure 3.1 English in the National Curriculum, Programmes of Study, Key Stage 3

For the sake of clarity, the list of the requirements for the programmes of study is divided into sections, but in practice, English lessons will nearly always include elements of speaking and listening, reading, writing, and language structure. Analysis of media texts is often integral to work on written texts or to writing activities (for example, when a media text is the stimulus). For this reason, it is not difficult for English teachers to identify elements of the programmes of study in their teaching. The difficulty is in identifying one or two objectives which are the focus for progression and which are to be assessed. In reading and responding to a poem about a cat, such as 'A Case of Murder' by Vernon Scannell, for example, the teacher needs to decide whether she is going to concentrate on improving the pupils' abilities to discuss, in which case she will organise the class into small groups, give them questions about the issues raised by the subject matter and assess them by the Speaking and listening level descriptions or whether they are to learn about the literary features of poetry and develop an informed response to their reading, in which case she may give them questions or set up activities on the poem which guide an exploration of the relationship between linguistic and formal features, such as vocabulary, rhythm and metaphor, and meaning; this work would be assessed by the level descriptions in reading. This does not mean, of course, that because the focus is on oral activities, pupils are not improving their reading skills or because they are looking at features of poetry as genre, they are not speaking and listening, but that there are clear objectives to which the pupils can work and which are consistent with the criteria by which they will be assessed. The identification and communication of objectives and the criteria for assessment enable pupils to know what they are aiming for and teachers to fulfil the statutory requirements of keeping records of their own assessment of pupils' achievements.

In your planning you should try to ensure that all the requirements of the programmes of study are fulfilled; you would also need to build in preparation for public examination, the Standard Assessment Tests (SATs). SATs are taken in May of Year 9 and consist of two papers testing reading and writing. From May 2003 there are to be three SATs papers similar to the optional Year 7 and 8 tests with separate reading and writing levels reported. These tests are an attempt to reflect the new content in the National Curriculum for English, and the requirements of the NLS at Key Stage 3. Paper 1 will assess reading based on a booklet of three texts followed by fifteen short questions (seventy-five minutes). In Paper 2 assessing writing, pupils will be required to write two tasks lasting forty-five and thirty minutes based on the National

Curriculum 'triplets' (e.g. 'Writing to imagine, explore, entertain', and 'Writing to inform, explain, describe'), and related to the themes in the Shakespeare paper. Paper 3 will require pupils to show a detailed knowledge of two scenes from a Shakespeare play, giving the two extracts in the examination, and asking for comparisons between them, but with a shortened time of forty-five minutes rather than the previous hour and a half. Early entry to the tests will be possible for those 'most able and gifted pupils', plus a range of optional tasks to support teacher assessment, and for those pupils working at levels 1 to 3 who do not have to take the SATs papers.

Schools have different policies about when the decision is made about which pupils should take the tests early or the optional tasks. These decisions are accompanied by decisions over whether to set the groups to prepare them for the exams. For example, if levels 1 to 3 become a 'bottom set', how are they to study the Shakespeare play which is a requirement for all pupils, even though they will not be assessed on it? The new requirements for Paper 2 demand that pupils understand both the sum and parts of a whole Shakespeare play, with enough comprehension to make comparisons between scenes. This tallies with the National Curriculum's new content under En2 Reading – Understanding the author's craft: 'Pupils should be taught (k) to compare texts, looking at style, theme and language, and identifying connections and contrasts.' For pupils with SEN this will be challenging, but will also avoid the fragmentation of a Shakespeare play into one isolated scene for revision and SATs purposes. Teacher assessment in the three Attainment Targets at the end of each year at Key Stage 3 is an important part of assessment, especially for speaking and listening. You will need to become familiar with matching the 'best fit' level descriptions to pupils' work so that you can accurately gauge their progress. However, it is the SATs levels in Year 9 that are reported in the published School League Tables, and that 'count' as the mark of each pupil's and each school's success, or failure, but the 'value-added' progress of each school now also reported helps to give a fairer picture of the achievements of that school.

To sum up thus far: you need to ensure that all aspects of the programmes of study have been covered by all pupils and have records to prove it. Pupils need to be: prepared for the SATs; provided with extension work for the top levels; and provided with appropriate and challenging work for levels 1 to 3. The Literacy Progress Units which are a part of the NLS will support your work here for those pupils working at Level 3 and below. In working with the requirements of the National Curriculum in conjunction with the Framework for teaching English, and your school's syllabus, you need to ascertain what the syllabus includes, what it tells you and what it does not. Table 3.1 is an example of a syllabus for Key Stage 3 to cover years 8 and 9. This syllabus is designed to meet the requirements of Key Stage 3, including the breadth of study, and acknowledges the objectives for each year group in the Framework for teaching English. These objectives would be mapped out in the far more detailed schemes for each unit of work. This model retains the principles of giving pupils opportunities to perform well in national assessment terms and also to be introduced to other work which is designed to meet their particular needs and interests and which allows the teacher some sense of autonomy.

Table 3.1 Sample English syllabus for Years 8 and 9

Year 8	Unit title	Speaking and listening	Reading	Writing
Autumn 1	*Skellig* – class novel	Group discussion – hypothesising, debating, exploration, role-play	*Skellig*, Blake's poetry	Writing to imagine, explore, entertain: diaries, story-boarding, narratives, poetry, drafting, proof-reading, book review
Autumn 2	Media product launch	Active listening, group interaction – presentations, scripting, language variation	Magazines, advertisements, TV scripts	Writing to persuade, argue, advise: scripts, storyboards, commentaries, reviews Planning, drafting on computer and video
Spring 1	*Our Day Out* – modern drama	Role-play, improvisation, evaluation, discussion	*Our Day Out*	Writing to analyse, review, comment: reviews, essays, scripts, narratives
Spring 2	Poetry on youth	Presentations, explorations, active listening, language variation	Anthologies of poems from pre- and post-1914	Writing to imagine, explore, entertain: poems, commentaries, essays
Summer 1	Refugees	Group discussion, analysis, listening to live talks, role-play	*The Other Side of Truth* – novel Articles on refugees to the UK	Writing to imagine, explore, entertain: stories, diaries, newspaper articles, letters, reports, for unknown audiences Planning, drafting
Summer 2	*A Midsummers Night's Dream*	Role-play, hotseating, story-telling, discussion, language variation	Shakespeare play – print and film text, Internet research	Writing to imagine, explore, entertain: descriptions, reviews, stories, captions, games, greeting cards
Year 9				
Autumn 1	Travelling	Group discussion and presentations, exploration, script-writing	Travel-writing brochures and adverts Media – travel shows on TV and radio, websites	Writing to inform, explain, describe: leaflets, brochures Writing to analyse, review, comment: essays, articles Scripts, video footage, radio broadcasts

Autumn 2	Texts from different cultures and traditions	Group discussion, analysis, exploring, debating, listening, role-play, improvisation	*The Wave/The Diary of Anne Frank*	Writing to analyse, review, comment: reviews, comparisons, editorials, storyboards, book covers
Spring 1	*Macbeth*	Role-play, hot-seating, directing, evaluations, debate	Shakespeare play – book and film texts for comparison Detailed analysis of two scenes	Writing to imagine, explore, entertain: poems, stories, essays, reviews
Spring 2	Preparation for SATs	Group discussion, exploring, debating	Range of pre-1914 and post-1914 short stories, articles, leaflets, editorials	Short stories, letters, reviews, articles, descriptions
Summer 1	Modern drama	Role-play, directing, hotseating, discussion	Play script	Diaries, reviews, playscripts, character descriptions
Summer 2	Pre-GCSE unit	Exploration, analysis, debate, presentations	War poetry – pre- and post 1914 Internet and library research	Analysis, commentaries, reviews, poetry

Lesson planning

Lesson planning also provides the means to identify the learning objectives in terms of pupils' progression which should be consistent with assessment objectives. With reference again to the poem 'A Case of Murder', it might seem like a good idea to ask pupils to rewrite the situation of the poem as a short story; it would be inappropriate, of course, to assess it on its demonstration of the features of a short story (surprise beginnings, twist in the tale and so on), if you had been talking about its poetry techniques or its treatment of fear or guilt. When beginning to teach, it is tempting to stick on a piece of writing at the end of an activity to give it value, but if it is an afterthought it may not be appropriate to the pupils' learning. You need to decide on your pupil learning objectives and what you are assessing before you start, drawing on past lessons, pupil records and the overall scheme of work. You will then be able to communicate these objectives to your pupils and give your lessons a sense of direction and clear focus. In your plenary at the end of a lesson you can identify what has been achieved and, in your own evaluation of the lesson, you should be able to ask yourself 'what has been learned and how?' in relation to your identified objectives (see 'Schemes of Work and Lesson Planning', Unit 2.2, in Capel *et al.*, 1995). Following the principle of working *with* but also *beyond* the National Curriculum, lesson plans can also identify objectives which are not specific requirements of the programmes of study; these may be procedural issues, such as ensuring that homework is understood and completed on time, cross–curricular issues, such as equal opportunities, or wider subject issues such as improving critical responses to film or television texts.

Figure 3.2 is a sample lesson plan which illustrates that any one lesson will include speaking, listening, reading, writing, and points about language. There is a clear aim in terms of what is to be learned and how that learning is to be measured. It is only a skeleton of a plan. It may be the start of a scheme of work which develops other objectives. For example, it could lead to writing a modern equivalent of a fairy story which would allow pupils to investigate the perceived 'authority' of received texts and to challenge gender stereotypes; their stories could be presented and assessed orally (to the class or read on to a tape recorder) or in writing. There are useful versions of fairy- and folk-tales from around the world in books such as *Changing Stories* (English and Media Centre, 1984) and *Inside Stories 3 and 4* (Benton, 1991).

The lesson plan (Figure 3.2) illustrates that in any lesson there is an integration of activities but that there should be a focus on one (in this case, speaking and listening) for progression. It includes consideration of appropriate teaching strategies: pair and group work are best for speaking and listening to allow for maximum participation. Worksheets, such as a table to fill in on selected aspects of each story, are used to clarify instructions, to provide differentiation through allowing pupils to work at different paces and to release the teacher to support individuals, and groups during the development phase of the lesson through guided reading (see Chapter 4 for further details on guided reading and writing). The plan is written with reference to the programmes of study and the Framework for teaching English, but is also informed by wider theoretical principles. These principles include:

- the importance of understanding how stereotypes work;
- that written texts are not superior to oral texts;
- that texts are constructed for particular purposes and are value-laden (e.g. the teaching to nineteenth-century children that virtue and vice work meritoriously);
- developing powers of narrative are important because:

> Stories are a way in which we represent the world to ourselves and, in the stories we tell ourselves or others, stories also become a way in which we represent ourselves to the world. They also help us to understand experiences we may never have had personally – of another time, another place, another culture. Stories allow us to speculate about 'what if . . .?' Stories are the foundation of religions and of history. The culture and the beliefs of a society are deeply embedded in its stories. For both individuals and societies live by the stories they tell themselves.
>
> (Benton, 1991, pp. 9–10)

Consequently, studying folk, fairy and short stories from different traditions may be seen not only as fulfilling curriculum requirements but also as introducing pupils to alternative systems of government, family life and responses to experiences. Such experiences will enable pupils to develop greater powers of narrative discourse themselves which will empower them to question and resist oppressive systems: 'The less constrained the discourse, i.e. censored by power, the more it is likely to have recourse to narrative. Spontaneous speech narrative is the most difficult kind of

Class: 8   **Lesson length**: 60 mins   **Levels**: 3–7
Date: June 4   **Position in scheme of work**:   1

National Curriculum aims: Develop ability to narrate and to listen helpfully; understand the origins of fairy stories in oral and folk culture; compare C19 and C20 written versions in terms of style, theme and language; consider stereotyping.

Framework for teaching English – pupil learning objectives: Speaking 2. Tell a story . . . choosing and changing the mood, tone and pace of delivery for particular effect.

Text level – Reading: Reading for meaning 5. trace the development of themes, values or ideas in texts; Sentence level: 13. Recognise some of the differences in sentence structure, vocabulary and tone between a modern English text and a text from another historical period.

Text level – Writing: 3. Use writing for thinking and learning by recording ideas as they develop to aid reflection and problem-solving.

Assessment: Speaking and listening – ability to narrate a story, and to listen actively and constructively.

Reading – Pinpoint some of the differences between the C19 and modern version in terms of sentence structure, vocabulary, and verbalise these to a partner/teacher.

Equipment/resources:
Worksheet 1 – Grimms' Stories, modern version.
Worksheet 2 – chart of gender types in four stories.

Lesson content and method

Activity	Content	Timing
Starter activity	Class brainstorm of all the fairy-tales they know. In pairs – list either the themes, settings, character types, plots – teacher to draw together on board.	10 minutes
Teacher introduction	Introduce scheme of work and pupil learning objectives for the lesson. Divide into pairs and instruct pupils in pairs (A and B) to retell story of *Cinderella* (A) and *Little Red Riding Hood* (B). Partner to listen carefully and add any omissions or differences.	15 minutes
Development 1	Teacher draws out points about no 'fixed' version until C19 (Grimm and Anderson). Give out worksheets with C19 and modern versions (e.g. from *Inside Stories* 3 and 4). Pupils to note differences between own version and C19.	10 minutes
Development 2	Give out worksheet 2 (chart of gender types – mother, daughter; other women, father, hero, other men – for *Cinderella*, *Little Red Riding Hood*, and two others of pupils' choice (e.g. *Hansel and Gretel*, *Snow White*). Pupils fill in worksheet. When finished or stuck join another pair.	15 minutes
Plenary	Feedback from groups to ensure understanding of stereotyping. Revert to aims of lessons, and draw conclusions about what has been learned.	10 minutes

Figure 3.2 English lesson plan for Key Stage 3

> **Task 3.1 Lesson Planning for Key Stage 3**
>
> The aim of this task is to become familiar with *The National Curriculum for England* (DFEE/QCA, 1999), the *Framework for Teaching English* (DfEE, 2001) and with your department's syllabus. With reference to your school's English syllabus for Key Stage 3, map out the long-term aims drawn from the National Curriculum. Plan a lesson for a Year 8 or 9 mixed-ability class, using the outline above (Figure 3.2) or the one advised by your mentor or tutor. Identify your aims for the lesson and the relevant statements from the knowledge, skills and understanding, and breadth of study sections from the National Curriculum. Use the *Framework for Teaching English* to identify specific pupil learning objectives. Teach the lesson plan and evaluate it with reference to your stated aims. After the lesson, discuss the suitability and success of your planning with your mentor.

language to censor. The narrative forms we master provide genres for thinking with' (Harold Rosen, in Prain, 1996, p. 10).

SUMMARY OF WORKING WITH THE NATIONAL CURRICULUM AT KEY STAGE 3

So far, the principle of working with and beyond the National Curriculum programmes of study has been emphasised and illustrated. In practice, you may find that your planning is dominated by the demands to provide evidence of pupils' achievement in terms of the objectives for each year contained in the Framework for teaching English, the Attainment Targets and, in Year 9, by preparation for the SATs. In addition, Key Stage 3 needs to be understood in terms of continuity and progression throughout the curriculum phases. Whatever the activity may be, it should take into account the pupils' prior learning: in Year 8 (or Year 9 of an upper school) you need to consider continuity from work at Key Stage 3; you also need to perceive work at Key Stage 3 as preparation for Key Stage 4. In *The National Curriculum in England* (DFEE/QCA, 1999) the programmes of study are combined for Key Stages 3 and 4; they are distinguished, however, in their assessment: SATs at Key Stage 3 and GCSE coursework and examinations at Key Stage 4.

ENGLISH IN THE NATIONAL CURRICULUM AT KEY STAGE 4: GCSE

The programmes of study and assessment requirements for Key Stage 4 have been adapted by QCA into common requirements for all GCSE syllabuses for English with additional requirements being specified for English literature. All GCSE examining groups rewrote their syllabuses to conform to the new regulations for *The National Curriculum in England* (DFEE/QCA, 1999). From September 2002, English departments have had to rethink their choice of examination board. Although there is, inevitably, much similarity in the content of syllabuses, there are differing priorities and philosophies implicit in the weighting, type of examination questions and choice of set texts. Some boards, for example, set different reading for each tier which is likely to preclude mixed-ability grouping. The requirements for GCSE English and GCSE English literature are shown in Figures 3.3 and 3.4.

So far you have been given a summary of what is common in terms of content to syllabuses for English and English literature. You have seen that you need to know how each aspect of the syllabus is to be assessed, whether by examination or course-work, and the skills which are the focus for assessment. Figure 3.5 shows in more detail what is required in terms of skills rather than content.

WORKING WITH GCSE ENGLISH AND ENGLISH LITERATURE

The following is an example of a scheme of work based on short stories. It deliberately connects with the sample lesson plan used in 'Working at Key Stage 3' (Figure 3.2) as a reminder that Key Stage 3 work is also preparation for Key Stage 4 (Figure 3.6). It uses the same principles about narrative and therefore further illustrates the possibility of working both within and beyond the programmes of study. It meets the requirements of an English and/or English literature syllabus if you choose prescribed or recom-mended texts. With reference to the AQA (A) syllabuses for 2004, for example, you could use five or six short stories in the detective fiction range, including Arthur Conan Doyle for the prose study in GSCE English, or use the anthology of post-1914 short stories from different cultures and traditions issued by OCR to make connections and comparisons.

The scheme of work is designed to meet the requirements of syllabuses for GCSE. It is also based upon principles which have long been common to English teachers, such as: the comparative analysis of texts sharpens critical awareness; a choice of tasks allows for differentiation; reading different discourses enlarges pupils' own language use; and telling and retelling develops thinking.

Therefore, although this scheme of work looks simple and clearly meets the require-ments of the GCSE syllabus, it is also securely founded upon objectives which are now specified for assessment. It allows you to retain aims for your teaching which underpin the activities; these are to do with the development of pupils in terms of their language competence through cultural analysis and use of language. It is nevertheless only a basic framework for a scheme of work and you would need to spend sufficient time engaging with each of the stories. Exploratory activities might include:

- Directed Activities Related to Texts (DARTs) such as predications, cloze procedures, colour-coding repetitions of phrases or vocabulary;
- group discussions relating the stories to their own personal experiences;
- pupils devising questions for each other;
- using pictures, illustrations, photographs and objects to represent the story;
- role-play or scripting for reading on the radio.

Worksheet 1 could be modelled on those provided in Heinemann *Core English* or *Contexts* folders. The point of Worksheet 2 is to ensure that redrafting is a meaningful

Speaking and listening

For the purposes of assessment, the programmes of study are clustered into three categories:

- explain, describe, narrate;
- explore, analyse, imagine;
- discuss, argue, persuade.

Reading

For the purposes of assessment, the range of reading assessed must cover prose, poetry and drama texts, with work from the English Literary Heritage by at least one major writer with a well-established critical reputation:

- play by Shakespeare;
- range of poetry, which must include the study of at least fifteen poems;
- range of prose, including a substantial prose text;
- media;
- non-fiction;
- texts from other cultures and traditions.

Writing

For the purposes of assessment, the programmes of study are clustered into four categories as follows:

- explore, imagine, entertain;
- inform, explain, describe;
- argue, persuade, advise;
- analyse, review, comment.

Assessment

1   Examination (60%):
    Two × 2 hr/1 hr 45mins examinations consisting of two sections each
    Section A – reading (including unseen reading test, media and non-fiction text).
    Section B – writing (including a test of 'argue, persuade, advise' and 'to inform, explain, describe'– all boards).
2   Coursework (40%):
    - 20% Speaking and listening by means of a group discussion and interaction, a drama-focused activity and an extended individual piece;
    - 20% Shakespeare play, response to prose or poetry, writing 'to explore, imagine, entertain'– all boards. Balance between reading and writing to be achieved in coursework;
    - three assessed assignments plus teacher's back-up record to be available for external moderator, if requested. (Oral assessment of reading and of literature texts allowed by some boards.) No dual assessment of coursework pieces for both reading and writing.

Notes

1   One text may cover several requirements: for example, coursework on Shakespeare and on literature pre- and post-1914 can be cross-over pieces for English literature coursework (although they may need to meet different objectives for the English or English literature syllabus).
2   Boards differ over how each category of reading is examined. For example, texts from different cultures and traditions are assessed through poetry in the exam (AQA A and B); through coursework and exam (Edexcel, WJEC)), exam only (OCR): media through exam only (AQA B, OCR, WJEC), coursework and exam (AQA A, Edexcel).

3   Boards differ over how each category of writing is examined. For example, 'analyse, review comment': Media coursework only (AQA);
4   AQA A and B, and OCR publish anthologies for poetry.
5   Most boards use pre-release material.
6   Grades are maintained but correspond to level descriptions.
7   Tiers of papers: foundation (F–C) and higher (D–A*) with no roll up or down: i.e. if a pupil fails to gain grade D at Higher, they are Unclassified.

The exam boards are as follows: Assessment and Qualifications Alliance (AQA), Edexcel, Oxford, Cambridge and RSA Examinations (OCR), Welsh Joint Examination Council (WJEC).

Figure 3.3 GCSE English (adapted from 'The New GCSE Specs', *English and Media Magazine*, 46, June 2002)

The requirements of English literature are demanding in terms of quantity and quality, the amount of content and the revised criteria which specify that considered responses to literature, including connections and comparisons between texts have to be made. Candidates are assessed on their understanding of literary tradition, and appreciation of social and historical influences and cultural contexts.

Set texts
● evidence of the study of three genres;
● each genre to include a pre-1914 and post-1914 text;
● one of these texts may be literary non-fiction.

Assessment
● coursework – 30%: three pieces;
● examination – 70%: one paper (1 hr 45 mins to 2hrs 15 mins) on specific set texts which must be in at least three genres;
● poetry questions for both English and literature must specify at least one poem which pupils must answer;
● two tiers as for GCSE English. Set texts common to both tiers;
● clean exam texts (i.e. without any annotations) will be required by 2005, and exam boards must specify the edition to be used.

Notes
1   Most boards state that pupils must not respond to texts which have been studied for the exam.
2   Three boards include literary non-fiction (Edecel, WJEC and OCR).
3   All boards assess poetry by exam; some through exam and coursework (AQA B, Edexcel, OCR, WjEC).
4   Cross-overs with English GCSE include Shakespeare, prose study, poetry.
5   Open Book exams (apart from WJEC).
6   Most boards publish anthologies (some for cross-over use with English GCSE), especially for poetry and short stories.

Figure 3.4 GCSE English literature

Speaking and listening
- communicate clearly and imaginatively, structuring and organising their talk and adapting to different situations;
- use standard English;
- listen to and understand varied speech;
- participate in discussion, judging the nature and purposes of contributions and the roles of participants;
- adopt roles and communicate with audiences using a range of techniques.

Reading
- read with insight and engagement, making appropriate references to texts and developing and sustaining interpretations of them;
- distinguish between fact and opinion and evaluate how information is presented; follow an argument, identifying implications and recognising inconsistencies;
- select material appropriate to their purpose, collate material from different sources, and make cross-references;
- understand and evaluate how writers use linguistic, structural and presentational devices to achieve their effects and comment on ways language varies and changes.

Writing
- communicate clearly, adapting their writing for a wide range of purposes and audiences;
- use and adapt forms and genres for specific purposes and effects;
- organise ideas into sentences, paragraphs and whole texts;
- use accurate spelling and punctuation, and present work neatly and clearly;
- use the grammatical structures of standard English and a wide range of vocabulary to express meanings with clarity and precision.

Literature (separate syllabus)
- respond to texts critically, sensitively and in detail, selecting appropriate ways to convey their response, using textual evidence as appropriate;
- explore how language, structure and forms contribute to the meanings of texts, considering different approaches to texts and alternative interpretations;
- explore relationships and comparisons between texts, selecting and evaluating relevant material;
- relate texts to their social, cultural and historical contexts and literary traditions.

The statements refer to the opportunities which pupils should have.

Figure 3.5 Summary of assessment objectives for 2002: GCSE English and English literature (adapted from 'GCSE '98: What's the Difference?', *English and Media Magazine*, 34, summer 1996, pp. 21–26, and QCA GCSE Subject Criteria)

activity and not just a copying exercise. It will include guidance about checking spelling and punctuation, but should also provide guidance on experimenting with structure, syntax and vocabulary. Response partners could also be used to act as friendly editors of each other's work.

Class: 10   **Syllabus**:

Title of scheme of work: Reading and responding to short stories.

Main objective/s: To understand genre (short story); to develop ability to write narrative.

Assessment:
Speaking/Listening –
Writing – write to 'imagine, explore, entertain' coursework in a range of forms (short story); develop
     vocabulary, syntax, structure; use standard English and accurate expression.
Reading – coursework essay for English literature, and useful practice for English prose examination;
     read with insight and engagement, making appropriate references to texts . . . understand and
     evaluate how writers use linguistic, structural and presentational devices to achieve their effects
     . . . explore relationships and comparisons between texts, selecting and evaluating relevant
     material.

Equipment/resources: five texts, worksheets 1 and 2.

Sequence of lessons – showing continuity and progression
1   Read story 1. Complete chart (worksheet 1) to identify characteristics of short story – point of
     view, characterisation, treatment of time, surprise, social comment.
2   As for lesson 1 with story 2, making comparisons and connections between them.
3   As for lesson 2 with story 3.
4   Develop thinking about short stories and the process of writing. Use supporting materials such
     as interviews with a short story writer. Clarify principles of planning and research before writing.
     Give out worksheet 1 and introduce choice of tasks (retelling a story provided, prequel or sequel
     of story provided, design own story, considering genre, e.g. romance; crime). Think about and
     make initial notes for homework.
5   Plan and draft story. Some pupils read out beginnings. Give out worksheet 2 which instructs (a)
     exchange story with partner and how to constructively criticise; (b) advice for redrafting.
6   As for 5. Complete for homework. Write a commentary discussing how you wrote your story,
     and what effect you hoped to achieve.
7   Read fourth story in the light of the experience of writing own stories. Compare with first three.
8   As for 7 with story 5.
9   Use jigsaw grouping to discuss point of view, characterisations, time, surprise, social comment.
10   Individual essays comparing and making connections between the five short stories. Complete
     for homework.

Figure 3.6 Scheme of work for Key Stage 4

AM I EQUIPPED TO TEACH THE NATIONAL CURRICULUM?

All teachers are likely to concentrate on the subject areas with which they are most
confident and these are likely to correspond most closely to their own educational
opportunities. Consequently, you may find yourself not only reproducing the attitudes
and activities which you have experienced, but also avoiding the areas where you are
less knowledgeable. Most experienced teachers have had to learn new curriculum

Task 3.2 Working with a GCSE Syllabus

The aim of this task is for you to become familiar with a GCSE syllabus and supporting materials and to see how they work in practice. It is tempting to avoid the documentation provided by examining groups but their booklets are invaluable for giving guidance about what is to be taught, marking criteria and sample examination materials. You should collect the syllabus materials and discuss them with your mentor.

1   Get a copy of the school's GCSE syllabus for English and English literature. Discuss with the head of English the reasons why this board was chosen. Read the syllabus and consider how it meets the common requirements for GCSE in terms of reading, writing, examination and coursework.

2   Look at sample materials provided by the examining group. Work out which knowledge and skills are tested in the examination.

3   Find out the departmental practice concerning teaching and assessing speaking and listening (e.g. Are lessons specified for assessment? How are records kept?).

4   What is the marking and assessment policy for GCSE work (e.g. are grades put on pupils' work?)

5   Study the department's syllabus for Years 10 and 11. Note how much time is allocated to each text or unit of work.

6   Plan your own scheme of work for a Year 10 class in conjunction with their GCSE syllabus requirements for English and/or English literature. Discuss it with your tutor.

requirements, such as media studies, using information communication technology and the not inconsiderable new demands for secondary English teachers on grammar. The need to keep up to date with contemporary fiction for teenagers and young adults, and with texts from different cultures and traditions for those who have a more traditionally 'English literature' degree should be viewed as welcome opportunities for personal development (and sheer enjoyment!) rather than as causes for resistance or anxiety. The final chapter in this book charts the curriculum requirements for English teachers in relation to their own educational opportunities. (See also Unit 1.1 and Task 1.1.2 in Capel *et al.*, 1995.)

Curriculum resources

When you consider the demands in terms of the range of knowledge and approaches required to teach English, it can be reassuring to know that educational publishers always respond to the needs of teachers, and excellent course texts and photocopiable folders, television programmes and educational software are produced. You will, of course, always need to know the resources well and adapt them for your class. Explore the resources in your school and training institution and ask colleagues in school for their recommendations. The following are particularly recommended to support your lesson planning with relation to the requirements of *English in the National Curriculum* (DFEE, 1999):

Task 3.3 Changing habits	

The aim of this task is to identify your own attitudes and insecurities when facing the requirements of the National Curriculum. In order to consider how your own experiences of English lessons at school may affect your approach to teaching, discuss the following questions with another student teacher, your mentor or tutor.

1   **Speaking and listening:** Were you actively encouraged to take part in discussions? What were the places of debate, role-play, small group discussion, producing media texts?

2   **Reading:** Were your progression and achievement measured by the number of classic writers you read? What part did television and film play in the classroom? What part did your own independent reading play here? Were records kept of this?

3   **Writing:** What proportion of time was spent in creating poems, plays and narratives? How were they marked – by spelling, handwriting or the teacher's judgement? Did you know what the teacher was looking for?

4   **Language study:** To what extent were you taught 'traditional' grammar? Were you taught to use standard English in writing or talk? Did you learn about language change and variety?

5   **Methodology:** to what extent was teaching didactic or pupil-centred? How did you best learn? What motivated your learning?

Bain, E. and Bain, R. (1996) *The Grammar Book*, Sheffield: NATE.

Broadbent, S. and Webster, L. (2001) *English and Media Centre KS3 English Series*, London: English and Media Centre (three books and accompanying videos on *The Media Book*, *The Poetry Book*, *The Non-Fiction Book*).

Buckley, K. *et al.* (1995) *Exploring Pre-Twentieth-Century Fiction: A Language Approach*, Lancaster: Framework Press.

Dean, G. (2000) *Teaching Reading in Secondary Schools*, London: David Fulton.

Goodwyn, A. (1998) *Literacy and Media Texts in Secondary English*, London: Cassell Education.

Goodwyn, A. (ed.) (2000) *English in the Digital Age*, London: Cassell Education.

Lewis, M. and Wray, D. (2000) *Literacy in the Secondary School*, London: David Fulton.

Neelands, J. (1998) *Beginning Drama, 11–14*, London: David Fulton.

Shepherd, C. and White, C. (1991) *Novel Ideas*, Carlisle: Carel Press.

SUMMARY AND KEY POINTS

The requirements of the National Curriculum consist of programmes of study, which set out what is to be taught in speaking and listening, reading and writing. When planning schemes of work, you need to refer to the statements under Knowledge, Skills and understanding, and Breadth of study, and the sections on language structure in order to identify long-term, overal learning aims. For medium- and short-term lesson planning you need to refer to the year group objectives in the Framework for teaching English. You also need to refer to the Attainment Targets and adapt the level descriptions into criteria for assessment. An emphasis on assessment by examination at Key Stages 3 and 4 means that pupils need to be prepared for the skills demanded by timed examination as well as for coursework. Although you may believe that 'archaic, limiting, timed end-of-Key-Stage exams have no place in the sort of wide-ranging assessment scheme that is necessary to reflect the complexities of the curriculum' (Hickman, 1995, p. 7) you will aim to enable all pupils to achieve their best in terms of national assessment, such as level descriptions, SATs, GCSE coursework and examination.

English teachers aim to underpin their adherence to the National Curriculum requirements with a rationale for the development of literacy in its broadest sense so that all pupils enjoy an enriching curriculum. As stated in the Introduction to this chapter, the reason for this is the belief in 'the connections between language, education and full participation in a political democracy [which] have lain behind debates round English throughout two centuries' (Burgess, 1996, p. 67). The challenge for English teachers, therefore, is to work within the requirements of the National Curriculum and the National Literacy Strategy, while continuing to develop and think about their own pedagogic practice and questioning new interpretations of what 'English' and 'literacy' teaching is all about.

The quantity and breadth of reading and other subject knowledge required to teach the full curriculum age and ability range means that you should be able to draw upon your strengths in the subject, but you also need to develop other areas: twentieth- and pre-twentieth-century literature in all genres; non-fiction work; literature from a range of cultures and traditions; contemporary writing, especially for teenagers; Shakespeare at all levels; media studies; drama techniques and conventions; formal and informal speaking and listening activities; grammatical terminology; language variety and language change; standard English; and information and communications technology.

FURTHER READING

DES and Welsh Office (1995) *English in the National Curriculum*, London: HMSO.
Protherough, R. and King, P. (1995) *The Challenge of English in the National Curriculum*, London: Routledge. This is an issue-based book which looks at working with *English in the National Curriculum* without losing sight of the values and practices which English teachers have seen erased by a skills-based, pragmatic and over-prescriptive curriculum. It looks at the controversial questions involved in all areas of English teaching including grammar, assessment and pre-twentieth-century literature.

4 The National Literacy Strategy

Jo Westbrook

INTRODUCTION

The debate to 'raise standards' in education stemming from Sir Keith Joseph's 1984 north of English speech reaches a conclusion in the present Labour government's National Literacy Strategy (NLS). This chapter looks at the background to the implementation of the NLS in its first stage in primary schools from 1997 to 1998, and then, following the brief pilot project, the introduction of *The Framework for Teaching English: Years 7, 8 and 9* (DfES, 2001) in secondary schools from September 2001. The Framework sets out detailed objectives for teaching at each Year group; these are linked directly with LEA, school and individual year group target-setting to ensure that the vast majority (85 per cent) of pupils achieve Level 5 or above at the end of Key Stage 3. The impact upon secondary English departments, and indeed on whole school policy, has been huge. However, considering the governmental commitment to the initiative in terms of infrastructure, training and school-based resources, the actual implementation of the strategy is also varied in practice in individual schools. You may find wide differences in the way departments have organised their planning, use of starters and plenaries, and assessment across schools that may surprise you. You will need to understand the initiative as a historical and political instrument for reform and development in schools, and the details of the content in order to grasp the opportunities offered by the Strategy, as well as be in a position to critique it. The Key Stage 3 Strategy originally had three elements which ran to schools: at departmental level there is the Framework for teaching English (DfES, 2001); at the department for pupils with AEN/English department interface there are the Literacy Progress Units (DfES, 2001) for those pupils working below Level 4; and at whole school level there is the relaunch of the 1980s initiative of Language across the Curriculum as Literacy Across the Curriculum (DfES, 2001).

The Framework has teaching objectives for years 7, 8 and 9, grouped into Text, Sentence and Word level work. These provide continuity and progression with the NLS

Table 4.1 Framework 1

Text level – Reading	Text level – Writing	Speaking and listening
• Research and study skills • Reading for meaning • Understanding the author's craft • Study of literary texts	• Plan, draft and present • Imagine, explore, entertain • Inform, explain, describe • Persuade, argue, advise • Analyse, review, comment	• Speaking • Listening • Group discussion and interaction • Drama

at primary level Year 6, and also align directly with the National Curriculum at Text level through the division into Reading, Writing and Speaking and listening. The main headings under these are similar to those in the National Curriculum (Table 4.1).

However, the 'new' heading of 'Research and study skills' picks out and highlights those skills subsumed in the National Curriculum within 'Printed and ICT-based information texts'. Conversely, while 'Media and moving image texts' has its own section in the National Curriculum, it is subsumed under 'Reading for meaning', and, under 'Writing', under 'Imagine, explore, entertain'. Interestingly, Drama retains its own separate heading under Speaking and Listening in the Framework for teaching English.

The sections in the National Curriculum on standard English and language variation in En1, En2 (punctuation, spelling, handwriting and presentation) and En3 appear under Word and sentence-level work in the NLS, and are greatly expanded 'to secure proper attention to the skills of spelling, vocabulary, sentence construction, grammar and style, which underpin excellence in Text level work' (DfES, 2001, p.11). They are positioned before the text-level objectives in the NLS that could inadvertently, and wrongly, suggest that English teachers work from the 'smaller picture' to the larger picture (Table 4.2).

The Framework therefore gives very detailed and focused teaching objectives using precise terminology for medium- and short-term planning, while the National Curriculum gives the longer term view, with a focus on Breadth of study. It is up to the professional judgement of the teacher, of course, to select appropriately from each document and to match up the two according to the specific needs of his or her class, maintaining a balance of speaking, listening, reading, writing, and text- sentence- and word-level work.

Table 4.2 Framework 2

Word level	*Sentence level*
• Spelling • Spelling strategies • Vocabulary	• Sentence construction and punctuation • Paragraphing and cohesion • Stylistic conventions • Standard English and language variation

It is the delivery of the lesson that marks the greatest change from past teaching and learning styles and the most challenge. There is a recommended four-part lesson plan, adapted from the primary 'Literacy Hour':

- **Starter activity** – a ten-minute interactive teaching focusing on sentence and word level.
- **Teacher introduction** – teacher exposition with modelling/demonstration/questioning.
- **Development** – the main teaching points developed and applied in context through scaffolded group activity, leading to independent work.
- **Plenary** – to draw out and consolidate the learning through reflection, feedback, presentation.

Within this the teaching is explicit, interactive, fast-paced and 'ambitious' (DfES, 2001, p. 16), with more time devoted to initial whole class teaching. Guided reading and writing in groups often formed by ability allow for development of the main learning points, with targeted teacher or LSA support. There is a new focus on genre, with pupils encouraged to explore a variety of texts in a critical light, recognising text types, analysing their effectiveness, and reproducing them for a specific purpose and audience. English secondary teachers are familiar and confident with the teaching of both fiction and non-fiction texts; it is in the explicit instruction of word and sentence level with the imperative to have a confident grasp of grammar in use, *and* grammatical terminology that is new and challenging. How many of us could readily give the definition of an adverbial phrase or explain the various functions and placements of the subordinate clause pre-2001?

The second element is the Literacy Progress Units. These give a tightly structured format of twenty-minute lessons for small groups of three to five pupils who need to 'catch up' with their peers in terms of the objectives for each year, as additional support apart from the objectives in the word- and sentence-level columns. The Units focus on: writing organisation; information retrieval; spelling; reading between the lines; phonics; and sentences. Pupils are taught these specific skills outside of the English lessons, at breaks or lunchtimes, often by language support assistants in consultation with the English department. There are also Literacy Progress Units adapted for larger groups, as practice showed that English teachers were using the Units for whole classes to focus on common areas for development, often as the starter activity. Student teachers in school are encouraged to teach these Units to small groups as good experience and induction into the NLS.

The third element of the NLS is the focus on Literacy Across the Curriculum. This redistributes responsibility for the improvement of literacy skills from the English and Special Educational Needs department to the whole school. Individual departments audit their own schemes of work and resources in response to whole school INSET days working through the most relevant of the thirteen training modules in the Literacy Across the Curriculum Training Folder. Schools select curricular targets for all teachers to aim for. Objectives from the Framework are also delivered by departments, for example, focusing, on the organisation of essays using writing frames in history, or encouraging pupils to understand the spelling roots of subject-specific terminology in

---

OBJECTIVES

By the end of this chapter you should:

- understand the historical and political development of the National Literacy Strategy at Key Stage 3;
- have gained a working knowledge of the aims of the National Literacy Strategy at Key Stage 3 in terms of objectives, planning, delivery and assessment;
- understood some of the impact of the National Literacy Strategy on the teaching of English;
- begin to form opinions to inform your own practice as an English teacher of a Key Stage 3 class with regard to the implementation of the National Literacy Strategy.

---

science. QCA's *Language for Learning* (QCA, 2000) gives broader objectives for cross-curricular work in the same vein as the National Curriculum.

BACKGROUND

The implementation of the National Literacy Strategy at Key Stage 2

The 'long tail of underachievement' at Key Stage 3 (Brooks *et al.*, 1996, p. 10) was of increasing concern both to the outgoing Conservative government and for New Labour. The varied range of intervention – or 'interruption' – (Bryan and Westbrook, 2000, p. 52) strategies designed to improve basic literacy, from reading recovery to basic skills lessons, to the panacea of the integrated learning system of SuccessMaker, were clearly not leading to a measurable rise in literacy standards. They also placed responsibility solely on either the Special Needs department or the English department for the literacy progress of all pupils. There was also growing concern for the underachievement of boys in schools reported in Graham Frater's study (Frater, 1997). Pupils leaving primary school found it hard to cope with the demands of the secondary curriculum, which assumed a secure command of literacy skills, and commensurate cognitive understanding. Many pupils simply failed to make that leap from primary to secondary, and so fell behind for good.

For a government elected partly on its 'education, education, education' slogan, a greater commitment to the raising of standards needed to be demonstrated, linked to New Labour's vision of inclusion 'to raise standards for the many' (Tony Blair, 1997, quoted in Fullan, 2001). This meant providing a cohesive all-embracing strategy to meet the needs of all pupils and referring to the same objectives and targets, so avoiding the 'sticking plaster approach' to underachievement (Bryan and Westbrook, 2000, p.

52) existing previously. The National Literacy Project set up by the outgoing Conservative government was therefore extended nationally as the National Literacy Strategy to all primary schools from September 1997. This attempted to give a clear focus to the teaching of basic skills – reading, writing, spelling, punctuation and grammar – through the setting of teaching objectives at Text, Sentence and Word level for each term. Explicit literacy instruction was to be delivered through the daily Literacy Hour consisting of:

- Whole class text-level work – 15 minutes;
- Word- and sentence-level work – 15 minutes;
- Shared, guided or independent reading and writing – 20 minutes;
- Plenary – 10 minutes.

This was a model of learning based on different research strands (Beard, 1998). The theories put forward by the Russian psychologist Vygotsky whereby children learned their language and culture through social interaction in which the adult (or peer) modelled and scaffolded the learning was a dominant strand. Higher order skills developed through working, and playing, with the symbolic nature of language. Well-planned 'literacy events' in the classroom emulated the way children learned language at home. This was a dramatic change for primary teachers when translated into the need for detailed long-term, medium-term and weekly planning to meet all the objectives, and a challenge in terms of their professional pedagogic practice, and as non-specialists, for their subject knowledge. The government provided top-down support through the appointment of literacy consultants for each school, a massive injection of money for resources, extra texts, and national training and materials for all primary teachers. As such, the Strategy has indeed been national reform on a large scale, and is globally the most comprehensive and fully developed example of educational reform. 'Expectations, Progression, Engagement and Transformation' is the newest 'slogan' used to encapsulate the Strategy, with the emphasis perhaps on the transformation of the teaching profession: 'strengthening teaching and learning through a programme of professional development and practical support' (DfES website, 7 August 2002). There was seen to be strong leadership and a sense of coherence 'cascading' from the Secretary of State, to the Regional Directors of the NLS, to the LEAs, and won the enthusiastic support of headteachers. Most crucially, targets set for the nation by David Blunkett as Secretary of State for 85 per cent of all pupils in Year 6 to achieve Level 4 or above in reading and writing by 2002, and devolved to individual LEAs and schools via the Performance and Assessment Report (PANDA), were seen to be on their way to being met. Estelle Morris as the new Secretary of State from 2001 wisely deferred from giving a figure to such national expectations, particularly for Key Stage 3. The explicit and direct teaching of phonics, including the use of terminology such as 'morpheme', 'phonemes' and 'graphemes' in Year R, was meant to give a secure start to reading for all pupils, and given a 'real' context at text level by the increased range and breadth of texts to be read. This 'balanced approach' to the teaching of reading aimed to appease what had been two fiercely polarised camps: the Phonics approach, and The Real books approach. Critics argued, however, that word-level work dominated the Strategy, and led teachers to select whole texts only for what they could offer in terms of examples of homophones or the use of the comma. Best practice coming through the experience of four years of the NLS in primary schools showed that making links between the lesson parts gave coherence for the learners, together with a relaxation of the lesson structure as appropriate. Figure 4.1 gives an example of a real lesson observed at Reception year. The links between each section are obvious, with a move from a phonics approach to writing whole texts as a class, and then individual reading and writing in 'real life' contexts.

The initial emphasis on reading resulted, not surprisingly, in improvements at Key Stage 1 and 2 in reading. However, measured standards in writing did not improve (83 per cent of pupils gained Level 4 in reading as opposed to 55 per cent in writing at Key Stage 2 in 2000). Speaking and listening was also seen to have been neglected in the pursuit of higher reading standards. Consequently the government set out training materials to improve writing, allowing time for extended writing, and guidelines on the integration of speaking and listening. Primary schools have become more flexible as the NLS has bedded down, and individual professional judgements are made more confidently. The NLS has raised the expertise and esteem of primary teachers, and given opportunities for shared planning sessions. The National Curriculum was revised in 2000 to align more closely with the NLS at all key stages, as we have seen in the previous chapter, and to provide greater support for the transition from Year 6 to Year 7.

Whole class teaching at word level 15 minutes	Teacher uses a puppet to focus on final phonemes. Puppet 'says' 'elephamp' and children have to listen to the endings and say the correct one. Developed into children holding up a large letter, and building up consonant-vowel-consonant (CVC) words.
Whole class teaching – shared writing 25 minutes	Circus poster up on board. Teacher with children point out importance of layout, placing of word 'Circus', visual impact of images.
Guided activities – 'independent group tasks' 15 minutes	Four different groups (alternating activities for that week): 1 Reading the text *Kipper* in the reading corner with LSA 2 Listening to initial sounds of objects with second LSA 3 Making circus posters with class teacher 4 Circus role-play in 'Circus tent' with tickets, dressing-up clothes, seats.
Plenary – 10 minutes	Saying initial letter sounds in a funny/shy/angry way. Quick reading of whole words.

Figure 4.1 Example of a lesson plan for Year R

> **Task 4.1 Observation of a Key Stage 2 literacy lesson**
>
> 1   Arrange to observe a Key Stage 2 literacy lesson in one of your school's feeder primary schools. Make notes on how the four phases of the lesson are developed according to the original 'Literacy Hour' format of:
>   - whole class text level work – 15 minutes
>   - word and sentence level work – 15 minutes
>   - shared, guided or independent reading and writing – 20 minutes
>   - plenary – 10 minutes
> 2   How far is the lesson observed similar to the example given in Figure 4.1? Discuss the variations with the teacher if possible.
> 3   What links can you make between the Key Stage 2 lesson observed and a lesson at Year 7?

THE IMPLEMENTATION OF THE NATIONAL LITERACY STRATEGY AT KEY STAGE 3

Following the success of the Literacy Strategy in primary schools some eighteen LEAs piloted the Strategy in secondary schools from September 2001. The draft Framework for the Teaching of English at Years 7, 8 and 9 took cognisance of the differences in secondary schools and allowed for greater flexibility of delivery. Clarity of objectives remained, and explicit word- and sentence-level instruction directed to take place in the starter activity of ten minutes. Modelling the writing of a ghost story or the skimming of a Contents page from a non-fiction book with the aid of an OHT as part of the teacher introduction became familiar methods of teaching, as did the use of Directed Activities Related to Texts (DARTs), and the use of writing frames to scaffold the learning. Pilot schools were required to give the 'Optional' NC tests at the end of Years 7 and 8 to demonstrate improvement. The pilot was very short, with little time to either learn from the three years of the primary experience of the NLS, or to evaluate what had worked best in secondary schools. By Easter 2001 all schools had begun national training for implementation of the Framework at Year 7 as a minimum for September 2001, with a roll-out for Years 8 and 9 in the subsequent years.

Continuity with Year 6

Pupils coming into Year 7 are well versed in grammatical terminology, whole class interactive teaching, collaborative and independent ways of working, and in the forms and functions of different genre. Teachers of Year 7 will have visited primary schools to observe primary colleagues as part of their training to support this continuity, and to make sense of the incoming data from each feeder school. You should discuss their observations and collaborations. There is now also transition training, and the Years 6–7 bridging units of work. These units are designed to support the transition to secondary school through pupils beginning a unit in the last two weeks of Year 6, and completing it during their first two weeks in secondary school.

Summary schools

Task 4.2 Transition between Year 6 and Year 7

The implementation of both the National Curriculum and the NLS aimed to support Year 6–7 transition, through continuity of curriculum and pedagogy. The notion of giving Year 7 pupils a 'clean sheet' (p.20 of the *Framework*) or fresh start is considered both too slow, and also redundant. Teachers can draw on the incoming Key Stage 2 data to pinpoint accurately where each pupil's 'starting point' or needs are. However, with some schools receiving pupils from over fifty different feeder primary schools, especially those in London and urban areas, the use of data may be variable in practice.

Task: Find out what information your placement school is sent from their feeder primary school – Key Stage 2 NC test results, folders of work, and details of pupils with AEN.
    What does the secondary school do with the information? How is this used to inform the planning and teaching of the *Framework* at Key Stage 3?

I have a caveat here; no matter how much data you receive as a new teacher of a class, there are dangers in planning to teach specific texts and clusters of objectives without actually knowing the class well enough to make your own professional judgement about what their needs are. 'Start from where the learner is' has always been the English teacher's mantra. The experienced teacher may well give him- or herself time to become acquainted with each class before spending time on detailed planning. As a student teacher you will be given two or three weeks' preparation time to observe the class, collaborate and team-teach with the class teacher, and so begin to judge how they will respond to particular texts, who needs to sit away from who, what individual strengths and weaknesses there are. The NLS is simply a strategy to support the planning of teachers. Strictly applying the four-part lesson plan with objectives plucked randomly from the Framework will not work with an unknown class who use whole class teaching to speak off-task, and show off to friends, and who do not know how to work constructively in small groups. In this case the NLS lesson structure may need to be drastically adapted until the class, and the teacher, have become more familiar with one another. The central premise of the NLS is that learning is social, and is indeed a 'sharing of the culture'; some classes and pupils will need to be trained to work in this manner.

Similarly, a lack of spontaneity in the initial stages of getting to know a class may backfire. One of my trainees tells a story of a primary teacher with whom she worked while on primary school experience who, pre-NLS, enjoyed having her Year 5 pupils clamber around her desk each morning sharing stories like 'Miss, my rabbit died last night'. This helped to build relationships upon which the learning, and the teaching, was based. With the implementation of the NLS with its firm structure and fixed timetable slot, the teacher missed this social interaction. She came to feel that she wanted to go into her classes now and again and ask 'Did anyone's rabbit die last night?' Teachers need not let go of past pedagogic practices that still hold true. Giving pupils time to respond individually, and the teacher to listen properly and with genuine interest and engagement, may be seen as both NLS objectives and good practice.

Planning

English departments are encouraged to adapt existing schemes of work by mapping the original objectives with the new ones, and rewriting objectives and content accordingly. There is great emphasis placed on planning in the NLS to ensure the full coverage of the objectives for each year:

- long-term plans give an overview of each term for each year group, ensuring that the content of the National Curriculum and the objectives from the NLS for that year are covered, and a balance of fiction and non-fiction texts and a range of activities;
- medium-term plans give details of the aims, texts and clusters of objectives to be covered over a half-term or three- to four-week period;
- short-term plans give an 'at a glance' weekly overview of each lesson;
- individual lesson plans focus on the teaching and learning of one or two objectives, detailing the four-part plan.

Planning formats and examples of schemes of work are available on the DfES website, and in the training materials given. English departments are using a practical mix of original schemes of work with some rewritten sections, and, within the time constraints allotted for the implementation of the Strategy at Key Stage 3, some completely new medium-term and short-term plans, so compromising with what is both familiar, 'tried and tested', and with using the new formats. The great advantage for you as a trainee is the given support of the objectives, plans and lesson structure, allowing you to make full use of your time in getting to know your class, and the 'how' of classroom practice.

Task 4.3 Becoming familiar with the training materials

Arrange a time with your head of department to go through all the training materials and folders, including videos, for the Key Stage 3 Literacy Strategy. A full list of all the documentation is given at the end of this chapter. Following this you will need to ask for the department's rewritten or newly written schemes of work to see how the NLS has been implemented in practice at school level. You will most likely be asked to teach a medium- and even short-term plan devised by the department, and so you will need to understand their rationale for selecting particular objectives and texts. Nametags given for each objective in the *Framework* provide a useful shortened way of recording each one.

About the unit

The unit focuses on features of personal record writing. Pupils read a range of biographical and autobiographical texts and write a short biography.

Prior learning

In order to complete this unit successfully, pupils should be able to draw on their knowledge and experience of:

- working in groups;
- language conventions of different types of text;
- skimming and scanning;
- using features of formal written language;
- cohesion in texts;
- spoken and written texts.

Expectations

Most pupils will: understand the differences between kinds of text that contain accounts of lives; select information from several sources, incorporating it effectively into their own biographical writing and making use of linking structures which render texts coherent. They will understand key differences between spoken and written texts.

Some pupils will not have progressed so far and will select information from texts that influences their own writing. They will use some linking devices and show some understanding of the differences between spoken and written texts.

Some pupils will have progressed further and will use information from texts with intelligent selectivity, and grasp subtler differences between spoken and written texts. Their own writing will be fluent, stylish and confident, using a range of linking structures.

Starters

- use of pronouns;
- pronoun/verb agreement;
- dictionary race;
- word association;
- positive/negative;
- abstract/concrete;
- comparatives;
- critical terms.

Stages

1 Biography and autobiography

An analysis of the features of information texts, including those which help text cohesion.
Writing sections of their own autobiographies and biographies.

2 Orations and obituaries

Exploring differences between spoken and written English.
Researching, planning and writing orations and obituaries about the life of a person.

3 Gathering the evidence

Reviewing different types of text that give accounts of people's lives.
Writing the biography of a well-known person.

Resources

Rediscover Grammar, David Crystal.
Internet and school library: examples of different types of historical and biographical text, for example: encyclopedia extracts, newspaper articles, autobiographies/journals, obituaries. Sample page of textbook focusing on a 'great life' (e.g. from *Religious Education or History*).

Great lives objectives stage 1: Biography and autobiography				
Word	**Sentence**	**Reading**	**Writing**	**Speaking and listening**
		R2 Extracting information R3 Comparing presentation	Wr10 Organise texts Wr11 Present information	S&L10 Report main points

Great lives objectives stage 2: Orations and obituaries				
Word	**Sentence**	**Reading**	**Writing**	**Speaking and listening**
	S5 Active or passive voice S11 Paragraph cohesion S16 Spoken and written	R13 Non-fiction style	Wr14 Description	S&L16 Collaborate on script

Great lives objectives stage 3: Gathering the evidence				
Word	**Sentence**	**Reading**	**Writing**	**Speaking and listening**
W18 Terms of qualification and comparison	S12 Sequencing paragraphs		Wr1 Drafting Wr10 Organise texts	

Figure 4.2 Medium-term plan for Year 7 (from DfES Standards website: www.dfes.gov.uk/keystage3/strands/publications/?template+dwon&pub_id=1480&strand=english)

Examples of long-term and medium-term plans at Key Stage 3 are given in Chapter 3, 'Working with the National Curriculum', and further examples may be seen on the DfES Standards website. As a new student teacher in the classroom you may be required to draw up medium-term plans, but certainly weekly short-term plans, and individual lesson plans which will need to refer to the aims and clusters of objectives given in the medium-term plan. The medium-term plan given in Figure 4.2 also specifies pupils' prior learning, and the expectations for pupils of differing abilities which support your short-term planning, in particular the developmental phase of the lesson.

Short-term plans

English teachers are used to producing half-termly units or schemes of work, encouraged by the implementation of the National Curriculum for English in 1990 to ensure coverage of content and breadth. The short-term plans, however, are a new development, and originate from the NLS in primary schools. They support the

Year: 7
Term:
Week: 1
	Frankenstein – unit focuses on Philip Pullman's adaptation of Shelley's *Frankenstein*.
	Week 1: Focus on introductory activities, Act 1
	Objectives
	Word W15 Dictionary and thesaurus
	Text R6 Active reading
	      R8 Infer and deduce
	      R12 Character, setting, mood
	      R14 Language choices
	      R18 Response to a play
	S&L1 Clarify through talk
			School priorities:
			
			Writing
			Spelling
			Inference

Lesson 1 1 hour	**Starter** Opening oral starter. Different groups have different key words related to themes of play (prejudice, outsider, difference, revenge, etc.). Each group has 2/3 minutes to discuss what the word means to them and then to refer to dictionaries/thesaurus. Feedback. 10 mins	**Teacher introduction** Picking up on the theme of difference/outsider/prejudice, class reading of Dylan Thomas's 'The Hunchback in the Park'. Have poem on OHT – come to class reading of 'story' of the poem. 15 mins	**Development** Working in groups, students then look more closely at poem. Use worksheet to encourage a close reading of the poem, and to encourage students to consider what the poem is saying about the way people treat each other. Teacher to work on guided reading with Group 1. Teaching assistant to work with Group 2. 25 mins	**Plenary** Class feedback – what has the poem got to say about the themes raised at the beginning? 10 mins
Lesson 2 1 hour	Brainstorm – give students 2/3 minutes to write down everything they know about Frankenstein. Take feedback. 15 mins	Introduce play version, giving some background in the sense that it is an adaptation. Shared reading of opening speech of play. Put on OHT and begin to look at way the piece draws audience in, raising questions and creating suspense. Underline together phrases that create questions – generate list of class questions from the piece. 15 mins	In pairs, students then look more specifically at the language used to create suspense, or an 'eerie' atmosphere. Work in pairs, then feedback particularly effective words/phrases. 20 mins	Feedback from one group commenting on effectiveness of speech. Why is it used as an opening? What effect does it have, etc.? Ask another group to discuss links to starter activity, and feedback. 10 mins

Lesson 3 1 hour	Introduction on character. Ask question: How do writers create characters? List on board methods of characterisation – through actions, words, language, tone, etc., drawing on previous texts read, and pupils' prior knowledge. Use this as a 'framework' for later character analysis. 5 mins	Shared reading. As whole class read to the middle of Act 1 (Elizabeth's arrival). 25 mins	In pairs, students fill in character sheet, showing what they have learned so far about Frankenstein (and detailing their evidence). 20 mins	Take feedback from pupils on the character, referring back to the start of the lesson, in terms of how writers create character. Ask one or two pairs to create a freeze-frame or statue denoting individual characters. 10 mins

Figure 4.3 Example of a short-term weekly plan (adapted from 'Year 7 Unit – Drama Text: *Frankenstein*', devised by Simon Gibbons, NLS consultant for Redbridge)

teaching to specific objectives, and, for the more experienced teacher, and indeed for the student teacher, obviate the need for detailed individual lesson plans. They give an at-a-glance weekly overview, and can be planned, and implemented in collaboration with a teaching assistant so that both teacher and assistant know exactly what their roles are, implications for resources and so on. The progression over the weeks, and from one lesson to another, can be clearly seen and understood.

Figure 4.3 gives an example of a short-term weekly plan that also meets the requirements of the NLS in its formatting. The starters in this plan are linked directly to the main lesson activity, and, for this introductory session, are mainly text-level based. They have also been planned to show progression from one lesson to the next. The text-level aim is maintained throughout the first week, but with a sharp focus on sentence level as the key to reading the poem, and the opening speech of the play. Word level comes into play when looking at the language used to create an 'eerie atmosphere' in the second lesson. Thus there is a kind of kaleidoscopic effect used to support the pupils' understanding here, moving from the larger picture to the smaller one, and back again as appropriate. The timings of each part of the lesson alter according to need, but maintain the overall four-part structure.

Individual lesson plans

Figure 4.4 gives an example of an individual lesson plan that would be the first lesson of the scheme of work on biography and autobiography given in Figure 4.2. This gives a word-level starter on the use of the pronoun, drawing on pupils' prior knowledge of pronouns, and oral pair work to employ the part of speech in a meaningful context, using autobiographical story-telling. This then links directly to the teacher comparing key features of two texts in a modelling carried out in front of the whole class. This supports the pupils in completing a similar activity, scaffolded by a reading grid, by group work, and possibly given targeted support for guided reading by the teacher or teaching assistant. The plenary focuses on drawing together the textual differences between biography and autobiography. The lesson is highly focused, but has a variety of pair, group and whole class activities, and a mix of talk and reading, which means that the lesson objectives can be met.

You should not assume that pupils will understand automatically what the objective is. Writing the lesson objectives in pupil-friendly language on the board, and referring back to them frequently during the lesson sharpens the focus and allows for measurable targets. Conversely there may be other, richer aims, which you either plan to come out, or occur as part of an unplanned discussion or surprise response from pupils. English classes deal with the imagination and with human emotions, as well as with direct literacy instruction, and teenagers have a wonderful capacity to pose awkward questions. One head of English involved in the pilot of the NLS spoke of the loss of 'sparkle' in the classroom through over-planning, and over-zealous adherence to the four-part lesson plan (personal communication, January 2000). You may want to refresh yourself with the overriding aims and spirit of the NLS for pupils at the end of Key Stage 3 which focus on producing independent, creative and questioning speakers, readers and writers:

> The overall aim of the Framework is to enable all pupils to develop sophisticated literacy skills. By the end of Year 9, we expect each pupil to be:
>
> an effective speaker and listener:
> - with the clarity and confidence to convey a point of view or information;
> - using talk to explore, create, question and revise ideas, recognising language as a tool for learning;
>
> a shrewd and fluent independent reader:
> - reflective, critical and discriminating in response to a wide range of printed and visual texts.
>
> a confident writer:
> - able to write for a variety of purposes and audiences, knowing the conventions and beginning to adapt and develop them;
> - able to write imaginatively, effectively and correctly;
> - able to shape, express, experiment with and manipulate sentences.
>
> (Adapted from DfES, 2001, p. 10)

Subject knowledge

Children in Year R are taught about alliteration, syllables and end-pages which, when I was teaching in the 1980s, were the terrain of Year 8. The subject knowledge level

Stage 1 Biography and autobiography: Lesson 1
Pupil learning objectives: W17 Word classes
                            R3 Compare presentation

Starter
- A revision exercise on pronoun use.
- Create lists with whole class of all the pronouns they know: first, second and third person, gender, etc.
- Put pupils in groups or pairs to take turns to tell the story of something they did recently. They must not use any pronouns, and if they do so, the listeners note down each pronoun used. As a class then discuss why pronouns are useful.

Introduction
- Shared reading of short biographical and autobiographical texts. Teacher compares key features of the two texts at word, sentence and text level, e.g. *person, use of subordination, voice, vocabulary, cohesive devices, authorial viewpoint, text structure.*

Development
- In groups, differentiated if appropriate, pupils are given a range of short biographical and autobiographical texts which they classify and analyse using a group reading grid which requires identification of the key features discussed. (See KS3 Strategy support materials for an example of such a grid.)

Plenary
Review of similarities and differences at word, sentence and text level between biography and autobiography.

Homework

Figure 4.4 Example of an individual lesson plan (from DfES Standards website)

Task 4.4 Observing English lessons at Years 7, 8 and 9

1   Observe three English lessons for Years 7, 8 and 9. In what ways do they adhere to the four-part lesson plan recommended in the Framework? In what ways do they differ? Are all the lessons NLS-style lessons, or are some non-NLS? Discuss with your mentor the reasons for any variations.

2   Discuss the implementation of the NLS in your placement school with your mentor and other English department colleagues. What are their views on the implications of planning, delivery, resources and assessments of pupils?

---

has been heightened in the NLS; some of the terminology and concepts in the word- and sentence-level objectives may well be new to you if your degree was primarily literature based. Much of your knowledge will be implicit; teaching the use of connectives or the use of the active voice will crystallise your understanding, and make your own understanding explicit. The sentence and word banks (See 'Materials to gather') give practical examples of the objectives in context. What is important is that pupils' learning is dependent upon your integrating the subject knowledge with the right balance of text, sentence and word-level work appropriate for your classes, and style of teaching.

Starter activities

Starter activities are designed as a 'warm-up' to the main lesson, with the explicit teaching of 'small' bits of language in a fast-paced ten-minute interactive style in which all the class participate in some way. The Framework gives two examples of the use of starters: one series of starter activities on spelling words with -'shun' endings linked to each other, but not directly to the main lesson; the other with each starter linked directly to the lesson (e.g. revising school site spelling words such as corridor and laboratory), linked to the creation of an alternative school plan in the main lesson.

The training video shows teachers focusing on word- and sentence-level work, using individual pupil whiteboards for immediate visual feedback to the teacher and whole class correction. Departments are building up a bank of resources to use for starters; publishers have also been quick to produce 'starter kits' where laminated cards and worksheets support teachers to teach in what is still relatively unknown or unfamiliar territory.

The most effective starters are those that have been planned to link with the lesson unfolding either immediately following or in subsequent lessons that week. The learning that takes place can then be enacted upon and transferred to real contexts, and consolidated. The examples given in Figure 4.3 illustrate such an approach.

Task 4.5 Devising a starter activity

Select one word-level objective or one sentence-level objective. Plan a starter which involves the whole class, and which leads to learning gains at the end of the 10 minutes.

Starters are popular with English teachers, who are now confident about adapting them to their own purposes. Starters at text level are used, for example, to revise the particular forms of a text type, or to recap on a chapter read during the previous lesson. Common errors of spelling, punctuation or grammar arising from class work can be 'blitzed' through the strategic use of starters to reinforce learning. You may find that not every lesson needs a starter; if pupils are busily engaged in the writing of a lengthy story, stretching over two or three lessons, a starter may distract them from the task at hand, or may more effectively be introduced half-way through the writing lesson to break up the task, and to remind pupils of particular grammatical or text-level points.

Teaching and learning strategies

The requirement for explicit and clear teaching and learning strategies has led to an increased repertoire of teaching activities and sequences. Most whiteboards in classrooms now have a section labelled 'Lesson aim' for the teacher to write, in pupil-friendly language, the learning outcome or objective: 'This is what we are going to learn today.' The teacher reinforces this verbally by clarifying the aim, and referring to it at points during the lesson, and as part of the plenary.

a) Shared reading and writing

In a 'classic' NLS lesson the teacher then provides an example of the text, whether a poem, chapter, newspaper article, TV advert, computer game or speech. The text is shared with the whole class through teaching from the front, modelling by composing a story on the board led by the teacher or ways of inferring meaning from a text by underlining key ideas, but drawing out contributions and ideas from the class, or a demonstration where the teacher-as-expert writes their own science fiction short story opening or gives an example of a persuasive speech. The investigative nature of the Strategy is reinforced by the use of DARTs to give an active, critical engagement with the text. The social, talk-based context is the key to these activities:

> The apprenticeship of children into the use of written language for these purposes needs to involve teaching/learning activities which deconstruct written explanations collaboratively talking out the text and shunting back and forth between the grammar of spoken and written language.
>
> (Unsworth, 1997, p. 47)

Recognition of text type is an important part of the National Curriculum and NLS, with its list of distinctive non-fiction types:

Year 7 – Sentence level 13 stylistic conventions of non-fiction

- a) Information
- b) Recount
- c) Explanation
- d) Instructions
- e) Persuasion
- f) Discursive

These come from the EXIT (Extending Interactions with Texts) model of writing from Lewis and Wray (Lewis and Wray, 1995), another example of the way in which the Strategy has drawn upon various research and pedagogic practices. Pupils are asked to analyse such texts, and to articulate how they are constructed, using word-, sentence- and text-level terminology. This may be seen to be a form of critical literacy where basic questions are asked of any text, and then used to reproduce such a text themselves. The option also remains to subvert genres, and to produce new text types or parody known ones to avoid an over-formulaic response, which meet the overriding aims given earlier of the Framework. You may also want pupils to simply write from their own experience or imagination, writing 'from the heart' in what used to be known as poetic and transactional writing, and choosing the most appropriate form.

b) Guided reading and writing

The immediate application of what has been learned from the teacher introduction or whole class teaching is another strength of the four-part lesson. Pupils work in teacher-directed groups – the communal sharing of the culture – that may be either by ability, interest, friendship or gender. Each group may have a different text or task to work on, or a writing task, or topic to discuss. This is where classes need to be 'schooled' to work independently from the teacher as mentioned earlier, in order to give the teacher time to sit down and work in a concentrated fashion for twenty minutes with a particular group.

A particular 'instructional sequence' for guided reading is given in the Guided Reading in English at Key Stage 3 training materials shown in Figure 4.5 This sequence scaffolds learning for a small group, and mirrors the overall four-part lesson strategy. The recognition of the need for more time for extended independent reading and writing in English lessons has been met by the development of guided reading. The

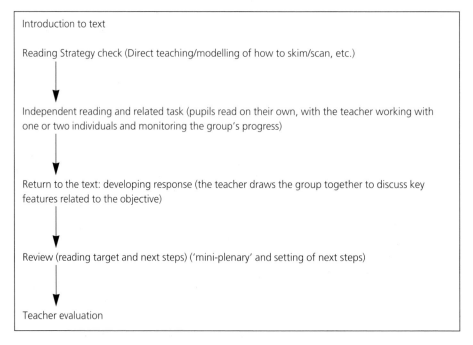

Introduction to text

Reading Strategy check (Direct teaching/modelling of how to skim/scan, etc.)

Independent reading and related task (pupils read on their own, with the teacher working with one or two individuals and monitoring the group's progress)

Return to the text: developing response (the teacher draws the group together to discuss key features related to the objective)

Review (reading target and next steps) ('mini-plenary' and setting of next steps)

Teacher evaluation

Figure 4.5 Instructional sequence for guided reading (Key Stage 3 National Strategy, 'Guided Reading in English at Key Stage 3' guidance folder published by the DfES and the Standards and Effectiveness Unit 02/02/Ref DfES 0044/2002)

Source: Key Stage 3 National Strategy 'Guided reading in English at Key Stage 3' guidance folder published by the DfES and the Standards and Effectiveness Unit 02/02 Ref: DfES 0044/2002

time for actual reading can vary according to need: in some lessons pupils may want to read for forty minutes to gain some sustained, uninterrupted reading of whole texts, as well as extracts. The teacher can then work with two groups for two twenty-minute focused sessions, allowing other groups a longer time to read as required.

The role of the teaching assistant has grown in importance in recent years along with the implementation of this part of the lesson, originating from the primary Literacy Hour. Indeed, it could be argued that without the in-class support of teaching assistants the Strategy could not be implemented at all. TAs are able to work alongside the teacher as professionals, leading the lesson at points, or modelling for the class, or recording pupil attainments. Teaching assistants also work with individual groups, especially groups of pupils with AEN in the development part of each lesson plan, and also teach the Literacy Progress Units with small groups of pupils outside of English lessons.

Task 4.6 Working with a teaching assistant

Discuss the role of the teaching assistants with the SENCo or your head of department. How much time is there for collaborative planning before lessons? How do English teachers work most effectively with teaching assistants in their lessons?

The Plenary

This is designed to 'draw out the learning and refer back to the lesson objectives' (effective use of the plenary Key Stage 3 National Strategy at www.standards.dfes.gov.uk/keystage3). It allows the pupils to reflect upon what they are learning, and to go out of the door with the explicit learning aim freshly relevant in their minds. The plenary also gives the teacher the opportunity to assess how much has been learned and to make explicit links between previous lessons and the next. Like starters, the plenary should be varied, and not rely on a routine formula of five minutes of quick lesson summary by the teacher. Involving the pupils through hot seating or by them asking the questions devolves the learning from teacher to pupils. You may also do 'mini-plenaries' all the way through a lesson at transition points, using it to round off one part and link to the next. Your pupils need to be shown where they are going and why as overtly as possible. Similarly you may want to use 'maxi-plenaries' at the end of a series of lessons. Here is one trainee discussing his adaptation of the plenary:

> 'I found it useful to do a "maxi-plenary" relating to the previous five or six lessons. I effectively recapped what we had learned about narrative writing and visualising characters, and scenarios. The plenary can occur almost anywhere and also relate to more than one lesson. If this is not the case then it is almost as if we forgot what had been learnt once the lesson (and accompanying plenary) are over.'

Task 4.7 Planning and teaching a whole lesson

Now that you have observed lessons at Key Stages 2 and 3, discussed the implementation of the NLS with your mentor, and explored the different lesson components, it is time for you to plan and teach your whole NLS lesson. It would be useful for your mentor to observe you teaching this lesson, or, alternatively, to take your lesson plan, and teach it him- or herself, observed by you.

- How explicit have you been about the objectives and timing?
- Are the links between each part of the lesson cohesive and obvious to the pupils?
- How did you go about organising your groups for the development part?
- How useful was the plenary in drawing conclusions about the learning in the lesson?

Assessment and target-setting

The Strategy requires each school to have curricular targets derived from the analysis of incoming cohorts' needs and test results. You will need to incorporate these wider aims into your own aims for each class, as well as those for each class for each scheme of work. Assessment will therefore focus on these objectives for major pieces of work produced at the end of units. In addition, pupils will have their own targets, and pupils with AEN will have their individual education plans with termly targets. The challenge is for you to maintain an overview of school and class targets in your records, while keeping a closer focus on formative 'daily' assessments. The constant and immediate 'in-the-head' assessments of pupils from the starter activity to the plenary will support you in making the right professional judgements needed both for on-the-spot assessments and for the subsequent lesson. Indeed, marking can become a whole class activity with very pertinent criteria for success shared with the class. With such an approach it may be possible to continue teaching the National Curriculum up until May for pupils to ready themselves for the optional Year 7 and 8 tests, and for Year 9 to revise more formally for the Year 9 NC tests. Some English departments had previously stopped teaching in the January of Year 9 in order to revise for the tests, which works against the spirit of continual assessment using the objectives from the Framework as stepping stones leading to learning, and the tests.

Differentiation

The original concept of the LPUs to support those pupils who had failed to reach Level 4 by Key Stage 2 has enlarged as the Strategy has been rolled out into Key Stage 3 and now also includes the following initiatives:

- Year 6–7 transition units and training;
- Summer schools/Easter schools/Saturdays;

- Year 7 catch-up based on the LPUs;
- Mentoring programme for Year 8 pupils who are falling behind;
- Key objectives at Year 8 (DfES, 2002) designed to avoid the dip in attainment at Year 8 and to keep energy levels up;
- Year 9 booster 'kit' (DfES, 2002) to 'maximise their success in the Year 9 tests', targeted at borderline pupils in the higher levels of 5 or above. The focus here is on revision for the tests, and targeted homework. The 'kit' contains a series of twelve tightly planned lessons analysing the requirements of the NC tests, and supporting pupils in their writing of, for example, persuasive writing and the shaping of a narrative. It offers practical 'tips' such as the 'PEE' paragraphs for giving quotations:
  P – What's your **point**?
  P – Give **evidence**.
  P – **Explain** it.
- Study support – a voluntary out-of-school scheme including Year 9 pupils reading with Year 7, and enrichment of the curriculum.

As the Strategy moves into its second year and embeds itself into school life, the increasing number of 'extra' intervention and support strategies or elements as outlined above does begin to replicate the patchwork of intervention which existed prior to its implementation in 2001. Whether this means that the Strategy has not been successful, or that the issues around literacy are more complex than a simple, single approach is difficult to gauge after a run-in of only one year at Key Stage 3. The difference from pre-NLS is that these further supports are centralised initiatives, all based upon the same objectives, forms of delivery and targets, supported by extra finance for schools, and, crucially, responsibility for their success devolved to all departments in school. The government's promise 'to raise standards for all' is also the driving force behind these new initiatives.

The danger remains, however, of reducing literacy to disconnected parts of language. As Colin Harrison puts it, 'critical literacy is just as important for weaker as for stronger readers' (Harrison, 2002, p. 3). The big text-level questions about where, why, how and for whom a text is produced should be asked of all pupils. Similarly, OFSTED found that, despite English as an Additional Language (EAL) support staff not being closely involved in the development of the strategy in the pilot, bilingual pupils 'benefited from the emphasis on oral work' (OFSTED, 2002, para. 35) and from 'the emphasis on engaging all pupils in a wide variety of activities, the attention given to the explicit teaching of grammar, and the building of vocabulary supportive of bilingual learners' (OFSTED, 2002, para. 50).

SUMMARY AND KEY POINTS

The drive to raise standards for all has seen the National Literacy Strategy firmly in place in primary schools from 1997, and, following the pilot in 2000, introduced to secondary schools from September 2001. The Key Stage 3 Strategy for Literacy has the three elements of the Framework for teaching English: Years 7, 8 and 9, the Literacy

Progress Units, and Literacy Across the Curriculum. Further developments focus on providing differentiated support for Years 8 and 9, and supporting teachers' practice in guided reading, and assessment. The Framework for English has objectives for Years 7, 8 and 9 grouped into five levels: word, sentence, text level – reading, text level – writing, and speaking and listening. The impact upon the teaching of English has been huge, with English teachers having both the content and the pedagogy of their practice challenged, and prescribed for the first time in history. When pupils in Reception class have a good understanding of morphemes, phonemes and graphemes, when lessons on alliteration and syllables previously taught at Year 8 and revised for GCSE are old hat by Year 1, then to a certain extent standards and expectations have been raised. Positively, this will mean that pupils coming to Year 7 should be well grounded in the 'basics', allowing secondary English teachers to teach the increasingly broad and rich number of texts, whether print-based, ICT or media texts, required in the National Curriculum. The word- and sentence-level objectives offer challenges in terms of subject knowledge for all secondary English teachers, but, to quote from the rationale on 'Knowledge about language' given in the 1989 Cox Report: 'Language is central to individual human development; human society is inconceivable without it. *Therefore it is intrinsically interesting and worthy of study in its own right*' (DES, 1989, para. 6.7; emphasis added).

Best practice in the NLS allows pupils to gain a sophisticated understanding about language within a meaningful context through investigation, armed with a cheerful confidence about how language works. The planning requirements for the NLS are considerable and necessary in order to ensure that all the objectives, or clusters of objectives, have not only been covered, but also understood, by the end of Year 9. English departments have been given time to rewrite schemes of work for Year 7, and are 'rolling out' Years 8 and 9 over the next two years. As a student teacher you will find it immensely helpful in your first year, and as a NQT, to have schemes of work ready for you to teach, so that you can concentrate on their delivery. The four-part lesson plan of start activity, teacher introduction, development and plenary is a recommendation only, and should be used flexibly to meet the particular needs of your pupils. There is a wealth of teaching strategies and ideas to support you here, from the NLS training materials published by the DfES, to the mountains of commercially produced materials, from starter activity kits with their laminated cards, to photocopiable writing frames and anthologies of non-fiction writing.

As a student teacher you will need to take the NLS on completely, and absorb all the materials, and teach your classes according to the objectives and the delivery. But you will also need to reflect upon what English teachers taught, and how they taught, before the implementation of the NLS, and consider what the future of the NLS might be once it embeds more firmly into secondary schools. You may want to teach a 'non-NLS' lesson for your own professional development, and engage in pedagogical discussion about directions the NLS may evolve into to avoid fossilisation. The greater flexibility of the NLS at secondary schools, and the encouragement to maintain existing good practice in English classrooms, ensures that a pedagogical debate around the nature of English teaching continues, and that the 'sparkle' in the English classroom is not lost.

MATERIALS TO GATHER

The following four NLS documents should be given to you from your training institution:

Key Stage 3 Framework for teaching English (DfEE, 2001)
Key Stage 3 Year 7 Spelling Bank (DfEE, 2001)
Key Stage 3 Year 7 Sentence Bank (DfEE, 2001)
Key Stage 3 Year 7 Speaking and Listening Bank (DfEE, 2001)

The following sets of materials should be available in schools, or from the following website:
http://standards.dfes.gov.uk/keystage3/publications
DfES Publications
Tel: 0845 6022260
E-mail: dfes@prolog.uk.com

Literacy Progress Units (DfES, 2001)
Guided Reading (DfES, 2002)
Key Objectives Bank for Teaching and Assessment for Year 8 (DfES, 2002)
Year 9 Booster Kits (DfES, 2002)
Making Assessment Work (DfES, 2002)
Key Stage 3 English Roots and Research by Colin Harrison (DfES, 2002)
Guidance for the Marking of Writing (QCA, 2002)

Also useful:
Key Stage 1 and 2 English Framework (DfEE, 1997)
Grammar For Writing (DfEE, 2001)
Language for Learning (QCA, 2001)

ACKNOWLEDGEMENTS

Thanks to Aylesham Primary School in Kent, my trainees on the PGCE flexible programme at Canterbury Christ Church University College and primary colleagues for their discussions and input – from 1996 to today.

REFERENCES

Beard, R. (1998) *National Literacy Strategy: Review of Research and other Related Evidence*, London: Department for Employment and Education.
Brooks, Cato, V., Fernandes, C., Gorman, T., Kispal, A. and Orr, G. (1996) *Reading Performance at Nine*, Slough: NFER.
Bryan, H. and Westbrook, J. (2000) '(Re) defining literacy: how can schools define literacy on their own terms, and create a school culture that reflects that definition?', in Davison, J. and Moss, J. (2000) *Issues in English Teaching*, London: Routledge.

DES (1989) *English for Ages 5 to 16*, London: DfES (The Cox Report).

Frater, G. (1997) *Improving Boys' Literacy*, London: Basic Skills Agency.

Lewis, M. and Wray, D. (1995) *Developing Children's Non-Fiction Writing: Working with Writing Frames*, Leamington Spa: Scholastic Press.

Fullan, M. (2001) *Watching and Learning – Reflections after Year One of the NLS/NNS*, Ontario Institute for Studies in Education, University of Toronto (OISE/UT).

Office for Standards in Education (2002) *The Key Stage 3 Strategy: Evaluation of the First Year of the Pilot*, London: OFSTED.

Unsworth, L. (1997) 'Scaffolding reading of science explanations', *Reading*, November.

5 Speaking and listening

Gabrielle Cliff Hodges

INTRODUCTION

Within the English curriculum the importance of reading and writing has always been uncontested, whereas the importance of speaking and listening has only recently been fully acknowledged. Before the 1960s oral work was very likely to consist of teacher-led question-and-answer sessions or formal activities such as reading aloud, debates and prepared short talks. However, during the 1960s the influence of educators such as Andrew Wilkinson (cited in Howe, 1997, p. 6) and a growing awareness of the work of psychologists such as Vygotsky led to more systematic studies of the role of classroom talk. New understandings about the relationship between language and learning emerged and led to significant changes in classroom practice. Speaking and listening were gradually afforded greater status and made a compulsory part of the assessment of English at GCSE. Subsequently, 'Speaking and listening' became the first Attainment Target for English in the National Curriculum.

Vygotsky's theories are helpful to English teachers in a number of ways. First, he argues that children learn to think by talking with others, by engaging in a social process which enables them to 'grow into the intellectual life of those around them' (Vygotsky, 1978, p. 88). At a certain stage in the child's development, speech divides into two distinct kinds: 'communicative' speech to be used for communication with others, and 'egocentric' speech or speech for oneself which will eventually turn inward to become 'inner' speech with its own idiosyncrasies of grammar, for individual thinking. Inner speech has different rules from communicative speech: with inner speech, speaker and listener form the same consciousness so there is much that can be taken as read; with communicative speech the need is to be understood by another person so more must be made explicit. Inner speech is not, therefore, a mirror image of communicative speech. It is essentially different because it is serving a different purpose. The distinctive natures of inner and outer speech and the power of the dynamic relationship between them to enable intellectual development are vital to an understanding of how children become effective learners and the part teachers have to play in that development.

In the late 1960s, with the aid of portable tape-recorders, researchers and teachers such as Douglas Barnes, James Britton and Harold Rosen were able to study much more systematically than ever before the kinds of spoken exchange that took place between teacher and pupil, and between pupil and pupil in ordinary classrooms (Barnes *et al.* 1969). They analysed how and when learning seemed to be taking place and the part played by home dialects, spoken standard English, the task set, the formality of the context, and the authenticity of the problem to be solved. New understandings emerged about the role of exploratory talk in cognitive development, of how talk might be used to learn through speculating, hypothesising, arguing, negotiating and so on. These understandings, in turn, led to new classroom practices. Teachers began to organise their classrooms for group work, to plan activities which involved solving problems, discussing texts, debating controversial issues more informally than hitherto. Time was also spent teaching about talk, making explicit what pupils knew implicitly about how, for example, spoken language is affected by the context and purpose of the communication and by the audience to whom it is addressed; about why and when people alternate between speaking in standard English or their regional dialect. Whether pupils were learning through speaking and listening or learning about speaking and listening, silent classrooms were no longer prized once it was realised that talk might sometimes have a greater role to play in the development of learning than silence.

Gradually the move was towards recognising the centrality of speaking and listening, and investigating how it might be assessed. Many felt that it never could be effectively assessed. Knowing that they were being assessed would affect how pupils performed and distort the outcome. Nevertheless, surveys into the development of oracy conducted by the Assessment of Performance Unit (APU) in the 1980s pointed the way to the development of assessment criteria and to exploring what constituted progression in speaking and listening (Johnson, in Norman, 1992, p. 51).

For those new to English teaching, the important point to remember is that speaking and listening in classrooms has not always been viewed the way it is now. It is worth familiarising yourself with how its current position has been arrived at (Howe, 1997, pp. 3–7; Johnson, in Norman, 1992, pp. 50–60), what some of the debates have been, and what theories have informed them so that you can begin to develop a rationale of your own for teaching and assessing speaking and listening. You may remember vividly what counted as speaking and listening when you were at school and have strong feelings about it, but however recently you were at school yourself, things will have changed. As a learner you need to trace for yourself the steps which will show you the moves from traditional patterns of speaking and listening in schools to new approaches adopted by many teachers nowadays. You have to make what is described in the Bullock Report as 'a journey in thought' (DES, 1975, p. 141) about speaking and listening for yourself. This chapter is designed to help you map that journey.

It is worth bearing in mind, however, that although maps will take you a long way there may be value in sometimes deviating from marked routes. An account of where the origin of Virginia Woolf's experimental work may have lain buried is recounted in her biography by Lyndall Gordon. Like her father, Virginia loved to step aside from the high road . . . to trust to innumerable footpaths, 'as thin as though trodden by rabbits', which led over the hill and moor in all directions . . . she followed natural paths which ignored artificial boundaries. The padlocked gates and farm walls were deceptive barriers for, when she climbed over, the path would continue quite happily.

(Gordon, 1984, pp. 78–79)

Thus, in her novels, she was inclined to ignore the signposts of birth, marriage and death; instead she tended to focus on 'those unlooked-for moments that shape our lives'. It may be the same with talk in classrooms: although there is much to be gained from thoughtful and reflective planning and organisation, sometimes the best talk occurs when and where it is least expected, precisely in those unlooked-for moments. Be ready to listen for them.

OBJECTIVES

By the end of this chapter you should:

- be aware of some of the factors which contribute to or inhibit effective, purposeful speaking and listening in English;
- be aware of how teaching about the differences between spoken and written language and about different types of talk can assist pupils in their development as speakers and listeners;
- understand how planning and the organisation of classrooms can contribute to pupils' language, learning and cognition;
- begin to understand how to assess pupils' speaking and listening against given criteria and to link assessment with future planning.

OBSERVING SPEAKING AND LISTENING

In order to enable pupils to develop their ability in speaking and listening it is useful to consider the range of talk which may occur within the boundaries of the classroom. In order to evaluate pupils' speaking and listening (so that you can identify achievement and plan for progression) there has to be consideration of audience, context and purpose. It is also important to understand the role of the teacher in providing opportunities for all pupils to participate and achieve (Table 5.1).

Table 5.1 Observing speaking and listening

Factors contributing to effective, purposeful talk	Factors inhibiting effective, purposeful talk

Task 5.1 Identifying helps and hindrances

In order to gain a clearer picture of the variety and value of talk in the classroom, find as many opportunities as you can to observe pupils speaking and listening. Draw up a table similar to Table 5.1 and use it to jot down your observations. Compare your findings with those of other student teachers observing in different contexts and curriculum areas.

At the start of any initial teacher education course a great deal of time is spent by student teachers in classroom observation. One of the best ways to begin thinking in depth about speaking and listening is to make diversity of talk and the range of classroom opportunities for speaking and listening key targets of that observation.

Contexts

While you are observing you will become increasingly aware of the difference made by the contexts in which speaking and listening are taking place. Small group discussions or question-and-answer sessions in English classrooms will involve pupils differently from drama lessons in which pupils are planning for performance or role-playing. In library lessons, pupils engaged in research will talk and listen differently to each other from how they will when working collaboratively on a screen in the computer suite.

Range, audience and purpose

You will begin to note the opportunities pupils are given to:

- talk formally/informally;
- talk in pairs/small groups/whole class discussions;
- use talk to explore and develop ideas at length;
- use talk to express their feelings and opinions;
- use talk to question and challenge what they hear;
- use talk to negotiate;
- use talk to instruct/listen to, and act on, instructions;
- use talk to ask questions as well as answer them;
- use talk to plan, explore and evaluate other activities;
- talk to a specified audience;
- talk for a specified purpose;
- talk about speaking and listening;
- plan and evaluate their talk;
- discuss different types of talk being used in drama and role-play.

The role of the teacher

The role of the teacher in developing pupils' speaking and listening is central. In terms of planning, organising, differentiating and so on, there is much to consider. In addition, however, teachers need to be conscious of how their own use of language affects the language used by pupils in their classes. It is therefore valuable to spend time in lessons observing teachers' as well as pupils' use of language.

A frequently used technique in many lessons across the curriculum, for example, is for teachers to ask questions of their pupils as a way of eliciting information, recapping on prior learning or checking instructions have been understood. It is worth considering, however, which are the pupils in any one class who are most likely to answer the teacher's questions. How long are pupils given to think before the chance to answer is passed on to someone else? Research reveals that:

> when questions are posed in everyday conversations, a response usually comes within less than a second of silence. This is also true of classroom questions. Teachers usually allow about a second for a reply and, if none is forthcoming, they take back the conversational floor. [But] where a longer silence was left – even one as short as three seconds – the quality and extent of pupils' responses improved dramatically.
>
> (Wood, in Norman, 1992, pp. 204–213)

Wood goes on to suggest that particular types of teacher talk create a classroom climate which affects how pupils themselves will talk. For example, where closed questions are common and are not followed up by the teacher with open-ended questions, pupils' responses are often single words and underdeveloped. On the other hand, where teachers themselves speculate, surmise, listen and ask questions to which they do not already know the answers, pupils will often respond in kind, i.e. hypothesise in response to hypothesising, speculate in response to speculating. As part of your observations you may wish to note how teachers develop pupils' speaking and listening through the use of questioning and to evaluate your own success in using questions in lessons.

EXPLORING DIFFERENCES BETWEEN SPOKEN AND WRITTEN LANGUAGE

Speech is fundamentally different from writing. It has its own characteristic grammatical features and is greatly affected by the fact that it almost always takes place when speaker and listener are face to face. Despite this it is very easy to make quick and erroneous judgements about people based on the way in which they speak.

Examining your own knowledge and attitudes

As teachers it is vitally important that we understand clearly some of the differences between spoken and written language so that our judgements about pupils' achievements are not the result of ignorance or misconception. As Katharine Perera points out in *Understanding Language*:

> There are two important points to be made that concern the nature of speech on the one hand, and the nature of writing on the other. First, there is a fairly widely-held but mistaken view that speech is some kind of careless or sloppy version of writing. This view leads people to make judgements of speech that are inappropriate because they derive from the written standard. . . .
>
> Secondly, it is necessary to realize that written language is not merely a transcription of speech; so learning to read and write means not just learning to make and decode letter shapes but also acquiring new forms of language. Some difficulties in reading spring from the language itself rather than from the written code, because there are some grammatical constructions which are common in writing but which occur very rarely in speech.
>
> (Perera, 1987, pp. 17–18)

Some characteristics of spoken language

Depending upon where, when, why and to whom they are talking, speakers will probably alter some or all of the following:

- their register (e.g. from formal to informal);
- their grammar (e.g. from clauses embedded in complex sentences to linked simple sentences peppered with gap-fillers, false starts and changes of direction);
- their dialect (e.g. from standard English to regional);
- their accent (e.g. from a regional accent to Received Pronunciation);
- the paralinguistic features of their speech (e.g. gesture, body language);
- the prosodic features of their speech (e.g. tone, speed, rhythm).

Many of us find that when we explore our views about spoken language we unearth prejudices and misconceptions such as those described by Katharine Perera above. However, the more we investigate language, the more we see how complex speaking and listening can be and how significant the apparently ordinary spoken contributions of pupils often are.

Transcribing spoken language

Taping and transcribing pupils' talk can be a very helpful way for you to enlarge your understanding about their achievements. Finding time to listen to, and transcribe, what you have recorded can be very time-consuming. However, it is important to do this from time to time, especially if you skim through what you have taped and only

Table 5.2 Analysing a transcript

	Transcript	Tape
Accent		
Tone		
Pace		
Fluency		
Gender		

transcribe the key moments which are likely to be worth looking at in more detail. The following example demonstrates what transcription can reveal (and see Table 5.2). Both of these transcripts record the words spoken by a pupil (D) in a piece of improvised drama. In the first transcript he is role-playing a villager being asked by an interviewer (I) about a play to be performed by the village drama group.

Transcript 1: The interview

D: Well, I'm Tom Evans, and I'm sort of the narrator in these plays. We're sort of re-enacting the story of another legend which was about the two monsters that supposedly are buried in the mine . . . they're supposed to have thousands of years ago came and . . . well . . . arrived in Tallybont and murdered a few people . . . of the village and the people caught them, put them away, but they escaped again not long ago.

I: How did you find out about this story? How did you know it in the first place?

D: Well . . . I was down the mine and I was um hacking, hacking away um ready to push the cart away full of coal and um I sort of found this book. I don't know why there was a book down there. It was a sort of diary.

An analysis of the way pupil D speaks in role here shows that he employs many of the features of spoken language. His speech includes examples of hesitancies such as 'um' and 'sort of' which give him time to think what comes next. His words are mostly a series of clauses linked by 'and'; for example, 'and I was hacking', 'and I sort of found this book', 'and it sort of told'. This is what Gunther Kress calls 'chaining' and it is characteristic of spoken as distinct from written language (Kress, 1992, p. 31).

   In the second transcript the pupil is the same villager, now performing in the play itself. The rest of the class, also in role as villagers, watch the play being acted out. The performance begins with the sound of drilling announcing that the characters are already down the mine. Pupil D then begins to speak as Tom Evans, the narrator of the play's events. While he narrates, the rest of his group mime the story. Putting down an imaginary drill, Pupil D then picks up a fairly large, fat dictionary, the group's only prop. His opening words explain what this dictionary is: it is an old diary, the book which was found down the mine. Turning the pages of this 'diary' he then proceeds to 'read' from it.

Task 5.2 Making a transcript

If you have not had the opportunity to do so before (e.g. as part of your own schooling or university course), try making a transcript of a short piece of spoken language. The purpose of the task is to encourage you to focus your attention on some of the characteristic features of spoken language texts.

- Using a tape-recorder, record someone, possibly another student teacher, talking about the school they used to go to. When you transcribe the tape you may end up with something similar to the following:

  Um I went to a quite a big private school and big red brick building with lots of very good facilities and swimming pool um and little well quite a big theatre as well where we put on quite a lot of shows and um I really liked doing English I had a really excellent English teacher who sort of inspired me um lots of poetry we did and also nineteenth-century novels which I particularly enjoyed um what I liked about the school was that everyone was you could enjoy the work without feeling that you were um being boring in fact it had a very academic purpose to it um you weren't meant to it wasn't there weren't ideas about being cool um by not working or pretending that in fact for lots of people it the school was quite difficult there was a lot of pressure to do well to er produce things not just academic but also creatively um creative writing or drama um also suited me because sport was not at all emphasised um you could in fact it was quite looked down on if you enjoyed um playing sport against other teams um so in that respect it's quite unlike other private schools with the sort of play up and play the game ethos.

- Ask other people to read the above transcript. Before the tape is played to them, jot down under the heading 'Transcript', in a chart similar to the one given in Table 5.2, what they predict about the speaker and how their words might sound.
- Play the tape. In the column headed 'Tape', jot down notes about what is actually heard.

(In this case the speaker is a young woman who sounds fluent and assured. The varied intonation and steady pacing of the spoken language mean that the whole hangs together and sounds more coherent than it appears when transcribed. The speaker does not have a regional accent, but certain features commonly associated with social class are prominent.)

Transcript 2: The performance

D: The story which I am about to tell is one which I do not believe myself. Recently, in the village, it is said that two monsters suddenly came out of the cave and started murdering and killing the people of Tallybont. Several were killed. They were finally caught after a lot of effort. While they were trying to come out of the cave they were grabbed and seized by the people. They took them and put them in a cast iron coffin. The coffin was set in a hill and covered up. This is all I can say.

   A hundred years ago when the mine was opened for the first time it is said they did not like having a mine built on top of their grave and so they came out of the coffin to take revenge . . . there was a murder down the mine and it is not known if it was the monster but it could've been. The victim was found screaming and shouting, 'Terror! Terror! It's coming!' He died of shock in hospital. They think it was the monsters that did it but that's only a legend.

The language of this second transcript is 'written' language, even though it has never been scripted. There is not a single example of hesitancy, unlike the many which featured in the earlier, 'spoken' version. Furthermore, the syntax shows all the signs of a 'hierarchical', embedded structuring which Kress says is distinctive of written language. Here we have relative clauses ('which I am about to tell'), adverbial phrases ('in the village'), use of the passive voice ('it is said') and so on.

   These many distinctive features of Pupil D's language, illuminated in the transcribing, suggest a highly sophisticated, internalised sense of the difference between spoken and written language. Because spoken language is ephemeral unless captured on tape or video, the achievements of many pupils are bound to pass us by. But two things can help to prevent us from underestimating what pupils can do: the first is to develop our own knowledge about language so that we may recognise more clearly what pupils' spoken language tells us about their learning and understanding; the second is to spend time, now and then, analysing transcripts to remind ourselves of the complexities of what we are teaching and assessing.

Making transcripts with pupils

Transcribing tape-recorded speech is an activity which can be adapted readily for use in the classroom, with any age group, as long as there are sufficient tape-recorders available to make it practicable. You may, however, wish to try out the task first with a small group of three or four pupils. Your planning will need to take account of the time allotted between lessons for you (or the pupils) to transcribe the recordings.

EXPLORING VARIETY IN SPOKEN LANGUAGE

Having established, for yourself and with your pupils, some of the differences between spoken and written language, you may now wish to focus on variety in spoken language.

Formality and informality

An interesting area to investigate with pupils is how the context, audience and purpose for speaking and listening affect the formality or informality of the language used. A

Task 5.3 Transcribing anecdotes and stories

The purpose of this task is to provide you with an activity, suitable for a Year 8 or Year 9 group, which you can use to discover how much pupils know or can learn explicitly about some of the characteristic features of spoken language texts.

- Equip yourself with a tape-recorder and blank tape.
- Set the tape-recorder running and ask each pupil in turn to recount a short anecdote about a topic such as the following:
  - How I got my scar
  - A time when I was really scared
  - My earliest memory
  - The most exciting time of my life.
- Transcribe the anecdotes and make enough copies for pupils to have one each.
- Ask pupils to do some oral redrafting of their stories, shaping them as a practised story-teller might, drawing on some of the techniques of traditional story-telling. (You might wish to refer to story-tellers such as Kevin Crossley-Holland or Hugh Lupton who discuss different aspects of their craft in *Tales, Tellers and Texts* (Cliff Hodges *et al.*, 2000). When they are ready to do so, pupils retell their stories, perhaps being recorded this time on video so that facial gestures and body language can be discussed afterwards.
- Ask pupils to redraft their anecdotes using a deliberately literary style.
- Discuss with pupils some of the differences between their original anecdotes and their more crafted story-telling. They may, for example, notice differences between beginnings: impromptu anecdotes often begin with initiators such as 'right' or 'well' whereas a prepared story is more likely to start with a formulaic phrase such as 'A long time ago' or even possibly 'Once upon a time'.

light-hearted piece of improvised role-play such as the following can result in a serious consideration of language registers.

Pupils (perhaps in Year 7 or Year 8) read an article entitled 'Teachers in Detention' (Figure 5.1) and improvise a series of different conversations afterwards.

- In pairs, the two teachers talk to each other when they first realise what has happened.
- In threes, the two teachers explain/apologise tactfully to the head on Monday morning.
- In fours, the teachers recount their experiences to two colleagues in the staffroom on Monday morning.
- In fours, one of the teachers explains to pupils in their form group on Monday morning (following the incident and the newspaper report) what has happened.

It is interesting to ask pupils to predict which of the four scenarios will result in the most formal or informal register and why. For example, will the conversation between the head and the two teachers be more formal than the one which takes place in the

---

Teachers in Detention

By our Education Correspondent

There were red faces all round last night when two local teachers found themselves locked in school until the early hours of Saturday morning.

Working late
They had been working late in the workshops in the centre of the school campus. They did not realise that they had been locked in until they tried to get out at 9.30 p.m. last night.

999 call
But the most embarrassing moment was yet to come. The school caretaker, Mr Arnold Jones, was woken up in the middle of the night when he heard a noise of banging and clattering.

> 'I thought it was vandals, so I dialled 999,' he said today. 'I can tell you, the police were not well pleased to be called out at two o'clock in the morning.'

Explanations
The teachers involved refused to comment – but they will certainly have some explaining to do on Monday!

Figure 5.1 'Teachers in Detention'

form group? Afterwards pupils can discover whether their predictions were accurate and what factors contributed to the various registers being used.

Accent and dialect

Several of the activities described above may lead to discussions about accent and dialect and the use of standard English. For example, pupils may discuss whether some of the roles in 'Teachers in Detention' are more likely than others to involve use of regional dialect words rather than their standard English equivalents. In these circumstances it is important to be absolutely clear yourself about the concepts and knowledge involved, about what the differences are, for example, between accent and dialect or between Received Pronunciation and standard English. Use of linguistic terminology, rather than labels from folk linguistics such as 'posh' or 'common', can help to move the discussion away from the stereotypical and towards a more precise knowledge and understanding of how spoken language works and is used.

PLANNING AND ORGANISING CLASSROOMS FOR SPEAKING AND LISTENING

Your observation of speaking and listening will have demonstrated to you how much talk goes on all the time in schools and how rich and varied it is. A good deal of what you have observed, however, will have been carefully planned for, with classrooms organised and tasks chosen to enhance opportunities for speaking and listening. Pupils need plenty of occasions to talk and listen informally and incidentally. They also need the chance to talk and listen in more formal and challenging contexts.

An important paragraph in the Bullock Report makes clear what the teacher's role must be:

> The teacher's role should be one of planned intervention, and his purposes and the means of fulfilling them must be clear in his mind. Important among these purposes should be the intention to increase the complexity of the child's thinking, so that he does not rest on the mere expression of opinion but uses language in an exploratory way.
>
> (DES, 1975, p. 145)

The next section of this chapter will look at some examples of how planning and organising classrooms for talk can develop pupils' language, learning and cognition and increase the complexity of their thinking.

Planning structured group work

What follows is a description of an activity which might be undertaken by a mixed-ability Year 9 or Year 10 group who are studying Shakespeare's *Henry V*.

The class has reached Act IV, scene vii, the point in the play when Henry is handed the two lists of those who have died in the Battle of Agincourt. The first is the list of the slaughtered French; the second gives the number of the English dead. The two parts, the King and the herald, are first read aloud by volunteers:

King:	Now, herald, are the dead numb'red?	
Herald:	Here is the number of the slaught'red French. . . .	
King:	This note doth tell me of ten thousand French	1
	That in the field lie slain; of princes, in this number,	
	And nobles bearing banners, there lie dead	
	One hundred twenty-six; added to these,	
	Of knights, esquires, and gallant gentlemen,	5
	Eight thousand and four hundred; of the which	
	Five hundred were but yesterday dubb'd knights.	
	So that, in these ten thousand they have lost,	
	There are but sixteen hundred mercenaries;	
	The rest are princes, barons, lords, knights, squires,	10
	And gentlemen of blood and quality.	
	The names of those their nobles that lie dead:	
	Charles Delabreth, High Constable of France;	
	Jacques of Chatillon, Admiral of France;	
	The master of the cross-bows, Lord Rambures;	15
	Great Master of France, the brave Sir Guichard Dolphin:	

> John Duke of Alencon; Antony Duke of Brabant,
> The brother to the Duke of Burgundy;
> And Edward Duke of Bar. Of lusty earls,
> Grandpre and Roussi, Fauconbridge and Foix,   20
> Beaumont and Marle, Vaudemont and Lestrake.
> Here was a royal fellowship of death!
> Where is the number of our English dead?
> [Herald presents another paper]
> Edward the Duke of York, the Earl of Suffolk,
> Sir Richard Kikely, Davy Gam, Esquire;   25
> None else of name; and of all other men
> But five and twenty. O God, thy arm was here!
>
> (*Henry V*, Act IV, scene vii)

Even for adults the speech is difficult to read aloud with feeling straight away. For pupils it is likely to prove even more so. The activity which follows is designed to encourage closer study of the language with a view to being able to reread the speech, speaking the words with greater intensity and emotion. The activity is structured to create maximum opportunities for purposeful talk which will involve everybody and extend their thinking and understanding.

1   The class of thirty pupils is divided into six groups of five. In the groups pupils are labelled A, B, C, D and E. The groups are told that they are members of different stonemasons' workshops in France at the time when the play is set. They have been given the possibility of a contract to create stone memorials to the French dead after the Battle of Agincourt. The list has arrived at their workshop just as it is in the King's speech up to line 22. Their task is to put in a bid for the contract. Every group member should keep their own record of the results of their discussions.

2   Groups should work their way through the list in the King's speech to establish the facts (e.g. about who has died, their names (if known), what their rank or position was).

3   Groups should then consider what type(s) of memorial might be appropriate: should there be just one or should there be several different ones? Why? Where should the memorials be erected?

4   One member of the group (A) should sketch out on an overhead projector transparency what their memorials might look like. The group should consider what should be carved on them and discuss why. They should instruct A in how they want the OHT to look.

5   During these discussions the teacher moves from group to group asking one pupil in each group (B) for an interim explanation of the group's findings, suggestions, decisions.

6   Once all the groups have completed this first stage, an envoy (C) is sent from each group to the next group to try out their group's ideas on another audience. The remainder of each group listens to the ideas of the envoy and notes any similarities with, or differences from, their own.

7   Envoys return to their own groups where one person (D) fills them in on what they have missed while they have been away. The group's ideas are adjusted as necessary in the light of anything that has been learned from the envoys.

8   Each group then sends a representative (E) to the front of the class with the OHT of their plans to summarise briefly to the rest of the class what their ideas are, using the OHT as a visual aid to support their talk. Class members may wish to question or comment on their plans.

9   Finally a decision can be made (perhaps by a representative group from each workshop, e.g. all the As) as to which stonemasons' workshop should receive the contract and why.

10   Then, of course, the speech can be put back into its context within *Henry V* to be reread or dramatised in the light of understandings which the activity, if successful, will have generated.

One criticism sometimes levelled at this kind of work is that it may take pupils rather a long way from the context of the original speech. You can decide for yourself what you think by going back to the stated learning objectives for the activity, namely: 'to encourage closer study of the language with a view to being able to reread the speech, speaking the words with greater intensity and emotion'; and 'to create maximum opportunities for purposeful talk which will involve everybody and extend their thinking and understanding'.

When the speech is finally reread and the study of the play itself is resumed, consider what difference the work might have made to the pupils' understanding of the significance of this deceptively awkward speech. A group of student teachers who tried out the activity for themselves found that it led them quickly into discussions about vocabulary (mercenaries, dubb'd), rank (barons, lords, knights), attitudes to warfare (volunteers, paid soldiers), word forms and functions (use of adjectives – gallant, brave, lusty), punctuation (commas to signal words or phrases in apposition; semicolons to separate the individuals listed). That they were in role as stonemasons bidding for a contract led also to thinking about ordinary people's attitudes to remembering those who die in battle and how those attitudes might be swayed by financial considerations. The student teachers differed in their views about whether the activity impeded or enhanced the emotive qualities of the speech. But they were not in doubt about the extent to which it promoted valuable focused discussion.

SPEAKING AND LISTENING AND IT

Observation of speaking and listening undertaken when pupils are working collaboratively using IT will have shown you how extensive and varied their talk can be. Tasks 5.5 and 5.6 are two tasks which you may wish to try for yourself before exploring them with pupils.

These two tasks, like most of the activities described in this chapter, show how different elements of the English curriculum may be integrated: poetry, language study, writing, IT, speaking and listening, media studies. There will be occasions when, as a teacher, you put speaking and listening under the spotlight, to teach specifically about

Task 5.4 Analysis of teacher's and pupils' roles

The purpose of this task is to analyse the roles of pupils and teacher in the *Henry V* activity. If you are able to try out or adapt the task for yourself before analysing it, so much the better.

1   Draw two columns on a sheet of paper, labelling one 'Teacher' and the other 'Pupils'. Work your way through each section of the activity making brief but precise notes about what the teacher and the pupils are doing in terms of speaking and listening.

Teacher	Pupils
1 Explains task	1 Listen to find out nature of task
2 Issues instructions	2 Listen in order to act on instructions

2   Discuss with other student teachers some or all of the following issues:

- *Involvement*. From your experience of reading or working your way through the activity, and from the notes you have made, assess what proportion of the class have been actively involved in purposeful speaking and listening.
- *Differentiation*. Are there noticeable differences between the speaking and listening tasks performed by A, B, C, D and E? If so, can you rank them in order of difficulty? Could the structure of the groups and labelling of group members be prepared by the teacher in advance so as to differentiate between the pupils in the class?
- *Equal opportunities*. How is the activity organised to try to pre-empt any individuals taking an unduly dominant role and to give space to those who are inclined to hold back? Is the subject matter likely to diminish girls' motivation to participate fully? Is the subject matter accessible to all pupils whatever their cultural background, or might the teacher need to provide some support materials (e.g. illustrations of the forms which memorials can take in a variety of cultural contexts)?
- *Envoys*. Using envoys is one of a range of ways of organising group work which can successfully promote speaking and listening in the class-room. Can you analyse why it is usually successful? Find out from teachers with whom you are working what some other commonly used methods for grouping and regrouping pupils are and note the differences between them.

an aspect of oral work which you want your pupils to develop. Much of the time, however, the richest and most fruitful speaking and listening will occur when the complexity of the activity demands it and when classrooms and resources are organised so as to maximise pupils' opportunities for purposeful talk.

The purpose is to discover the extent to which the collaborative use of IT relies on and
encourages particular kinds of speaking and listening.

Find two other people to work with you. Two of you collaborate, writing a poem on screen;
the third person observes the speaking and listening which takes place between the two
writers. The first task involves poetry writing and using IT to draft and edit, moving text
around on the screen, deleting and inserting as necessary.

A What the writers do
1   Using a picture as a stimulus, list on screen, one beneath the other, five things
       which you can see in the picture.
2   Add a verb and an adjective to each line of the list.
3   Underneath, type a list which consists of:

       ● four colours you can see;
       ● four textures;
       ● four sounds you might hear;
       ● four similes or metaphors which the picture suggests.

Your screen might now look like this:

1   ● woman
     ● table
     ● chair
     ● doors
     ● wallpaper

2   ● old woman looking sad
     ● table set out for tea
     ● straight-backed chair standing in the background
     ● wooden doors painted orange
     ● old-fashioned patterned wallpaper peeling off the walls

3   ● orange, brown, rust, yellow
     ● smooth, rough, scratchy, glossy
     ● woman breathing, clink of tea cups, muffled murmuring, wind outside
     ● single button like a buttercup; hair like unspun cotton; little jug like a
       fairy's mirror; scarf knotted like a tulip

4   Now that initial ideas have been gathered, reassemble them using commands such
       as insert, delete, cut and paste, so that they form a poem of at least four lines in
       length. Each line should have a specified number of syllables to give it a regular
       rhythm.

5   When you are happy with the poem, read it aloud or print it out.

Here is how two student teachers, working from a reproduction of *Mrs Mounter* by Harold Gilman (1917) which hangs in the Walker Art Gallery in Liverpool, turned their notes into a poem.

Mrs Mounter

Dejected lonely. Hair like unspun cotton,
Sits rough and pink by table set out for tea,
Woman's old breathing and muffled murmuring,
The clink of tea cups and turquoise wind outside.

Yet an ethereal mirror before her,
Dazzles with images of a buttercup
Of smooth surfaces ripe as a young woman,
Of rich, full, scarlet tulips ready to burst.

Dejected lonely. Sits in contemplation,
Her scratchy thoughts scouring her mind clean away
To happier times of orange and olive.
Straight backed and hopeless but her life not yet dead.

B What the observer does
Make a note of all the different kinds of speaking and listening you observe while the poem is being written. Here is a list that you could photocopy and use as a checklist, adding to it as well where necessary:

- listening to instructions;
- interpreting instructions;
- giving instructions;
- seeking clarification;
- questioning (e.g. meanings of words);
- disagreeing;
- negotiating a consensus;
- discussing (e.g. layout, word choices, spelling, punctuation);
- reading aloud;
- explaining;
- thinking aloud;
- dictating;
- asking direct questions;
- answering questions;
- commenting on sounds of poetic words;
- modifying others' suggestions;
- talking oneself into understanding;
- rephrasing ideas;
- hypothesising.

The second IT task involves editing a newspaper article, locating particularly emotive words and changing them so as to alter the bias of the piece in some way. Work in pairs with an observer in order to assess the effectiveness of the activity in encouraging speaking and listening.

You will need a short newspaper article which has been retyped and copied into two columns so that the two versions can be viewed side by side on screen.

Fen tiger spotted at scene days before SWAN KILLED IN SAVAGE ATTACK By Suzanna Chambers	Fen tiger spotted at scene days before SWAN KILLED IN SAVAGE ATTACK By Suzanna Chambers
ANIMAL welfare experts were investigating today after the headless body of a full-grown swan was discovered.	ANIMAL welfare experts were investigating today after the headless body of a full-grown swan was discovered.
The grisly find at a park and ride site used by hundreds of commuters each day heightened local fears that the bird may have been the victim of the Fen Tiger.	The grisly find at a park and ride site used by hundreds of commuters each day heightened local fears that the bird may have been the victim of the Fen Tiger.
The swan had been dragged from the lake, probably last night, and mauled to death by a large animal.	The swan had been dragged from the lake, probably last night, and mauled to death by a large animal.
It was found lying by the side of a lake in the Madingley Road park and ride early this morning.	It was found lying by the side of a lake in the Madingley Road park and ride early this morning.
Derek Neville, a car-park attendant at the site, said: 'I saw it this morning and I thought it was a white paper bag. There were feathers everywhere and its head had been bitten off.'	Derek Neville, a car-park attendant at the site, said: 'I saw it this morning and I thought it was a white paper bag. There were feathers everywhere and its head had been bitten off.'

1   Read through the article to see what it is about and whether it is biased in any particular direction.

2   Read through the article again to identify any emotive words which are contributing to the bias of the piece.

3   Highlight each emotive word, as it occurs, in the version in the right-hand column, and discuss a replacement for it which will help to bias the article in a different direction.

Fen tiger spotted at scene days before SWAN KILLED IN SAVAGE ATTACK By Suzanna Chambers	Fen tiger spotted at scene days before SWAN KILLED IN *SURPRISE* ATTACK By Suzanna Chambers

ANIMAL welfare experts were investigating today after the headless body of a full-grown swan was discovered.
 	
    The grisly find at a park and ride site used by hundreds of commuters each day heightened local fears that the bird may have been the victim of the Fen Tiger . . .
	ANIMAL welfare experts were investigating today after the headless body of a full-grown swan was discovered.
	
	    The *unusual* find at a park and ride site used by hundreds of commuters each day supported local theories that the bird may have been the victim of the Fen Tiger. . . .

PROGRESSION AND ASSESSMENT IN SPEAKING AND LISTENING

You have now been introduced to a number of classroom ideas for encouraging speaking and listening. However, it is also necessary to think about how pupils make, and can be helped to make, progress in oral work. There are several issues which need to be considered simultaneously:

- How will the task set engage pupils in speaking and listening and make appropriate demands of them?
- To what extent will the learning objectives for the lesson be focused on learning through talk or learning about talk?
- How will pupils' oral records influence the setting up of the task and the pupils' involvement?
- Are there any aspects of speaking and listening within the task which need teaching, (e.g. the difference between asking each other open and closed questions when trying to elicit information; explanations of concepts such as register or dialect)?
- How will pupils' contributions be recorded? Will they be taped or summarised by the pupil and commented on by the teacher on a speaking and listening record sheet (Figure 5.2)?
- What criteria will you use to assess their involvement?
- Are pupils aware of the criteria by which they will be assessed?

As these questions suggest, progression involves a cycle of planning, teaching, task-setting, pupil activity, recording, assessing against criteria, pupil review, teacher reflection and evaluation. You will need to find out how speaking and listening is

Activity 1 Debate about animal rights – pupils in role   *2 October*
You worked hard to put a strong case from the floor. You listened to others' points of view but you seldom challenged any of the points raised even though they conflicted with those you had made earlier. You chose to be in role as a character rather like yourself – you were convincing in role, but you didn't really have to adjust your language to any significant degree, as you would have done if you had been role-playing someone very different.
Target: To sustain an argument in a debate or discussion, rather than just to present it. To role-play a character who holds different views to your own and who is likely to speak rather formally in a debate or discussion.

Activity 2 Talk on karate   *12 December*
Your talk was delivered clearly. It engaged the attention of your listeners, especially when you used video clips to illustrate a point. You responded well to questions asked afterwards. For example, when you were asked what people think about girls doing karate you gave two points of view, making both clear but indicating which one you supported. ('Some people think . . . but others, including myself, think . . .)
Target:

Activity 3 Small group discussion about short story   *15 March*
You didn't make many comments. You rather relied on others to lead the way. You made a good point, however, when you were asked directly what you thought about the way the writer built up the suspense, namely that he used lots of questions rather than stating facts. Was there a reason why you didn't contribute this observation voluntarily, earlier in the discussion?
Target:

Activity 4 Directing the banquet scene in Macbeth   *25 June*
You listened carefully to views offered by others in your group. You were able to see quite quickly which to accept and which to reject. You obviously had strong ideas of your own, too, and managed to communicate them to the relevant actors effectively. You gave reasons for your suggestions (e.g. 'Lady Macbeth should smile wickedly because the audience must see the murderous thoughts she's having.'). Giving a reason like that lends weight to your point and helps to convince those who are listening to you. Well done!
Target:

1   Look at the GCSE criteria for speaking and listening and try to establish which level description best suits this pupil at the end of Year 10.
2   Drawing on any speaking and listening activities you think would be appropriate and referring to the speaking and listening criteria, set targets for this pupil for activities 2, 3 and 4 which will help her to aim for a higher grade at the end of Year 11.

Figure 5.2 Speaking and listening record sheet

recorded across the age range in your department and to familiarise yourself with whatever systems are in place for ensuring continuity of pupil records from year to year. When you are preparing to teach a lesson or unit of work which involves speaking and listening activities and assessment, you will need to look back at pupils' oral records in order to plan for progression and continuity. It is worth discovering early on what technology is available to enable audio-visual recording of speaking and listening, and how to use it.

SUMMARY AND KEY POINTS

Pupils need opportunities to speak and listen in a wide variety of contexts and for a wide range of purposes, in order to increase the complexity of their thinking, to develop their powers of communication and to provide examples of language in use through which to develop their explicit knowledge about speaking and listening.

As a teacher you will need to learn when and how to intervene in pupils' discussions to help them to move on, and when just to listen to what they have to say unprompted. When considering pupils' progression it is necessary to analyse and reflect on their oral work and to plan subsequent teaching accordingly. Activities often need to be carefully organised and classrooms deliberately arranged to maximise the chance of all pupils being able to participate to the best of their ability. Pupils' achievements need to be communicated to them both in general terms and in relation to specific assessment criteria.

You also need to be able to recognise and make explicit to pupils their achievements. This can be done by teaching about spoken language and how it differs from written language, as well as by assessment, recording and reporting.

Task 5.7 Setting targets

This task is designed to help you develop your ability to plan for progression in speaking and listening, taking into account a pupil's prior learning and achievements across a range of oral activities and making use of given criteria.

Look at the speaking and listening record sheet for a pupil in Year 10 (Figure 5.2). The teacher has commented on the pupil's performance in four different activities. A target has been set after Activity 1, but not after the remaining three activities.

FURTHER READING

DES (1975) *A Language for Life*, London: HMSO. Commonly referred to as the Bullock Report, this is an important work for anyone wanting to explore ideas raised in this chapter in greater depth. Chapters 4 and 10, on language and learning and oral work respectively, are well worth reading.

Howe, A. (1997) *Making Talk Work*, Sheffield: NATE. A survey of some of the many different ways in which talk may be employed in the classroom. The book contains a particularly good chapter on the organisation of classrooms and pupil groupings.

Mercer, N. (2000) *Words and Minds: How we Use Language to Think Together*, London: Routledge. A fascinating book for anyone interested in exploring further the relationship between thought and language in everyday settings, including the home, the workplace and the school.

Videos produced by bodies such as the examination boards, QCA or the DfES (for the Key Stage 3 National Strategy) offer examples of pupils of various ages and abilities engaged in a range of speaking and listening activities. Time spent with other student teachers and with more experienced teachers, analysing pupils' contributions and trying to assess them against given criteria, can be a very valuable way to familiarise yourself with the process of assessing oral work.

ACKNOWLEDGEMENTS

The author would like to thank the many colleagues and students with whom the ideas in this chapter have been developed over the years.

6 Reading

Caroline Daly

INTRODUCTION

When we teach pupils to read, we enter an area of seemingly awesome responsibility: for we are teaching individuals something which affects so many aspects of personal and social development, and which plays a special role in language development. Through reading we are able to interpret, comprehend and respond critically to the ideas of others. We learn about the particular ways in which text helps to formulate and express those ideas; we reflect upon the relationship between our own experiences, and those we discover in what we read. Pupils' experience of reading impacts upon their participation in wider learning; it has implications for: personal enrichment; economic viability and employment prospects; social relationships; leisure activities and cultural identity. Reading in the social and cultural context is bound up closely with concepts of citizenship, civilisation and national identity.

There is much at stake for pupils at any stage in their development as readers. Views on what constitutes reading, and what counts as literature worth studying in school, are deeply polarised. It is important to consider the range of views on what reading is *for*, and the differing emphases which will affect your aims and decisions about methods and texts. Consider the following statements:

1   How do we ensure there is a common core to produce citizens? The book must be at the heart of our culture. We must preserve the distinctive culture of this country.

(Nick Tate, in SCAA, 1996)

2   Children [should be helped] towards a critical understanding of the world and cultural environment in which they live. Children should know about the processes by which meanings are conveyed, and about the ways in which print and other media carry values.

(DES and Welsh Office, 1989, para. 2.25)

3   Now that there are more readers than at any time in the past, more books to
        choose from and new literacies, we must accept that differences among readers
        and among texts are normal. There is no going back to a single text, a single
        way of reading, a single way of defining 'good readers'.

                                                                (Meek, 1991, p. 36)

4   Effective literacy is the key to raising standards across all subjects, and equipping
        pupils with the skills and knowledge they need for life beyond school.

                                            (*Key Stage 3 National Strategy*, 2001, p. 9)

What cultural assumptions underlie these four statements? What issues are raised here,
to do with the role of reading in contemporary society? What special significance is
ascribed to the study of books? What are the implications for the part played by English
teachers in cultural development?

The first statement was delivered by Nick Tate at the conference on 'Information
Technology, Communications and the Future Curriculum' (SCAA, 1996). It reveals
some of the factors which lie at the heart of debate about reading, literacy and the
selection of appropriate reading material for schools, as they prepare pupils to be readers
in the twenty-first century. This statement makes explicit the connections between the
books which carry authorised value in our society, and the forging of national identity.
Such texts form 'the canon', the collection of literature from the English literary
heritage, which has characterised literature courses in schools and universities since the
institution of English as an academic subject. Authors include Chaucer, Shakespeare,
Austen, Milton, Pope and Dickens. The centrality of these texts indicates a close
connection between 'reading' and 'literature study' as part of a cultural process aimed
at national cohesion. It implies a shared value system into which pupils may be
inducted, and a reading of texts which can be agreed upon as containing values within
a common cultural heritage (see Chapter 2).

By contrast, the cultural analysis view, which is acknowledged in *English for Ages 5
to 16* (Cox Report 2) (DES and Welsh Office, 1989), identifies the need to teach pupils
to be critically aware as readers. This view asks questions of the cultural heritage model
for reading, and seeks to empower pupils by teaching them to examine texts as being
culturally produced. It emphasises the way in which readers are positioned in
relationship to authorised literature, and helps them to understand that relationship.

Contemporary society makes demands on its members to acquire an ever-widening
repertoire of communication skills. Meek's statement reveals how our understanding of
what it is to 'read' has become increasingly diverse. To have studied the entire works
of Shakespeare may, in one sense, be an indication of being 'well-read', but this concept
of literacy is not likely to prove helpful to someone who needs to 'browse' pages of
electronic text in order to find information. The increasing complexity of what it
means to be a reader is illustrated in Chapter 9's treatment of teaching media and
information technology in English. Reading as literacy today requires pupils to
experience texts that variously represent the world through written, digitised and
visual language which the reader can interpret. Margaret Meek's analysis of contemporary literacies helps us to understand the need for diversity in our choice of texts
and ways of reading with pupils. The National Literacy Strategy (NLS), 1998, and the

National Strategy for Key Stage 3 (English), 2001, have further contributed to a particular skills-based concept of literacy, in which reading is part of a 'tool-kit' which equips school leavers for participation in national life.

Peter Benton (1996) reminds us that we can think of literature study as a particular aspect of reading: other aspects feature non-literary, printed information texts, media texts, electronic and audio-visual texts, all of which form a reading culture in which many of our pupils are already highly experienced. This reading culture forms the rich basis from which to develop our objectives for teaching texts within the contemporary classroom:

> Teachers will be at a disadvantage in understanding their students' responses to reading and to literature unless they have at least some understanding of, and interest in, the reading and viewing culture that adolescents are busily constructing and reconstructing in their everyday lives. Official texts are read in the context of a multitude of unofficial texts both literary and visual. There is no reason to believe that such unofficial texts are any less important in shaping students' imaginative capacity and view of the world than those promulgated by the formal demands of the curriculum. . . . Texts offered from on high without an understanding of students' own reading and viewing background are likely to be rejected.
>
> (Benton, 1996, pp. 77–78)

OBJECTIVES

By the end of this chapter you should be able to:

- understand the significance of 'making meaning' for pupils' engagement with texts;
- plan for pupils to experience a broad range of texts, both literary and non-literary;
- develop activities which build on pupil difference, to teach reading in the mixed-ability classroom;
- consider ways of creating a reading environment in your classroom;
- consider ways of assessing progress in the reader.

READING IN THE NATIONAL CURRICULUM

It is worth highlighting the concepts of breadth, independence and enjoyment of reading, which underpin the opening declaration about the teaching of reading in secondary schools, in the National Curriculum for English. It represents an acknowledgement that, without the pupils' *own* engagement in a text which has meaning *for them*, reading lessons become an empty ritual.

During Key Stages 3 and 4 pupils read a wide range of texts independently, both for pleasure and for study. They become enthusiastic, discriminating and responsive readers, understanding layers of meaning, and appreciating what they read on a critical level.

(DFEE, 1999b, p. 34)

Task 6.1 Reading the National Curriculum

1	At this point try listing the types of text which you think might help to achieve the goals outlined in the above extract.
2	Compare your list with another student teacher's, and discuss your predictions for how prevalent this type of reading is in schools.
3	If you are in England or Wales, read pages 34–36 of *English in the National Curriculum* (DfEE/QCA, 1999b), which contain the reading requirements for 11- to 16-year-olds. What conclusions do you draw about what reading is and what reading is for, as it is presented in the document?

Note down how the guidelines in the document relate to the four statements that begin this chapter and to the extract from Benton.

The National Curriculum Orders for English (DfEE, 1999b) set out an agenda for what counts as reading, in a way which places high emphasis on reading as a particular form of *literary* practice. The National Curriculum for English presents two areas of statutory requirements, both of which will relate to your lesson planning, though they will not necessarily be your starting points. They relate to the 'Knowledge, skills and understanding' and 'Breadth of study' which must be incorporated into your English teaching. The relation of the two requirements is important to understand: 'During the key stage, pupils should be taught the **Knowledge, skills and understanding** *through* the following ranges of literature and non-fiction and non-literary texts' (italics added). It is here that contention lies in the way of what might have been a genuine attempt to allow English teachers to make professional judgements about their pupils' needs in relation to learning about 'understanding texts' (including 'reading for meaning' and 'understanding the author's craft'); English literary heritage; texts from different cultures and traditions; printed and ICT-based information texts; media and moving image texts, and language structure and variation. The required 'Breadth of study' is in fact drawn mainly from the traditional heritage of canonised English literature, with specific authors appearing on approved lists of 'major writers' and 'poets' . . . published before 1914'. The decision that English teachers could be trusted to choose for themselves only writers whose work was published post-1914 offers a culturally exclusive definition of 'authorised' literature. It is largely texts from the English national heritage which form the foundation for reading development at KS3 and 4. The requirements for 'range' from the English literary heritage include two plays by Shakespeare, drama by major playwrights, two works by major writers published before 1914, two works by major writers published after 1914, poetry by four major poets published before 1914, and poetry by four major poets published after 1914. By comparison, the reading of contemporary literature, and that 'from different cultures and traditions' is marginalised by its summary appearance.

A teacher wishing to develop a broad experience, and to promote the individual pleasure of reading, needs to undertake a careful and critical reading of the document. You will need to acknowledge the diversity of pupils' experience and preferred texts, and reconcile this with teaching prescribed literature; you will need to manage the transition from reading at Key Stage 2, which is less prescriptive of reading material, to meeting the requirements at secondary school which lead ultimately to class preparation of 'set' examination texts and core practice questions; you will aim to develop confident personal and critical readings of texts, while inducting pupils into the literary discourse of examinations, with its assumptions that some readings are more acceptable than others. You need to reconcile the broad range of demands made by these versions of reading, in how you organise your schemes of work.

THE NATIONAL STRATEGY FOR KEY STAGE 3

The National Strategy for Key Sage 3 includes a 'Framework for teaching English: Years 7, 8 and 9' (2001). The Strategy is non-statutory, and attempts to build on the work of the National Literacy Strategy (1998) in the primary phase, by focusing on the teaching of literacy at word, sentence and text level (see Chapter 7). At Key Stage 3, the non-statutory Strategy has attempted to 'map' its recommendations on to the statutory Orders for the English National Curriculum. A critical difference between the two is that the National Curriculum does not prescribe pedagogy – it sets out what must be taught, but leaves the teacher to make professional decisions about methods, which can be informed by further knowledge about individual pupils, cultural contexts and learning as a highly complex process. The non-statutory Framework prescribes teaching methods, and offers to provide 'full coverage' of the English Order at KS3. Literacy objectives at 'text level' are set for reading, and they form a strand for planning throughout Years 7, 8 and 9 of the Framework. These objectives are mapped on to the National Curriculum programmes of study for 'Reading for meaning', 'Understanding the author's craft' and the combined study of literary texts from the NC's 'English literary heritage' and 'Texts from different cultures and traditions'. In addition, the Strategy has set 'Research and study skills' as a literacy objective for reading, but currently has no strand of literacy objectives for 'Media and moving image texts'.

MAKING MEANINGS OUT OF TEXTS

It is easy to lose sight of the readers in the midst of debate concerning appropriate school literature, manageable assessment procedures, the National Framework and differing classroom methods. This chapter is based upon the centrality of the reader in the reading process, and highlights issues of difference in the cultural and social histories which pupils bring to their reading. If we are building upon a popular reading and media

---

Task 6.2 Implementing the Framework?

Discuss with your mentor the English department's policy on implementing or rejecting the Framework.

Then either:

1   If you are in a school following the Framework, watch a lesson in which an English teacher is focusing on 'literacy' teaching at text level. Discuss beforehand what the literacy objectives for the lesson are, and ask the teacher how they have planned the lesson. You might talk about the three-part lesson, 'guided reading', the deployment of classroom assistants or provision for pupils who are still working at Level 3 of the National Curriculum.

2   If you are in a school which is not following the Framework, watch a lesson in which an English teacher is focusing on teaching language use and effect through literature. Discuss beforehand what the learning objectives for the lesson are, and ask the teacher how they have planned it.

Watch the lesson and focus on how the pupils respond to the methods used, in particular how the methods appear to meet their individual needs. Make a list of findings and share them with another student whose school has adopted a contrasting policy.

---

culture in which pupils are already immersed, we need to consider how we present *choice of texts*, *range* and *relevance* in ways which encourage *variety*, *breadth* and *critical reading skills* to be developed upon new ground. The diversity of texts encountered outside the English classroom contributes to the continuum of pupils' reading histories: popular fiction, television programmes, videos, computer games, newspapers and magazines, comics and hobby books. Pupils *expect* a text to mean something – this has been their experience in their own choice- and needs-led encounters with texts outside the classroom, where an unsatisfactory text can be switched off, left unfinished or replaced by readily available alternatives.

What are the aims of reading?

If the starting point is the pupil, then that pupil's experience of culture, gender and social environment will all help to compose her understanding of why any text should be significant: in other words, she has her own *reading position*, her individual perspective from which to interpret what she reads. Our teaching aims need to take account of the pupil's development as a reader over time, and will be relevant beyond the particular text of the moment. Questions to ask yourself before embarking on teaching any text should include:

●   What can my pupils already do as readers?
●   What can help to develop my pupils as readers?
●   What do pupils need to know about this text?

It is easy to assume the existence of a body of uncontested knowledge about a literary text we are about to teach: volumes of 'pass notes' are testimony to the view that knowledge can exist in an uncomplicated way for pupils, which can be handed on by teachers in order to produce standard responses about what a text means, for test purposes. Underneath lies the assumption that the book's meaning is not subject to the reader, whose own individual history will in fact confer an infinite range of significance on that text.

Consider the following possible aims for a scheme of work to teach Charles Dickens's *A Christmas Carol* to a KS3 class. Make brief notes on what each aim implies about reading development, and how it can be achieved:

- to widen the reading experience of pupils already knowledgeable about ghost stories;
- to develop strategies for pupils to make meaning out of unfamiliar forms of written language;
- to teach characteristic features of Dickens's style.

The first two aims relate to what pupils can *learn* about how to read texts; the last is more concerned about what can be *taught* about the book, and will probably feature in schemes of work which are aimed increasingly towards common exam preparation.

If your aims are to do with the development of enthusiastic, confident and independent readers, you must make explicit for them the unique path which each follows to becoming experienced with text. A good place to start is a conscious examination of your own reading history.

READING STRATEGIES: INDIVIDUAL, GROUP, WHOLE CLASS

Demands made upon readers today, both in and out of school, are huge, varied and growing. If we aim for pupils to read traditional and contemporary material, including electronic and media texts, and to develop individual preferences as well as an awareness of shared cultural ones, then pupils will benefit from learning a variety of ways to read, and from understanding that we treat texts differently for different purposes. Different ways of reading may be incorporated into schemes of work to satisfy the varied demands of pupil difference and curriculum requirements. Not all pupils in the same class will read the same amount of the same types of books: schemes of work throughout a key stage should ensure that the requirements of the National Curriculum can be met, and beyond that, that pupils are able to develop different reading patterns. 'Wide range' is achieved through the combination of class and group shared texts, and individual reading. Within 'range', in addition to the National Curriculum, you can include popular fiction, comics, picture books, books by pupil-authors, books which ensure that an overall balance is achieved in the representation of cultural diversity and gender. Your sources for texts will vary, as will some of the tasks, according to the way you group pupils for reading. The importance of *grouping* pupils for differentiated reading activities cannot be overstated:

Task 6.3 Constructing a reading autobiography

A reading autobiography charts out your history of reading, and attempts to include your most influential experiences with printed texts, which includes non-fiction. It is useful to divide texts between authorised ones studied at school (and in higher education in your case), and unauthorised reading, chosen entirely for your own pleasure or needs. The autobiography indicates texts which have had a powerful impact on the reader, either positively or through their rejection. It can go back as far as you can remember, to comics and nursery favourites. The important thing is to highlight those moments in your personal reading history which made an impact on your choices and preferences about reading. A simple format for it is suggested below.

Age	Authorised texts	Unauthorised texts
11	*A Midsummer Night's Dream* – we acted it out, abridged version, but I still didn't understand it.	Serial read of Enid Blyton – couldn't put it down. Read the entire Mystery series, and *Malory Towers*.
13	*Tale of Two Cities* – teacher read it out to us with a grim look on her face – she obviously would rather have read something else as well. Took all year.	Don't remember reading anything else that year.

When you have completed your reading autobiography, compare it with another student teacher's. It is very unlikely that you will have a common appreciation of 'the best' literature, and in non-fiction it is probably even harder to find a common text or genre that was powerful for both of you. Differences between you both in terms of age, gender, ethnicity and schooling might make even broader diversity in your reading experiences and responses to texts. Discuss what made those highlighted texts successful or not, and examine the balance between school-taught texts and 'unauthorised' reading choices.

Discuss how you could account for your differing reading histories and what impact your findings make on how you might make decisions about choosing texts in school.

it is surely important to ensure that teaching and resources do match the learning needs of pupils. . . . Since group reading is very seldom used in many classrooms, and individual reading often lacks the focus needed to produce a fully differentiated diet, it is usually through work based on the class reader that reading is being most consciously developed. Thus overall differentiation in the diet is often inadequate.

(Daw, 1995, p. 15)

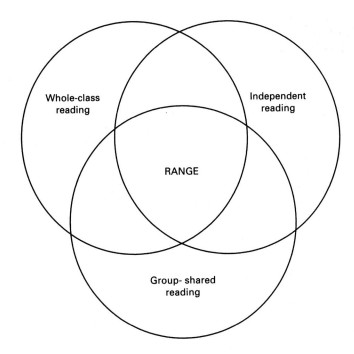

Figure 6.1 The range of reading in the secondary classromm

Independent reading	Group-shared reading	Whole-class reading
School library	Book box/class library	Thematic schemes of work
Pupils' own books from home	Small class sets by author	GCSE set texts for exams
Peer-swapped texts	Small class sets by theme/genre	KS3 SAT texts
Book box/class library	Play scripts	National Curriculum list of authors
Local library	Library project loan	Literature by visiting writers
School book club	Computer-generated/ on-screen texts	Theatre in Education texts

Figure 6.2 Sources for texts

Consider how your learning objectives are best matched by the differing models for grouping pupils for reading, offered in Figures 6.1 and 6.2. The rest of this chapter examines teaching based on these three approaches: *independent reading, group shared reading* and *whole class reading*. It considers how you can plan for your pupils in their individual development as readers, and what strategies might best achieve your aims.

Of course, no grouping of pupils has to exclude the treatment of particular texts. You might decide that a small number of pupils would benefit from a shared reading of a further Louis Sachar novel, having studied one as a class, and there will clearly be overlaps in how texts are approached. The important point is that pupils are introduced to texts in a way which offers structured guidance to meet their individual needs and pleasures as readers.

Individual reading

Pressure to prepare classes for common examination texts can make it seem a luxury to allow pupils the time to read their own choice of books in English lessons, especially to allow sufficient time for real engagement in such texts. This is allied with concerns about how we know what is being learned – evidence of progression in individual reading can appear elusive at secondary school. Some schools operate a short fixed reading period at the start of English lessons, which has the benefit of guaranteeing time for private reading, but which also emphasises it as something fairly dispensable when the lesson proper begins, and can lead to it being used chiefly as a tool to achieve quiet; individual reading needs to be accommodated elsewhere as a sustained activity which is not fragmentary.

Private reading is crucial to meeting the different needs of pupils, through access to appropriate reading material and tasks tailored to the individual. Special Needs pupils (slow learners – gifted pupils also need to be guided in their individual reading, but not in order to complete it) need to spend time with a text of their choice to be able to *complete* it, and they sometimes receive additional support for reading with a class-room assistant or specialist teacher. It is important, however, that they spend time reading with the rest of the class during sustained reading time, if they are to identify themselves as part of a community of readers, and to learn that able readers also experience preferences and difficulties with texts which do not work for them. The organisation of space for all pupils to find a quiet spot to read, and to read sometimes with a teacher, is an important factor in planning for differentiated reading activities. How many of us gain much from reading in an upright position on a hard wooden chair for a ten-minute period? Finding appropriate time and space to read is crucial. Try to observe a teacher using the library with a class as a *space* to read and respond to books.

In your school, find out about the different strategies used for monitoring and assessing individual reading. These can range from those which stress reading as a private activity, to those which form a bridge with the shared reading activities going on in the class, and so allow for pupils to develop experience of active interrogation of texts with their peers, and ways of responding to literature. The range might include:

- Keeping a personal reading diary, with some common criteria to be considered but mostly emphasising the particular significance which a text has for the reader. For pupils with English as an Additional Language (EAL), the diary offers scope for reading in a first language to be recorded, and for pupils to develop reflective reading of those texts. First language reading is crucial to developing confidence in the transferability of critical reading skills between texts.

Task 6.4 What makes a supportive reading environment?

Make a detailed observation of an English classroom in your school. Analyse how the following factors send messages about reading to pupils. Consider especially how these factors influence the reading environment for pupils with Special Educational Needs and with English as an additional language:

- Book displays and class libraries. What types of books count as reading? Literary, non-literary, information, hobby books, picture books, books written in languages other than English, comics?
- What provision is there for 'quick reads' which can give a sense of achievement to slower readers?
- What access is there to material written and printed by pupils, both in English and in the languages of multilingual pupils?
- Wall displays. Do pupils read the walls? Is pupils' work presented so that it can be read by others? Are the displays interactive, requiring a response to what is read?
- Book boxes. If they exist, what is their intended audience? Again, consider the range of materials they contain which counts as 'reading';
- Information about school book clubs, sponsored or national reading events, the school library, local library.
- How is space and furniture organised inside/outside the classroom to accommodate individual and group reading?
- How is gender and cultural diversity represented in the books and other materials displayed?
- Is information material available in the local community languages?
- How easy is access to information technology texts?
- What types of books are on the teacher's desk – is the teacher seen as a reader too?

Discuss with another student teacher, your mentor or tutor what you think the environment says about what it means to be a reader in that classroom.

- Private reading as a basis for written work, or taped oral response: this means that the teacher needs to recognise that he frequently *does not know as much* as the pupil about the text being used. It confers real power on the reader to *make her own meaning* within a guided context. Your job is to engage in a dialogue about the text, which helps her to reflect upon its meaning, in a way that can be communicated to a broader audience. She begins to develop awareness that texts can have shared significance for some people, and, through a negotiated task, can consider her reading as something which might interest others. Responses might include: designing a book jacket for the text; selecting a key passage for reading on to a tape and explaining the selection made; designing the advertising materials which would accompany the 'film of the book'; a book review with recommendations.
- Pupils also need to share individual reading in a way which looks at common criteria, to establish a foundation of common discourse to which they have access. An example of this is the group preparation of a 'book programme' or

literary magazine, in which pupils bring together their individual reading, and present it in a format which builds on their familiarity with the language conventions of media presentation. In this way, pupils use their language experience of media texts to couch their exploration of the critical discourse about texts they have chosen to read.

Group shared reading

This method of reading is suitable for small groups of pupils reading a core text, author or genre, and working on a task, either as a group or individually: pupils show that they have taken account of the responses and views of others in their reading of the text.

Group reading is demanding in terms of class organisation and sufficient resources. It is, however, a critical bridge between individual reading and class set texts, between pupils exercising their own purely personal criteria for responding to a text, and learning about the prevailing literary discourses of examinations, and how to be critical readers. It allows for guided choice, for the teacher to ensure range, while supporting the autonomy in readers. It is a way of keeping a personal dialogue going, and maintaining an individual reading position, while pupils move towards examinations which increasingly prescribe what to read and how to respond.

Group reading is an important way of addressing difference, and requires both the class and support teachers to give guidance and allocate appropriate targets for reading. In the multilingual classroom, shared language groups can read in a first language to develop critical reading skills. Pupils at different stages of reading fluency in English can be directed to texts which they are ready to try. Areas of study for group reading might include the following examples:

- further texts by an author already introduced as a class reader;
- genre (e.g. horror), with different groups reading Point Horror books, Stephen King, nineteenth-century short horror stories, Mary Shelley's *Frankenstein*, *The X-files*, Arthur C. Clarke's *Mysterious World* series;
- a study of texts as preparation for a class reader, John Steinbeck's *Of Mice and Men*, to include a library project loan on the Great Depression, atlases of North America, Harper Lee's *To Kill a Mocking Bird* and Mildred Taylor's *Roll of Thunder: Hear my Cry*.

Reading and gender

Since the early 1990s there has been a considerable revival of interest in gender differences in reading across the key stages, sparked initially by the OFSTED report, *Boys and English*, which expressed concern that 'In all year groups girls read more fiction than boys' (DFE, 1993, p. 3). The reluctance of some adolescent boys to read fiction may be seen as part of a broader pattern of underachievement in English, relative to the continuing higher performance of girls in tests and examinations. Gender differences in attitudes towards reading are complex and stereotypical categorising of 'boys' and 'girls' reading are to be resisted as advised by Elaine Millard: 'For many pupils, boys and girls alike . . . their current reading cannot be described as personal choice in any true sense, but as a chore imposed on them by others, mainly their English teachers' (1997, p. 97). Some generalisable features, however, may be summarised as follows:

- Boys and girls can perceive the act of reading itself as a gendered form of behaviour. Much of the reading undertaken in classrooms is performed as a quiet, still, passive, compliant and constrained physical process. This conforms to stereotypical 'feminine' behaviour, at a time when adolescents are increasingly conscious of sexual identities.
- Reluctant male readers frequently express a pragmatic perception of what English is *for*. They see it as equipping them with basic literacy skills to get a job – and therefore dismiss the reading of fiction, in particular, as irrelevant to the real world as they see it. It is not seen to be empowering.
- Female pupils find compensatory power in the lives of heroines in teenage romance novels, at a time when they are becoming more aware of gender differences in the economic power roles in society.
- Male pupils are often not interested in the main texts which count as reading material, i.e. 'literature', in many classrooms. Their expressed reading preferences are infrequently met beyond occasional private reading opportunities. Factual information books, hobby books, graphic novels and comics are rarely given a high-profile whole class focus.
- A main emphasis on character study, personal response and empathy as approaches to literature is alienating to many boys, while preferred by girls. Boys in general have expressed greater interest in events and plot development, and analytical ways of writing about literature.

In the light of the points made here, you will need to consider the following questions:

1   How can your planning aim to motivate both boys and girls to develop wider reading habits?
2   How, in particular, can you plan to prevent boys from effectively opting out of reading from age 12 onward?
3   Are boys *and* girls encouraged actively to interrogate texts, to change them, rewrite them, talk about them, dramatise them, compare them to their world as they see it?
4   How will you treat the gendered reading of adventure game books and teenage romance?

It is important to explore gender preferences in texts with pupils. As individuals with a reading history, they can learn about why some genres are so important to them at that stage in their lives – to reflect upon their own changing self-perceptions during adolescence. Single-sex group reading is very supportive of this, and of the fact that these texts are often experienced as serial reads. Space should be given for gender preferences to be validated in the classroom. This is not to legitimate a narrow reading experience, but to acknowledge that serial reading is a real need for many pupils, and should be seen as part of a continuum which counts as reading. Pupils need to be able to reflect upon it as part of their reading history in a *conscious* way. Gender groupings can help pupils to explore texts of particular interest to them, and offer opportunities for a critical re-examination of gendered attitudes to reading. Through shared group reading, pupils are particularly enabled to examine their own reading position. Between themselves, they can ask questions about how their attitudes towards reading and their responses to texts have been formed by their social histories. Encourage the broadest definition of what it is to be a reader: this means evaluating the *range* of texts which feature in the curriculum, and the *variety* of methods by which pupils can respond to them.

Task 6.5 Learning about reading positions

Learning to be a critical reader means learning about what it means to read. If we want pupils to engage *consciously* in a text, we need to teach about how it positions them as a reader. They need to learn how the text was culturally produced, to treat it as a product of a particular person's experience of culture and history, to demystify its origins and thus its meanings. They need to understand what has influenced their own development as a reader.

Take a short teenage novel with a multicultural focus, such as *Face* in *Come to Mecca* (Zephaniah, 1999). Read the first five chapters yourself, and ask yourself the following questions. What is your own experience of:

- the inner-city setting for the story;
- its cultural context;
- the main character types;
- non-standard dialects?

What difference does it make to read this story:

- as a speaker of a non-standard dialect;
- as a reader from a particular generation – a grandparent, parent, teenager;
- as a male or female;
- as a person living in the East End of London, or another inner-city area?

Assess how these factors will influence your own response to this story, and your own desire to continue reading the novel. Now, consider how important these factors are to pupils' reading of *all* literature. By understanding their own reading position, pupils bring a personal voice to their treatment of texts.

Class readers

The predominant experience of reading for most pupils in secondary schools is that of a single text, chosen by the teacher or an examination board, which is read with the whole class, usually, therefore, at a common pace, with core aspects of the text focused upon for detailed study and the preparation of examination-type assignments. Class readers, however, are used to achieve specific aims beyond examination preparation. They can:

- provide a common experience which has a part to play in the emotional, social and cultural development of pupils growing up in society. Issues such as racism and the experiences of child refugees are explored in novels like Beverley Naidoo's *The Other Side of Truth*: gender roles and parenting are scrutinised in Anne Fine's *Flour Babies*;
- provide a foundation for an integrated approach to the English curriculum, in which language study is embedded in the exploration of language in use: literary texts provide the *contexts* for meaning, in which pupils can explore their responses to written language;
- be used as a focus for critical reading, in which pupils explore the cultural factors which have influenced a text's construction, and begin to understand that all texts exist within particular social and historical contexts – it is interesting to discuss with pupils *how* their set examination texts came to acquire that privileged status.

Core texts have been used frequently to structure an English curriculum around a theme. Prior to the centralised curriculum development which followed the Education Reform Act (1988), many departments claimed 'we teach English through literature', and this approach is still popular: a common core is established for the class through the teacher's selection of a text, from which springs language study, literary approaches and creative writing. The text is central here to curriculum planning, and is used to embody the concept of a fully integrated approach to English teaching. For example, a scheme of work based on Steinbeck's *Of Mice and Men* might include: a study of accent and dialect in spoken language; a diary written by George; a dramatisation of one scene; an alternative chapter ending and a tracking of events to examine the unities of place and time in the plot development of the novel. Today, a different concept of *core* language experience will often underpin the planning of schemes of work: a film text, drama experience or a study based on language in use could all be used as the foundation for units of English work. More recently, within the KS3 Framework, curriculum planning is centred around literacy objectives, sometimes resulting in reduced opportunities for the study of complete works of literature. It is important for you to consider the benefits of sharing a complete text or 'class reader' as one among several core curriculum experiences, all of which will draw on differing areas of pupil expertise and culture.

Reading with the class: some pitfalls

In your observations of pupils reading a class text you will probably note a range of methods used in different classrooms, which might include: reading undertaken in silence; reading targeted amounts or different sections of text; following the teacher's

---

Task 6.6 Choosing texts

You may be free to select a class reader or you may have to read a text which forms part of a departmental scheme; either way, you need to consider how you 'prepare the ground' for a class reading of a text. Teachers' criteria for choosing texts may be quite different from pupils'! When you are selecting, meet with your tutor or the head of English to discuss your/their reasons for the choice. Include in your discussion whether the text is:

- a focus for the KS3 Framework objectives;
- part of a departmental scheme of work;
- a complete set in the book cupboard;
- one which works well with a particular theme;
- personally enjoyed by the teacher;
- recommended by pupils;
- recommended by colleagues;
- a text that the teacher feels will fulfil the needs of a particular class;
- set for an examination.

Will these reasons, and any others, be made explicit to the pupils? They need to understand the circumstances surrounding any text which is chosen for class study, so that a careful appraisal can be made of the status this confers on the text, when they come to make critical responses to it themselves. Some teachers are able to offer pupils the opportunity of choosing class readers, where stock is available: giving a choice depends on your *aims*, which determine whether your scheme of work ties the text very closely to a thematic approach, or is to do with developing experience of text, which can be achieved through a variety of literature.

Task 6.7 Beginning a class reader

Observe the first two lessons where a teacher introduces a new text. Make notes on the following:

- What objectives are set? How are they communicated to pupils?
- At what stage in the lesson do pupils actually begin to read the text?
- What form of preparation takes place for beginning to read – introduction to themes/issues; reference to other works/authors already familiar to pupils; discussion; group/pair work; improvisation?
- How do pupils establish their own possible relationships with the concerns of the text?
- At what place in the text do pupils begin to read?
- How much does the teacher read in each lesson?
- How are lessons ended in relation to the place that is reached in the text?
- What use is made of writing and speaking and listening in these introductory lessons?

> Discuss your observations with the teacher following the lessons. Points made here should help you to formulate ideas for starting reading with your own classes. It would be useful to look at how a different teacher begins reading with a class in another year or Key Stage, and to compare methods.
>
> Now, use your notes based on these principles to start planning your own scheme of work for the text which has been chosen for you to teach.

reading; reading 'around the class', where pupils take turns to read aloud from the set book, and reading some sections of the text for homework.

Many pupils love to read out loud to the class, some with an enthusiasm that is not always matched by competence. The dynamic of the text is quickly lost by just a few minutes of inexperienced, hesitant reading which frustrates more able readers. Listeners with English as an Additional Language, and less experienced readers, gain little by listening to poor reading. It lacks the necessary pace and inflexion which imparts comprehension. For other pupils, being asked to read aloud is the chief dread of any school day, and holds up an uncompromising public confirmation of what they cannot yet do well. You need to consider the needs of all those who do not raise their hands to read, because they lack confidence, or because of peer pressure. They need a different environment to show what they can do, and to develop skills through constructive and sustained activities. Further disadvantages lie in the use of 'reading around the room' to exact punishment on those 'caught out' not following the text: reading their 'bit' without misadventure becomes the main focus of the exercise, and we impart the notion that once their 'bit' is over, they can relax and switch off again. None of this has very much to do with becoming 'enthusiastic, discriminating and responsive readers'.

Pupils can, however, develop further competence by reading aloud, and who among us has outgrown the pleasure of listening to someone reading to us really well? We aim for all our pupils to feel able to read aloud confidently, and this will take place in different contexts. When a whole class is sharing a text, practice in reading can be built into the scheme of work, which gives *everyone* an opportunity to develop reading skills. Variety of reading approach is important. Pupils need to hear good models for reading on a whole class basis, from the teacher, and from pupils who have a mutual agreement with the teacher about reading aloud sometimes. Much individual progress can be made in group readings of the class text, both in reading competence and in understandings of the text. All pupils can have an opportunity to read aloud within their group and to prepare their reading, with support from a teacher if necessary. You will, however, still need to consider whether it is appropriate for every pupil to take part.

The next task pursues the principle that a variety of approaches is important in order to provide sufficiently diverse opportunities for the range of pupils within a class; in addition, it is important to select an approach which matches the learning objectives of the lesson. The following are examples of ways of reading a core text, having divided pupils into groups:

- reading the dialogue in the roles of speakers and narrator;
- taking the dialogue only, and turning it into a script;
- choosing a section which lends itself to dubbing with sound-effects and background music;

Task 6.8 Class readers: varying the approach

Find a short story or a chapter from a class reader; decide on your lesson aims and select which of these approaches would be most suitable. Try it out with a group of pupils. Following the readings, discuss with them how they decided to treat the text in order to read it. What have they learned about the way it is written, about the plot, the characters, the style?

- dividing into narrative sequences, and preparing an individual reading of each one by group members;
- making an abridged reading and performing/taping it;
- selecting passages for choral reading.

You might add to this list of possibilities.

SUPPORTING PROGRESSION: READING THE UNFAMILIAR

The 'unfamiliar' might be a new author, a pre-twentieth-century literary text for some pupils, an information text that is packed with specialist terms and which is intended for a particular audience, or a text which is culturally excluding for some pupils: consider the challenges offered by Dickens's *A Christmas Carol* to pupils not of Western European Christian origin. What is the significance of 'Bah! Humbug!' in this context? Such a text has become increasingly popular at Key Stage 3, since it meets the requirements to study literature published before 1914 (in a *short* novel), covers an author from the approved list, and suits the desires of many English departments to do seasonal work in the latter part of the autumn term. Whatever the reasons for a text being particularly challenging, active interrogation of it by pupils can develop *progression* in a way which helps them to bring their own language into play. Progression is achieved when pupils can develop language by: practising it upon texts; by hypothesising about meanings; guessing and estimating the intended effects by comparisons with what is already known from other narrative experience; by transposing what they already know to their reading of new or altered versions of it.

Strategies which interrogate texts actively can take many forms; these have been well documented in summary form in *The English Curriculum: Reading 1 Comprehension*. It includes the following statement in its rationale:

> by providing specific, problem-based but open-ended points of entry to peer-group discussion round a text these activities may dispel the inertia that tends to descend on many of us when under instruction in a classroom.
> (Simons and Plackett, 1990, p. 82)

This book is well worth reading. It acknowledges the contribution made by the work of Lunzer and Gardner (1979) in their reading research project out of which arose the

Task 6.9 Using DARTs

For this task, DARTs activities will be considered as a way of reading the following extract from *A Christmas Carol*, in which we learn about its central character Scrooge.

> Oh! But he was a tight-fisted hand at the grindstone, Scrooge! A squeezing, wrenching, grasping, scraping, clutching, covetous old sinner! Hard and sharp as flint, from which no steel had ever struck out generous fire; secret, and self-contained, and solitary as an oyster. The cold within him froze his old features, nipped his pointed nose, shrivelled his cheek, stiffened his gait; made his eyes red, his thin lips blue; and spoke out shrewdly in his grating voice. A frosty rime was on his head, and on his eyebrows, and his wiry chin. He carried his own temperature always about with him; he iced his office in the dog-days; and didn't thaw it one degree at Christmas.
>
> (Dickens, 1985, p. 46)

- **Cloze procedure** involves deleting key words prior to pupils' reading. Decide which words or parts of words you would delete to help pupils to explore Scrooge's character, using their own understanding of what a mean person might be like. Would you focus on adjectives, colour, temperature, getting the pupils to complete the similes? Ask them to reflect on how they made their choices.
- **Underlining/highlighting the text** helps pupils to identify the ways in which ideas are structured, and to pool ideas which have a common significance for them; for example, the words/phrases which seem to be critical of Scrooge or the ones which identify the story with a particular season. What you would ask them to highlight would obviously be relevant to the learning objectives.
- Try asking pupils to highlight words about which they would like to find out more; get them to try out predictions for meanings in their pairs/groups, before using a dictionary or asking you.
- **Prediction**. Pupils use their knowledge of other narratives to estimate some of the possible situations and outcomes for this character.
- **Dividing up the text** to explore how meaning develops. Here, appreciating the punctuation is a key to coping with the long sentences. Ask groups to highlight all the punctuation, or use it to cut up the extract, maintaining the sequence. They then use this as a basis for a choral reading. Afterwards, they are ready to talk about the significance of reading punctuation for meaning and emphasis, in texts where the complexity of the language may be new to them.

development of DARTs (Directed Activities Related to Texts). There are many well-tried strategies you can use to match the learning aims which you set for your pupils.

These activities would be particularly valuable for pupils to undertake using word processors (see Chapter 9). The example lesson outline in Figure 6.3 shows how some of these strategies can help to achieve learning aims. The lesson uses the extract as an introduction to the text.

Lesson outline

Main aims for scheme of work on *A Christmas Carol*:
To broaden the reading experience of pupils, to include literature published pre-1914; to develop approaches to 'reading for meaning' in texts containing unfamiliar language.

Learning objectives:
1   To develop strategies to explore for meaning the extract which introduces Scrooge.
2   To learn about this character through reflecting on the language used, both by the author and the pupils.

National Curriculum:
Eng2   Reading
        1a   Pupils should be taught to extract meaning beyond the literal, explaining how the choice of language and style affects implied and explicit meanings
        8 iii   The range should include works published before 1914 . . . Dickens

Resources:
Extract in cloze form; text: *A Christmas Carol*

Inclusion/support:
1   Pair work as a learning strategy – sharing ideas and vocabulary.
2   Supplementary sheet with suggestions for cloze procedure to choose from.
3   Glossary for the original text.

TIMING	TEACHER ACTIVITY	PUPIL ACTIVITY
5 mins	• register and settle	
5 mins	• explain the aims and objectives to pupils • ask pupils to work in pairs • introduce the reading activity: pupils to read the cloze extract; discuss to complete it	• pupils ask for any clarification
15 mins	• supporting pairs and monitoring • guide individual pupils on use of supplementary support	• pair work on the text • prepare to feedback suggestions to class
5 mins	• respond to small sample of pupil suggestions for cloze exercise – monitor understanding • focus on the impact of language choices	• two or three pairs feedback • contribute to discussion about language choices
2–5 mins	• explain next task: pairs are to discuss their language choices, and write a brief statement about their understanding of Scrooge at this point	
10 mins	• support pair work and monitor	• pupils discuss and write the statement in pairs
5 mins	• distribute the original text • ask pairs to read it out loud to each other • set the task: pairs are to discuss how Dickens presents Scrooge and write a brief statement	

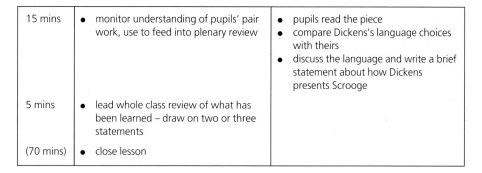

15 mins	• monitor understanding of pupils' pair work, use to feed into plenary review	• pupils read the piece • compare Dickens's language choices with theirs • discuss the language and write a brief statement about how Dickens presents Scrooge
5 mins	• lead whole class review of what has been learned – draw on two or three statements	
(70 mins)	• close lesson	

Figure 6.3 Lesson outline: exploring text

Non-literary texts

Pupils living in the 'age of information' have access to a proliferation of texts which qualify as 'non-literary'. The range is enormous, and is growing constantly: pupils have daily access to materials which make varied reading demands, including newspapers, magazines, leaflets, brochures, instructions, advertisements, timetables, food packaging, not to mention the whole spectrum of electronic and audio-visual texts.

Informative and persuasive texts pose particular challenges for pupils. Their power lies in their relationship with the 'real' world, being so explicitly a product of it, and having direct bearings upon it. Teaching pupils to read information texts critically involves an evaluation of the sources of the facts which they contain. As with the study of literature, pupils need to learn about the *context* of the text's production, and how the author's intentions will inform the selection of language and form.

Strategies for reading these texts can be particularly helpful in developing pupils' critical awareness of language. Many of the texts are short, serving a pragmatic function as well as contributing to a cultural consciousness of the type of society in which we live. Reading these texts involves learning how to:

- scan;
- sift the relevant from the irrelevant;
- alter text through deletion and substitution;
- collate textual evidence;
- summarise;
- produce alternative text;
- evaluate;
- account for findings.

Information technology has an important role in developing critical reading skills. Access to ICT means that pupils can see themselves increasingly as producers of authoritative-looking text: using the language and conventions of 'factual' presentation for themselves is a way of exploring its authority. Meaning may be viewed as something which is subject to the composer of the text: when more than one person is involved in that composing, the pair or group discussion shows what different possibilities for meaning exist within each decision about language and form.

ASSESSMENT

The assessment of reading is as complex as what we mean by reading itself. For assessment to have a purposeful role in the learning process, you will need to consider two main factors:

1   How will you *know* what has been learned?
2   How can you *describe* what has been learned, so that you and your pupils can see the pattern of progression in a way that is motivating, and helps to set new aims for reading?

How will you know what has been learned?

You need to have assessment objectives in mind when planning your scheme of work around reading. Ask yourself which assessment objectives you are aiming at with your pupils. The following are some examples:

- developing fluency in reading aloud;
- developing reading for pleasure, based on heightened awareness of what texts can offer;
- developing pupils' comprehension of texts;
- developing skills for reading for information;
- increasing confidence in tackling unfamiliar texts;
- developing a new strand of reading (e.g. graphic novel, pre-twentieth-century literature);
- development of critical reading skills – 'decoding';
- developing proficiency in literary discourse.

All of the above are part of an overriding objective, which is the development of reading for meaning in individual pupils.

Consider how you can gauge progression in your chosen area. The most simple and manageable form of reading assessment is also the most reductive: the comprehension test. It has been resurrected within recent examination reform, and provides a singular perspective on what a pupil has understood in his or her (usually solitary) reading of disembodied text. It has little to do with the assessment objectives listed above, which view *meaning* as negotiated continually through language experience in the social environment of the classroom. You will need to consider what appropriate means are available for you to obtain a record of pupils' progression, and to assess it. It might take the form of:

- oral responses to what has been read, either taped or presented to the class;
- dramatisation based on a text;

- visual/graphic accounts of the text;
- written responses, where pupils have been made aware of the *reading* objectives embedded in the task;
- pupils' personal reading journals.

Describing the learning

The following criteria for planning and assessing what pupils can do are not hierarchical. They evolve through the integration of speaking, listening and writing with reading. They indicate areas of development which will correspond at different times to the range of texts and different ways of reading, as seen in Figure 6.1. Learning here is described in a way which is *formative*. The criteria can form the basis of an ongoing profile of progression in reading, in which both pupils and teacher can map out the reading experiences of a class throughout a year or particular schemes of work.

- **Making individual meaning:** using a reading diary; constructing a reading autobiography; identifying and explaining preferences; identifying emotional responses to events; explaining responses to characters; empathising; identifying a reading position; imaginative and creative manipulation of texts (e.g. adding a chapter or changing an ending); interrogating 'fact' in non-literary text; rewriting texts in different genres; transferring personal responses to imposed texts; learning to examine the cultural context of texts; examining assumptions about gender and race; understanding the individual's relationship with a canonised text.
- **Broadening reading experience:** confirming preferences for types of texts; serial reading; exploring particular genres; exploring an author; rereading texts; developing meaning through peer discussion; communicating responses to others in oral/written/visual forms; finding that a text's significance is social and cultural as well as individual; learning about the responses of others; learning that texts have a cultural role; learning about writing conventions such as plot, structure, character development.
- **Approaching the unfamiliar:** understanding how some texts become canonised; learning about relationships between texts ('intertextuality'); exploring recurring themes within canonised literature; comparing media and literary texts; using drama improvisation to develop a personal perspective on a text; using DARTs; developing pupils' own questions about written material; learning about literary discourse; exploring new texts through familiar genre and language.

SUMMARY AND KEY POINTS

This chapter has raised issues about teaching reading as a classroom activity, while acknowledging that we are engaging in a wider cultural process. What happens with reading in school has implications for the society beyond, and vice versa. The society beyond is complex and continually changing, and you need to respond to that in establishing a rationale for teaching texts.

Mary Hilton has described the teaching of reading in a way which celebrates the relatedness and interdependence of new and traditional texts in contemporary society:

> Through new forms of story *and* through understanding the workings of traditional narrative desire, we get children hooked on books. Through books *and* media texts, through the new and the popular *and* the ancient and traditional, their worlds of cultural possibility are enlarged and enriched. They learn, ideally, to move from one text to the other with intellectual grace and ease.
>
> (Hilton, 1996, p. 191)

Such a view emphasises how this chapter and Chapter 9 need to be read together: together, they examine the spectrum of experiences which constitute 'reading' in the contemporary classroom. The cultural diversity of your pupils is your starting point in planning for broadening and deepening the reading experience.

The *pleasure* and *power* of reading is something which is easily lost or distorted, at a time when texts are screened to meet approval for national testing, and reading development has become synonymous with acquiring basic skills for the world of work. By planning for a range of texts, to be experienced through varied groupings and tasks, you can aim to develop readers who find many sources of *pleasure* and *power* in reading. Power comes with knowing about the different types of reading that are available, and how they are regarded in wider society. An independent, critical reading position is essential if pupils are to appraise the texts which are available today, both in the classroom and in the world beyond school.

FURTHER READING

McRae, J. and Vethamani, M.E. (1999) *Now Read On*, London: Routledge. The book's subtitle, *A Course in Multicultural Reading*, indicates the multiple benefits of this very accessible volume for new teachers whose experience of international literature and critical approaches is limited. It introduces a range of literature of varying genres, and models ways of reading which support teachers' own subject knowledge development and detailed planning for teaching a broader range of texts.

Meek, M. (1991) *On Being Literate*, London: The Bodley Head. Meek describes how teaching reading today is bound up with changes in contemporary society. She explains how a modern concept of literacy must embody full recognition of the texts which people actually need and use, and how children develop their reading across a broad spectrum of these texts.

Millard, E. (1997) *Differently Literate: Boys, Girls and the Schooling of Literacy*, London: Falmer Press. This book offers a contemporary analysis of the literacy development of boys and girls in secondary schools. There is a particular focus on the relationship between gendered reading preferences outside school, and how these impact upon engagement with reading in school, and boys' and girls' progression as 'readers'.

Simons, M. and Plackett, P. (eds) (1990) *The English Curriculum: Reading, 1: Comprehension*, London: English and Media Centre. This is an invaluable resource for all teachers who are interested in helping pupils to make real meanings out of text, and in helping them to gain access to texts. The book is divided into four sections: the reading process; comprehension; using information books; whole school policies.

See also Pennac, D. (1994) *Reads Like a Novel*, London: Quartet; and Bloome, D. and Stierer, B. (1995) *Reading Words*, Sheffield: NATE.

7 Writing

John Moss

INTRODUCTION

Some people may tell you that teaching writing is a simple business. They may tell you that when they were at school all pupils were given a title and did one piece of writing each week in their exercise books for their English teacher. They may add that the teacher corrected all the mistakes, which the pupils then wrote out three times. They may reassure themselves that this practice led to effective learning by pointing to all the evidence of hard work which accumulated in those exercise books. However, there are numerous false and dangerous assumptions in these apparently straightforward suggestions.

The assumptions include the ideas that: writing can be usefully isolated from the rest of the English curriculum; producing a large quantity of writing necessarily improves quality; finished pieces of writing can be produced with little preparation; the products of writing tasks are more important than the processes used to create them; school writing consists of exercises, and so presentation and layout can be standardised; the teacher is the audience for school writing; the teacher's main function in assessment is to check technical accuracy; pupils can improve their technical accuracy by mimicking correct forms introduced to them by teachers adopting this copyediting role.

In this chapter, you will be challenged to question all these assumptions by thinking about: the relationship between writing and other language processes; the development stages which many successful pieces of writing pass through; the ways in which writing makes use of the possibilities and conventions of different genres; the influence of a writer's perception of a real or imagined audience on all aspects of his or her writing, including technical accuracy. A central tenet of the chapter is that, when teaching writing, you will need to support pupils *both* by providing time, opportunities and experiences which allow them to work through a creative, interactive and evaluative process building on their initial ideas, *and* by making them aware of the possibilities of the different genres they may choose to adopt and adapt for particular purposes. In other words, to explore the world of writing, pupils need *both* a compass to orientate themselves, plan and follow routes, *and* a map which identifies possible writing destinations.

OBJECTIVES

By the end of this chapter you should understand the importance of the following to the effective teaching of writing:

- the relationships between writing, speaking and listening, and reading;
- the contribution that writing can make to learning;
- the social dynamics of writing in the classroom;
- drafting and the development of pieces of writing;
- writing models, and explorations of genre;
- audiences for writing and publication;
- the formative assessment and evaluation of writing;
- the writer's or writers' experience of making meaning;
- the possibility of developing technical skills through real writing tasks;
- a critical interpretation of the definition of the writing curriculum in *The National Curriculum for England: English*.

WHAT YOU KNOW ABOUT LEARNING TO WRITE

Writing and language autobiographies

Margaret Meek, one of the most important writers on literacy, asks her readers to find out what they think they don't know about reading by searching their memories for significant moments in their reading autobiographies (Meek, 1988). This activity can usefully be extended to cover other aspects of language development: it draws attention to truths about our own learning experience which we should allow to influence our search for good professional practice.

Here is an example of a story about writing from one teacher's language autobiography:

> One of my earliest memories of infant school is of being taught to use the letters of the alphabet by drawing pictures of things that started with each letter in succession and then writing appropriate accompanying sentences. After each piece of work, the teacher marked our books using a three-star marking scale. This practice has stayed in my mind because of the shock I had when I received only two stars for the letter 'v'. The teacher told me it was because the handwriting went downhill. The first discussion I remember ever having about writing was about this surface feature of my

work. I corrected the error and continued to the end of the alphabet, having this new idea that 'writing in straight lines makes it perfect', literally rubber-stamped. The experience was not in any sense about learning that I was just beginning to explore the limitless possibilities for making meaning that those twenty-six letters make available to us.

Learning to Write

We had to write a sentence
For each letter: *a, b, c, . . .*
I did all right at first
And got three stars for each
Until we got to *v.*
I drew a van, and wrote:
'This is a van.'

I only got two stars,
And asked the teacher why.
She said; 'It slopes
From left to right.'

My writing's
        gone downhill
                since then.

Thirty years later I wrote this short poem about the incident, at a teachers' training day during which I had been asked to search my language autobiography for significant events. After ten minutes the course leader asked if anyone would like to read out a piece he or she had written. Since I had finished a draft of the poem I put my hand up. No one else did. The course leader ignored my hand and used the general response to demonstrate that it is dangerous to make pupils share personal writing with a large audience, especially when they have only had the opportunity to work briefly on a draft. This may be true, but for me, the meaning of the exercise was entirely different: it had enabled me to illustrate, from my own experience, why I think mechanical approaches to the teaching of writing can be dangerously arid. I wanted to share that perception with the other teachers present.

WRITING AND THE PROCESSES OF ENGLISH

One of the central orthodoxies of English teaching is that development in each of the processes of speaking and listening, reading and writing is best promoted by work in which the processes are integrated. It is important to examine the implications of this idea for the teaching of writing.

Task 7.1 Your history as a writer

This story points towards some of the issues about the teaching of writing which this chapter will address. Search your own language autobiography for a significant moment and work out what questions your story, and/or the one quoted above, raise(s) about the teaching and learning of writing. Listen to the stories of some other student teachers. Brainstorm a list of issues to keep in mind while you read the rest of the chapter.

Note

Exploring your pupils' language biographies always pays dividends, and is especially valuable when you are getting to know them. It provides opportunities for you to learn about where they have come from in terms of their language development and previous English teaching experience. The information can be more useful for planning and target-setting than the results of formal reading tests and assessment scores. Work of this kind also raises pupils' reflective awareness of their own language development and enables them to become more usefully self-evaluative. It can also provide you with a means of validating pupils' home language or languages in the classroom, whether they are multilingual or experts in a particular regional dialect.

Talking and reading before writing

The sequence in which the three core language processes are presented in *The National Curriculum for England: English* may be seen to suggest that speaking and listening and reading should precede writing. This impression is strengthened by the fact that the requirements for writing emphasise the products more than process writing. Of course, language development begins with oracy, and there are many human situations in which we choose to talk something through before writing about it. The content of material we read can also be important in stimulating writing, and reading provides models for writing, by suggesting forms, conventions and structures which we can choose to adopt, modify or challenge.

Much classroom practice exploits ways in which speaking, listening and reading can contribute to the development of writing. There are many opportunities for collaborative activities, such as small group brainstorming of ideas about a text, which pupils record to provide ideas for a later writing task. However, individual tasks can also make use of the primacy of speech to develop writing: one example would be provided by a pupil tape-recording herself telling a story she knows, which she or a teacher will later transcribe to form the first draft of a written version.

Writing before speaking or reading

While writing is, then, often dependent on the stimulation of speaking and listening or reading, it is important to note that there are also many situations in which writing can support effective speaking, listening and reading. Examples of writing which supports speaking include carefully planned activities such as the preparation of prompt cards to be used in delivering a formal speech or presentation, and much more spontaneous tasks, such as five-minute bursts of silent writing during which pupils are asked to record their first impressions of a text before a class discussion of it. Examples of writing contributing to the development of reading include writing in a particular genre to gain insights into the problems that constructing a particular kind of text presents, which may inform later critical analysis of similar texts.

Analysing talk and texts to support writing

Another important aspect of the relationship between writing and the other core language processes concerns the analysis of talk and texts to support writing. Analysis of the language of speech and of related reading material can help pupils to understand the special character of the language commonly used in writing. For example, pupils who are asked to compare a tape-recording of a person being interviewed about an event and the interviewee's written account of that event can be guided to notice organisational features of the writing which may be different from those of the spoken account.

Some of the questions which can be asked when reading any text draw attention to the decisions which writers frequently make, and which pupils will need to make themselves when writing. Examples of such questions include: What do you think the writer's purpose was in producing this text? Who do you think the writer imagined reading the text? How has the writer organised the material that has been used in this text? What other texts like this can you think of – what kind of text has the writer chosen to make?

Writing in planning sequences

A fundamental planning issue that arises from these observations concerns the sequencing of activities in teaching. Teachers should be able to explain and justify the function and positioning of writing activities in the sequence of a lesson or scheme of work: often the emphasis is on using speaking, listening or reading to help develop achievement in writing, but writing should be used much more than *The National Curriculum for England: English* suggests to help develop speaking and listening and reading skills.

Task 7.2 Writing to support talk and reading

Explore the *The National Curriculum for England: English* programmes of study for speaking and listening and reading for requirements which could be supported by writing activities. Generate a varied list of writing activities which you think would be particularly useful.

WRITING AND LEARNING

The National Curriculum for England: English pays much attention to the purposes of writing. It emphasises that pupils should be taught appropriate compositional techniques to learn how to write: to imagine, explore and entertain; to inform, explain and describe; to persuade, argue and advise; and to analyse, review and comment. It pays less attention to the use of writing 'for *thinking and learning* [for example, for hypothesising, paraphrasing, summarising, noting]'. The distinction, which should be given more emphasis is between writing which sets out to convey the results of learning to an audience and writing through which learning takes place.

The distinction is not, of course, watertight: drafting processes, for example, may enable writers to work out what they think about something and then communicate this to an audience. However, some forms of writing are more concerned with processes of learning than with communication, and their development is much more important than the brief reference to them in *The National Curriculum for England: English* suggests. There are a number of ways of defining categories of writing to learn. One useful division is between retrospective writing, which has the primary purpose of recording and making sense of experience or material, and prospective writing, which is concerned largely with reorganising and reordering that experience or material for new purposes.

Retrospective writing includes diary and journal writing. In work of this kind, pupils can be given complete freedom over what they select to include, or their attention can be focused in particular directions. A diary could be used to net whatever strikes a writer as memorable or significant, say on a school trip. A reading journal could filter out predetermined categories of information, such as reflections on the characters in a novel. Retrospective writing can be as coherent as a series of reflections on a photograph, written in continuous prose, or as fragmented and architectural as a set of marginal notes and marks on a page of poetry. It can be as personal as a private diary, written with the self as the only intended audience, or as public as notes on the writer's first impressions of a television documentary, written as a contribution to a planned group or class discussion. It can be as unstructured as a commonplace book in which memorable quotations are collected in random order, or as structured as a set of notes on the techniques of newspaper advertising written under headings and gradually compiled from looking at examples.

Prospective writing includes a wide range of ways of planning writing. Some of this may be quite disorganised, such as brainstormed lists of ideas and questions, and some may show rudimentary elements of structure, such as schematic plans, columnar or grid-based maps of ideas and spider diagrams, and expressive fragments like those which may become either poems or the opening paragraphs of stories in later drafts.

Writing, thinking and learning

In general, learners often make use of thinking processes such as: reflecting on what is known; connecting what has been understood and what is new; analysing and selecting material and ideas which are relevant to a purpose. Consequently, schemes of work which make use of cycles of related retrospective and prospective writing activities are likely to make powerful contributions to learning. The sequence may start in either mode, but teachers should be conscious of the implications of decisions they make about this. For example, a group working on producing a class newspaper could start by brainstorming ideas and outlining the proposed structure of their paper, or they could start by reviewing the contents of a number of different published papers. There are advantages and disadvantages in both methods. The teacher should know why one method is chosen, or why the class is given a choice.

This discussion has suggested that the writing activities through which learning takes place can vary in the extent to which they are structured and selective. For example, while many teachers believe that writing journals makes a particularly useful contribution to learning, they may have very different expectations of the pupils using them. Moreover, some teachers see a journal (for retrospective writing) as something quite different from planning or drafting a book (for prospective writing), but others would expect pupils to carry out both kinds of work in one place.

Some pupil questions which teachers need to be able to answer, and justify their answers, when introducing writing tasks and different kinds of writing include:

- What will I be learning by doing this writing?
- What is the precise nature of the writing I am being expected to produce?
- Who will be reading it?
- How is this writing connected to other work I have done or will be doing?
- How much freedom do I have to adapt what I am being asked to do to according to my own priorities and preferences?

Any particular kind of writing raises its own questions. For example, teachers promoting the use of writing journals need to decide, sometimes with their pupils:

- Who will have access to the material in the journal (e.g. only the pupil, the pupil and teacher, pupils in the class, parents)?
- To what extent is the journal a place for personal responses to ideas, experiences and material which may not be transformable into 'publishable' writing?
- If the journal is to be a resource for later work, how much guidance (e.g. in the form of prompt questions) should pupils have about selecting appropriate material so that their writing is relevant, but so that they are not strait-jacketed by the teacher's expectations and perceptions of the task?

Task 7.3 Writing and learning across the curriculum

Consider what opportunities pupils in your placement school are given to use writing for learning across the curriculum by shadowing a group of pupils for a day and listing the range of writing activities they are asked to engage in. How much of the writing is primarily to aid learning, and how much of it is primarily to show the results of learning?

THE SOCIAL DYNAMICS OF WRITING IN THE CLASSROOM

School writing can sometimes appear a very isolated human activity in which one person, the pupil, independently produces a text, fed by information from one source, the teacher. This work may then be read by the same teacher, not for the purpose of any kind of communication, but for the assessment of this isolated performance. However, important functions of writing in culture and society are clearly dependent on matters such as the relationship between any piece of writing and what other writers have said or are saying, and the relationship between the writing and the range of actual and potential readers of it. Becoming a writer is partly about learning to see your writing as a contribution to various forms of social and cultural dialogue. It may be argued that pupils are only empowered as writers when they come to recognise their right to participate in this dialogue. To engage meaningfully in writing to meet the compositional purposes, *The National Curriculum for England: English* identifies pupils need a growing awareness of the reality of the social and cultural functions of writing. Some of the teaching which can contribute to the development of this awareness concerns genre and audience, which are discussed later in this chapter, but teachers also need to make use of the microcosm of culture and society that exists as the pupil's world, and to see the social dynamics of the classroom itself as a particularly powerful resource. There are at least four functions which individuals and groups available to pupils inside and outside the classroom can perform in developing an awareness of the social dynamics of writing processes, namely: adviser or information source; co-writer; critical reader, consultant, editor or publisher; and audience. Many of these roles develop the integration of speaking and listening, reading and writing, since they stimulate talk about writing and the reading of writing at numerous different stages before, during and after its composition.

Some of the most interesting teaching of writing takes place when individuals and groups to which pupils have access are placed in specific roles of this kind. For example, younger children (in other classes, feeder primary schools, or siblings) are often used as real audiences for story writing, but this kind of work is enhanced further when these children are also allowed to act as consultants earlier in the process, providing the writers with information about matters such as their likes and dislikes in stories they know.

Some examples of methods which make use of the social dynamics of the classroom to develop writing are as follows. Pupils can provide information sources for each other by conducting and responding to interviews and questionnaires, and by reporting on expert knowledge which they already have (e.g. about a hobby), or have researched for a particular purpose. Pupils telling stories that they know to each other can be a particularly powerful resource.

Pairing pupils with writing partners can provide them with temporary or more permanent writing consultants, trusted colleagues who will read their work at different stages and comment on it. Some pupils may need guidance on appropriate responses to the work of others until they have experience in this role, but it is possible to support them by devising prompt sheets with appropriate questions which might be asked. With experience, pupils can become expert at prompting their peers to think about their writing in many different ways, addressing issues such as: the meaning and authenticity of the work (they can be particularly good at talking about what is convincing); the kind of text the writer is producing (especially if they are able to compare it with other texts they like in the same genre); the way in which the writing is organised and whether or not its surface features such as spelling and layout enhance its power of communication.

Experience of collaborative writing can enable pupils to learn that contributions to various cultural and social discussions are sometimes more powerful when constructed by groups. In principle, it is easy to see that one of the potential advantages of collaborative writing is that a number of minds working together are able to keep a whole range of considerations about the writing more constantly in view. A disadvantage may be that the increase in the number of possibilities considered leads to an impasse of indecision and total loss of momentum. Strategies which support collaboration include the allocation of different tasks to individuals in a group. For example, pupils working on a class magazine may write different sections and then act as the editors of other contributors' work. Group story writing may benefit from individuals writing first drafts of different chapters after a structure for the whole story has been negotiated. Pupils word processing in pairs or groups may function more effectively if they vary the roles of composer and secretary, one controlling content and the other concentrating on accurate recording of ideas on the screen.

It is very easy to overuse silence in work on writing. While it is important for teachers to create opportunities in which sustained concentration on writing tasks can be developed, it is often appropriate to earmark short periods for intensive silent work which are supported by times in which various forms of consultation with the teacher and other pupils can take place.

Task 7.4 The social dynamics of writing in practice

Devise a scheme of work to develop writing in which you make use of the social dynamics of the classroom to place pupils in one or more of the roles of adviser or information source; co-writer; critical reader, consultant, editor or publisher; and audience.

Drafting and the development of pieces of writing

The National Curriculum for England: English makes a brief statement in the programme of study for Key Stages 3 and 4 to confirm that the importance of the processes which contribute to the development of pieces of writing is understood: 'To improve and sustain their writing, pupils should be taught to: plan, draft, redraft and proofread their work on paper and on screen' (DfEE/QCA, 1999b, p. 37). The description of these stages of writing is expanded upon in the programme of study for Key Stage 2, but earlier Key Stage 3 National Curriculum Orders (1989) gave a much more detailed account of the developmental process which is envisaged:

- drafting (getting ideas down on paper or computer screen, regardless of form, organisation or expression);

- redrafting (shaping and structuring the raw material – either on paper or on screen – to take account of purpose, audience and form);
- rereading and revising (making alterations that will help the reader (e.g. getting rid of ambiguity, vagueness, incoherence or irrelevance));
- proof-reading (checking for errors (e.g. omitted or repeated words, mistakes in spelling or punctuation)).

This model of the stages of the development of a piece of writing, even when it is presented in the very abbreviated manner of *The National Curriculum for England: English*, has some merit since it makes explicit the complexity of the processes which pupils often need to use to produce good writing. It also identifies separate activities which teachers can plan for pupils to experience. However, it does not fully represent all the possibilities. For example, earlier in this chapter it was noted that the prospective writing which marks the beginning of the reordering of material or experience, and often precedes attempts to write in a particular genre, can take many forms. Experimental fragments of a text as well as planning diagrams of the overall structure of a piece may both appear in a 'first draft'. In fact, the different processes defined in the 1989 Orders may take place in repeated cycles or other patterns, rather than in a linear sequence, and teachers must be careful not to frustrate pupils by insisting that the development of pieces always follows the same line.

Moreover, whereas *The National Curriculum for England: English* indicates that the functions of drafting are to enable pupils to improve and sustain writing, in fact, writers sometimes choose to translate material into a different genre to try something out in a much more experimental way. Classroom teaching may be used to encourage pupils to think flexibly about their own use of different genres by creating tasks in which they learn to translate material which they or others have written in one genre to another. Drafting processes provide many opportunities for other pupils and teachers to contribute to the development of an individual's work. The role of writing partners and writing groups has already been discussed, but teachers can, of course, also inter-vene productively in the writing process. In particular, various methods of conferencing are used by many teachers. One method which emphasises pupil ownership of the work while allowing for teacher input involves pupils in making appointments to see the teacher individually during writing sessions, and coming to the meeting with questions about the writing for the teacher. It is possible to draw up lists of sample questions to prompt pupils engaging in this kind of dialogue. Whatever method is used, intervening in the writing process through conferencing enables teachers to examine the decisions which pupils are making as they write, and what they understand about what will help their readers. This is invaluable knowledge for the planning of further work and individual target-setting.

It is important to note that GCSE Examination Boards have precise regulations about teachers' involvement in the development of writing which is to be submitted as coursework for examination. Normally, teachers are allowed to comment in ways which might influence redrafting, but they are absolutely forbidden to act as revisers or proof-readers. Pupils find it helpful if teachers explain the limitations on them, particularly if the regulations cause them to modify their role and behaviour.

The National Curriculum for England: English notes that pupils need to 'judge the extent to which any or all of these [drafting] processes are needed in specific pieces of writing' (p. 37), adding, in a later paragraph, that they should also be taught 'to write with fluency and, when required, speed' (p. 38). There are numerous situations in which adult writers have to work at speed which can be simulated in the classroom in ways which pupils find challenging and exciting. Some examples include preparing a press release or writing a radio news bulletin to a tight deadline.

SATs and GCSE examination papers provide all pupils with particular kinds of compulsory writing situations in which writing at speed and with no time for drafting is obviously necessary. Many teachers believe that the current emphasis on written examination papers at the end of Key Stage assessment forces them to spend an inappropriate proportion of teaching time on this kind of writing. Pupils are sometimes confused by the messages this kind of work gives about writing as a human activity, since they appear to conflict with the lessons they learn through their experiences of collaboration, drafting, choosing genres and writing for particular audiences. This sense of conflict can be reduced if other kinds of speed writing are explored as suggested above, and if examination writing is regarded as a genre which has its own conventions that need to be learned. It is also important that teachers have the confidence to teach according to the belief that the development of pupils' understanding of texts and of the writing skills which they are required to demonstrate is best supported by a rich experience of a wide range of reading and writing experiences, rather than by excessive practice on past papers, sample papers, or in other activities which simulate the examination or test.

Task 7.5 Making drafting processes explicit in the classroom

Devise a writing task for a group of pupils you are teaching which gives them good opportunities to make use of the processes of drafting, redrafting, revising and proof-reading. Design a classroom wall poster which includes a flow chart showing these processes and which defines them in language which is accessible and appropriate for your class.

GENRE

Teaching a range of writing genres

You will find that many books on the teaching of writing emphasise the importance of giving pupils experience of writing in a wide range of genres. Some of the reasons for this are that: each genre is likely to develop different aspects of a pupil's linguistic competence; work in each genre is likely to enable each pupil to demonstrate particular achievements and development needs; working on a variety of genres helps teachers to address a broad range of the aims of the English curriculum. It may also be argued that participation in the various discourses which take place in society is dependent on being able to recognise and manipulate the conventions of particular genres, especially those which are favoured by certain power groups.

The National Curriculum for England: English identifies a number of textual forms or genres which it is suggested that pupils at Key Stages 3 and 4 should learn to write. It is important to note that some of these genres can be subdivided into different kinds. For instance, subgenres such as ghost stories, science fiction, romance stories and detective fiction could be included under 'stories'.

A teacher or department's view of English is likely to influence which genres are prioritised in the school curriculum: for example, adherents of the 'cultural heritage' view may give creative writing genres such as stories and poetry more space than those who, with an 'adult needs' view of English, emphasise the writing of formal letters and reports. Similarly, a department's view of how writing development occurs may influence which genres are taught most to different year groups: for instance, many pupils are given more opportunities to write stories in Key Stage 3 than in Key Stage 4.

Task 7.6 Genre in the school curriculum

Examine the Key Stage 3 and 4 schemes of work at your placement school. Which genres are given most curriculum space, when and why? How do SATs and GCSE requirements influence decisions about which genres are emphasised in Years 9–11?

Genre and voice

The National Curriculum for England: English suggests that the development of pupils' work in particular genres should be a consequence of their exposure to and study of various kinds of models, through their 'reading and knowledge of linguistic and literary forms' (p. 37), and the conscious development of technique, through learning, for example, to 'exploit choice of language and structure to achieve particular effects and appeal to the reader' (p. 37). In the 1995 Orders there was a suggestion, if only in one paragraph about the writing of poetry, that there is a difference between using the conventions of particular genres and writing distinctively with an individual voice: 'pupils should be encouraged to . . . write poetry closely related to the poems they read, in their own distinctive style.'

The tension between exploiting what other writers have learned about genre and developing a personal style, which is not acknowledged at all in *The National Curriculum for England: English*, is highly significant in the development of writing. In fact this tension is highly significant in the development of writing. The conventions of a particular genre can be a frustrating strait-jacket which limits pupils' opportunities for self-expression, or, if these conventions are unknown or ignored, the writing may be formless and lacking in structure. Many teachers have at one time or another set newspaper writing tasks, for example, and have been disappointed by what they have received. Some of the work will have consisted largely of fragmentary, shallow and irrelevant examples of different sections of a paper ('the stars' and football results figuring frequently), and some will have paid lip-service to genre, having perhaps a headline and a page divided into two columns, but the content could equally well have been submitted as a short story. However, with appropriate preparation and support, such as the careful analysis of 'models' and access to desktop publishing packages, teachers find that many pupils are capable of writing newspapers with witty headlines and subheadings; catchy lead paragraphs introducing articles which are economically written to a word limit and deadline; appropriately cropped and captioned photographs; the consciously chosen style of a broadsheet or tabloid. Pupils can learn to do this even if new information is deliberately introduced by the teacher to mimic the conditions in which professional journalists work, making revision necessary during the writing process. In other words, pupils need to understand what kinds of things can be included in particular genres, and to develop a sense of how other writers produce texts in those genres.

In general, writing is often particularly successful when the writer has sufficient control of the conventions of a particular genre to be able to use them with some individuality or originality. It follows that immersion in the conventions of genres of the kind described above needs to be balanced in the writing curriculum by opportunities for pupils: to explore ideas for writing without preconceptions about which genre(s) they will adopt; to select the genre which they consider it is most appropriate to use to develop and express a particular set of ideas, and to be free to change their minds about this. Some tasks can be designed which emphasise these choices: for example, pupils engaged in autobiographical writing can be invited to choose which genres to use to tell their stories. Some possibilities which pupils exploit successfully include diary entries, interviews with a relative or friend, school reports, poems and magazine-style 'focus' articles. Writing with this kind of attitude to genre can give pupils new insights into their own thinking, by liberating material from the assumptions which are associated with its expression in a particular textual form. Writing activities in which pupils are given opportunities to take material from a text and re-present it in another form can also be liberating in this way. To sum up, the development of a writer's voice is partly about developing confidence in manipulating genre.

The manipulation of genre

It is important to recognise that writers can be manipulated by being forced to use particular genres, and that they can be empowered by being allowed to manipulate genre.

There are culturally significant ways in which working in particular genres can contribute to the empowerment or disempowerment of pupils. For example, the traditional discursive essay is a specialised genre in which writers are expected to debate issues in an open and balanced way. Since the essay, to some extent, suppresses the expression of committed opinion and has a limited, academic audience, it does not appear to be a particularly empowering form. On the other hand, learning how to write a campaign leaflet, which in theory can be distributed to a wide audience with the specific purpose of presenting the case for an opinion in such a way that others may

---

Task 7.7 Planning to explore genre

Plan a sequence of lessons for a class you teach on a teaching placement, in which a primary aim is to enable pupils to use the conventions of particular genre/s to express their own ideas.

Some of the planning questions which the successful teaching of genre writing will often need to address include the following:

- How familiar are pupils with the conventions of the genre(s) the lesson(s) will give them opportunities to adopt?
- What examples/models can be used to reinforce pupil familiarity with the genre(s)?
- How/when will the introduction of these examples/models in the sequence of activities in the lesson(s) best support the pupils' own explorations of the genre(s)?
- How much choice can pupils be given in finding genre(s) which are appropriate for the expression of their ideas?

Some practical activities which could be incorporated into planning include:

- whole class, group and individual reading of texts which provide interesting genre models (including some which challenge conventions) followed by discussion identifying similarities and differences between texts;
- teacher exposition of the stages involved in his or her production of a text in a particular genre (especially useful if this is shown to be a messy process including drawing diagrams, false starts, the rejection of material, checking spelling, gaps in composition, rather than a dauntingly smooth linear process);
- prediction exercises and other DARTs which draw attention to the generic characteristics of a text;
- pupil brainstorming and compilation of lists of the conventions of particular genres.

---

be influenced to adopt it, gives a writer power in much more obvious ways. One irony, of course, is that access to further educational opportunities is more likely to be achieved through proficiency in writing essays than campaign leaflets.

There are a number of ways in which teaching can empower pupils by enabling them to work flexibly with genres. Teaching some pupils to use difficult genres for their own purposes may be a long-term goal. Writing soap-box-style opinion pieces can be a staging post towards the production of a discursive essay. Work on descriptive writing or dialogue can anticipate their incorporation in story writing. On the other hand, some pupils can be stretched by being allowed to use the possibilities of more than one genre in a single task: for example, in writing pieces which, like a considerable number of twentieth-century texts, make use of the conventions of several different genres. IT word-processing facilities provide a valuable resource for manipulating and experimenting with genre.

Pupils also need opportunities to find an individual voice by making use of the conventions of genres in different ways. For example, whereas some writers of discursive essays will make extensive use of illustrations which are, in effect, short narratives of their own experience, others will make more use of generalisations supported by information gleaned from reference sources. Both approaches may result in convincing argument. When asked to write a science fiction story, some pupils may concentrate on parodying the conventions of the genre, while others will demonstrate its capacity to explore human problems in unexpected ways. Although work on differences in the ways boys and girls use writing to learn and choose to interpret writing tasks is at an early stage, it may be the case that boys and girls tend to manipulate particular genres differently. Certainly, the manipulation of genre is a high-order skill, so it is important that writing tasks and the methods which are used to assess them create opportunities for pupils to demonstrate and develop it and to reward their successes.

Task 7.8 The value of writing in different genres

A Year 10 pupil's last pieces of written work in English have been a campaign leaflet calling for a lowering of the school-leaving age and a postmodern narrative containing elements such as a screenplay and a series of letters to a newspaper. With a partner, role-play a discussion between the pupil's teacher and a parent, who is concerned about the appropriateness of this work as preparation for A level. Discuss the arguments used in your conversation with other student teachers.

AUDIENCE AND PUBLICATION

The National Curriculum for England: English indicates that 'The range of readers for writing should include specific, known readers, a large, unknown readership and the pupils themselves' (DfEE/QCA, 1999b, p. 39). There is substantial evidence that writing for real audiences improves the quality of writing that pupils produce. It encourages them to employ the drafting processes described above, to engage in consultation with other writers and potential readers, and to take care over features of presentation including technical accuracy. It also prompts them to develop their ideas beyond the point where the writing represents a message to themselves (which does not need to be developed further because 'they know what they meant'), or a message to the teacher (which does not need to be developed because the teacher already knows 'the answer'). Writing for real audiences gives pupils real writing purposes and enables them to discover the real power which writers can access.

This chapter's discussion of writing and learning identifies a number of types of retrospective writing which pupils can be encouraged to use to make sense of material and experience for themselves, and possibly for future use in writing for an audience in a particular genre. The 'specific readers' available to pupils can usefully be divided into audiences inside and outside the school.

Audiences within the school

The audiences within the school provide one of the most valuable resources available to teachers teaching writing. It is important that teachers planning to use pupils as real audiences think about ways in which the expertise of the pupils doing the writing can be ensured: it is often a writer's sense that he or she, either individually or as a collaborator, has something to say which the reader could not have said and wants to know which gives him or her a sense of purpose and power. Many creative genres, such as poetry, stories, plays and film scripts, clearly allow writers to make unique imaginative statements. However, other genres which communicate information, such as guides, journalistic pieces and prepared oral presentations, can make use of expert knowledge held by writers, and audiences may be found for these within the class or among other groups of pupils in the school.

It is also important to note that there are many modes of publication available in schools, including reading aloud, booklets, wall displays and posters, audio- and video-taped presentations, and web pages. Moreover, it is frequently possible to make publication interactive, not only by creating opportunities for other pupils to respond by writing reviews and replies, but also by encouraging writers to produce material which incorporates decision-making roles for the audience, so that the writers have to anticipate choices and plan routes through the material accordingly. Examples of such interactive writing might range from a short play for assembly which is rehearsed with two different endings so the audience can choose one, to a web page with hyperlinks which allow readers to pursue their own lines of enquiry in reading it.

The value of using pupils as real audiences for writing about reading also needs to be emphasised. Some examples of writing of this kind include: anthologies of poetry and collections of material on a topic with introductions from the editors; classroom displays and presentations on books which have been read as group readers; and files of reviews of books with recommendations, found in the library. Pupils working towards SATs and GCSE can produce materials on particular aspects of texts to be used as revision aids by other groups within the class.

Audiences beyond the school

Pupils in other schools are often used as audiences for letter exchanges, but the results are often richer when writing in other genres is included so that there is a purposeful exchange of creative endeavour, the results of research, or ideas for and about reading.

Specific groups of adults such as parents and relatives, visitors to the school, figures in the local community, and authors of stories or other texts read by the class can also provide audiences for writing across a range of genres. Using parents as audiences provides an opportunity to develop their understanding of the English curriculum. For example, using them as sources of information on dialect or language change can be followed by the production of booklets containing work which demonstrates the variety of language(s) used by members of any single class of pupils. Published writers and other adults who recognise the value of young people learning to see themselves as writers and as contributors to various social and cultural debates are often prepared to respond to writing sent to them, although it is sometimes useful to check their willingness to do this in advance.

Promoting writing for real audiences is one of the most important means by which teachers can encourage pupils to pay attention to technical and presentational matters such as spelling, punctuation, vocabulary, language register, syntax, paragraphing, discourse structure, layout, and handwriting or choice of font. Having real readers helps pupils to think about the needs those readers will have if communication is to be effective. It reinforces one of the learning points which emerges from learning to write in a range of genres: writers make choices at all levels of textual construction.

Task 7.9 Writing for a real audience

Devise, teach and evaluate a scheme of work in which pupils write for a real audience outside the school. Consider ways of incorporating the audience, or a sample of it, in the writing process at an earlier stage.

Effective teaching styles for teaching writing

The NLS *Framework for Teaching English: Years 7, 8 and 9* recommends to teachers the following range of 'effective teaching styles' for teaching writing:

- direction: to ensure pupils know what they are doing, and why;
- demonstration: to show pupils how effective readers and writers work;
- modelling: to explain the rules and conventions of language and texts;
- scaffolding: to support pupils' early efforts and build security and confidence;
- explanation: to clarify and exemplify the best ways of working:
- questioning: to probe, draw out or extend pupils' thinking;
- exploration: to encourage critical thinking and generalisation;
- investigation: to encourage enquiry and self-help;
- discussion: to shape and challenge developing ideas;
- reflection and evaluation: to help pupils to learn from experience, successes and mistakes.

(DfEE, 2001, p.16)

Two of the most commonly used teaching techniques for supporting pupils' writing development are 'modelling' and providing the 'scaffolding' of writing frames. The value of both techniques is that, when used well, they make explicit how the relationships between productive writing processes and the requirements of particular genres are worked through by successful writers in the course of their work.

Effective modelling means more than *explaining* the rules and conventions of language or texts, or simply presenting pupils with what may be quite intimidating examples of successful work by others. The most effective modelling practice involves the teacher showing pupils, *by doing it in front of them*, how he or she would undertake a writing task or a particular part of it, such as annotating a text, brainstorming ideas, developing a set of topic vocabulary, organising ideas into a table or diagram, selecting and discarding material, sequencing points, finding examples or illustrations from a text, or writing an opening paragraph.

Interactive whole class teaching using an OHP with partially prepared material which can be added to during the lesson provides a successful basis for this kind of modelling. Pupils can be invited to contribute to the development process the teacher is working through, and to annotate their own copies of the material the teacher is using. They may then be invited to carry out a similar task as the basis for their own pieces of writing or to carry out the next stage of the writing process using the material that has been developed. Good practice is likely to involve lots of opportunities for pupil questioning of the teacher, short bursts of pupil activity in which pupils experiment with the techniques which are being modelled, and evaluation, including evaluation of the teacher's work by pupils, as well as, say, peer evaluation using writing partners: the most effective evaluation will also feed forward into revision of the writing.

Writing frames are templates for writing which provide pupils with systematic guidance on the structure of a writing task. In a sense, two extreme approaches to teaching writing could be regarded as providing writing frames. The cliché instruction to write a story with a beginning, a middle and an end does at least indicate that the story should have three parts, even if it does not help pupils to understand what any of those parts should contain. At the other extreme, a cloze passage exercise, in which pupils are required to insert a selection of missing words into an otherwise complete text, provides such a detailed structure for writing that some teachers would contest whether this kind of work could be called 'writing' at all.

Between these extremes, writing frames consist more typically of visual guidance on the construction of each paragraph or section of a piece of writing, which includes all or part of a topic sentence and bullet points identifying items which pupils should include, and which may be defined quite specifically or more generally. One benefit of this technique is that the teacher has infinite scope to adjust the level of detail provided to meet the learning needs of individual pupils or groups. It is, however, vital that, while writing frames self-evidently provide 'direction' and 'scaffolding' in the terms described above, teachers should use them with pupils in ways which also include questioning, exploration, investigation, discussion, and reflection and evaluation. Very often, the writing process which is being supported should be planned collaboratively by the pupils and teacher together through discussion and critically evaluated. Some questions which should be considered at an appropriate level by the pupils concerned include: What is the purpose and audience of the piece of writing? What can we learn from this about how to organise it? What kinds of material is it appropriate to include? How will these things help the writing to achieve its objectives of communicating something to a particular audience? What will it be hard to understand that an illustration or example will help to explain? What order shall we put things in to make them clear? It is also important not to forget that the term 'scaffolding' is linked with the Vygotskian concept of the zone of proximal development: 'writing frames' should be used to help pupils to attain the next stage of development on the road to independent writing, and not as a means to allow them to write with less thought at a level at which they are already comfortable.

FORMATIVE ASSESSMENT AND EVALUATION

The National Curriculum for England: English indicates that 'Pupils should be taught to . . . analyse critically their own and others' writing' but does not provide any kind of rationale for this. A number of earlier sections in this chapter have suggested that writers thrive on processes through which they reflect on the development of their writing and share thoughts about it with others, especially, in the school context, teachers and their peer group. The practice in the teaching of writing commended in this chapter will create many opportunities for various types of responses to be given to ideas for writing, drafts of writing at different stages in its composition and finished writing.

Both self-evaluation and peer evaluation can be guided by prompt questions established by the teacher, or in negotiation, which draw attention to matters such as the total impression a piece of writing is intended to make on readers, and the effect it actually has; specific strengths in relation to matters such as its use of genre, its selection of content, its appropriateness for its audience and its technical accuracy; general points which the writer could address in redrafting or revising the text; specific changes which the reader thinks are particularly important. It is always useful if the teacher can intervene in peer evaluation processes and respond to self-evaluations before the writer takes action, both to provide further advice and to monitor the responses which are being made to writing. Pupils' comments can be highly informative about the writing development of those who make them, and will need occasionally to be counteracted when they make unhelpful suggestions.

Self-evaluation is especially valuable when pupils produce particularly sensitive or personal writing, or when they use genres such as poetry, in which they may invest a great deal of emotion but have difficulty with technical matters. Writers who are asked to discuss what they were trying to achieve and to consider how successful they have been, and to indicate the source of their ideas, can provide a teacher with very important guidance as to what kind of response is appropriate. The self-evaluation forms a kind of objectification of the personal, and the teacher needs to pay attention not only to the quality of the work, but also to the extent to which the writer is able to distance him- or herself from the content, in deciding how to respond.

Teacher assessment of writing should also draw attention to the issues indicated for peer and self-evaluation. Many teachers begin their responses to writing with comments which indicate their reaction to the way in which the piece has made meanings, and may include emotional as well as analytical responses. Many teachers combine these kinds of comments with some form of recognition of the individuality of the writer, at the very least by addressing him or her by name. Positive achievements should always be identified and the teacher should then target a limited and manageable number of areas for further development, if this is appropriate. Sometimes it may not be, because of the content of the piece, or because a pupil needs a simple affirmation for a range of reasons, or because the teacher chooses to respond entirely in relation to the human communication which has taken place.

If areas for development are identified, the advice should be as specific as possible, and it should be clear what opportunity the pupil will have to make use of it in the near future. In other words, the advice is effective when it becomes a form of precise target-setting. General advice, such as 'Watch spelling!' and more specific advice which does not create such an opportunity, such as 'You could have extended the description in the first paragraph' is of little use. Technical and presentational errors should be addressed sensitively, in a way which will support learning. One approach is to to select a limited number of patterns of errors, such as a repeated failure to paragraph, or patterns of spelling errors, and to provide information which will help the pupil to learn.

Teachers can fall into tired, repetitive habits of wording, so that every comment always starts 'I enjoyed this, because . . .' followed by the inevitable 'but . . .'. This can be avoided if the teachers' comments form part of an ongoing, open dialogue with pupils about writing. If this is attempted, it is important that the opportunity for pupil response is real. It is no use writing 'See me' on work unless you create the time to do this. If you ask questions in comments, you should acknowledge answers which pupils write later. Some teachers like to carry on this dialogue in writing journals or planning books rather than on or underneath individual writing tasks.

Assessment strategies of the kind described above can be very time-consuming, and teachers need to ensure that they do not miss opportunities to improve their communication with pupils which involve them in writing less. For example, one very valuable marking technique is to read enough examples of pupils' work to predict issues which will arise in the work of the majority of pupils. There is little point in repeating these points in thirty places when making a general note of them can allow you to use them as whole class teaching points. You can then spend more time responding to the individual achievements of pupils in the written comments you make.

Task 7.10 Exploring drafting and assessment through your own writing

Produce a piece of writing which meets the specifications of a task you set for one of your classes. Use this writing in a number of ways. Keep the different drafts of your writing and show them to your pupils on an OHP. Evaluate the impact of this technique on the writings your pupils produce. Ask four different student teachers to write comments on your piece of work, and consider which responses are most helpful to you as a writer and why.

SUMMARY AND KEY POINTS

It has been suggested in this chapter that you should take into account the following points when planning sequences of work which involve writing:

- the relationships between writing, speaking and listening, and reading can be formulated in many different productive ways in teaching;
- writing can make important contributions to learning, both when it is used retrospectively to respond to experience and material, and when it is used prospectively to plan, reorganise and develop material and ideas;
- the social dynamics of writing in the classroom reflect the social functions of

writing in society and must be addressed if pupils are to understand what writing is for;

- pupils benefit from teaching which offers them scope for *both* the drafting and development of pieces of writing *and* the exploration and manipulation of genre;
- writing becomes more purposeful when pupils perceive real audiences and opportunities for publication, and when they see that they have opportunities to make their own meanings;
- pupils pay more attention to the presentation and technical accuracy of purposeful writing;
- the formative assessment and evaluation of writing should take the form of a developmental dialogue between teacher and pupils and among groups of pupils;
- the teaching of writing should be informed by a critical interpretation of the definition of the writing curriculum in *The National Curriculum for England: English*.

FURTHER READING

Andrews, R. (ed.) (1989) *Narrative and Argument*, Buckingham: Open University Press.

Brindley, S. (ed.) (1994) 'Part IV: Writing', in *Teaching English*, London: Routledge.

Foggin, J. (1992) *Teaching English in the National Curriculum: Real Writing*, London: Hodder & Stoughton.

DfEE (2001a) 'Key Stage 3 National Strategy Literacy Progress Unit Writing Organisation', London: DfEE.

DfEE (2001b) 'Key Stage 3 National Strategy Literacy Progress Unit Sentences', London: DfEE.

Lewis, M. and Wray, D. (1997) *Writing Frames: Scaffolding Children's Non-fiction Writing in a Range of Genres*, University of Reading: Reading and Language Information Centre.

LINC (n.d.) 'The Process of Writing' and 'The Writing Repertoire', in *Language in the National Curriculum* (unpublished).

Meek, M. (1988) *How Texts Teach What Readers Learn*, Stroud: Thimble Press.

NWP (1990) *Ways of Looking: Issues from the National Writing Project*, London: Nelson. This text provides an overview of issues which can be pursued further in a set of books produced by the project.

Styles, M. (1989) *Collaboration and Writing*, Buckingham: Open University Press.

Wilkinson, A. (ed.) (1986) *The Writing of Writing*, Buckingham: Open University Press.

8 Teaching Language and Grammar

Elspeth and Richard Bain

INTRODUCTION

Language is a key part of our identity as human beings, expressing both our individuality and our sense of belonging to a group. This is as true of school pupils as it is of adults. Young people are immersed in language during their waking hours. They use it to establish relationships, to understand and interpret their environment and to interact with the world around them.

In the English classroom pupils experience language in three different ways:

1. *Learning through language.* Language is the medium through which much of their learning will take place. Pupils will learn by listening to the teacher and to each other. They will learn by reading written or media texts as well as comments from their teacher or from each other. They will explore and develop their ideas in both speech and writing.

2. *Learning to use language.* Pupils learn to use language by practising it in a variety of different ways. They practise speaking and writing many different types of text for a range of purposes and to a variety of audiences. They practise reading and listening for many different purposes and in many different contexts.

3. *Learning about language.* Pre-school children already know a tremendous amount about language at an implicit level. In every conversation they make sophisticated choices of vocabulary, grammar, emphasis and register in order to achieve the tone and effect they want. At primary school they will have received a good deal of explicit language teaching. The task of the secondary English teacher is to build on this existing implicit and explicit knowledge and to help them reflect on language use – their own and other people's – in order to develop the confidence and subtlety of their own use of language.

In most schools the content of lessons on knowledge about language and grammar will follow the framework for English teaching at KS3 and the requirements of the GCSE

OBJECTIVES

By the end of this chapter you should:

- have considered the role of knowledge about language and grammar teaching in the English classroom;
- have explored your own attitudes to language and grammar;
- understand the relationship between standard English and other dialects;
- have considered the principles that should underpin developing a scheme of work on a grammar topic;
- have considered ways of making the classroom a stimulating language environment.

---

specifications at KS4. This chapter suggests ways in which this teaching should be approached and undertaken.

WHY TEACH CHILDREN ABOUT LANGUAGE?

English teaching has evolved and developed over the years to suit differing perceptions of need. Attitudes to the value of teaching children about language have changed considerably. Four hundred years ago at his grammar school in Stratford, the schoolboy Shakespeare would not have studied English. Instead he would have been drilled in Latin grammar.

During the first five decades of the twentieth century, English teaching included a great deal of prescriptive grammar teaching with a focus on repetitive exercises, artificial examples and parsing, when students had to identify all the component parts of a sentence. Pupils were taught rigid rules such as that you cannot begin a sentence with the word 'and' – despite the fact that many writers choose to do so. This work was based on a theoretical model of formal standard English rather than on examination of language as it is actually used. Such work neither helped pupils to understand a text better nor to make more accurate judgements about a text's success.

By the 1960s many teachers felt that this formal and formulaic approach to language teaching was ineffective and that teachers should instead develop their pupils' implicit knowledge of grammar. Systematic teaching of grammar disappeared from most schools. Instead there was an emphasis on language variation and the significance of audience, purpose and context. Many schools stopped using course books – which tended to rely on short out-of-context extracts from books – and instead based their teaching on whole novels, poems and plays. Specific teaching about language continued but usually in a limited and sporadic way, and often did not go beyond identifying the different parts of speech.

The introduction of the National Curriculum in the 1980s led to much greater uniformity about what was taught. It placed an emphasis on standard English and specified the terminology of parts of speech that should be covered. It also made more systematic the coverage of the range of topics English departments had been addressing called 'Knowledge about language'. This title covered work on:

- language acquisition and development;
- history of languages;
- language and society;
- language variety;
- language as a system.

How these topics were tackled in schools still varied greatly. Some teachers still felt that work on grammar stifled a pupil's individuality. Very often these would be teachers who had themselves been taught in a very prescriptive, narrow way concentrating on error. Other teachers grew to believe that language was a crucial and powerful influence in pupils' lives and that everyone needed to learn more about how it worked. These teachers viewed grammar as a process of describing and exploring the patterns whereby we make sense of words and create meaning.

The introduction of the National Literacy Strategy with its compulsory Literacy Hour in primary schools in 1997 represented the beginning of a major change that would eventually reach secondary schools. The literacy hour required a great increase in explicit teaching of language forms and functions and has undoubtedly led to cohorts of pupils entering Year 7 in secondary schools with much more explicit knowledge and understanding of language than before.

One influential aspect of the National Literacy Strategy is its division of topics between word level, sentence level and text level. In relation to work on grammar:

- Word level (which includes spelling and vocabulary which lie outside grammar teaching) corresponds to the study of morphology – the way inflexions can change the meaning or effect of a word (e.g. table and tables or walk and walked).
- Sentence level corresponds with syntax – the ways words are put together to produce complex meanings. This can include word order and the ways clauses are deployed.
- Text level corresponds with the study of discourse – the ways in which whole texts build up meaning through the relationships and patterns of component paragraphs, verses, chapters or sections.

The introduction of the National Literacy Strategy to secondary schools in 2001 and in particular the introduction of the Framework for English teaching brought significant changes to teaching at Key Stage 3 in many schools. The Framework prescribes what should be taught in Years 7, 8 and 9 by listing the objectives that need to be met. This invited a switch from studying grammar as it arises in what is read or is needed for what is written to making the various language topics themselves the chief focus. The Framework requires that teaching be planned around objectives rather than texts.

There is a broad consensus among English teachers that explicit language teaching does feed back into improvements in reading and writing. Surprisingly, however, there

> **Task 8.1 Pupils' entitlement**
>
> The purpose of this task is to reflect on what you think children should be taught about language and why. Try to decide what (in a Utopian state where you were completely free to choose) should be covered in work on knowledge about language and grammar. Consider and then discuss with your mentor or tutor points (a), (b) and (c) below. Use as your starting point the following list of entitlements which was suggested by a group of English advisers in 1993:
>
> All children have a right to learn important things about language:
>
> - there are many Englishes;
> - language changes over time and place;
> - language is at the centre of who we are, of all the relationships we make, and of what we are able to become;
> - awareness of the systems and patterns of language can help towards more assured and effective communication;
> - as language users, children themselves are language experts.
>
> (a) Do you agree with the ideas listed and could you put them into an order of priority?
> (b) Are there any ideas you would wish to add or omit?
> (c) For each idea, explain why it is important and what impact on your classroom practice it should have.

is not much research evidence to prove this, an issue addressed in the booklet of essays *Not Whether but How* (QCA, 1999).

Of course English teachers are not working in Utopia and are subject to various constraints:

- the legal demands of the National Curriculum;
- the non-statutory (lacking legal force) but virtually compulsory Framework for teaching English at KS3;
- what they perceive OfSTED will want to see;
- the demands of KS3 SATs (national exams at the end of Year 9);
- GCSE specifications for exams and coursework;
- the need to follow their own school's policies (e.g. on teaching gifted and talented pupils);
- pressure to improve results.

The requirements of the National Curriculum for teaching knowledge about language and grammar are shown in Figure 8.1.

WHAT MAKES STANDARD ENGLISH 'STANDARD'?

There is a very strong focus in the National Curriculum requirements on standard English, which is the dominant dialect of English. It is used for almost all writing and

Task 8.2 Language autobiography

The purpose of this task is to help you reflect on your own development as a language user so that you can come to a better understanding of pupils' development as language users.

(a)   Plan and write your own language autobiography. This could include the following:
- your memories of learning to read and write
- times when you have felt proud or ashamed of your language
- your experience of standard English and regional dialects
- differences between your home language and school language
- learning new languages
- your experience of slang and the language of the playground
- your experience of jargon (including acronyms)
- words you love
- words you hate
- circumstances when you felt it easy or difficult to talk or read or write
- how you feel when your language is criticised.

(b)   Share your language autobiography with other student teachers or your mentor.
(c)   How do you think your experiences of learning language compare with those of your pupils?
(d)   What do your experiences of learning and using language suggest to you about how you as a teacher should teach language?
(d)   What should the future chapters in your language autobiography consist of? What do you feel you need to learn to make yourself a more effective teacher of language?

for most public or formal communication. As such it has a special place in English teaching and all pupils need to be aware of standard English and be able to use it alongside their regional dialects as appropriate.

Unlike most other dialects of English, it is spoken by people all over the country, and does not have a regional base (although historically it developed from an East Midlands dialect). Most people in Britain are able to use at least two dialects: standard English for writing and formal communication, and a regional dialect for informal communication. However, standard English is also a class dialect: it is used much more consistently by middle-class and upper-class people. As with all dialects of English, standard English has a distinctive vocabulary and grammar; however, unlike most other dialects, standard English does not have its own accent.

Although a great deal of fuss is made about standard English in the Press and it is given such prominence in the National Curriculum, the differences between it and other dialects of English are very slight. The majority of the vocabulary and grammar of English is used in common by all the dialects: there are slight (though very noticeable) differences at the margins.

Many people misunderstand what is meant by standard English. The Cox Report (DES and Welsh Office, 1989) which formed the basis for the first version of the English National Curriculum, took pains to identify what standard English is and to emphasise that it is not what many people take it to be. In particular:

English KS3:

En1 Speaking and listening
Standard English
Pupils should be taught to use the vocabulary, structures and grammar of spoken standard English fluently and accurately in formal and informal situations. A note then adds: When teaching standard English it is helpful to bear in mind the most common non-standard usages in England:

- subject–verb agreement (they was)
- formation of past tense (have fell, I done)
- formation of negatives (ain't)
- formation of adverbs (come quick)
- use of demonstrative pronouns (them books)
- use of pronouns (me and him went)
- use of prepositions (out the door).

Language variation
Pupils should be taught about how language varies, including:

(a)   the importance of standard English as the language of public communication nationally and often internationally
(b)   current influences on spoken and written language
(c)   attitudes to language use
(d)   the differences between speech and writing
(e)   the vocabulary and grammar of standard English and dialectal variation
(f)   the development of English, including changes over time, borrowings from other languages, origins of work, and the impact of electronic communication on written language.

En2 Reading
Language structure and variation
Pupils should be taught to draw on their knowledge of grammar and language variation to develop their understanding of texts and how language works.

En3 Writing
Standard English
Pupils should be taught about the variations in written standard English and how they differ from spoken language, and to distinguish varying degrees of formality, selecting appropriately for a task.

Language structure
Pupils should be taught the principles of sentence grammar and whole-text cohesion and use this knowledge in their writing. They should be taught:

(a)   word classes or parts of speech and their grammatical functions
(b)   the structure of phrases and clauses and how they can be combined to make complex sentences (e.g. co-ordination and subordination)
(c)   paragraph structure and how to form different types of paragraph
(d)   the structure of whole texts, including cohesion openings and conclusions in different types of writing (e.g. through the use of verb tenses, reference chains)
(e)   the use of appropriate grammatical terminology to reflect on the meaning and clarity of individual sentences (e.g. nouns, verbs, adjectives, prepositions, conjunctions and articles).

Figure 8.1 National Curriculum requirements for teaching knowledge about language and grammar

- *Standard English is not the same as 'good' English.* An insurance claim form will be written in standard English but could be overly complex and full of jargon, and therefore not effective at communicating meaning. Regional dialect, appropriately used, may deliver very effective communication.
- *Standard English is not the same as 'correct' English.* Although standard English has a special status among English dialects, its grammar and vocabulary are no more 'correct' than those of any other dialect. It is, of course, possible to make mistakes in any dialect.
- *Standard English is not the same as 'formal' English.* Standard English can be formal or informal, just as can any other dialect. It is perfectly possible (and extremely common!) for people to swear in standard English. A phrase such as 'I'm bloody knackered' uses the vocabulary and grammar of standard English and yet is extremely informal. A phrase such as 'I be very tired' uses a regional dialect form, and yet is much more formal. Which would you prefer in your classroom?
- *Standard English is not the same as logical English.* Standard English forms are no more logical than those of any other dialect. For example, standard English uses 'themselves' where many regional dialects use the more 'logical' 'theirselves'.
- *Standard English is not the same as Received Pronunciation (RP).* Standard English is the one dialect of English that can be spoken in any accent. It is defined by its vocabulary and grammar and not by its pronunciation. Received Pronunciation is an accent which, like standard English, has a class basis rather than a regional basis, but is only one of the many acceptable ways of pronouncing standard English.

HOW CAN YOU TEACH STANDARD ENGLISH EFFECTIVELY?

In the past, standard English was taught in schools to the exclusion of pupils' regional dialects. Pupils would be corrected and even punished for using regional dialect forms. The effect of this was to drive a wedge between pupils' home and school experiences. Some pupils would respond by deliberately speaking standard English less in order to distance themselves from the school's values. If teachers reject a pupil's home language, they reject an important part of the pupil's identity and also lose a valuable resource for language exploration.

It is essential to remember that regional dialects are not standard English gone wrong, but are just as ancient and have developed in parallel. It is not necessary to reject regional dialects in order to teach standard English: indeed, pupils' awareness of regional dialects can improve their use of standard English.

Standard English may be taught through:

- a focus on writing: as most writing is in standard English, a focus on writing is almost inevitably a focus on standard English;
- contrasting speech and writing: looking at the differences between spoken forms and written forms will highlight many features of standard English;

- contrasting regional dialects: contrasting local dialects with standard English will highlight the standard English form and make pupils more aware of the subtle choices which they make subconsciously when they switch dialects;
- creating situations where pupils need to use standard English: if pupils are put in formal or public situations where they need to use standard English, this will develop their competence in using it; such situations may be created through drama or by providing adults as an audience for pupils' speech.

Task 8.3 Exploring standard English and a regional dialect

The purpose of this activity is to develop an awareness of the local dialect and its differences from standard English.

1   Find out as much as you can about the local dialect in the area where you undertake your teaching practice. You can achieve this by listening to pupils and making notes; listening to adults; talking to pupils and teachers; recording and transcribing.

2   Ask a class of pupils to find as many differences as they can between their local dialect and standard English. When they have brainstormed or collected a long list, try to sort them into different words (vocabulary), different patterns and forms (grammar) and different sounds (accent).

3   Familiarise yourself with correct regional dialect forms that tend to slip into written standard English and appear as mistakes (e.g. 'The car needs washed' is a north-east construction where standard English requires 'The car needs washing'). (NB: The list of common errors taken from the National Curriculum section on speaking and listening is entirely made up of 'errors' which arise when the correct grammar of a regional dialect is at variance with standard English.)

4   Research the origins of the regional dialect (e.g. north-east dialects use words that are very close to words still used in modern Scandinavian languages: bairn for child (barn in Norwegian) and spelk for splinter (spjelke in Norwegian)). These words are, presumably, direct survivals from Viking days. Understanding this gives pupils more pride in their local dialect and a clearer sense of its origins.

5   Using your research, devise a unit of work that involves pupils investigating standard English and regional dialects. (This could address an objective from the Framework: Year 8: sentence level: standard English and language variation: objective 11.)

SOME PRINCIPLES FOR EXPLORATION OF GRAMMAR

Any approach to grammar in the English classroom should:

- *Acknowledge and build on what the children already know.* This will involve real familiarity with work undertaken at KS2 and in lower classes, within your own school, for Year 8 and above. It also means showing awareness of the children's substantial implicit knowledge. Always seek to make a link with something already known at the start of a topic then the pupils have something to relate it to and are more likely to absorb new information.

- *Involve children in exploration and investigation.* Don't just tell them what they will find. Let them research for themselves.
- *Be descriptive and not prescriptive.* Focus on effectiveness rather than on simple 'correctness'. Correct use of a language is the usage of an educated, adult user of that language. We observe the patterns but the 'rules' or 'laws' that we detect cannot restrict the language or prevent it from evolving. Never be afraid to draw attention to writing which breaks the 'rules' (e.g. advertisements which contain sentences with no main verb or the opening of *Bleak House* which includes several one-word sentences.
- *Address the grammar of informal writing, spoken English and regional dialects in addition to the grammar of formal standard English.* You can encourage research into current teenage non-standard language or the specialised grammar of the text message or e-mail.
- *Encourage interest in and respect for all forms of language.* Set a tone of interest and curiosity which accords respect to different ways of expressing ideas.
- *Focus on the functions of grammar in real texts.* Try not to invent examples; concentrate on what a grammatical device achieves in the text and not just what it is. Collect samples of text. Encourage pupils to bring in examples of different types of text from a bus ticket to unwanted baby books or even old Christmas cards. Be on the lookout yourself for interesting samples of real language use (estate agents' details with numerous pre-modifiers before the noun or the various grammatical patterns used to ask people not to smoke in restaurants) and share these with classes where appropriate. Don't just collect mistakes!
- *Exploration at word and sentence level should feed into the examination of whole texts.* Don't use significant texts simply as a quarry for grammatical features. Don't use a poem or the climax of a novel as the source for a trivial grammatical point. There are probably better reasons to read them than to observe the use of the semicolon or verb tense. Any work on a detail should lead on to how that detail contributes to the effectiveness of the whole.
- *Be explicitly related to children's own reading and writing.* Make links between what you happen to be reading and work already done. Keep making those links or encourage pupils to make them for you.
- *Relate directly to the issue of how language changes in relation to purpose and audience.* You could make it a policy that whenever anything is read to the whole class or a piece of writing is being planned that the question of purpose and audience is addressed and that you make explicit the effect they have on language chosen and grammar used.

Exploration of grammar should not:

- focus predominantly on errors;
- rely on invented sentences out of context;
- ignore or stigmatise regional dialect.

BUILDING ON THE FRAMEWORK

This section takes the topic 'Stylistic conventions of non-fiction', Year 7 sentence level, objective 13, and attempts to apply the principles given above. This work would obviously touch on numerous other objectives covering speaking and listening, reading and writing but its main focus is a grammatical investigation.

- *Acknowledge and build on what the children already know*. This topic will have been covered in primary school. Not everyone will remember it well, so present it and check on understanding. Ensure that everyone understands what 'conventions' means and that unusual 'unconventional' approaches could be especially successful. Consider what implicit knowledge the pupils might have (e.g. most people giving instructions would meet the conventions for that type of text).
- *Involve children in exploration and investigation*. Homework could require pupils to find an example of non-fiction writing – perhaps sharing out the job of locating the different types of text among members of a small group. The type that is least likely to be found is discursive writing but you can anticipate this by looking for some examples yourself. You could send pupils around the school to find examples of the text types. Before they set off they could hypothesise about which types they are most likely to find and why. Incidentally, don't worry if they come up with a question you cannot answer. You should be setting an example by being investigative not omniscient! Think it through or find out later and get back to them.
- *Be descriptive and not prescriptive*. You are very likely to find that several examples of text types are hybrids or do not follow the very categoric list of conventions given in the Framework. Encourage pupils to work out why this is. Get them experimenting with attempts to mingle different types or to write instructions using the conventions for persuasion. It can be useful to have a language box or a language wall (with dozens of examples of texts) in your classroom so that there are various types of text easily to hand.
- *Address the grammar of informal writing, spoken English and regional dialects in addition to the grammar of formal standard English*. Pupils could speculate about which types have the most obvious spoken equivalents. They could plan and perform a radio commercial (persuasion) in local dialect. You could ask them whether local dialect could have any place in a national advertising campaign. They could compare the grammar of Jamie Oliver and Delia Smith when giving instructions on television. This could be followed up by a comparison of the grammar of the two cookery experts in their written recipes.
- *Encourage interest in and respect for all forms of language*. The writing of very young children can be useful in the classroom. Your pupils may initially think it very inaccurate or simple but can probably learn from reflecting on it. A group of infant pupils who were asked to make a poster encouraging children to wash their hands after using the toilet came up with a sign above the sinks with an arrow pointing downward and the one word: 'Look.' Ask pupils to consider why this might have been chosen and whether it would be effective. Ask what they can suggest instead. Ask what might be an appropriate poster

for the toilets in their own school. When children are engrossed or challenged by an investigation they are bound to come up with questions and ideas that are not relevant to your objectives. Never brush aside the unexpected but relevant and, while you should not ignore the irrelevant but interesting, don't get distracted by it. Tell them you will follow it up another time and try to do so, whether with an individual or with the group.

- *Focus on the functions of grammar in real texts.* Don't just identify a grammatical feature but think about its effect. Look at invitation cards. Some are information, some instructions and some persuasive writing. What works best and why? Sometimes a task that encourages pupils to attempt, knowingly, to subvert the conventions will reveal the function of grammar. Grammar study is of no value if it does not lead to a better understanding of the text or a clearer judgement of its effectiveness.

- *Exploration at word and sentence level should feed into the examination of whole texts.* Looking at details should help pupils judge the success of the writer in the text as a whole. In other words, the grammar should illuminate the text rather than the text only being read to fillet out a grammatical point.

- *Be explicitly related to children's own reading and writing.* Look for any possible examples from what the children have been reading anyway – not necessarily only in English lessons. Get pupils to peer-mark written work using a checklist of likely features of the different types of writing. Try to find real audiences: a poster marking a door as one way only or a discursive essay on school uniform for the school newspaper.

- *Relate directly to the issue of how language changes in relation to purpose and audience.* A recount of events for different purposes (e.g. police statement and newspaper report of the same event) will share some features but not all. Encourage pupils to reflect on the differences in the grammar.

Task 8.4 Developing a scheme of work on grammar

This task will give you the chance to plan a sequence of lessons. You could use the topic explored above or a different one that you need to address with a class you are teaching. Your department may have planning sheets you can use to do this.

(a)   Can you devise starter activities that will relate to aspects of the work or does the department you are working in have a regular timetable for starters which do not need to link with your main activity?

(b)   Plan a sequence of two or three lessons on this topic and pick out which other objectives you will be addressing. Aim to build in progression so that your pupils are tackling more demanding tasks at the end than they were at the start. Consider what resources you will need.

(c)   Show your scheme of work to your mentor or actually tackle the tasks you have devised for the pupils yourself.

(d)   Teach the lessons and evaluate your success.

Work on a topic such as this could take several lessons and in one sense never finishes. For as long as you continue to teach the class you will find that what they have learned can be used in their own writing or to assess the success of a piece of writing. With older pupils this knowledge could be used to detect bias; for example, in a piece of persuasive writing that masquerades as a discursive text.

LITERACY ACROSS THE CURRICULUM

Over the past twenty years there has been a growing awareness in schools of the simple fact that language is being 'taught' by anyone who teaches – not just by English teachers. Teachers of other subjects have become increasingly well informed about the contribution they make to the language development of their pupils. Most teachers of other subjects accept that they both contribute to this language development and also benefit, as subject teachers, from aspects of language teaching that will have been covered elsewhere in the curriculum. Thus, a science teacher will usually make explicit the fact that writing up an experiment involves following the usual conventions for writing instructions and that the same conventions will be found in a recipe from a food technology textbook, because a recipe is also a set of instructions.

In some schools a selection of the non-fiction text types described in the Framework will be covered in detail outside English lessons. In most schools there will be agreed approaches to marking language and teaching spelling.

Task 8.5 Looking at language across the curriculum

The purpose of this task is to help you see how teaching language across the curriculum works in practice.

1   Discuss with your mentor or the professional tutor in your placement school how the teaching of language across the curriculum is co-ordinated in the school. You may be able to speak to the literacy co-ordinator or the senior manager responsible.
2   If you have an opportunity to observe lessons outside the English department (for instance, if you shadow a pupil for a day) you could make language teaching the focus of your observation. If you have the opportunity, ask teachers what explicit contribution they make to the language development of their pupils.
3   Find out what the school's future plans are for the development of language across the curriculum.

WHAT WILL A 'LANGUAGE-RICH' CLASSROOM BE LIKE?

The environment of an English classroom needs to be conducive to the exploration and study of words and meanings. All English teachers needs to consider what this will involve and decide how they can adapt their surroundings, attitudes and teaching styles to achieve it.

A 'language-rich' classroom should provide:

- varied and challenging opportunities to use language;
- many opportunities to reflect on and talk about language;
- easy access to a wide range of resources: the Internet, moving image texts, fiction, poems, comics, newspapers, pupils' own writing on display and language samples from other cultures or times.

In it pupils and teacher will:

- show real enthusiasm for enquiry about language;
- use specialist terminology when appropriate;
- use their knowledge of language from home and the media, knowing it will be treated with respect;
- show concern for effectiveness and appropriateness rather than for mere 'correctness';
- make comparisons between texts;
- speculate about how texts could have been different (e.g. if spoken not written, or if for a younger audience rather than for an adult audience).

Task 8.6 Auditing the language environment of a classroom

The purpose of this task is to reflect on what opportunities can be provided for language reflection in the classroom environment. Read through the list above and consider the items either in relation to your own classroom or to one of the classrooms you have observed.

1   Can you add anything to the list of qualities of a 'language rich' classroom?
2   List three things you could do to make your present classroom a richer environment.

SUMMARY AND KEY POINTS

Knowledge about language and the exploration of grammar are not added extras but at the heart of most of what goes on in the English classroom. A fascination with words and meanings and forms and patterns should be a fundamental part of all English teaching, inseparable from the planning, writing, thinking, acting, reading, researching and telling which goes on as a matter of course.

The ability to examine a text rigorously could contribute to:

- Demanding work on literature (e.g. comparing the opening thirty lines or so of *A Christmas Carol*, *The Chimes* and *The Cricket on the Hearth*) by looking at sentence type and sentence length and use or omission of main verbs connecting this analysis to Dickens's purpose and use of authorial voice.

- Trying to work out what makes a sign such as 'This door is alarmed' funny.
- Understanding why a teacher might refuse to accept the response 'Aye' from a pupil being reprimanded, yet the Speaker in the House of Commons might expect it and refuse to accept a 'Yes' as a positive vote.
- Appreciation of the power of advertising language.
- The effective redrafting of a speech to be delivered to Year 6 pupils about life at secondary school.
- All our pupils developing a lifelong enquiring approach to language and an awareness of its power and significance.

FURTHER READING

Bain, E. and Bain, R. (1997) *The Grammar Book*, Sheffield: NATE. Photocopiable materials for teaching grammar at secondary school. It provides a range of classroom activities for developing grammar in the context of pupils' own reading and writing. A new edition will be published in 2003.

Bryson, B. (1994) *Made in America*, London: Martin Secker & Warburg. A highly entertaining account of the development of American English. It provides interesting insights into language change and an understanding of why American and British English have diverged.

Bryson, B. (1991) *Mother Tongue*, London: Penguin. A very readable exploration of the development of English including its role as a world language.

Crystal, D. (1995) *The Cambridge Encyclopaedia of the English Language*, Cambridge: Cambridge University Press. A fascinating book covering an immense range in an accessible way. A very useful reference book for an English teacher.

Crystal, D. (1987) *The Cambridge Encyclopaedia of Language*, Cambridge: Cambridge University Press. This book covers all languages. Browsing through it will generate many ideas for classroom investigations.

9 New(ish) Literacies: Media and ICT

Elaine Scarratt and Rob McInnes

> The school and the family share the responsibility of preparing the young person living in a world of powerful images, words and sounds. Children and adults need to be literate in all three of these symbolic systems, and this will require some reassessment of educational priorities. Such reassessment might well result in an integrated approach to the teaching of language and communication.
>
> (UNESCO Declaration on Media Education, 22 January 1982)

INTRODUCTION

This chapter will explore the ways in which media and information communications technology (ICT) may be seen as central to the teaching of English in the twenty-first century. Although media and ICT are discussed here in a separate chapter, they should not be seen as separate, 'bolt-on' aspects of English, but as integrated with what might be considered good practice in English teaching. In the same way that all aspects of English are inextricably interlinked in the English classroom, as you read the other chapters – which for the purposes of discussion have focused on key aspects of English teaching separately – you should be looking for opportunities to bring what you learn from this chapter to your practice. The chapter also considers approaches to the teaching of Media Studies examination specifications.

The past fifty years have witnessed rapid development in the technology associated with communication in all its forms. 'Interest in and attachment to the media begins, for most children, well before they attend school and continues throughout their adult lives' (Masterman, 1985). Many pupils come to school with experience not only of viewing, listening to and reading a wide range of mass media forms, but they have grown up creating and publishing with DTP packages on powerful desktop computers. In addition to direct social interaction, their personal communication includes e-mail, mobile phone texting and the Internet (all producing new forms of writing, spelling and uses of punctuation); and they can participate in interactive mass communication via radio and television broadcasting. The advent of affordable user-friendly technology has invited broader and more exciting opportunities for teachers, first in terms of texts – since the early 1980s VCRs have brought the moving image more easily into the classroom, for instance – and second as a shift in pedagogical identity – since the late 1980s digital technology has enabled more teachers to see themselves as producers and creators. Few English teachers would consider themselves to be poets and novelists. If teachers are to engage with the notion of literacy in its widest sense, media and IT should be central to the work of the English classroom.

OBJECTIVES

By the end of this chapter you should:

- have an understanding of the key concepts and areas of knowledge of media education;
- understand the difference between media education and Media Studies;
- begin to understand how work on the media may be incorporated into your English teaching;
- begin to understand GCSE, A Level and vocational Media Studies specifications;
- understand why the use of ICT should be central to the teaching of English;
- be aware of the debates about the nature and role of media education, and its positionings in the school curriculum.

DEFINING 'MEDIA'

'The media' has two aspects, first as the plural term of 'medium', thus referring to diverse forms of communication. There are slight differences between Media Studies and media in English (see 'What's in a name?' below) regarding what products are appropriate for study. Media Studies considers predominantly mass media forms (i.e. nationally and internationally distributed to large audiences of at least thousands); however, specifications may also include alternative versions of those forms, which naturally entail small-scale niche audiences. Mass media forms are television, film, radio, magazines, newspapers, comics, advertising, popular music, websites, computer games, new technologies; examples of alternative versions include fanzines and 'art' films. Media education includes all of these and additional print texts produced for local or specified consumption such as leaflets and brochures: holidays, leisure, schools, campaigns.

The second version of 'the media' is a unified one as an institution akin to others such as education, politics and the Church. Issues related to their cultures, legislation, ideologies, finances and working practices are integral to the dynamics of society – hence the media concept of institution is vital media education and, indeed, such understanding is empowering which has led to the inclusion of media education in citizenship.

CULTURAL ATTITUDES

The fact that Media Studies is the fastest growing subject at all levels of education and that, although Media Studies examinations have been available for at least three decades at secondary level yet not all schools offer them, is testament to the tentative process of change in dominant cultural attitudes and certain types of education institutions. Chapter 2 showed the passionate conflicts in the early twentieth century about the worthiness of English as an educational field, yet English is now naturalised as a core subject. The evolution of media education has been similarly a site of cultural struggle, such as moments of high-profile debate in the news press running up to new versions of the National Curriculum. Those earlier debates about English revealed almost universal antipathy towards popular culture; popular fiction, radio, advertising, film and television were regarded with deep hostility and suspicion because of their perceived detrimental effects upon the minds and behaviour of the young. Latterly there are similar moral panics about physical health, violence, and pornography attributed to the assumed negative 'effects' of videos/DVDs, computer games, the Internet and certain music genres. There is a prevailing assumed simplistic hierarchy of texts that deems reading to be beneficial whereas television viewing is detrimental; for example, America and Canada have an annual television Turn-off Week 'in order to promote healthier lives and communities' (www.tvturnoff.org).

The explicit presence of media components in the National Curriculum 2000, the National Literacy Strategy and all GCSE English specifications thus entitling all pupils to media education marks a significant shift to education validating popular culture. It must be acknowledged that since the 1960s the evolution of media study has not only been due to a pioneering 'movement' (Stafford, Bazalgette) of individual teachers, academics and media education organisations such as the English and Media Centre, the British Film Institute and NATE. There have been several government reports recommending the study of media in their own right: The Newsom Report, *Half our Future* (DES, 1963) and the Bullock Report, *A Language for Life* (DES, 1975). *Popular TV and Schooling* (DES, 1983) commissioned by the then Education Secretary Keith Joseph concluded that television should be put to 'constructive use in the classroom' and that 'all teachers should be involved in examining and discussing television programmes with young people'. In 1989, Angela Rumbold, Kenneth Baker's Junior Minister for Education, stated that the 'ability to "read" media texts . . . is an important skill for contemporary and future citizens'. As Chapter 3 shows, the first National Curriculum English Order (DES and Welsh Office, 1990) directed teachers of English to encompass media texts in their teaching. There was, though, minimal requirement, and more explicit advocacy and detail were relegated to the *English Non-statutory*

Task 9.1 Attitudes to the media

Consider the UNESCO statement which opens this chapter and the following statements:

All media forms are worthy of study. All media texts should be subject to the same scrutiny, whether produced for entertainment, information, as learning resources, or by pupils themselves. . . . The most effective media teaching is non-judgmental, rather than about 'good' or 'bad' texts.

(Grahame, 1990)

Is it no wonder that children struggle at school when they are allowed by their parents to spend more time in front of the television than they do in front of the blackboard.

(Patten, 1992)

Widespread media literacy is essential if all citizens are to wield power, make rational decisions, become effective change agents and have an active involvement with the media. It is in this much wider sense of 'education for democracy' that media education can play the most significant role of all.

(Masterman, 1985)

What children get from television depends on what children bring to it. Depending on how old they are, how bright they are, how tired they are, what sort of family they belong to, what sort of skills they already have, television will affect them differently. And the same child will react differently to television programmes at different stages of his or her life.

(Messenger Davis, 1989)

The existence of an informed citizenry, essential to the democratic process, is increasingly sustained through the moving image media. This unique and vital language must surely, therefore, become part of basic literacy at the start of the third millennium.

(Report of the Film Education Working Group, 1999)

'English is always treated as a general subject: everybody should do English, English is non-specialist. But English A-Level to me is very specialist, and yet it's not regarded as a specialist subject.'

(A level Media Studies student quoted in
Buckingham and Sefton-Green, 1994, p.181)

The best schools struggle to outdo the influence of peer pressure and the teenage culture created by the pop and fashion industries. But struggle they must.

(Woodhead, 2000)

> Literacy is the flexible and sustainable mastery of a repertoire of practices with the texts of traditional and new communications technologies via spoken language, print and multimedia.
>
> (Luke, 2002)
>
> How do you react to these statements? Do you agree with, or reject, some of them completely? Are there some statements with which you agree/disagree, but have reservations about part of their assertions?
>
> Discuss these statements and your reactions to them with another student teacher or your tutor/mentor. Keep any notes you make. They will be useful when you come to Task 9.2.

Guidance (NCC, 1990). That said, the inclusion of media at a basic statutory entitlement was welcomed simply for its presence.

It is important, then, to be aware of media education, even in Curriculum 2000, not as the fixed natural entity but as the latest form of a highly contested and constantly negotiated field. Historically, fierce debates within the various Conservative governments (1979 to 1997) led, for instance, to the almost complete disappearance of media in English from the rewritten Order of 1993 (see Chapter 3). Strong protests following its first draft led to a hasty ill-thought-through inclusion as a cross-curricular 'strand' that proved virtually impossible to implement. Media in English was reintroduced in 1995 albeit in a lesser form than the Cox Report envisaged. Given this historical context the statutory study of the moving image and audio-visual language in the National Curriculum 2000 is a positive landmark. It is important to thoroughly scrutinise the media provision, however, and to reflect upon the tensions arising from grafting one field of study on to another (see 'Some issues to consider', below).

MEDIA EDUCATION

What's in a name?

The controversial and shifting dynamics of media study are reflected in its names(s) and terminology(ies) and places in the curriculum. Debate about appropriate nomenclature flourishes even within the subject; for example, it is not unusual to find the terms 'media education' and 'Media Studies' used as if they were interchangeable. The following is offered as a simplified introduction and observation of most common usage but it is by no means definitive – you will find several variations in your reading. *Media Studies* (and the capitalisation is deliberate) refers to a discrete field of study, distinct from other subjects. Like other discrete subjects it has its own history, mode of enquiry, concepts and content base. It is constructed into formally assessable courses such as GCSE, A Level, GNVQ, VCE (advanced) and a wide range of degree courses.

Media education was proposed by Bazalgette (1989) as an 'umbrella term' that encompasses all forms of teaching about the media, including Media Studies. It has, however, become ascribed more specifically to teaching about the media within another subject, such as sociology (representations of families) and of course English. Some clumsy, long-winded phrases have evolved – 'moving image in media within English' being one example, but you may find 'media in English' more fluent. It is important to be clear about the distinction between Media Studies and media education because although there is a conceptual framework common to media education and Media Studies, knowledge, understanding and assessment requirements are highly variable.

For instance, in their research about experienced media teachers, Hart and Hicks found that the most common film texts used were literary adaptations and the learning focuses were on literary issues such as narrative, character and themes. These was understandably passive and indeed active avoidance of unfamiliar but relevant knowledge; for instance, film's institutional issues related to creating meaning, such as budget, technology, studio styles, star persona, audience targeting. It is also inevitable then that each host subject gives media education an idiosyncratic inflection, and one area of debate is how we perceive these hybridised versions of media study.

You are also likely to encounter *media-across-the-curriculum* or *cross-curricular media*; these terms refer to a whole school policy and organisation of media teaching. They also signify pre-National Curriculum imaginative proposals to get media education on to the curriculum map (see Bowker, 1991). A second concern was, and continues to be, about token inclusion but potential marginalisation of media education. The ubiquity of the media has meant that cross-curricular media study has remained a powerful idea; experience has shown that whole school organisation is vital to its sustained effectiveness (Robson *et al.*, 1990), but there are invigorating exceptional institutional examples; Burn (1998) is a recommended read. *Moving Images in the Classroom* (BFI, 2000) is a well-focused guide, with learning objectives, activities and outcomes demonstrating how the moving image can be integrated into a range of subjects, including citizenship. It is worth noting that pioneers for media education operated in several disciplines as well as English such as sociology, art, communication studies and film studies. Nowadays, pupils at KS4 and KS5 also find informative similarities with subjects such as business studies and technology.

Some issues to consider about media in English

Because of lack of clarity about expectations of learning and, in particular, assessment for media in English, it is important that your department and you have a well-formulated, educational philosophy. The lack of explicit Attainment Targets and grade descriptors means that if schemes of work are too assessment-led then there is a danger of inadequate media education or that ICT becomes merely a set of technical skills. *Moving Images in the Classroom* contains a useful guide for monitoring pupil progression. Naturally your main responsibility is for English, so the following are some broader issues to consider for departmental discussion.

National Curriculum 2000 maintains the distinction between 'media texts' and 'literary texts' in line with its dominant cultural heritage version of English. The crude alliance of 'media and non-fiction' is highly misleading and fails to encourage teachers to study fiction forms written for television such as dramas; listing 'films' as examples of 'Non-fiction and non-literary texts' (En2 9c) is more than careless – should that be 'documentary films'?

How are you going to apply terminology? There is some hybridisation of common terms which can be confusing, especially for Media Studies teachers and pupils. 'Style' in English refers specifically to writing, whereas visual image, font design, layout, choice of colour and lighting are also considerations of style in media products.

Consider the range of teaching methods which media education has to offer. One of the reasons English was thought to be a conducive environment for media education in the 1970s and 1980s was the predominant active pedagogy that encouraged pupils' creativity and critical autonomy. Hart and Hicks's research published in 2002, however, found that much of the media in English pedagogy was whole class teacher-led analysis of the text. Consider how you can break down the learning, transfer responsibility for learning to the pupils and promote more interactivity with the media text studied. For instance, more productive learning arises from studying short sequences of moving/ aural images and short sections of printed texts.

Research has found an over-reliance on printed texts, despite the fact that teachers recall their best experiences being with teaching moving images. Consider how you can use film, radio and television more.

Many English teachers are 'edgy around practical work' (Buckingham and Grahame, 1998). Explore low-tech activities; there are many ideas in *Picture Power* (English and Media Centre), and see 'Media in English' below.

Some teachers question the 'assumed relationship between concepts and production and analytical skills' (Buckingham, 1993) but if the broad view of literacy is applied we can consider media production as 'writing'. Any English teacher recognises the development of conceptual and analytical understanding in both creative and analytical writing.

Researchers have found the majority of English teachers to be positive about media education, but there is also a prevailing philosophy to help pupils to 'discriminate' and, further, to help pupils to 'resist media manipulation' (Hart and Hicks, 2002). There are issues about cultural bias, engaging with the pleasure of the text and audience relationships with texts that need to be addressed here. Bias also, of course, applies to accommodating pupils who have different ideological readings of texts from those of the teacher (see Grahame, 1990; Lemin, 2001).

Task 9.2 Why study the media?

By now you should have a clear idea of the reasons for including media education in the English curriculum. Similarly, you should have developed an awareness of a variety of ways in which media work will underpin your teaching.

Imagine you have to write a letter to parents explaining what happens in the English department in your school in relation to media education. Write a statement on the reasons for and purposes of studying the media in the English classroom. Remember that parents are likely to hold a range of views in relation to the worth of studying media in school.

MEDIA LITERACY

Media products are, in the context of the classroom, texts to be read critically like the printed texts with which English teachers are familiar. Your training will have made you well acquainted with literacy in English, and it is a notion written about abundantly in media theory. Bazalgette provides a succinct list of the wide range of skills that media literacy entails of which the most obvious parallel skill to reading books is 'the mastery of a repertoire of semiotics-based techniques for the analysis of visual images' (1996, p. 35). However, though such decoding is essential, it is only one aspect of media literacy. McLaren (1988) provides a highly informative and recommended account of three 'positions' of literacy which informs much media theory, and indeed some English theorists (see Chapter 1). The key position is critical literacy which includes the other two: functional literacy (technical decoding of texts) and cultural literacy (cultural competence gained from literacy in selected works). Critical literacy involves decoding texts in the contexts inherent in the unified definition of 'the media' in an actively critical way which may include oppositional readings as well as 'appreciation'. The emphasis here is on decoding the institutional, especially ideology and power relations.

Critical literacy is a more active model akin to Cox's 'cultural analysis' model of English; whereas the dominant 'cultural heritage' model in the English curriculum is closer to cultural literacy. In this way, and in the differentiation between literary and media texts, all books are subject to the same economic and industrial determinants as newspapers, television programmes, films and so on. Such a distinction is, of course, anchored firmly in beliefs about the respective cultural worth of the product. A collection of poems or a novel does not spring fully formed from the writer's brain to the bookshop shelf; it undergoes lengthy negotiation between author, literary agent, editor, publisher, designer, marketing department and bookshop, among others, before the reader glimpses a single word. This is the case whether it be the work of Jane Austen or Jeffrey Archer; Christina Rossetti or Benjamin Zephaniah.

The aims of media education

Media work in the English classroom will enable pupils to develop a range of skills, knowledge and understanding about their lives as critical readers and writers of media texts. Media education aims to enable students to:

- understand the similarities and differences between the many media around us;
- reflect on their own experiences of media;
- develop a critical language to describe, categorise and analyse;
- express themselves in the widest range of media possible.

(Grahame, 1990, p.10)

While pupils following a Media Studies course may well develop in a similar way, their focus of study is prescribed by the requirements of a specification constructed by an examination board.

Media Studies pupils will, of course, have the further aim of achieving a qualification at GCSE or A Level. Therefore, while most English teachers find it useful, relatively easy and even enjoyable to develop the skills and knowledge to engage in media work in the English classroom, as the section on Media Studies later in the chapter shows, teaching Media Studies demands a greater depth of knowledge and understanding of media concepts in relation to examination syllabuses.

MEDIA CONCEPTS

The common ground between a wide range of media products means that in order to achieve a 'consistent line of enquiry' (Masterman, 1980, p. 3) a conceptual, rather than a content or text-based framework is more appropriate for media study. Such a framework also invites the culturally contextualising analysis that is the aim of critical literacy. However, since the debates about media education have not only been external (should it exist?) but also internal (in what form(s) should it exist?), you will find several variations of the Key Concepts. They cover very similar ground however, and are all informative for your media teaching and indeed of any text.

As the Cox Report states: 'the kinds of questions that are routinely asked in media education can fruitfully be applied to literature' (DES and Welsh Office, 1989, para. 7.23). Some Media Studies teachers like to use their examination specfications to organise their media in English teaching. The key questions and aspect of media education in Figure 9.1 provide a comprehensive outline that is useful for both media and English.

Many teachers use or adapt this framework to focus their learning objectives for KS3. As both the National Literacy Strategy and the National Curriculum include the moving image it is worth considering the simpler version recommended in *Moving Images in the Classroom* (BFI, 2000, pp. 52–57). The concepts are streamlined into three areas which reflect their interrelated nature: Language, producers and audiences, Messages and Values. It also usefully proposes an informal model of learning progression. It is best to find the system that is comfortable for you. Implicit in the key concepts is an active method of interrogation; we do not necessarily have all the answers but it is salutary to remember that pupils often have sophisticated understandings about the media (Buckingham 1993).

Objects of study need to be chosen with care; it is empowering for pupils to study familiar texts, but examining texts at a 'distance' can be a useful method of avoiding too much personalisation, a sense of invasion into personal territory, unwelcome teacher 'inoculation' and off-task chat. Obviously texts should not be so rarified that they are completely remote from pupils' lives, and some connection to the texts which they encounter should be made. The conceptual investigative approach will guide their development to 'critical autonomy' (Masterman). Media work in the English classroom should be founded upon practical, active investigation of aspects of the media which allows pupils the opportunity to both read and write a range of media texts. Media education can supply the vocabulary which will enable pupils to articulate, to make explicit, their growing knowledge and understanding of the media.

WHAT TYPE of text is it?	Media categories	Different media (TV, radio, cinema, etc.); forms (documentary, advertising, etc.); genres (sci-fi, soap opera, etc.); other ways of categorising texts; how categorisation relates to understanding
HOW is it produced?	Media technologies	What kinds of technologies are available to whom; how to use them; the differences they make to the production process as well as the final product.
HOW do we now what it means?	Media languages	How the media produce meanings; codes and conventions; narrative structures.
WHO is communicating and why?	Media agencies	Who produces a text; roles in production process; media institutions; economics and ideology; intentions and results.
How does it PRESENT its subject	Media representations	The relationship between media texts and actual places, people, events, ideas; stereotyping and its consequences.
WHO receives it and what sense do they make of it?	Media agencies	How audience are identified, constructed, addressed and reached; how audiences find, choose, consume and respond to texts

Figure 9.1 Key questions and aspects of media education (adapted from DES/BFI, 1989)

MEDIA IN ENGLISH

Arguments for the centrality of teaching media in English are more powerful today than ever before. The pace of technological change has been so dramatic that many of the proposals for the teaching of media made in the 1980s by influential writers such as Len Masterman now resemble ancient history. This is not principally because the debates regarding media 'literacy' have fundamentally changed (although they have certainly evolved with the influence of ever more complex cultural theories such as postmodernism) but is more a reflection of the kinds of classroom activities suggested. Not only have the facilities for students to make their own media become increasingly more affordable and accessible, but we have witnessed the astonishing growth of the Internet and the world wide web; effectively a completely new medium, with its own textual conventions and complexities of ownership. With such change it has not only been difficult, at times, for teachers to keep abreast of developments and research, but the theoretical waters of 'English', if they were ever pure, are surely now more muddied than ever. Technological convergence promises a future (already a reality in some schools) where every student has a laptop capable of editing digital video, creating web pages or e-mailing students in Australia, and yet the presence of mobile phones in classrooms is routinely seen as a 'problem' and handwriting is still regarded as the primary mode of presentation.

Among the numerous discussions and conferences about the future of English, most views that stress the importance of critical literacy admit the need to focus on the 'production, distribution and reception of texts' in the *widest* possible sense. English, in other words, should be about students' experience of the 'now' (i.e. the contemporaneous) at least as much as their experience of 'then' (i.e. the historically valued). But with the profusion (and confusion?) of communications and information available in every conceivable form, one might be surprised that the latest version (1999) of the National Curriculum for KS3 and KS4 includes only a few lines describing media texts suitable for EN2 Reading: 'for example, newspapers, magazines, advertisements, television, films, videos.' It is evidently felt that an outline of forms is all that is necessary. Yet the same page contains several columns detailing lists of set authors 'before and after 1914' (DfEE/QCA, 1999b, p. 36). The message to teachers here is surely qualitative: study *any* media text you want, but *these* authors are the *real* deal. The names would surprise few English teachers (they include Chaucer, Keats and a brace of Brontës) but is inescapably canonical – based on assumed notions of 'quality' and 'tradition'. It is difficult to conceive of a similar list of prescribed media texts that would not look either terribly arch (*Cathy Come Home, Citizen Kane*?) or selectively populist (*The Simpsons, Spider-Man*?).

The vacuum of prescription around media texts within the National Curriculum (and we are not arguing *for* prescription) does of course have its advantages, insofar as there remains a fair degree of freedom about how one delivers the media requirements. The extent therefore to which English departments focus on media work will often depend on the levels of expertise and the interests of individual teachers. It undoubtedly also reflects the fact that, by its nature, media education is resistant to notions of a canon based predominantly on 'quality'. In fact, many critics have noted that a quite different view of the media has tended to dominate English teaching; that is, as something that it is necessary to inoculate students against. In this view, critical literacy becomes an ideological tool that should be nurtured in students through texts deliberately chosen to represent objectionable or reactionary viewpoints.

As a new teacher you may find the embarrassment of choice and lack of prescription refreshing and exciting when compared to the lengthy guidance of the National Literacy Strategy, but you are more likely to find the issue of practical work more dependent upon available resources – as well as your own expertise. It has often been said that practical work in media – designing magazine pages, film posters, editing radio programmes and filming television commercials – is the equivalent of *writing* in English. This analogy is perhaps more meaningful than ever before thanks to the ICT revolution.

Technology has changed media teaching enormously, both within English and the specialist subject areas of Media Studies, and, as we discuss at the end of this chapter, it has also placed responsibility on some English departments to 'deliver' some of the programmes of study for ICT as well as those for English. In the past, practical media activities were dominated by 'low-tech' approaches involving scissors, glue and tiny pieces of paper left all over the classroom floor. We would argue that, while these approaches still offer excellent potential, access to even a small number of computers can transform lesson and student outcomes in any number of ways. Inexpensive digital cameras (such as the Sony 'Mavica') can save images to smart media or even floppy disc. These can be transferred easily to computer and included in student publications or web pages. Software packages are equally affordable, from Adobe's easy-to-use yet powerful 'Photoshop Elements' (a stripped-down version of the industry standard Photoshop) and Microsoft 'Publisher', a simple Desktop Publishing (DTP) package. Digital video cameras continue to offer value for money and, together with a higher specified computer (such as the Apple iMac), can provide an easy-to-learn desktop non-linear video-editing package capable of creating DVDs.

In their important study of practical media production in education, Buckingham and Sefton-Green (1995) describe four main traditions of practical work that have historically informed English and media teaching. These traditions view practical work as:

1   A tradition of self-expression, deriving largely from 'progressive' art and English teaching.
2   A method of learning such as the use of video to present aspects of oral history.
3   Vocational (or more accurately pre-vocational) training, modelling work upon professional practices.
4   Deconstructionist, often with the explicit aim of opposing or subverting dominant modes of professional practice.

What is evident here is that media production work has been subject to just a similar set of debates and controversies to those that have inflected the role of 'creative' writing in English. As a new teacher, you may find it useful to sound out the attitudes to practical work of your departmental colleagues. It may also be valuable to consider how far each of these traditions might inform the practical activities that you undertake with students.

Buckingham, Grahame and Sefton-Green's accounts of their research into production work in schools raise many of the key issues that you will want address in planning, managing and evaluating practical work in either English or Media Studies lessons. They conclude with three 'principles for practice' which (simplified) are as follows:

1   *Practical work has to provide students with genuine opportunities to develop their own insights and theories.* It should not *simply* be used as vehicle for addressing a set of prescribed assessment criteria.

2   *Practical work must be recursive.* It should occur regularly, with any 'product' not being seen necessarily as the 'end of the process'. A key comparison here might be with the process of drafting and redrafting.

3   *Reflection is a central and indispensable aspect of practical work.* It does not necessarily have to be 'written'. The relationship between theory and practice needs to be 'equal and dialectical'.

Media in English at KS3 and KS4

There are many ways for teachers and departments to find and make opportunities for media work in English, and in recent years the number and quality of specially designed resources has increased significantly. It is now widely recognised that work on the media should be central to English teaching and learning.

There are two main approaches to integrating media work into the English curriculum. One approach is to build media work into already existing units; another is to offer discrete units with a media focus. Both of these approaches are supported in resources such as the KS3 *Media Book* (English and Media Centre) which claims with considerable legitimacy to include 'everything you need to teach Media within English at KS3'. The *Media Book* provides an excellent range of teaching materials, covering: popular culture case studies (*Big Brother*, *The Simpsons* and *The Teletubbies*); debates about young people and advertising, and examples of mainstream and alternative texts. The book is accompanied by a video with clips to accompany the case studies and a selection of original short narratives which raise issues of representation, ethnicity, identity and disability. The teachers' notes provide concise and valuable introductions to the main media concepts involved.

For an introduction to and resources for practical work, the English and Media Centre's *Production Practices* offers a range of well-tested materials, ideas and simulations including publishing, video and news production.

Media tasks in English units

Poems are extremely useful for media-based work because, by and large, they tend to be short, complete texts. The practice of storyboarding, or making a video poem, can be one way of beginning to get pupils used to 'writing' with a video camera. A storyboard is the beginning point for all TV, video and film productions (see the two previously mentioned texts for examples). It comprises a number of blank frames on a sheet into which are drawn or pasted approximations of what will appear on screen. Beneath each frame are written details of music, sound-effects, dialogue and camera movement. Storyboard work enables pupils to begin to understand how visual images are constructed and how technical and narrative codes and conventions determine the 'look' of television and film drama.

Working in groups, pupils can produce storyboards of poems they are studying. Details of camera angles, lighting, movement and music and sound-effects can be added to the line from the poem which will accompany the image in the frame. For longer narrative or pre-twentieth-century poems, the text might be divided up among groups to storyboard. There will, of course, need to be some discussion by the whole class beforehand related to the tone or mood of the poem and how this will influence the visual style of the storyboard.

Images from magazines and Sunday supplements might be used to create a video poem. Images are pasted on to caption cards, which are then shot on video. Pupils decide whether the image is static and full-frame, or whether different close-up details from the same image might be used; if the camera will pan or zoom, and so on. The text of the poem can be read out as a voice-over at the same time as the image is recorded, or read out to accompany images as they appear on the TV monitor when they are shared with the class. The second approach is often more successful as it limits the number of opportunities for mistakes at the recording stage.

Many novels commonly found in English departments lend themselves to media work. At KS3, novels such as Morris Gleitzman's *Two Weeks With The Queen* open up many opportunities for work on, for instance, media representations of boys and masculinity. When beginning a new class reader it is not unusual to spend some time discussing what can be learned about the book from its cover. For example, what clues does the title give about the content of the story? How does the blurb on the back cover raise the reader's expectations? Can the illustration help us to predict what the characters will be like, or what might happen in the story? Media work based on a class reader may include examination of the book cover in media terms in order to make apparent to pupils the industrial nature of a book's production and circulation. For example, what messages are conveyed by the choice of illustration, the nature of the image? How is the cover laid out; what typefaces and font size are used; what use is made of colour? What is the importance of the bar code and ISBN? What does the price tell us about the intended market for the book? Why are sales restricted to certain countries? What do we know about the publisher? What is the importance of logos, imprints and particular series? Such analysis and discussion fits naturally into the type of work English teachers will do on front covers, but it develops a pupil's awareness of the economics of marketing and publishing. Further work related to book covers might include repackaging the book for a new audience. Pupils design a cover aimed at a slightly older or younger audience, or perhaps as a school text. A range of covers, posters and promotional flyers all reinforces pupils' understandings of the industrial/technological nature of publishing.

While working on a class reader pupils might make a poster for a television adaptation, after doing some analytical work on posters – particularly those used to capture the attention of a potential television audience. Without such preparatory work, pupils might well produce something that looks like a poster with an image and text, but their knowledge and understanding of the conventions of this media text will not have been developed.

Further related work could involve the pupils in making a two-minute radio commercial for a radio adaptation of the story. Limiting the length of the product and making the focus of the exercise the commercial rather than the adaptation of the whole story is useful in two ways. It clearly constrains the amount of work that pupils have to do and it makes the focus of the exercise media as opposed to literary. Such an exercise involves pupils thinking about: audience (how different might the commercial be on Radio 3 or 4 compared to Radio 5 Live or a commercial station?); technical and narrative conventions of radio drama; and purposes and practices of radio advertising. Equally, older pupils might produce a television trailer for an adaptation of the story for Channel 4, Children's BBC or a local cable channel. Once again similar media concepts might be explored. It is but a short step from this type of work to considering promotional campaigns, marketing and merchandising related to television and films. Many pupils will have tangible proof of the efficacy and ubiquity of such marketing either as part of their collection of toys, their clothing or their pencil cases and lunch boxes they bring to school.

Finally, when planning media work, remember to build into your English lessons opportunities that allow your pupils to both *read* and *write* in a variety of media. Similarly, before beginning any new media-related topic, you should ask yourself two questions: 'What do I need to know in terms of the media?' and 'What do my pupils need to know in terms of the media?' Remember: getting them to draw a newspaper masthead, a banner headline and dividing the page into two columns for the *Verona Times* or the *Soledad Enquirer* might enable pupils to develop their knowledge of the texts they are studying, but it is not media education unless you have done some preparatory work on, for example, newspaper ownership, distribution, stance and so on. Similarly, a class magazine is only really a collection of English work unless you have previously explored such areas as conventions of magazines, audience and so on to make the work a valuable experience in terms of media. After media-related work you should, or you should enable your pupils to, make explicit what has been learned in terms of the media.

MEDIA STUDIES – KS4 AND KS5

As has been said earlier, Media Studies and media education are separate, though related, disciplines. The first part of this chapter has shown how media education can be located within the work of the English classroom in order to develop pupils' literacy in the widest sense. The focus of this part of the chapter, however, is to consider Media Studies in relation to the preparation of pupils in order to pass public examinations.

Although teaching Media Studies has historically come to be located within the English department, such teaching requires particular knowledge, skills and understanding to be developed in the teacher, which are in many ways separate from those that a teacher uses in the English classroom. For the many media teachers who have also taught English, the attractions and strengths of the subject are often associated with its conceptual framework, which they find significantly enhances their English teaching. The main concepts of Media Studies appear in various formulations, but are generally variations of media language (forms and conventions); media narrative (modes – such as realism, non-narrative); media categories (formats and genres); media audiences; media representations and ideology; media institutions (ownership, working practices) and media technologies.

It is often assumed that because there are some similarities between media and literary texts – for example, in common narrative elements such as plot, themes, character, setting – that 'English' reading skills can be transferred to analysing media texts. However, as examination boards have regularly noted, 'Media Studies is a specific subject with its own body of knowledge, theories and debates'. 'Textual analyis' is an important element of the discipline but it is rarely possible or desirable to study media texts in isolation from their social, cultural and production contexts.

If you are keen to teach Media Studies but have not studied it as an undergraduate, it is best to do so with experienced teachers in an established GCSE and/or A level course in your placement school. They should therefore have units of work based on clear conceptual and theoretical aims and a range of well-focused materials for you to browse through. Should you wish to go on to take up a post which includes Media Studies teaching you need to be aware that the responsibility for further training lies with you. Ironically, despite the exhortations for pupils to be prepared for twenty-first-century technology and literacy, training for teaching Media Studies still does not reflect its massive growth as an examined specialist subject – partly because since 1992 teacher education has to be provided in National Curriculum subjects.

If, as a student teacher with little or no Media Studies education, you are offered a post in a school which wants you to start up GCSE or A level Media Studies that September, you should consider the matter very carefully before you accept. Some schools can be very insistent because, since Media Studies is a growth area, it brings in funding and potentially keeps students who might otherwise leave to do A levels in the local college. Ideally you might ask them to consider postponing the introduction of the course for a year. You should, though, make it clear to the school that you would like the resources and time (a year) to go on courses, read, collect materials and buy equipment. Without such support, the quality of teaching and the quality of pupil learning will be likely to undermine the purpose of having the course in the first place. If the school is unable to give you such support, you need to be aware of the ramifications on the quality of your professional life. As the HMI report *The New Teacher in School* (OFSTED, 1993) shows, you are likely to be under considerable pressure as an NQT with the physical demands of teaching full time, learning classroom management with new pupils, handling marking and administration, without undertaking the equivalent of a self-directed undergraduate course in Media Studies in the small hours of the morning.

Even if you do have a degree in media, you should still be equally cautious. As an NQT you will have had only limited experience of examination teaching and little, if any, experience of managing an examination course. Running GCSE Media Studies could be possible provided you already have teaching resources relevant to the syllabus and are given a budget to buy equipment. However, we would stress that as an NQT you should not have to deal with the responsibility of managing examination board administration – for example, being solely responsible for marking coursework – when you have not had the experience of knowing what levels of achievement are appropriate. Indeed, you are no doubt aware that it takes a while to understand the syllabuses themselves. Remember, it is the pupils who pay the price of mismanaged courses. Again, we would suggest being given a year to choose your syllabuses and plan your courses; for A level in particular there is much which has to be covered and it has to be very tightly managed. In addition, the practicalities of organising and monitoring practical work, for instance, are ones learned through classroom management experience.

Training

You may be lucky to be on an English course which includes a Media Studies unit, but if you intend to teach Media Studies in school, you will need to become acquainted with the opportunities for short courses and qualifications via part-time courses. Once you have secured a teaching post, contact your local English adviser or the English and Media Centre in London; their courses include one for an accredited qualification which is the Diploma in Media Education. There are also many regional media teaching support groups. The English and Media Centre is a good starting point. The British Film Institute Education (BFI) section can also provide details of regional groups. Specialist institutions such as Film Education, Bradford Museum of Photography, Film and Television, NATE and local projects such as video, photography and radio workshops run good-quality short courses with professionals. There are also several independent education companies which provide courses specifically geared to aspects of examination syllabuses.

Resources

There are several excellent books which offer accessible and succinct explanations of the key media concepts, debates and theories, as well as a range of case studies with good-quality visual images. The following books are also worth considering as text-books for pupils: for GCSE, *Media Studies: An Introduction* (Dutton and Mundy, 1995), and *GCSE Media Studies* (Wall, 1996); for A level, *Studying the Media* (O'Sullivan, Dutton and Rayner, 1994) and *The Media Student's Book* (Branston and Stafford, 1996). The latter has a comprehensive glossary of key terms. A book which more advanced students may find useful and is certainly useful for you to extend your knowledge and feel that you are more than one step ahead of the students is *Media Studies* (Price, 1993). *Media Education: An Introduction* is an erudite Open University (1992) distance learning package, written by experienced media teachers, containing activities and opportunities to analyse case studies of media lessons at Key Stages 1, 2 and 3. While it clearly has a media education focus, the teaching and learning skills are sound ones that may be applied to examination courses. You will also need to read a range of specialist books for particular areas of study; most examination boards have bibliographies printed in their syllabuses or available as support materials.

There are some excellent packs of photocopiable materials which may be used for GCSE, GNVQ and A level courses. As they are expensive they should be bought as departmental resources, such as the English and Media Centre's *Advertising Pack* and *Panic Attacks*. The *Advertising Pack* in particular is exemplary in that it offers work appropriate at every key stage and enables departments to begin developing a sense of progression (from KS3 to GCSE, for instance).

Whether you wish to teach media education and/or Media Studies, you will need your own bank of materials for use in the classroom such as TV listings magazines, music magazines, newspapers (local and national), magazines targeted at men, women and teenagers, comics, and film marketing merchandise. Label them and/or keep an inventory which you can check at the end of each lesson. Also encourage pupils to bring in items of interest. Invest in a good VCR at home for film and television resources.

As you are teaching about contemporary businesses it is important to gain insights from the viewpoints of the practitioners. Obtaining trade magazines such as *Campaign* for the advertising industry, and information about audiences such as BARB figures and press packs, provides active research material for both academic and practical work. Annuals such as *The Guardian Media Guide* and *The BFI Annual Review* publish lists of professional media organisations. One of the stimulations (and demands) of teaching this subject is the need to keep up to date: ownership changes regularly; legislation is amended; new technologies and attendant debates proliferate; there are constant new spins on old moral panics and issues of freedom and regulation, ethics and so on. You can easily inform yourself via newspapers such as *Media Guardian*, *Observer* and *Sunday Times* and their respective websites. The Guardian media website is an excellent starting point for media news of every shape and size (www.guardian.co.uk/media) and the BFI website has excellent educational and industry links.

Qualifications

There is a range of courses currently available, although it is in the sixth form where the largest growth in Media Studies has taken place in recent years. The principal courses you will come across at this key stage are the more traditionally academic A level and the recently developed GNVQ (General National Vocational Qualification) Media Production and Communication and VCE (Vocational Certificate of Education) Advanced. The main examination boards all have websites where specifications, additional guidance, past examination papers and examiners' reports may be accessed and/or downloaded. They are AQA (Assessment and Qualifications Alliance), EdExcel, OCR (Oxford, Cambridge and RSA) and WJEC (Welsh Joint Education Committee).

GCSE Media Studies

The GCSE Media Studies is now well established and is fairly straightforward to teach without significant additional specialist training. The AQA specification, for instance, requires that students produce three pieces of coursework covering all the main concept areas, and a practical production. They must complete the course with a terminal examination based on a prescribed topic which changes every year, but which can be prepared for in advance by students. GCSEs from all the boards make relatively few demands on practical resources and should be considered by all schools as a useful addition to achieving a broad and balanced curriculum.

Your school may offer a single GCSE as an option or may even choose to offer *all* KS4 students a dual award course by teaching Media Studies alongside English. This option should generally only be considered once there are sufficient levels of expertise within the department. It can, however, be a serious and attractive alternative to teaching the (more common) dual award English and English literature. Occasionally you may find a school that offers all three subjects to their entire cohort.

A level Media Studies

You will find that the A level specifications, like the GCSE, state that their overall aims are to engender critical autonomy, conceptual understanding, creative engagement and practical production skills. Since the introduction of Curriculum 2000, all A levels consist of two distinct courses: the AS level and the A2. The AS level can be offered to students as a one-year qualification and is worth 50 per cent of the full A level (AS plus A2). You will need to bear in mind that the A2 is intended to be more academically demanding than the AS. In order to satisfactorily deliver the full A level course, many schools begin teaching it as soon as the summer exam period is over.

With the introduction of the AS and A2 and the merging of examination boards at the end of the 1990s, the differences between each specification became less marked than had previously been the case, and perhaps the most noticeable difference is the greater emphasis placed upon production work in the specification offered by OCR. All specifications are unit- or module-based and all include opportunities for students to conduct independent research. A further result of the review of A levels that led to Curriculum 2000 is that specifications are now more detailed than ever before and provide plenty of guidance on how units might be taught, along with explanations of terminology and concepts and detailed mark schemes.

In order to adopt or plan schemes of work to achieve the specification aims, you need to be very clear about what you want pupils to learn and why, in terms of knowledge, study and technical skills. You will need to set graduated specific tasks to build up skills and confidence over each year of the course. The following suggested list of skills is a general one which you can select or adapt as appropriate to the level or specification. Pupils need to be:

- keeping themselves informed about current media issues, collecting materials from their own viewing, reading and listening;
- developing observant, detailed reading of media texts;
- learning and using theories, debates and terminology;
- contributing to class and group discussion;
- writing clear, detailed, succinct notes which can be used for planning practical work, essays and for revision;

- reading independently: selecting relevant information, recording key points in their own words, recording quotations;
- writing well-structured discursive essays in a clear, detailed and succinct style;
- illustrating their arguments with examples, case studies, quotations and references;
- learning technical skills associated with at least two media: for example, audio, video and DTP;
- taking responsibility for the organisation of their productions, including research and planning;
- making products to the best of their ability;
- ensuring the products are used to explore media concepts;
- writing clear, succinct, critical commentaries which use terminology and are well focused around theory, concepts and debates;
- participating co-operatively in group work;
- working independently on individual tasks and seeking support when necessary.

There are not necessarily better or worse specifications: the choice lies in what suits your educational philosophy, your department's resources and your school's action plans. You should examine all of the specifications, support and exemplar materials, and past examination papers. When you read the documentation, elements to consider are:

- the amount of practical work;
- the quality and quantity of support materials;
- what teacher support is offered;
- how supportive is the administration;
- the ratio of examination board/teacher examination marking;
- where there is practical or unseen criticism, what is the quality of reproduced materials;
- the clarity and accessibility of examination questions.

VCE (advanced) and GNVQ (intermediate); media communications and production

These courses are broadly described as 'pre-vocational' and are usually both offered at KS5. The GNVQ (intermediate) qualification is the equivalent of four GCSEs but is due to be replaced by vocational GCSEs. The VCE (advanced) is often described as a 'Vocational A level' and may be taken in two forms: a single (six-unit) award or a double (twelve-unit) award (worth two A levels in terms of UCAS tariff points). Like A levels, they are unit-based and there are relatively few differences between each board's specifications. As with the other courses outlined here, space prevents a detailed account of their content, but it is reasonable to describe them as more production orientated than GCSEs and A levels. It is important to note however that neither course lacks theoretical and conceptual content and each requires students to adopt a reflective and critical approach to their own work.

Resourcing is a more important issue for departments wishing to deliver these courses and they should not be undertaken unless you are able to provide something approaching industry–standard facilities.

Task 9.3 ICT skills audit

No doubt your ITE course provides opportunities for the development of your ICT skills. The ICT skills test is intended to show student teachers' progression in their ICT capability, so at whatever level you begin your course you are expected to improve. The following checklist may be used to assess your current capability and to create an action plan for development.

ICT skills	Aspects developed Level of knowledge/ competence (1 Very good to 3 Basic)	Aspects in need of development	Strategies to enable development
Word processing			
DTP			
Spreadsheet/ database			
CD-ROM			
Curriculum packages			
Electronic mail			
Internet			

When you have completed your audit, discuss with your tutor or mentor in school opportunities and strategies for development.

ICT and the English curriculum

Information and communications technology (ICT) and the English curriculum have historically experienced an intricate and at times uneasy association. Evidence, often in the form of enthusiastic firsthand accounts, suggests that many individual teachers and schools have had significant success using ICT to underpin and enhance teaching and learning. However, despite truck-loads of guidance and fresh National Curriculum requirements, the subject still lacks a coherent tradition of computer use and much of the innovation of practitioners working in classrooms for over two decades has yet to coalesce into a recognised set of subject-based mainstream principles and practices. This may be explained partly by the existence of several different models of how ICT resources are organised and used in the classroom. A variety of situations, from network rooms used by many different subjects to single computers in English classrooms, have arguably made it more problematic for good practice in one establishment to be transferred to another.

Education policy and investment have seen intense activity in recent years and ICT has been used to spearhead much needed change. In 1998 the government introduced the National Grid for Learning (NGfL) strategy, which was intended to help learners and educators benefit from ICT. A consultation paper *Connecting the Learning Society* (1997) was followed by the NGfL challenge document *Open for Learning, Open for Business* in November 1998, which set targets to be met by 2002. These targets included:

- connecting all schools, colleges, libraries, universities and as many community centres as possible to the Grid;
- ensuring that serving teachers feel confident and are competent to teach ICT within the curriculum, and that librarians are similarly trained;
- enabling school leavers to have a good understanding of ICT, with measures in place for assessing their competence in it;
- making Britain a centre for excellence in the development of networked software content, and a world leader in the export of learning services.

To support these aims the British Educational Communications and Technology Agency (BECTA) was established to provide, promote and evaluate advice and resources for ICT use in education. Further injections of funding were to come from the DfES along with the National Lottery's New Opportunities Fund (NOF) providing hardware and training for teachers, albeit in a selective series of stages. DfES statistical research published in 2002 (available at DfES website www.dfes.gov.uk/ictfutures/) certainly indicates a significant increase in computer availability in schools. In the secondary sector there is now an average of one computer for every seven students and devices such as interactive whiteboards and digital projectors have become increasingly commonplace.

A site of struggle?

The beginning of the twenty-first century is undoubtedly an exciting time for English teachers but it is also fraught with difficult challenges and uncertainties. At its heart, ICT has the potential to challenge many of our fundamental notions of what constitutes teaching and learning. However, the everyday reality is probably far more mundane, with teachers across the country bidding for scarce periods in network rooms, attempting to familiarise themselves with the use of new software, or grappling with online support (and all with ever-increasing demands on their time).

Although such positive and ambitious government initiatives have sought to cement the use of ICT firmly into the National Curriculum, it has remained a matter for individual schools precisely how they develop and implement ICT. This has inevitably led to some often very difficult decisions about how best to spend money and use resources. Most schools have invariably opted for networks of computers located in discrete areas, often the preserve of maths, modern foreign languages or IT and business studies. The massive growth of ICT courses at KS4 and KS5 has placed even greater pressure on such networks and it has not always been easy for English teachers to gain access to computers for their lessons.

As investment in computing infrastructure in schools has continued to expand so have the expectations of pupils, parents, employers and government. Pupils entering secondary schools are likely to be familiar with multimedia activities. They may well have designed websites or made PowerPoint presentations to their class. However, as Leask and Litchfield (1999, p. 192) point out,

> The disparity in the pupil experience of ICT in different schools in the UK
> is already unacceptably high. . . . Experiential learning in ICT from a
> young age seems to enable users to develop problem-solving capabilities, so
> that they are often able to use intuition to work their way around technical
> problems. Others, who are denied the opportunity, may well struggle to
> keep up for the rest of their lives.

Even in the secondary phase, approaches to ICT across the curriculum have clearly varied greatly from school to school. Some of the greatest successes of ICT usage have been built around a cross-curricular topic-based approach encompassing a host of subject areas such as drama, art and dance (as described in Leask and Williams, 1999). However, given the rigid timetabling and balkanisation that so many teachers experience, it is difficult to see how the successes of isolated pilot schemes that may attract extra funding through research grants and so on can be made to work on a more regular basis without either severe compromise or through excessive teacher goodwill.

A major problem for English teachers working with ICT has often been the degree to which they have been able to control and manage the environment within which they are expected to deliver the curriculum. Although, as we have pointed out, there are several models of ICT resourcing, by far the most dominant has been that of the computer network room. It is comparatively rare for secondary schools to adopt the practice, common in primary schools, of locating a small number of computers in each classroom. This has generally been justified through either the (lack of) availability of support staff or managerial pragmatism. It is still rarer for laptops or other portable devices to be commonly available for all students. One result of this has been to restrict the range of activities that computers can be used for. Small group activities, involving speaking and listening targets, for instance, tend to be discouraged simply by the physical arrangement of computers in a standard network environment, whereas interactive whiteboards and digital projection facilities tend to favour teacher-led whole class discussion and modelling activities.

The government's aim has been explicitly to challenge these restrictions and open up the ways in which computers can be used in education. When new funding becomes available in a school, departments should look closely at what opportunities could open up for them to develop their curriculum offer. Occasions should also be sought regularly for teachers with varying degrees of experience in a department to train together in order to be able to collaborate on new units of work or fresh modes of delivery. There is also encouraging evidence (particularly from schools with well-established ICT resources) to suggest that schools are developing and opening up their ICT provision in more flexible ways and that the once-dominant 'network room' may be giving way to clusters of computers in a greater number of classrooms.

Task 9.4 ICT in schools

Some questions to ask about ICT in your new school:

- How much access is there for students and teachers to ICT?
- What is the nature of the access (network rooms, library, English classrooms, other)? Is sufficient time available for classes/students to properly develop their skills?
- What expectations are there around how your department uses ICT? Are you expected to participate in the assessment of the ICT programmes of study?
- How does your school use the Internet? What is its policy regarding safe use and how does it convey this to students and parents?
- How far can ICT be used to facilitate practical production work and media-orientated outcomes?
- What opportunities are there for staff training? How is existing knowledge and expertise shared?

Using ICT

This section considers the main areas in which you will need to integrate ICT into your work as an English teacher. These fall broadly into four categories:

1   *Pupils' learning and attainment* – the ways in which ICT is used to enhance teaching and learning in the classroom and at home.
2   *Pupil assessment* – both of 'traditional' English skills and of ICT skills themselves.
3   *Professional development* – teachers learning new skills, such as web design, new

software packages and the use of hardware devices, such as digital cameras, video-editing.

4   *Preparation of materials* – the days of the handwritten worksheet are surely past. With many resources already online, we are entering the age of the 'virtual learning community'.

Pupils' learning and attainment

Although the National Curriculum Orders for English make relatively few references to ICT, there exist several threads of expectation regarding pupil entitlement. Under reading (EN2) pupils are required to:

(4) – develop their reading of print and ICT-based information texts, and pupils should be taught to:
a)   select, compare and synthesise information from different texts
b)   evaluate how information is presented
c)   sift the relevant from the irrelevant, and distinguish between fact and opinion, bias and objectivity
d)   identify the characteristic features, at word, sentence and text level, of different types of texts.

Under writing (EN3), pupils are required to:

(2)   a) plan, draft, redraft and proof-read their work on paper and on screen 5c →
ICT opportunity: Pupils could use a variety of ways to present their work, including using pictures and moving images as well as print.

ICT clearly has much to offer your pupils in the English classroom. ICT in English:

- improves the quality of content and form of pupils' outcomes;
- significantly supports the processes of drafting;
- benefits those pupils who have problems with writing, as their final drafts will look as good as work produced by any other pupils, thereby increasing their self-esteem;
- has much to offer the quality of pupil talk and the nature of discussion;
- enables pupils to operate in a range of genres;
- offers *real* publishing opportunities (both paper and virtual);
- enables pupils to communicate flexibly with a variety of audiences from within school to the wider community (and, via e-mail and the Internet, through video-streaming, video-conferencing and website design, across the country and globally).

Reading (EN2)

The growth of hypertext (as used in the Internet and the world wide web and in DVD and CD-ROMs) has profound implications for the way we read and process information. Texts need no longer be approached in a linear way but can be opened up in innovative ways. Hypertext-based approaches to traditional texts can allow students to develop different and more positive relationships to Shakespeare and so on. However, students' use of the Internet needs to be carefully managed within the classroom to ensure it is used appropriately and usefully. (Guidelines for safe use of the Internet may be found through the NGfL website.) Practically all schools are now online and most operate some kind of software 'protection' against students visiting inappropriate sites. So rapid has change in these technologies been that CD-ROMs are often now seen as a dying medium. This is unfortunate in some ways since they still have much to offer educationally. For reluctant readers, or those who have difficulty reading in KS3, the development of CD-ROM interactive books – the *Living Books* series, for example – has demonstrated real potential for motivating and supporting pupils. And there still exist a whole range of informational texts (e.g. encyclopedias) for which the DVD or CD-ROM remains an ideal educational medium.

Use can also be made of word processors with a speech facility for reading text, a feature also useful for encouraging students to write. Perhaps one of the most powerful programs for English teachers was *Developing Tray* (*DevTray*) developed by English teacher Bob Moy and the Inner London Educational Computing Centre in the 1980s. The beauty of *DevTray* was that it was an extremely 'teacher-friendly' suite of programs, which provided a skeleton structure into which teachers could type any text they wished to use with a class. *DevTray* involves pupils in creating the meaning of the partial text in front of them and in getting into the *deep structures* of the text. Using the program to investigate texts which are being read as class readers, or for GCSE or A level, involved pupils in a detailed, active investigation of the text at word and sentence level which was difficult to sustain in any other way. The teacher could use *DevTray* with one computer via a large screen monitor or projector, or by individuals, or groups of pupils in a network room. Several versions of the program currently exist, including *Sherlock: The Case of the Missing Text* and Spelling *it Out: Context*. Although their use tends to be most commonly at KS2, there continues to exist a huge potential for reading activities using ICT at Key Stages 3 and 4.

Writing (EN3)

> The essential factor . . . is that the writing process changes when we use the computer as a tool. . . . Children do not only write more with computers, they write differently. . . . Where so many of us misunderstood word processors when they first appeared in the classrooms was seeing them as devices which related to what had gone before, such as the typewriter and the printing press. Word processing is not copy typing followed by printing, but a revising and drafting activity.
>
> (Abbott, 1995, p. 136)

You should not feel that only the most up-to-date package is of use in the classroom, or that only one particular word-processing program may be used. It is important to recognise the power of the basic facilities of all word-processing packages, facilities that allow you to:

- *cut* and *paste* blocks of text;
- insert new text at any point of a document;
- *search* and *replace* words or phrases;
- check spelling (and increasingly grammar and style).

Much of the time spent redrafting handwritten work involves pupils in copying out what was good in the first place: a chore that is unnecessary with a word processor. Pupils should be encouraged to move whole blocks of text, reshape and resequence stories using cut and paste. They can find/search and replace to change the tone, mood and genre of writing; explore texts at sentence and word level by searching and replacing nouns and adjectives – try using this facility to change the tense of a story, or a character from male to female by replacing *his* with *her*, and the anomalies provide a very real context for grammar work. Abbott (1995) notes how some writers have suggested that engaging in the practices of word processing 'alters the thinking processes involved with writing, so that the person involved thinks in blocks of meaning rather than in individual words or ideas' (p. 32).

In word processing, the use of spell and grammar-checking facilities echoes the debates about the use of calculators in maths and you will have to check what your department's policy is towards word-processed homework, or the examination board's regulations related to the number of pieces of word-processed coursework which may be submitted. Spell and grammar checks provide a very useful support for less able writers and place fresh emphasis on the ways in which we might teach proof-reading skills. The limitations of the word processor's dictionary can be a useful opportunity for word- and sentence-level work, as many of them use American English and will suggest substituting, for example, *color* or *center* for the UK equivalents. Those word-processing packages that include a thesaurus can enable pupils to use, search for alternatives and replace synonyms in their work with ease and enjoyment.

To begin with, you may wish to introduce Year 7 pupils to short, structured pieces of writing, which do not demand much keyboard expertise on their part. The mini-saga, a complete story written in exactly fifty words including the title, can be a motivating starting point for pupils new to word processing to develop a number of writing skills. The *word count* facility enables them, and you, quickly to check how close they are to their target.

For poetry work, the haiku or even the limerick can be structured, clearly constrained starting points. Similarly, a file containing the topic sentences of six paragraphs to which pupils add further sentences can be useful for work on paragraphs. Although all pupils have the same starting points, their results can be very different. Pupils enjoy being able quickly to share the very different outcomes of such 'paragraph work' with their classmates. Similarly, providing them with a short story or news report that they change in mood, location, genre, stance using *search* and *replace* produces excellent results. Such an approach may be used to support work based on almost any class reader.

Speaking and listening (EN1)

> The computer is an effective catalyst of talk both at the screen and away
> from it. . . . Of particular interest is the talk which takes place at the
> computer screen, for it can differ significantly from small group talk in
> other contexts. . . . While some aspects of computer-stimulated talk will be
> recognisable as characteristic of small group talk in any context, others arise
> as a direct result of the children's response to the resource.
>
> (Kemeny, 1990, p. 7)

The series of case studies reported in *Talking IT Through* (Kemeny, 1990) were a result
of research conducted jointly by the National Oracy Project (NOP) and the National
Council for Educational Technology (NCET) based in Coventry. The report shows
clearly the benefits of using IT in the classroom to promote and enhance the quality of
talk in a variety of contexts. 'One consistent and powerful observation is that speaking
and listening *arise naturally and purposefully at every stage of learning in the classroom*' (ibid.,
p. 2; emphasis in original). Chapter 5 (this volume) has shown in detail how speaking
and listening may be approached in the English classroom; you may wish to consider
how some of the approaches described in it might be developed further using ICT.

However, as noted above, the ways in which computers are arranged in classrooms
often militate against speaking and listening activities, although paired work is often
possible, with two students negotiating their way through a task. The introduction of
interactive whiteboards into many classrooms has increased dramatically the possibilities
for pupils presenting their work to each other, using programs such as Microsoft
PowerPoint.

If you are fortunate enough to have control over where computers are placed, then
arranging a small group of pupils around one screen can produce fruitful possibilities
with programs that promote structured talk. These may be CD-ROMs such as *Picture
Power* (and *Picture Power 2*, available from the English and Media Centre) which allow
students to edit their own short video, using pre-filmed clips. Or they may be cloze
reading programs such as those (see above) based on *Developing Tray*, which can
stimulate discussion most effectively.

Pupil assessment

This area has caused more difficulty than most, for a number of reasons. The main one
is possibly the confusion caused by having different sets of assessment criteria for both
English and ICT. As an English teacher you should ascertain precisely how the
department and the school sees your role here. Many English departments have resolved
the issue by simply stating that their assessment role should be limited to the programmes
of study and so on for their subject.

A further difficulty undoubtedly hinges upon the inevitably conservative nature
of assessment in English. Where the use of computers in education has increased
dramatically in recent years, English examinations have yet to embrace any technology
more advanced than the biro (In maths, the use of calculators is now widespread). At

KS4 it is now common for students to produce word-processed coursework at home, which may be considerably better written than anything they achieve in class. It can become difficult to ascertain whether the degree of support they have received is acceptable and examination board criteria will need to be carefully consulted. Many schools have attempted to address issues of equality of access to ICT by providing facilities in libraries and study areas for use after lessons and so on.

In the 2002 exam session a further phenomenon was noted by a senior examiner; that of the use of phone-texting language in a question which required candidates to write a letter to a friend. A spokesperson for the DfES commented; 'Text message language holds no sway with us. There is no place for slang in exam papers. Pupils should err on the side of traditional grammar.' Again, this suggests that it will be some time before we see attitudes to traditional assessment reflecting the full diversity of student work and achievement using 'new' technologies.

Professional development and the preparation of materials

An effect of the government's determination to properly embed ICT into the whole curriculum has been to highlight the huge disparity of skills and expertise from teacher to teacher. This has led to an expansion of the independent training and consultancy sector. Care needs to be taken, if and when INSET is brought in, that it is appropriate to teachers' needs and will have practical application in the classroom with regard to actual available resources. One benefit of the Internet is that it has allowed for the establishment of professional 'virtual' communities. Many of these have been set up by the NGfL, LEAs, examination boards, professional associations and individual schools, and there currently exists a considerable support structure for English teachers.

The advantages of preparing materials using ICT hugely outweigh the disadvantages. Word-processed worksheets can be adapted more readily for different purposes. They can be shared, with details changed from class to class. They can be magnified for students with sight problems or projected on to a whiteboard directly from a computer. Many schools and LEAs operate an Intranet, which allows for materials to be made available to pupils online, although, without effective management and safeguards, this form of publishing and communication can simply make greater demands on individual teachers' time.

SUMMARY AND CONCLUSION

The second part of this chapter has explored some of the key ways in which ICT must interact with the English curriculum and has outlined some of the challenges facing English teachers. We are clearly at a crossroads in education and society's use of ICT, and as a teacher you can expect significant change to occur throughout your career. In the foreseeable future, powerful portable computing devices are likely to become as common as pens and paper; indeed, they may simply evolve from the next generation of mobile phones. Debates about handwriting may conceivably become as redundant as handwriting itself as voice recognition software becomes commonplace. The proliferation of multimedia with its hypertext foundations has already begun to revolutionise the way we read and process information. And questions of assessment in English will once again have to confront the issues of precisely what it is we wish to assess and how we should most effectively and accurately assess it.

REFERENCES

Websites

http://www.nc.uk.net/servlets/Subjects?Subject=En The National Curriculum online.

http://www.becta.org.uk/index.cfm/ Becta is the government's lead agency for ICT in education. It supports the UK government and national organisations in the use and development of ICT in education to raise standards, widen access, improve skills and encourage effective management.

http://www.ngfl.gov.uk/ Portal for the National Grid for Learning. Has news and links and operates a 'Virtual Teacher Centre'.

http://besd.becta.org.uk/ Educational software database. Useful for tracking down specific programs.

http://www.teem.org.uk/ Teachers evaluating educational multimedia.

http://www.englishandmedia.co.uk/ English and Media Centre. Leading training organisation and publisher of materials, including *Picture Power 2*.

http://www.learn.co.uk/ *Guardian* newspaper's run site for teachers with online resources for pupils.

www.english-teaching.co.uk/ Resources for English teachers.

http://www.avp.co.uk/ One of many publishers of educational software. Publishes *Spelling it Out: Context*, a program based on *Developing Tray*.

http://www.topologika.co.uk/ Publishers of *Sherlock: The Case of the Missing Text* also based on *Developing Tray*.

www.dfes.gov.uk/statistics/ Statistical information on schools' connectivity; 'ICT in Schools' may be accessed here.

http://www.dfes.gov.uk/ictfutures/ The government's ambitions for ICT development in education may be found here: 'Transforming the Way We Learn: A Vision for the Future of ICT in Schools.'

Further reading

Buckingham, D., Grahame, J. and Sefton-Green, J. (1995) *Making Media: Practical Production in Media Education* London: English and Media Centre.

Grahame, J. (1996) *Picture Power*, London: EMC Publishing.

—— (2002) *The Media Pack: Units for GCSE Media and English*, London: EMC Publishing.

Grahame, J. and Domaille, K. (2001) *The Media Book*, EMC KS3 English Series, London: EMC Publishing.

Grahame, J. and Simons, M. (1999) *Picture Power II* (CD), London: EMC.

Leask, M. and Pachler, N. (1999) *Learning to Teach Using ICT in the Secondary School* London: Routledge.

English and Media Magazine, quarterly publication, aimed at media students and teachers, London: EMC.

10 Drama

John Moss

INTRODUCTION

If you already know that drama teaching is a distinct and complex skill, that it is possible to train as a specialist drama teacher, and that some secondary schools have separate drama departments, you may wonder why this book contains a chapter on teaching drama. First, it is the case that *The National Curriculum for England: English* places considerable emphasis on drama: all English teachers have a legal responsibility both to use practical drama methods in a substantial part of their teaching and to stimulate pupils to create and respond to drama texts. Second, much of the drama teaching which goes beyond these requirements is, in practice, undertaken by teachers who have trained primarily as English specialists. Indeed, many English teachers find that the special opportunities of drama both enrich their professional experience, and allow them to challenge and develop their pupils in ways which are excitingly different from those available to them using other parts of their teaching repertoire. It is important that this book should make you aware of both the responsibility that English teachers have to teach drama, and the opportunities this responsibility gives them. However, this chapter can only be a starting point: the suggestions for further reading at the end of it will point you to a number of important book-length studies which will help you to develop your theoretical and practical knowledge.

DRAMA AND THE NATIONAL CURRICULUM FOR ENGLISH

The position of drama within English has been strengthened in each of the revisions of the National Curriculum since 1990. In order to meet the requirements for speaking and listening, English teachers must now provide pupils at Key Stages 3 and 4 with the following learning experiences, which, for the first time, in *The National Curriculum for England: English* (DfEE/QCA, 1999b), are listed under the discrete subheading, Drama.

OBJECTIVES

By the end of this chapter you should:

- be able to assess the rationale which underpins the drama teaching in your placement school;
- understand how to create the working conditions for 'risk-taking' drama;
- understand a range of drama teaching methods and their applications.

To participate in a range of drama activities and to evaluate their own and others' contributions, pupils should be taught to:

a) use a variety of dramatic techniques to explore ideas, issues, texts and meaning

b) use different ways to convey action, character, atmosphere and tension when they are scripting and performing in plays [for example, through dialogue, movement, pace]

c) appreciate how the structure and organisation of scenes and plays contribute to dramatic effect

d) evaluate critically performances of dramas that they have watched or in which they have taken part.

(DfEE/QCA, 1999b, p. 32)

There is a further requirement that the range of activities experienced by pupils will include: improvisation and working in role; devising, scripting and performing in plays; and discussing and reviewing their own and others' performances. In addition, plays 'from the English literary heritage', 'recent and contemporary drama', and drama 'from different cultures and traditions' must all be studied to meet the requirements for reading; and the range of forms of writing to be covered includes playscripts.

However, the National Curriculum Level Descriptions for speaking and listening make no reference at all to drama! If we seek guidance on what progression in pupil attainment in drama might consist of, the NLS *Framework for Teaching English: Years 7, 8 and 9* provides a little more help. It includes discrete teaching objectives for drama in Years 7, 8 and 9 which are intended to help teachers to determine when it is appropriate to prioritise different aspects of the four main objectives the National Curriculum defines. Nevertheless, it is difficult to make clear sense of the model of progression and continuity implied in the guidance the NLS offers. For example, it states that, in Year 7, pupils should 'extend their spoken repertoire by experimenting with language in different roles and dramatic contexts' (p. 25), but there are no references to language repertoire in the National Curriculum drama objectives or in the NLS teaching objectives for Years 8 and 9. If we search other parts of the National Curriculum requirements for speaking and listening, there is, however, a related requirement for pupils to 'use gesture, tone, pace and rhetorical devices for emphasis'.

THE IDENTITY OF SCHOOL CURRICULUM DRAMA

Drama as a service subject for English

The facts noted above need to be seen in the context of long-term, ongoing debates about the identity of drama as a school curriculum subject and its strategic location in the National Curriculum. These debates are complex, but the most important considerations in them for you as a student teacher of English are as follows.

One kind of rationale for drama in the school curriculum is hinted at in the learning objectives concerned with the use of gesture, tone and pace, and the extension of a spoken repertoire noted above. It is based on recognition of the contribution that drama methods can make to the development of pupils' skills in each of speaking and listening, reading and drama. Drama's role in supporting speaking and listening has long been understood. For example, in *A Language for Life* (DES, 1975, p. 159) it is argued that: 'Drama . . . has the capacity for sensitizing the ear for appropriate registers and responses. It encourages linguistic adaptability, often accustoming the children to unfamiliar modes of language.' Pupils' engagement in the dramatisation of parts of literary texts, whether these are originally plays or not, is also known to help develop their reading responses, such as their ability to analyse plot and character. In a similar way, improvisation can provide a stimulus for writing which is powerful in its capacity to generate vocabulary for dialogue and ideas for narrative. The use of drama methods can also benefit pupils' work on the media. For example, pupils who are asked to use, in practical drama activities, the conventions of a media genre, such as soap opera, can develop insight into the important media education concept of representation. Recognition of these benefits justifies the incorporation of drama in English, which is where it is currently located in the National Curriculum. If, as it might appear, drama's role is in a service capacity, there is little need for reference to it in the National Curriculum Level Descriptions, which define important planned learning *outcomes* for English rather than the methods by which they are to be achieved.

Drama as an independent arts subject

While the rationale outlined above may explain the inclusion of drama *within* speaking and listening *within* English and the English Level Descriptions' curious silence on drama, the new National Curriculum requirements for drama are not those of a service subject. Instead, they reflect the progress of a long-term campaign for recognition of drama as a curriculum subject with its own integrity, and which may be defined as a discrete set of knowledge, concepts, skills and processes which have their own language.

This point may be illustrated through comparison of the *The National Curriculum for England: English* drama requirements with the content of the most comprehensive attempt that has yet been made to define a coherent National Curriculum for drama: *Drama in Schools: Arts Council Guidance on Drama Education*, published by the Arts Council in 1992. This document was originally produced because of the low status accorded to drama in the 1990 National Curriculum generally, and because of the very limited recognition of its possibilities in the first *English in the National Curriculum* (DES and Welsh Office, 1990).

The guidance acknowledges that English departments carry much responsibility for drama teaching, and recognises that they often use drama primarily to promote language development and enhance literary analysis. However, it insists that effective drama teaching must draw attention to the special character of drama experiences and drama texts. For example, the guidance argues: 'Making and performing drama . . . is fundamental to drama in schools. . . . It is important that the study of plays as dramatic literature in English at the same time recognises their essential existence as pieces of live theatre' (Arts Council, 1992, paras 5, 8).

Most importantly, *Drama in Schools* proposes a National Curriculum for drama, centred, as is the English curriculum, on three core processes. The processes are all concerned primarily with developing pupils' knowledge and experience of the unique characteristics of drama:

> *Making* drama is the ability to generate and shape dramatic forms in order to explore and express ideas;
> *Performing* drama is the ability to engage and communicate with an audience in a dramatic presentation;
> *Responding* to drama is the ability to express understanding, discernment and appreciation of drama in all its forms.
>
> (Arts Council, 1992, para. 8)

These processes are interpreted in programmes of study for each Key Stage. At Key Stage 3:

Pupils should be taught to:
- Use increasingly complex drama styles and conventions;
- Respond constructively to direction given by other pupils;
- Use a variety of technical effects;
- Devise and perform plays in different styles;
- Edit and refine their work in the light of constructive criticism;
- Develop voice and movement skills, including mime;
- Understand drama from different cultures and times;
- Analyse and evaluate performances with an understanding of style and purpose.

Pupils should be given opportunities to:
- Develop themes from other curriculum areas in drama;
- Read and perform plays from different cultures and times;
- Take part in plays as actors or technicians;
- Learn how drama has developed through the ages;
- See a range of professional performances;
- Evaluate performances using appropriate specialist vocabulary.

(Arts Council, 1992, para. 20)

This programme of study affirms: that drama has its own skills, conventions and language; that, as a creative art, it stimulates the development of personal, social, cultural and aesthetic understandings which are vital to the well-being of a mature individual; that it makes reference to an historically rich and culturally diverse body of texts and practices; and that its explorations require access to appropriate working spaces and technical resources, such as studios equipped with stage lighting. The programme of study also implies that progression and continuity will be most sustained when substantial dedicated curriculum time and resources are available.

To sum up the discussion so far, the current National Curriculum largely *locates* drama within speaking and listening as a service subject for English, but *defines* its requirements as those of a discrete arts subject.

Task 10.1 Progression in drama

Working in a small group, imagine you have been asked to define a drama syllabus for Key Stage 3 which reflects National Curriculum and NLS expectations, and the vision of the Arts Council curriculum. With reference to the drama teaching objectives in the NLS *Framework for Teaching English: Years 7, 8 and 9* (pp. 25, 29 and 32), the current National Curriculum requirements for drama, and the Arts Council programme of study for Key Stage 3 quoted in this chapter, draw up a progression statement identifying what your learning objectives will be for each of Years 7, 8 and 9. Compare and contrast your statement with one produced by another group of student teachers.

THE CHARACTER OF DRAMA IN SCHOOLS

It is important for you to understand that within current national requirements different interpretations of the educational purposes of drama are possible, because you will find these differences reflected in practice in schools.

Many drama activities can be interpreted so that emphasis is placed either on their function in developing language or on the possibilities of drama as an art form. For example, one teacher might describe 'role-play' as an activity in which pupils adopt the attitudes of people with particular roles in society, to consider topics and issues from a number of different perspectives. She might point to the example of some Year 10 pupils who are discussing the rail transportation of nuclear waste. They are working in pairs sitting at their desks with cue cards which describe respectively some of the viewpoints of a Greenpeace activist and a spokesperson for British Nuclear Fuels, and arguing with each other in these roles. The planned outcome is a piece of persuasive writing, such as a pamphlet to be distributed to members of the public.

Another teacher might describe role-play as an activity in which pupils explore the tensions between personal identity and public roles through the processes of experimental drama. She might point to the example of Year 7 pupils engaged in a whole class spontaneous improvisation of a sea voyage in which the vessel is about to be wrecked and there are a limited number of lifeboats. The pupils are exploring roles such as those of captain, ship's cook and child passenger. Within limits imposed by their roles, each pupil is interacting with many other members of the group. This work may lead to the development of a polished improvisation for presentation to another class, in which costume, props and lighting would be used, but it is also possible that the teacher's objectives for the class will be met entirely through the improvisation.

Moreover, some schools have views of drama which have little to do with language development or drama as an art form. Some other perceptions of drama you may encounter are as follows.

A school with an 'adult needs' view of drama will tend to justify the drama curriculum in terms of its development of skills which are transferable to the world of work. As *English for Ages 5 to 16* (DES and Welsh Office, 1989, 8.13) put it: 'Drama provides a discipline for the development of co-ordination, concentration, commitment, organisation and decision-making that depends upon self and group awareness, observation, imagination and co-operation.' Very many teachers see drama's development of these skills as of at least equal importance to its role in developing language or aesthetic understanding.

In a school with a 'cross-curricular' view of drama, teachers in a range of subjects may use role-play and other activities to support subject learning, and/or to explore moral, personal and social issues. Pupils may make frequent use of drama in activities such as year group assemblies. In a school with an integrated arts policy, drama may be incorporated into the curriculum time made available for 'expressive arts' or 'performing arts', and pupils may be particularly confident about creating multi-discipline art events. A school or individual teacher's rationale for drama, especially as this is represented by the previous experiences of pupils and the resources available, must guide the direction of the drama teaching which a student teacher initially attempts with any particular class. Teaching methods and learning objectives will need to build from those with which the pupils are familiar, and differences introduced

---

Task 10.2 A rationale for drama

Establish what kind of rationale underpins the teaching of drama in your placement school. Watch some drama lessons and use the questions which follow as a starting point in your discussions with teachers.

- Is there a scheme of work for drama at Key Stage 3 either within the English department or across the curriculum?
- Is drama taught as a separate subject, as part of an integrated arts programme, or within English?
- Are drama methods used by teachers across the curriculum?
- What resources and how much curriculum time are available for drama?
- What examination courses in drama are available to pupils?
- Are there regular school drama events, and if so, are these, for example, 'cultural heritage' school plays presented by elite casts, or experimental works and festivals involving large numbers of pupils across the age and ability range?

gradually, especially with older pupils. For this reason, you should start your work on drama in your placement school by identifying the rationale for drama that operates there.

The integration of drama and English

A long-term aim for drama *within* English at Key Stage 3 for any class may be what could be called 'integrated practice'. The identification of drama requirements in *The National Curriculum for England: English* which do not merely service English is encouraging teachers to find ways of achieving this. The identification of a more coherent drama progression statement in the NLS, and the definition of drama-specific outcomes in revised National Curriculum Level Descriptions would help to promote this work, although, of course, some drama teachers would prefer the subject to have its own, entirely separate National Curriculum at Key Stage 3, reflecting its independent existence at Key Stages 4 and 5.

In integrated practice, the skills, knowledge and processes of drama are developed *together with* the core processes of English in dynamic learning experiences. Where this integration is achieved, pupils who are habitually making, presenting, remaking and responding to texts, in the form of English which is defined as critical literacy in Chapter 1 of this book, will also be making, performing and responding to drama. They will be using drama as a resource to develop a wide range of speaking and listening skills, but also using English as a resource to develop a wide range of drama skills.

Much of the rest of this book is concerned with the contribution which different aspects of English teaching could make to such integrated practice. The rest of this chapter provides an introduction to the classroom environment and atmosphere, teaching strategies and lesson structures which can help to make possible the making, performing and responding activities and culture which drama can contribute to such integrated practice at Key Stage 3. For drama to make this rich contribution, teachers need to cultivate what may be called 'risk-taking' drama.

WORKING CONDITIONS FOR RISK-TAKING DRAMA

Anyone who makes a dramatic gesture takes a risk. The risk involves a person in exposing part of his or her understanding of and response to something, and in exploring or projecting this, with commitment, through an act of pretence. This act makes the actor extremely vulnerable to the responses of others, who, whether participants in the drama or observers of it, may reject what is offered because of what they consider to be poor understanding, poor projection or both. However, risk-taking is essential to any kind of educational drama which is not going to settle for superficial work such as the endless re-presentation of tired stereotypes in unchallenging exercises. All drama lessons should be planned to support the risk-taking that is expected of pupils. Some of the practical considerations which need to be taken into account to make risk-taking drama possible are as follows.

The classroom and resources

In a well-equipped drama studio, stage lighting, costume, props and stage blocks may be used to create the atmosphere of many different locations and so support pupils who are being asked to risk behaving other than as themselves in some other world than their own. These resources can and should be used to support drama development processes, as well as to contribute to the multi-sensory impact of performance work. In an ordinary classroom it is usually possible at least to create an open working space by placing the desks against the four walls with the chairs in front of them, so making an inward-facing rectangle. In these more difficult conditions it is all the more important for the teacher to provide video clips, pictures, music, artefacts, documents or indications of costume, such as hats, to help create the idea of the drama.

Such strategies can compensate meaningfully for the lack of more substantial resources. However, this is not to say that drama teachers should ever simply make do with poor accommodation. There are a number of severely limiting problems teachers may encounter using ordinary classrooms for drama, including: insufficient space for movement, or for groups to work far enough apart to hear themselves; a 'fish-bowl' effect during the presentation and sharing of work which may inhibit performers who have the sense of a large, very close audience. For these reasons, it is always important to make a case for the best room available, even if this is only the largest room in the English department suite.

Expectations and signals

Pupils gain confidence from knowing how their risk-taking will be supported by the teacher and the group. Expectations need to be discussed and sometimes negotiated openly, with their purposes being made explicit, although they need not all be introduced to a class new to drama at once. One important expectation is that all pupils in a group will be prepared to work with everyone else. This can usually be achieved with a new class if pupils have plenty of experience of changing partners and groups frequently for several lessons so that mutual trust is established before the expectation is explicitly defined. Another vital expectation is that pupils will respect each other's work when it is shared, both by listening and watching attentively and by offering constructive criticism when appropriate. It is important for teachers to ensure that sharing serves a useful purpose in the development of the whole group's work, so that attentiveness is encouraged, and that their own observations about shared work build from the identification of praiseworthy features. It is rarely useful to share all the work produced in a lesson: this can be repetitive and always counteracts momentum, so another expectation should be that all pupils will get opportunities to share their work, but on a longer time-scale.

A clear set of signals for controlling the lesson and moving the drama on also contributes to the confidence necessary for risk-taking. Signals help the teacher to maintain pupil concentration by allowing rapid movement from one activity to another. This avoids lengthy, disruptive delays in which concentration is broken while pupils work out that something new is expected of them. A signal for silence is vital: the word 'freeze' which means 'stop immediately and hold whatever position you are now in' is useful because it gives teachers a number of options for continuing the work. For example, short pieces of new information can be added before all the 'frozen' pupils are asked to carry on an improvisation at the point at which it left off. Alternatively, using the technique known as 'spotlighting', one group can be asked to carry on its improvisation while the rest of the class is invited to 'relax' and observe. 'Freeze' is valuable because it is more than a control word: it can be used to introduce pupils to the idea of the 'freeze frame', 'still photograph' or 'statue' which has many applications in drama. These include the identification of key moments in scenes, and the examination of the physical representation of the relationships between characters in a drama.

Drama routines

In general, the human capacity for risk-taking is enhanced when we have a strong sense of security. In drama, routines can make a powerful contribution to the establishment of a sense of security, as well as developing concentration through each pupil's association of a particular set of repeated actions with drama lessons. We must always remember that the expectations of drama are usually very different from those of the lesson pupils have just come from; drama routines help them to make the adjustment. For example, many teachers like to begin and end drama lessons with pupils sitting in a circle. Circles are useful for the democratic sharing of ideas: every member of the group can see and hear all the others, and everyone is in the front row. A number of warm-up activities and drama games use circles, which means that it is very easy to make transitions from discussion to activity. A circle can also provide a focused acting space. One use of it in the development of pupils' confidence about sharing work involves devising a flexible drama situation, set perhaps in a public space, which different characters can easily enter and leave. A rule is established that only three members of the class can be inside the circle at any one time, but with this constraint, pupils are allowed to enter or leave the circle at any time.

Group dynamics and the difficulty of the work

Although it is important for pupils to learn to work flexibly with all other members of the group, it is also important for the teacher to recognise that some of the confidence necessary to risk-taking comes from a person's trust in his or her working partners and audience, and that this will be affected by the difficulty and sensitivity of the work. For some activities it will be appropriate for pupils to work individually, following guidance or instructions from the teacher: for example, pupils who are unused to mime might follow a sequence of actions 'narrated' by the teacher, and concentrate more effectively without the self-consciousness which may be induced by apparently having an audience. Friendship pairs and small groups also provide pupils with security, and it can be a very big developmental step for some pupils to change to working in random groups or to kinds of drama which involve interacting with the whole class, at least for activities which are sustained for any length of time. Similarly, there is a big step for some pupils between, say, showing their pair work to another pair of pupils and being able to present it to the whole class.

Sharing and reflection

Regularly stepping out of a situation in order to evaluate its progress and direction is another means by which human beings can develop the sense of security they need to be able to take risks within that situation. Some of the most valuable techniques for sharing and reflection in drama teaching provide security by generating ideas for the next stage of the development of the work. For example, 'hotseating', a technique in which actors are interviewed in role about their characters' motivation, intentions and relationships, provides a form of reflection on the drama which an actor can use to develop greater subtlety of characterisation.

Task 10.3 Observing drama strategies

Observe some drama lessons and note how the teacher uses the classroom, resources, expectations, signals, drama routines, pupil groups, sharing and reflection to provide the foundations for risk-taking drama. After a lesson, ask the teacher to discuss with you the reasons behind the strategies you have observed.

The next section of this chapter is concerned with some of the working methods available to drama teachers. Rather than attempting to provide a handbook or index of working methods, it aims to consider some of the issues involved in choosing to use methods which appear to be concerned primarily either with developing drama techniques or with engaging pupils in making meaning through drama. Games, movement and mime exercises are discussed as an example of the former, and improvisation as an example of the latter.

DRAMA GAMES

If risk-taking drama is dependent on security, that security is partly dependent on trusting others. A Year 7 pupil who mimes passing a cup of tea to his or her partner trusts in that partner's acceptance of the dramatic gesture which has been made, and on the concentration which has made possible its recognition. Trust is partly about being able to take the risk of pretence with confidence in the capacity of others to concentrate and accept the pretence for what it is. Concentration depends on sensory alertness and attention, watching what other actors do, and listening to what they say. Acceptance makes the continuation of the drama possible.

Writers on drama games frequently make use of at least part of the argument of the last paragraph, maintaining that games contribute to the development of some of the essential drama skills of looking, listening, trust, attention and concentration. In her book *Drama Guidelines* (1977), Cecily O'Neill points out some other benefits: 'many games provide secure frameworks within which communication can easily be established. They are also a means of releasing tension, giving enjoyment, establishing relationships, and increasing the group's level of self-control.' However, when making use of games there are two very important considerations: the first concerns the appropriateness of the games chosen; the second the relationship between the games and the rest of the drama work.

Clive Barker's book *Theatre Games* (1977) provides a thorough and convincing rationale for the use of games in drama, and includes much useful discussion about the purposes of different games and their influence on the work of a drama group. He stresses the need for the teacher or leader to choose games which match the developmental level of the group. This is important not least because some trust exercises in particular could be very dangerous if attempted by pupils with poor concentration. For example, a number of exercises require pupils to support each other physically or take responsibility for the safety of blindfolded partners. When leading a partner as a school pupil myself, I completely forgot he was blindfolded and walked him into a brick wall, with rather bloody results!

The games which contribute most to learning will often be linked by the teacher to the topic of the drama lesson or scheme of work. One example from my own practice occurred when I made use of a simple cat-and-mouse game to develop some movement ideas for work on the story of *Theseus and the Minotaur* with some Year 7 pupils. In the game, the class forms a grid, and individual pupils join hands to form rows or columns, alternating on the instruction 'change', while one pupil as cat pursues another as mouse through the grid. The game clearly develops listening, watching and concentration skills. Playing it in slow motion and talking about how it works suggested how the class could work on using bodies to represent the Minotaur's labyrinth, and exposed some of the central themes of the story for them: power, fear, frustration, the subconscious, brain against brawn. You may now wish to plan a drama lesson in which you use games or exercises to introduce a topic in such a way that the games establish, develop or extend learning which is integral to your teaching and learning objectives.

MOVEMENT AND MIME EXERCISES

Movement and mime exercises can help pupils to develop an awareness of the physical resources available to them, and also provide them with a drama vocabulary to describe the quality of particular effects they have observed or are attempting to achieve. Progression can be achieved through the experience of increasingly subtle and complex exercises, but movement work, like games, is enriched by opportunities to make meanings.

Many teachers make use of a technical vocabulary to describe physical positions, which has as its starting point the word 'freeze' discussed above. When half a class is 'frozen', the others can be invited to describe the physical positions which their classmates have taken up, and the value of some shared terminology soon becomes apparent. A basic vocabulary might describe a physical position using the term 'level'. In a 'high-level' freeze, part of the body will be in a position above head height; in a 'middle-level' freeze, the most expressive part of the body will be between standing head height and standing waist height; in a 'low-level' freeze, most of the body will be in a position below standing waist height.

If we want to progress from describing physical positions to movements, Bronwen Nicholls demonstrates in *Move* (1974) how pupils can be equipped with an increasingly sophisticated vocabulary. With an inexperienced class, you might begin by defining the pace and quality of movement respectively as 'fast' or 'slow' and 'smooth' or 'jerky'. This already creates the combinations 'fast and jerky', 'fast and smooth', 'slow and jerky' and 'slow and smooth' and opens up the possibility of describing movements along two continuums (Nicholls, 1974, pp. 10, 30).

With a more experienced class it is possible to suggest an extended vocabulary for describing quality of movement, such as part of the Laban analysis (see Figure 10.1).

It is possible to devise sequences of activities which explore quality of movement in a manner which is abstracted from any dramatic context, which makes use of pupils' interest in exploring space and in comparing and contrasting ways of using their bodies to achieve different kinds of dramatic effect. However, many pupils would benefit more from exploring fewer categories of movement in ways which related them to the exploration of a dramatic theme. For example, a gliding movement could be developed in an exercise centred on the experience of weightlessness, as part of the preparation for improvisation work on space voyages. Thus a technical vocabulary for an aspect of drama can be a source of ideas for teaching, even when not all of this language is shared with pupils.

Work on mime can lead to further progression in pupils' use of movement because it extends the range of dramatic gestures which it is possible to make using the body alone. Mime can provide a useful means of developing the physicality of any drama work,

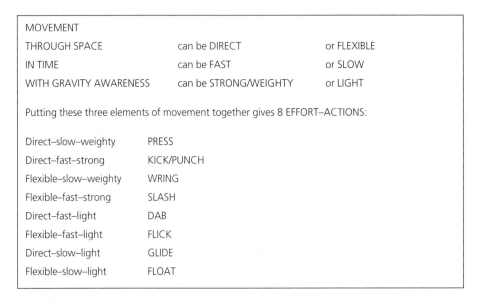

Figure 10.1 Qualities of movement (adapted from Laban, 1948)

especially with pupils whose previous drama experience has focused on the verbal. Pupils with limited experience of movement work will sometimes show this by taking chairs with them and conducting any task they possibly can sitting down. When asked to develop a mime, they may also respond by miming a conversation. You might consider doing some work on mime with a class you observe behaving in this way.

Some books on educational drama argue that mime is limited in its capacity for character development and draws pupils towards atrocious stereotyping, and it is true that the knees-bending policeman is not dead. However, miming social experiences which already have powerful physical dimensions or ritualistic elements, such as home decorating, discos and weddings, can teach pupils to express the relationships between different characters and to develop narrative direction using an entirely physical language.

There is a technical vocabulary for mime which teachers can use, and will teach pupils to help them describe their work. Some key terms are defined by Kay Hamblin in *Mime* (1978), a book which is careful to present exercises in which technical understanding is developed in contexts which make use of imagined situations. Some examples include: 'snap', a sudden precise movement with a clear start and finish; 'neutral', a balanced position from which movements originate; and 'mask', a face which can be 'snapped into' from neutral. All these concepts and techniques can also be incorporated into forms of drama in which speech and props are used.

Isolating different aspects of technique in drama can give pupils more control of later work in which they have more freedom and choice, because it gives them a repertoire of techniques to choose from. However, work on technique is likely to be most effective when it makes use of situations in which pupils can begin to make meaning. The next time you take drama, devise a lesson in which you incorporate some work which deliberately focuses on technique and extends pupils' vocabulary for talking about drama, but which also enables them to use the newly learned technique to make meaning.

IMPROVISATION

In contrast to drama games or movement and mime work, improvisation seems to be much more directly concerned with making meaning. Many drama teachers place improvisation at the heart of their practice for reasons which are closely linked to this. Improvisation is seen as fundamentally democratic, because it involves pupils in developing and using a range of negotiation and co-operation skills. It is also seen as empowering because it allows pupils to focus on the exploration and communication of their own ideas, by freeing them from subjection to the constraints involved in responding to texts or developing particular formal techniques.

However, these freedoms are dependent on the teacher providing strong support for the work. The key tasks of the teacher are: to provide pupils with a structure which supports the processes of negotiation and experimentation through which progress is made; to direct pupils to stimulating topics and ideas for exploration through their drama; to guide the development of the work as drama by alerting pupils to techniques they can make use of, and forms they can adopt and adapt.

When planning improvisation lessons, a key decision the teacher needs to make concerns the extent to which the work will be based on contexts which are familiar to the pupils. Pupils' own personal, social and cultural experiences are one very important source of ideas, not least because accessing these immediately gives them the role of experts and considerable control over the direction and outcome of the work. There are many methods whereby teachers may help pupils to access these experiences, including discussion and writing tasks which stimulate memory, as well as through work which is more directly dramatic in character, such as bringing to life a real or imaginary photograph. Drama will nearly always require pupils to interpret even their most familiar experience in new ways, because the act of dramatisation will make them focus on the experience of characters other than themselves. However, pupils can be challenged to build the unfamiliar out of the familiar in numerous other ways. For example, known fictional characters may be placed in new situations, or drama may explore gaps in texts to account for what happens between two appearances of a character in a play. A further step is to create drama from situations which make few references to what pupils already know, using historical events, situations from different cultures or pure fantasy. The further the work moves in this direction the more the teacher will have to do to provide contextualising information or some resources in which pupils can find it.

A second responsibility of the teacher is to provide guidance on the shaping of the drama. Such guidance may include some specific work on matters of technique which are important in all dramatic forms, for example: effective beginnings and endings; establishing the motivation for movement which takes place in the drama and communicating its meaning to an audience; making entrances and exits dramatically effective. It may also include work on the many dramatic forms and conventions pupils can adopt other than soap opera realism. For example, pupils working on comic plays could be introduced to some of the conventions of Shakespearean comedy, such as overhearings, disguise, confusions of identity, misplaced letters and malapropisms.

It will sometimes be more appropriate to focus work on character development rather than on dramatic structure. Security and confidence in character building can be supported by the use of role-play exercises which establish attributes, qualities or habits in structured contexts. For example, in improvised interviews pupils can experiment with the need for a character to speak and behave in a manner which is appropriate to the situation and yet 'in character'. The discoveries which are made can be fed into work which places the character in less structured situations. Another method of developing character is based on work on 'stock characters'. These may be contemporary stereotypes, which are often introduced by classes to their drama lessons, but there is value in exploring the stock characters of other historical periods and theatre styles such as Restoration comedy, and *commedia dell'arte*. When the typical behaviour of the stock characters has been explored by pupils, character can be enriched by the addition of information which undermines stereotyping: for example, the pupil working on the role of an aggressively dressing teenager is told the character spends his weekends looking after his grandmother. Work on movement of the kind described above can be used to help pupils make choices about the physical presence of characters. Similarly, the power of props and clothing in helping to establish characters physically should not be overlooked: these items are sometimes only added to enhance performance, and may well fail to do so if actors have not become accustomed to working with them.

Spontaneous and prepared improvisation

Many teachers include opportunities for pupils to engage in both spontaneous and prepared improvisation work at different times in the course of a sequence of lessons. It is important to be clear about the opportunities and limitations of each method in relation to the development of the drama work of a class.

In some definitions of spontaneous improvisation, only work in which the teacher calls for an immediate response to a stimulus is included. However, other practitioners would extend the definition to include group work with limited preparation time. This would be a few minutes to establish some ideas about the location, characters who will be needed, and the order in which they will arrive, so that the drama can establish itself without too many people trying to define its direction at once.

In all cases, spontaneous improvisation work is concerned with the processes of interaction achieved by members of the group. In particular, pupils need to learn 'acceptance skills', namely willingness to perceive and respond appropriately and creatively to the ideas of others. This willingness contributes to the seeking of 'slow solutions', the ability to continue dramatic situations long enough to explore the ideas and feelings they contain, and often, also, long enough to avoid heightening confrontation in the drama without adequate preparation. Good spontaneous improvisation experiences which make use of these skills will encourage pupils to explore their ideas for prepared improvisation by acting them out, rather than through discussion.

Prepared improvisation challenges participants to develop their understanding of the situation the drama is concerned with by giving it dramatic form and structure. This involves them in making use of their imagination, their understanding of dramatic shape, and in working collectively to develop character, perhaps using some of the methods indicated above, as well as discussion, research and spontaneous improvisation. Very often success is dependent on the teacher providing an appropriate balance of choice and constraint in relation to both form and content: pupils can be overwhelmed by excessive choice and frustrated by too closely defined tasks. Prepared improvisation work can be extended to incorporate the development and appropriate use of presentation skills, which will need initially to be defined for pupils. Effective communication with the audience, by means ranging from audible speech to appropriate costumes and set for a rehearsed improvised play, should be gradually developed, and represented in the assessment criteria for the work at a corresponding rate.

Opportunities for discussion and reflection need to be built into the development of the work. Group members need to feel strong commitment to the work, not least because there is often a period of difficulty between the establishment of a group's perception of the dramatic potential of an idea they are working on and the emergence of confidence about its realisation. Pupils will sometimes press to start on a new idea when they reach a difficulty which blocks the development of the work. The teacher's job is often to suggest techniques and methods, such as some of those for exploring structure or character described above, to help move the drama on, if there appears to be a shortage of ideas. If groups have too many different ideas, and are unable to make decisions for this reason, it can be helpful to provide them with a sequence of limited tasks which will allow a number of options to be attempted before a decision is made. Since work on prepared improvisation often spreads over a number of lessons, teachers need to be prepared to help groups to continue their work when members are absent, by identifying ways of moving forward which the group sees as appropriate.

This section of the chapter has suggested that just as games, movement and other work which obviously focuses on technique should be adapted into meaning-making activities, so meaning-making activities such as improvisation need the support of some explicit work developing both pupils' repertoire of dramatic technique and their collaborative working skills.

Task 10.4 Researching drama methods

Research a range of drama teaching methods in the books listed under Further reading at the end of this chapter. Consider how much emphasis there is on developing technique and the making of meaning in the methods you read about. Design and teach some lessons in which you offer pupils an appropriate sequence of work combining the development of technique and opportunities to use drama to make meaning.

WORKING WITH TEXTS

It is important to approach work on drama texts with the understanding that playwrights expect their work to be interpreted by a group of actors in a production. Most play scripts concentrate on the words which are to be spoken, but it is understood that actors will supply the movement, gesture and intonation which will communicate an interpretation of the script. Actors develop this interpretation through rehearsal methods. When working with plays in school, it follows that it is very beneficial for pupils to explore texts in ways similar to those used by actors. Although there are clearly other ways of working productively with play texts, experiences which reinforce pupils' perception of them as drama are essential. National assessments including the Key Stage 3 SATs and GCSE English literature examinations increasingly ask questions which reflect an expectation that plays will be studied in this way.

Exploring character

Many actors work by trying to develop a coherent (or incoherent and paradoxical) characterisation from the fragmentary information presented in a drama text. This involves asking questions about what happens to the character during off-stage periods, and sometimes in extending this way of thinking by considering everything that has happened before the character first appears on stage. This work requires an actor to make use of clues about characters in the text, including its margins and omissions, and to develop his or her thinking about these clues by making reference to research, his or her own life experience, and other resources. This thinking is brought to bear on the improvisation of events such as those which are only referred to in the text, or which will enable the actors to explore relationships which are only briefly represented in it. It can also be useful to make use of techniques which help an actor to see a character objectively or through the eyes of other characters in the drama, for example, by exchanging roles temporarily, or describing the character's thoughts, feelings and motivation at particular points in the action in the third person. These activities, which develop forms of empathetic and analytical understanding of character, are related respectively to the dramatic theories of Stanislavski and Brecht, and are as useful in preparing pupils to write empathetic and analytical essays as they are in rehearsing a stage performance.

Exploring contexts

It is useful to research the societies and cultures in which a play is set. This research may involve referring to historical and sociological texts, but drama methods may be used to make the full significance of the information which is discovered clear. Improvisation can explore the daily lives of the characters in a play which is being studied, outside of the situation with which it is primarily concerned, or, in other words, it can establish what the 'normality' is from which the events in the play dramatically deviate. A closer focus can be established by working on off-stage events, both those which are reported in the text and those which are implied, by, for example, the opening lines of scenes which show that the text joins conversations and events after they have begun. Improvisation work exploring these events can explore questions about the reliability of the reporters who describe events, and what the dramatist has found is most important to represent.

Exploring the languages of drama

One way of making connections between the idea of drama as a specialised kind of language study and the idea of drama as a performance art is to search the verbal language of a text for ideas and images which can be translated into the language of theatrical performance. For example, the imagery of clothing and blood in *Macbeth* can be re-presented through design ideas for set, costume and lighting. Rehearsal methods and the process of putting on a production of a play or part of a play may be the best way of exploring such relationships between text and performance, but there are many aspects of this process which can be isolated in classroom work, including the design and preparation of posters and programmes, producing designs for set, costumes or lighting, producing the director's staging notes, finding or producing music and sound-effects for particular scenes, tape recording readings of scenes, creating tableaux, working on choric readings of soliloquies, or improvising key situations from the play having transferred them to different contexts.

Task 10.5 Director's notes

Working either individually on paper or using rehearsal methods in a group, produce director's notes on a scene from a play which you plan to teach in school. Cover as many aspects of production as you can, including instructions for the actors, costume and lighting notes. Use your notes as a source of ideas for the lesson or sequence of lessons in which you will teach the scene.

WORKING METHODS IN DRAMA TEACHING

Drama teachers can choose the methods and combinations of methods they use from a wide range of possibilities. If you watch a number of different drama teachers you will see how the repertoire of methods they use contributes to their personal teaching style. There is only scope in this chapter to consider two of the many areas where choice is available: methods of introducing the drama, and methods of supporting the development of the drama.

Story-telling and the provision of focusing material are two methods which may be used to provide an initial stimulus for drama which can give pupils varying degrees of control and responsibility for the development of the work. For example, very controlled individual work can be achieved if the teacher tells a story which pupils 'follow' through solo mime. Alternatively, the teacher can pass control gradually to groups of pupils by telling them part of a story, allowing them to improvise the next stage and report what happened to the whole class. The discussion may be used to generate ideas for the further development of the work. Providing focusing material is one strategy for giving some narrative guidance while allowing pupils to construct their own story. For example, a map of a journey to an interesting destination such as a treasure island could be 'found' in the classroom along with a manual describing the crew needed to sail the *Hispaniola*. This method could stimulate the development of a whole class improvisation.

If we consider how the teacher might support the development of an improvisation of this kind, again a range of methods is available. One method would be to start by supporting groups of characters in developing their sense of what their role in the drama will be. For example, groups of ships' officers, crew and passengers would work separately on matters such as their reasons for being on the voyage, their living conditions, and their interactions with members of other groups. Discussion, writing, drawing, items of clothing, pictures, and/or research information from books and other stimuli could be used to help each group develop its idea of itself. The role of the teacher, once the improvisation began, would be that of an observer who is able to steer the drama from the outside, by occasionally stopping it and holding discussions.

It would be possible for this role to be disguised as that of the ship's chronicler, who needs to find out information for his or her reports. This method of involving the teacher in the drama is known as 'teacher in role'. It would be possible to develop the same kind of improvisation entirely by using the 'teacher-in-role' method, if, for example, the teacher took the role of ship's captain and explained what the rules of the ship are for officers, crew and passengers rather than allowing groups to work this out by the method described above. This role would also make it easy for the teacher to intervene by, for example, calling for 'all hands on deck' when the drama needed a steer. When pupils are used to 'teacher-in-role' methods of working, it is possible for the teacher to take less powerful roles and so give the pupils more autonomy. The role of information provider, in this case of ship's navigator, for example, would allow the teacher to give the drama some structure without appearing to make decisions. The role of an apparently powerless person such as a very sick passenger could also be used with an experienced class, because the pupils would recognise that they were required to make decisions which would affect this character's situation.

All these variations of the development of the work give pupils different degrees of control and are related to different expectations of them. It is important for the rules of different working methods to be made explicit to pupils when they are introduced, so that the number of drama 'genres' in which they can work confidently is gradually extended. When using a drama method which is unfamiliar, it will often take time for the whole class to become committed to the work, and some pupils may be very slow to become involved. Some pupils may challenge the drama. The teacher's awareness of this will affect such things as the number of times the work is interrupted for the purposes of discussion and the provision of additional stimuli and ideas. It is also helpful if the teacher is prepared to accept and put to positive use remarks and contributions which do not take the drama seriously. This sense of commitment and seriousness helps to give whole class work momentum in the early stages. It may involve the acceptance of ideas from pupils which take the work in unexpected directions, or which are based on a misunderstanding of factual matters which needs to be corrected later.

Of course, it is possible for whole-class work to combine the strategies described here, and to link them with others. This flexibility allows a teacher working with an experienced class to focus on particular aspects of a story in detail, and to represent others more economically: for example, a series of group photographs could represent a long sea journey where the drama is concerned primarily with events on arrival at a destination, such as discovering the treasure.

STRUCTURING DRAMA LESSONS

When beginning to plan drama lessons, you may find it helpful to adopt the following outline structure:

1   Teacher-centred activity with the whole class working together as individuals
     reflection/discussion
2   A series of activities in pairs (activities make increasing demands)
     reflection/discussion
3   A series of activities in small groups (activities make increasing demands)
     reflection/discussion
4   An activity with the whole class/large groups working together
     reflection/discussion.

This sequence could take place in a double lesson, but it may take months to progress from stage 1 to stage 4 with some classes. Of course, some lessons will omit some of the stages suggested here, and, as your confidence and skills develop, you are likely to want to try other approaches.

Examples

1   *Teacher-centred activity with whole class working together or as individuals*: teacher in role introduces topic of drama; teacher organises drama games related to topic; teacher tells a story or uses artefact as stimulus (e.g. photographs, music, costume, document); teacher leads individual mime or acting sequence; teacher leads improvisation work in circle.
2   *A series of activities in pairs (activities make increasing demands)*: students work with friends, teacher supplies detailed ideas, closed familiar situations and roles *at first*; improvisation work preceded by lengthy discussion, or, for example, the use of a piece of drama text or video.
3   *A series of activities in small groups (activities make increasing demands)*: for example, students work in random mixed groups, teacher supplies limited stimulus; open, unfamiliar situations and roles *later*.
4   *An activity with whole class/large groups working together*: teacher in role (later a supportive rather than dominant role) establishes situation and provides structure for groups to see the need for interaction with other groups in the drama.
5   *Reflection/discussion stages*: teacher/pupils interview others in role (hotseating); after sharing or spotlighting of work of several groups with same task, pupils discuss what it felt like to play certain roles; pupils keep journal of drama experiences or write letters following up improvised events.

SUMMARY AND KEY POINTS

Many drama activities may be interpreted so that emphasis is placed either on their function in developing language or on the possibilities of drama as an art form. The programme of study for drama in *The National Curriculum for England: English* (DfEE/QCA, 1999b) challenges teachers to teach drama in a way which addresses its own discrete learning objectives. 'Integrated practice' can bring English and drama learning objectives into alignment by focusing on the opportunities for making, presenting and responding which are common to both. Within your placement school and in your future department, you should develop a clear understanding of the rationale which underpins the use of drama. Similarly, you should develop a realistic sense of the constraints and possibilities for drama work within the particular context in which you are working. In order to enable your pupils to develop their creativity, imagination and language skills in either spoken or written form, you should look for opportunities to include drama as part of your teaching.

FURTHER READING

Arts Council (1992) *Drama in Schools: Arts Council Guidance on Drama Education*, London: Arts Council.

Barker, C. (1977) *Theatre Games*, London: Methuen.

Bolton, G. (1992) *New Perspectives on Classroom Drama*, New York: Simon & Schuster.

Bolton, G. (1998) *Acting in Classroom Drama*, Stoke on Trent: Trentham.

Burgess, R. and Gaudry, P. (1985) *Time for Drama*, Buckingham: Open University Press.

Byron, K. (1986) *Drama in the English Classroom*, London: Methuen.

Fleming, M. (1994) *Starting Drama Teaching*, London: David Fulton.

Hamblin, K. (1978) *Mime*, London: Lutterworth.

Hodgson, J. and Richards, E. (1974) *Improvisation*, London: Methuen.

Laban, R. (1948) *Modern Educational Dance*, London: Macdonald & Evans.

NATE (1993) *Move Back the Desks*, Sheffield: NATE.

Neelands, J. (1984) *Making Sense of Drama*, London: Heinemann.

Neelands, J. (1992) *Learning Through Imagined Experience*, London: Hodder & Stoughton.

Neelands, J. (1993) *Structuring Drama Work*, London: Cambridge University Press.

Neelands, J. (1998) *Beginning Drama 11–14*, London: David Fulton.

Nicholls, B. (1974) *Move*, London: Heinemann.

O'Neill, C. (1977) *Drama Guidelines*, London: Heinemann.

Rawlins, G. and Rich, J. (1985) *Look, Listen and Trust*, London: Macmillan Education.

Woolland, B. (1993) *The Teaching of Drama in the Primary School*, London: Longman.

11 Approaching Shakespeare

Jane Dowson and Jo Westbrook

INTRODUCTION

Shakespeare is prescribed reading at Key Stages 3 and 4 and on GCE AS/A2 level syllabuses. Approaching the Shakespeare play therefore provides a means of considering continuity and progression throughout the secondary English curriculum. The approaches to reading and responding to Shakespeare discussed here may, of course, be applied to any text. The compulsory study of Shakespeare also crystallises many of the debates within teaching English, such as: the need to balance an English literary heritage and skills model of English teaching with a cultural analysis model which includes texts from different cultures and traditions and media texts, as reflected in *The National Curriculum for England* (DfEE/QCA, 1999) (see Chapter 2); the contradiction of assessment by external examination at the end of Year 9 but assessed as coursework by the majority of examination boards at GCSE; the lists of pre-1914 prescribed texts in the National Curriculum. English teachers are conscious of the correlation between Shakespeare in school, particularly Shakespeare for examination, and a person's future relationship with Shakespeare. The significance of this relationship is that because Shakespeare continues to be used as an emblem of high culture and synonymously British cultural identity, a person's relationship with Shakespeare determines an individual's, and social or ethnic group's, *affection for* or *alienation from* British culture. Consequently, teachers find themselves torn between aiming for the greatest access to Shakespeare texts for all pupils and resisting the force-feeding of Shakespeare. The implications for a class-ridden pluralistic society are keen. As David Hornbook puts it:

> The unavoidable identification of Shakespeare with the examination system is seen as in itself alienating and prohibitive of creative growth.
> Furthermore, Shakespeare for most children is inescapably associated with social snobbery . . . outside the school, a routine dismissal of his plays as

part of an inaccessible middle-class ritual of 'theatre-going' further strengthens this sense of alienation.

(Hornbrook, 1988, p. 146)

Another tension for the teacher is the increasing gap between the cultural studies approach to English studies in higher education courses and the focus on what amounts to literary criticism (disguised sometimes in the SATS as giving director's notes for a 'performance') required for assessment in the school curriculum. Teachers are also sensitive to the implicit perception that by studying the same text at the same time young people will become dutiful citizens; the assumption goes like this: *force the same text on all children and we will once again become a unified society; give them Shakespeare, and children, like Caliban through learning Prospero's language, will become tame and subservient.* The paradox is that, on account of its demands in terms of language competence, maturity of experience and conceptual thinking, instead of becoming an instrument of social unity, the Shakespeare play is the means by which social divisions are endorsed, as registered in a tiered examination system where the Shakespeare play is often used to 'sort out' ability groupings. In order to dissociate Shakespeare from the exclusive world of adult upper- or middle-class theatre-goers, teachers need to bring the theatre into the classroom through drama activities and through pupils acting out parts of the plays themselves. These approaches help them to 'own' the plays, and by association the culture they represent, as well as to understand them.

OBJECTIVES

By the end of this chapter you should have:

- considered the attitude towards studying Shakespeare by pupils of different abilities and cultural identities;
- become familiar with the curriculum requirements for teaching Shakespeare at Key Stages 3 and 4 and GCE AS/A2 level;
- explored a range of strategies for teaching a Shakespeare text (and other texts) for coursework and for examination.

BACKGROUND TO THE TEACHING OF SHAKESPEARE IN SCHOOL

Before the 1988 Education Reform Act and the 1989 (Cox) *English in the National Curriculum*, the study of Shakespeare was not compulsory but was common practice in secondary schools and in some measure, albeit often in the form of an introduction to the theatre, life and works of Shakespeare, in primary schools. Changing selections of plays were set for GCE O and A level exams; the introduction of GCSE changed assessment to coursework and assessing Shakespeare by coursework also became common at A Level. Schools and teachers could choose the texts according to their enthusiasms, what was in the stock cupboard, which productions were on locally or being offered by Theatre in Education groups. The 1989 National Curriculum simply prescribed one Shakespeare play at KS3. Brian Cox envisaged that achievement would be measured by teacher assessment which would have allowed for the continuation of successful practices. These included a variety of 'ways in' to the plays, an emphasis on role-play, recreative work and thematic approaches. These were common starting points for study of the language and structure of the plays in coursework GCSE syllabuses and to some extent at A level.

The first Standard Assessment Tasks (SATs), however, introduced a controversial anthology with differentiated demands for each of three tiers of ability. One major difference between the bottom tier and the top two tiers was that the compulsory Shakespeare element was one speech – 'All the world's a stage' from *As You Like It* – whereas the other tiers could enjoy a whole play (but *As You Like It* was not prescribed so there was little chance of mixed-ability teaching). The tiered papers and rigid comprehension questions were severely criticised and teachers objected to the suggestion that Shakespeare was not deemed suitable for low attainers. These 1993 SATs were boycotted. Sir Ron Dearing's draft proposals for the revised Orders, however, maintained the tiered papers – reduced now to a standard and extension tier – and a compulsory Shakespeare text (Paper 2) but the plays were the same for all children: a choice of *Romeo and Juliet, A Midsummer Night's Dream* and *Julius Caesar*. The KS3 examination consisted of a choice of two predetermined scenes from each play with quite open questions about character, meaning and response. The assessment objectives also allocated marks for handwriting, spelling, grammar and style. The pressure to achieve good examination results because of reporting to parents and league tables enforced setting in many departments, so that pupils believed capable of the extension tier could be tutored for it. There was inevitably a self-fulfilling prophecy concerning achievement. In the national survey, *The Real Cost of SATs* (LATE, 1995), heads of English reporting on the SAT results in 1995 reflect that the Year 9 curriculum has become 'SAT driven' and dominated by the Shakespeare play. They tried to maintain good practice in teaching Shakespeare and resented reverting to the type of approach which is alienating – flogging one prescribed scene of one prescribed play – and to using the threat of examination performance as a stick:

> We did quite an extensive preparation of the Shakespeare texts. This took a large amount of curriculum time and was quite prescriptive. I think teachers should have a choice whether to teach Shakespeare at this age. The class found *Romeo and Juliet* difficult even though we did pupil-friendly activities to do with text. I found that the students became more demotivated as the SATs test loomed near and they had to do 'practice' tasks . . . A far better, educationally worthwhile assessment procedure is one based on teacher assessment, especially at this age.
>
> (Head of English, Enfield, in LATE, 1995, p. 31)

The prescription of texts and the nature of the SATs from 1993 to 2002 revived the debate over the position and politics of Shakespeare. During the *Shakespeare in Schools*

Project (Gilmour, 1992–1994), teachers expressed their anxiety about being able to sustain stimulating approaches to the themes and language of Shakespeare's plays while meeting the assessment requirements of the National Curriculum. The implications of prescribed plays and tiered examinations were articulated from several perspectives: academics saw it as social engineering; Theatre in Education groups were concerned that they would be squeezed out by curriculum demands – they were already being squeezed out by lack of funding; actors talked about being condemned to perform the prescribed plays relentlessly in order to attract school audiences; inspectors spoke of the threat to widespread good practice; heads of department told of stock cupboards bursting with *The Tempest* or *The Merchant of Venice* while having to purchase literally hundreds of copies of *Romeo and Juliet*; classroom teachers talked of being forced to return to dull teaching methods.

In response to the above concerns The Qualifications and Curriculum Authority (QCA) has reduced the amount of time pupils spend on the Shakespeare paper within the new Paper 1 Reading for May 2003 (down from seventy to forty-five minutes) and tried to prevent the teaching-to-the-test fragmentary approach by asking pupils to make connections between two key scenes. This theoretically ensures that pupils are taught the whole play rather than, as was previously possible, one key scene, and encourages an active approach to Shakespeare which should include all pupils. However, this may still mean that pupils are trained in the Shakespeare SATs Paper 1 format, rather than educated to enjoy Shakespeare, and does continue the contradictions inherent in an assessment system whereby 14-year-olds are tested in their understanding of Shakespeare in formal paper and pen exams, but the more mature 16-year-olds are tested through coursework at GCSE.

WHY SHAKESPEARE?

Addressing initial hostility can be the experience of teachers who have to tell adolescent pupils that Shakespeare is compulsory, that they have to 'do' a play for an exam for, or after, which they are likely to be setted. At the same time, pupils often have a sense of pride and achievement when they have acted out a piece from one of the plays, or know titles, quotations or the stories. Recurring objections to the plays are that they are too 'difficult', 'irrelevant' or 'elitist'. These may be based on a child's experiences but are often grounded in hearsay. Rather than be instantly defensive, the teacher can find out the prior experiences of pupils. The Royal Society of Arts initiative, the *Shakespeare in Schools Project*, aimed to give opportunities for working on and through Shakespeare throughout and across the curriculum. In interviews, pupils and teachers in primary and secondary schools expressed how their prejudices against the plays before the project had been changed:

> 'People think that Shakespeare is posh and serious, but when we did it, it was fun.'
> (John, aged 9).

Task 11.1 Prejudices and expectations about Shakespeare in the classroom

A Personal history

It is likely that your own experiences of school Shakespeare have influenced your interest in continuing to read or watch Shakespeare's plays. In discussion with another student teacher or your tutor, consider the following questions to identify negative and positive influences upon your engagement with Shakespeare.

1   What was your first experience of seeing or watching a Shakespeare play? To what extent did it influence your perception of Shakespeare?
2   What were your experiences of reading and viewing Shakespeare plays at school, at university or on your own?
3   How have you been examined on Shakespeare? How well did you do?
4   Do you have preferences concerning plays? On what are these based?
5   What is your response to the following article: 'Was Shakespeare a Tory?' by David Lister?

Was Shakespeare a Tory?
The Bard is now a subject of political controversy
DAVID LISTER reports

SHAKESPEARE, anarchist or Tory, upholder of traditional values or subversive? The struggle for the Bard's soul is being fought in the world of academia.

Lining up on either side of the argument are some of the country's most respected Shakespeare scholars, and on one thing they all agree: his works are undergoing a fundamental reappraisal.

Michael Bogdanov, founder and artistic director of the English Shakespeare Company, says that schools should not teach Shakespeare for 20 years and neither should any of his work be performed, while a rethink takes place. To get things going, he has decided that he will not direct a Shakespeare play for five years.

Others, including Lord Lawson, the former chancellor of the exchequer, argue that some of the plays were written from a Tory standpoint and that Shakespeare was a strong royalist.

Mr Bogdanov, who is currently rehearsing *Romeo and Juliet*, says: 'The only way Romeo's and Juliet's parents can measure the worth of their children is in gold. Look at Romeo's speech to the apothecary: "There is thy gold, worse poison to men's souls,/Doing more murders in this loathsome world/Than these poor compounds that thou mayst not sell:/I sell thee poison, thou hast sold me none." He is saying that money is the real poison in the world. This nice, romantic wimp gives a whole social and political comment on the value of money.' Not perhaps how this play – one of the Government's prescribed three texts for 14-year-olds – will generally be taught. But that, says Bogdanov, illustrates the problem.

In fact, he says, Shakespeare is full of 'invisible bullets', the elements that are potentially embarrassing and are often ignored or cut by those who want to see the plays as 'shoring up the system with its class divisions and government by divine right'.

'We must reclaim Shakespeare for the anarchists,' Bogdanov goes on. 'He was a challenge to society, but this is not the Shakespeare that is taught or, on the whole, performed. Shakespeare is never used as a social and political dramatist. He is used as a moral dramatist.'

Lord Lawson does not see Shakespeare as an anarchist. He said in an interview that 'Shakespeare was a Tory without any doubt', adding that Coriolanus, espousing 'the Roman virtues, the Tory virtues', was 'written from a Tory point of view.'

Brian John, an English teacher at King Edward VI Grammar School in Chelmsford, adopts a similar approach to literary criticism, showing that the Lawson philosophy continues down the line into the classroom. He told a recent conference: 'Shakespeare was a great enthusiast of royalty and a true Conservative.'

Elaborating on this, he explained to me: 'I do feel that he must be generally a Conservative in asserting the basic principle of the desire for stability and order. Just look at the "degree speech" in *Troilus and Cressida*. Take his whole philosophy of history. He has a low opinion of rebellion: look at the Jack Cade example in *Henry VI Part Two*. And as a person he knew how to handle his finances and was upwardly mobile.'

The dispassionate Shakespeare Institute in Stratford-upon-Avon, an academic centre for the furtherance of understanding of the Bard, recognises that the battle lines over Shakespeare are changing.

Its director, Professor Stanley Wells, says: 'There is an academic conflict over Shakespeare. A lot of critics of the cultural materialism school are arguing that the plays contain elements of subversion which haven't been adequately recognised in the past.'

Alan Sinfield, of Sussex University's English department, ought to be a leader of the Young Turks preaching cultural materialism. He has just written a book entitled *Fault Lines: cultural materialism and the politics of dissident reading* and claims cohorts at several universities outside Oxbridge.

'Cultural materialism,' he explains, 'is materialism as opposed to idealism. Idealism says there's an ideal conception of a Shakespeare play, a reading that transcends all performances. Materialism says it is located in a political and historical context, his context but also ours.

'In the old days the thing you were meant to do with a literary text was to point out how whole and complete it was. The trick now is to do the opposite, to look for the gaps and silences and stress and pressure points.

'As you start looking for the fault lines, the text reveals its project. If you look at Desdemona, for example, she starts off incredibly spunky. She tells the Senate she wants to go off and have sex with her husband. Later she has turned into a nagging wife. Then she lies back and says "I've done wrong but don't kill me yet". It's not really a continuous character, it's a series of stereotypes and the play is deploying those stereotypes as a political representation to explore gender politics.'

(David Lister, *Independent on Sunday*, 3 January 1993)

B Questionnaire

Based on the above questions, devise a questionnaire in conjunction with your tutor or mentor. Interview a range of pupils, preferably across the whole age range, of differing abilities and of different cultural identities. To what extent are gender, class, age, race and past experiences relevant to pupils' attitudes to Shakespeare? Find out their experiences of watching plays and films as well as of reading the texts. Make a note of the reasons why pupils may be hostile to studying a Shakespeare play.

'Students were excited by their ability to understand something called Shakespeare which had primarily seemed alien to them and their lives.' (Teacher, Market Bosworth High School)

(Gilmour, 1994, frontispiece; p. 26)

The *Shakespeare in Schools Project* culminated in quality presentations which involved all pupils in a class. The presentations demonstrated a range of skills from several curricular areas:

> 'Beginning a new project in a way that arouses curiosity and a desire to learn is perhaps the most important part of the process. If effective the students' own enthusiasm usually carries it along and they meet not only the academic demands more readily, but also develop perceptive, artistic and social skills.'
>
> (Teacher, Brookvale High)

> 'The use of choreographed dance and live improvised music gave the production an exciting edge. The students worked excellently and within six weeks "Lear's Dance of Death" had been created.'
> (Teacher, Groby Community College)
>
> (Gilmour, 1994, pp. 31, 33)

The findings of the *Shakespeare in Schools Project* support the following arguments *for* teaching Shakespeare:

1   The plays are entertaining because they work dramatically: they have good stories and interesting characters; they mix comedy and tragedy; they contain conflict and produce mixed feelings in the audience; they require special effects to show magic, shipwrecks or fights; there is plenty of action.
2   The plays are examples of good theatre and are suitable for developing critical analysis of drama as a genre.
3   The language provides a valuable model and resource.
4   The characters and situations can be made relevant.
5   All are entitled to have access to the dominant culture.
6   The plays offer alternative ways of perceiving.
7   The stories and themes challenge and therefore extend the imagination, from which can come new ideas.
8   The plays stimulate a range of reading, oral and writing activities.
9   The range of linguistic registers and frames of reference can be liberating not restricting; through reading and analysis pupils develop powers of rhetoric and discourse.
10   A cultural materialist approach to the texts – for example, the analyses of government and authority in the plays – can be empowering.
11   The exploration of identities through universal experiences, such as marriage or death, in different cultural contexts can promote cultural exchange, especially through productions of the plays.
12   Like it or not, taking part in the plays engenders a sense of ownership rather than alienation and enhances self-esteem.

Shakespeare *can* therefore promote rather than inhibit personal and social development through opportunities for extending language awareness and usage, through the representations of complex relationships and through the debates explored in the plays; there is plenty of scope for cultural analysis through the study of power systems or the nature and structures of family life and marriage. There are debates about individual responsibility, the concepts of loyalty and duty and the relationship between religious and state laws; the plays depict people falling in love, telling lies and quarrelling. Since Shakespeare is performed across the world the productions can mediate between cultures as any production will reproduce the values and conventions of its social context. This is what Michael Bogdanov also discovered in his project of taking Shakespeare to a Birmingham housing estate (*Shakespeare on the Estate*, BBC 2 Television, 1994): as the plays were appropriated by different groups – for example, a single mothers' group worked on scenes with Lady Macduff; sequences were rewritten and performed as rap; one group acted out the Capulet/Montague brawl in a mixture of 'Shakespeare's' and contemporary English – there can be an exchange and understanding of different cultural codes. Progression in teamwork, creativity, commitment and self-confidence, as was demonstrated in *Shakespeare on the Estate* and the *Shakespeare in Schools* projects, is difficult to measure. Consequently, examinations have tended to prioritise a literary appreciation approach in reading and writing rather than an involvement with the narratives, characters and themes of the plays which can be enjoyed across the ability and social range. For example, the 2002 SATS question on *Henry V* asked: 'How does Shakespeare make this scene exciting and tense for the audience?' which does allow for a more dramatic interpretation, but the four bullet-pointed prompts point candidates to answer through an accurate translation of the key scene, including putting in appropriate quotations. GCSE coursework essay examples from the examination boards, however, do allow for both 'critical essays with textual reference which shows understanding of the plot and main characters' and also 'makes a personal response to the themes and ideas in the play' (AQA GCSE Specifications, 2004). This reflects the wider demands for GCSE which assume a literary appreciation plus an informed personal response – which is what is required for the highest grades at AS/A2 level. The SATs continue, therefore, to be out of step with GCSE and A level.

APPROACHES

In the long-standing and continuing debates about teaching literature in schools, the 'why Shakespeare?' question will not and should not go away. The immediate problem for the new and established teacher alike is not only 'why teach Shakespeare?' but also 'how to teach Shakespeare?' One reason why teachers find themselves locked into a hostile situation is because pupils get 'switched off' at the reading stage. The common practice of reading plays in the classroom is to distribute characters to the good readers; as these readers go through their speeches, which are often long and read without understanding, the non-participants become disaffected. There is no simple answer to this problem, but there are different strategies with which you can experiment.

A valuable learning model is that proposed in *Small Group Learning in the Classroom* (Reid *et al.*, 1989). This model sets out the stages of learning in the classroom as 'Engagement, Exploration, Transformation, Presentation and Reflection'. There are

Engagement. The teacher introduces the learning activity. With Shakespeare especially, pupils actually need to know what is happening before they read because comprehension is unlikely at first reading. You need to give enough away to arouse their curiosity and provide guidance about the plot and character development without telling them everything. Consider the following points:

- What pre-reading activities could introduce the central themes and situations of the play or scene (e.g. brainstorm what makes a good crime story before reading *Macbeth*)?
- How should the reading be managed – whole class/groups/audiotapes?
- How will the whole class get to know the play and characters – e.g. through scene summaries, acting out key extracts or 'keeping track' activities such as timelines or ongoing character profiles?
- What use can be made of film or television production (e.g. the *Animated Tales* series on video) before starting the text; watching film sequences in conjunction with reading?

Exploration. The pupils are given opportunities to become involved with the text. Activities might include:

- comprehension questions which demand close reading and individual exploration of the text and which deal with difficulties in vocabulary;
- using film, such as *Shakespeare Shorts* (BBC Education, 1996); pupils should script or storyboard passages before viewing alternative productions;
- use of drama conventions and improvisation such as interviews, hotseating, freeze frames;
- guided group discussion or activities (e.g. character profiles);
- projects on social or theatre history (e.g. marriage customs); researching different productions.

Transformation. At this stage there is a focus on a particular aspect of the work and the understanding gathered so far; tasks could be:

- writing up a project;
- preparing a draft for an essay;
- polishing up a script or improvised piece for performance;
- recreative writing: (e.g. a character's journal or letter); a modern English version; a cartoon strip.

Presentation. The process of feeding back and sharing ideas and information: it gives value to the work achieved and can sharpen critical awareness through the response of a sympathetic but critical audience. Tasks can include:

- exchanging work within a pair, followed by redrafting;
- handing in work to the teacher;
- a wall display;
- talk, performance or presentation to the class;
- word processing a review for a newsheet;
- timed examination practice.

Reflection. The vital stage where teacher and pupils discover what has been learned and what still needs learning. It may take a variety of forms, such as:

- feedback from the teacher after marking work;
- peer response to a presentation;
- whole class feedback;
- evaluation sheet.

Figure 11.1 Learning model for approaching texts

a variety of activities which are appropriate for each part of the learning process as illustrated in Figure 11.1.

It is assumed that most of these stages can be the same for all pupils. There are possibilities for differentiation by task – with projects of varying difficulty, for example, and at the transformation and presentation stages where there may be choice of tasks or essays; presentation and performance tasks can provide opportunities for pupils who are stronger at research or speaking and listening than at writing. Because Shakespeare's plays include debates about complex issues, such as power relations in domestic and national contexts, it is easy for the teacher to jump from the level of narrative, 'What is going on in the passage?', to a highly conceptual question, 'Should this character behave in this way?' Work will be accessible to most pupils if there is progression through the levels of thinking, identified as record, report, generalise, speculate/hypothesise and theorise (Reid *et al.*, 1989, p. 9). The questions on the extract from *Romeo and Juliet* given in Figure 11.2 illustrate these in practice.

Each of these questions is a process which needs time and varying degrees of support from the teacher, depending on the ability of the pupils: the more structure the better. The practice of structuring exploration of the plays along these lines can help not to lose the pupils who are working at the lower levels and need to be engaged at the level of description and narrative. For this reason, the most able pupils can underachieve if they do not have opportunities to respond to the more complex issues of the plays because the teacher does not include the more theoretical approaches for fear of 'losing' other pupils, who may misbehave if the work seems 'above their heads'.

The following questions are based on Shakespeare's *Romeo and Juliet*, but the principles of developing progression in thinking may be applied to setting questions on any scene in any play, or a passage in any text.

Read *Romeo and Juliet*, Act III, scene v. Focus on lines 104–200 and answer the following questions:

1   What is the 'joyful news' that Lady Capulet brings to Juliet? (*record*)
2   Discuss with a partner how you would produce Capulet's speech, lines 160–168, for play or film. Describe his facial expressions, volume and tone of voice, movements around the set/stage and body language in relation to the other characters. (*report*)
3   Read Capulet's speech beginning line 176. Sum it up in modern English. Jot down: (a) what you learn of Capulet as a father; (b) whether you think that fathers now behave like Capulet. (*generalise*)
4   Read the rest of the scene. Write the letter which Juliet might have written to Romeo that night. Tell him of the conversations between herself and her parents. What would her feelings be? What will she say to Romeo? (*speculate/hypothesise*)
5   Arranged marriages were common in Shakespeare's time. Look back over this scene and decide whether you think Shakespeare was suggesting that Juliet should have obeyed her parents. Work out what the reaction of the audience will be at different stages of the scene. Write a paragraph starting: 'I think that Shakespeare wanted us to sympathise with. . . . Give reasons by referring to speeches in the play. (*theorise*)

Figure 11.2 Questions to encourage progression in thinking

Curriculum phase	Teaching strategy
Throughout the curriculum • Know the play: plot; characters; themes • look at language use and change • understand the historical, social and cultural background.	• Read through the text – whole class; in groups; in conjunction with film/TV/audio adaptation; use 'keeping track' strategies • use the Internet for research on The Globe, and Shakespeare's background.
Possibilities for the text in performance and in film • Write structured essays, using references and quotations: write reviews, commentaries, director's notes	• see productions • role-play; interview; hotseating; acting out; scripting film; comparison of film productions. *Essay practice*
Key Stage 3 • Character work • personal response to characters at different stages of the play • understanding of some dramatic functions (e.g. irony) – and structures (e.g. tragedy) • understanding and analysis of the use of language to build character, tension, scene-setting • plot overview and comparison between scenes • practice for SAT, Paper 1.	• Group work on different characters with key references and quotations and present to whole class • hotseat or trial characters • transpose into modern equivalents with a focus on language • use productions to record individual responses and how these have been achieved • close study of set scenes to be compared • timed essay with open questions.
Key Stage 4 (GCSE) • Historical and social background • objective analysis of characters • detailed study of productions • comparison of plays • understanding of themes • coursework.	• Project work on different aspects of the times (e.g. marriage; idea of kingship; key laws and events; religious movements) • choice of essays, as suggested in the syllabus • empathetic tasks (e.g. diaries, letters, writing in a scene).
AS/A2 Level • Ability to interpret a character in two or more ways • explore themes and concepts (e.g. revenge; love; suffering) • engage with critical debate, and refer to different readers' interpretations • argue a point • write well-structured essay in examination conditions.	*As for KS3 and 4, and also:* • Students prepare papers on characters, introducing questions for debate • put Shakespeare on trial with a *J'Accuse* type or other TV question-time programme – (e.g. of being anti-monarchy or anti-women) • give two opposing articles on the play or a production • take a passage for small group discussion • exam practice.

Figure 11.3 Teaching approaches across the curriculum

SHAKESPEARE THROUGH THE CURRICULUM

The chart shown in Figure 11.3 is a starting point for considering continuity and progression through the curriculum stages. It is important to build upon prior learning. You may also need to address resistance to studying Shakespeare, caused by prejudices or previous experiences. Photocopy and add in your own observations and ideas.

Figure 11.3 is not exhaustive in identifying the requirements of each curriculum phase and possible teaching strategies. It is intended to illustrate that much work is common all the way through from Key Stage 3 to GCE AS/A2 level. Consequently, It is appropriate to use a range of approaches, including acting out and recreative work, at the engagement and exploration stages at all levels. Your observations, however, may show that the more active strategies are usual at Key Stage 3 and below, intermittent at GCSE and invisible at AS/A2 level. Assessment requirements do, of course, mean that pupils must have a close knowledge of the text and must practise particular skills at each stage, but a range of approaches enables them to perform well because they have genuinely engaged with the plays; it will also enable them to engage with the texts beyond what is assessed. Any of the approaches, whether acting out or writing a character's diary, will require pupils to look closely at the texts and explore their possible meanings. Looked at in this way, you do not have to choose between providing opportunities for pupils *either* to explore the plays for their own development, for cultural analysis and for improving drama techniques, *or* to prepare for assessment; broad learning objectives and the narrow requirements of assessment can be seen to interrelate. The active exploration of the plays is preparation for responding to assessment tasks and assessment validates the exploration of the plays. The problem is in safeguarding time from being swallowed up by specific examination work.

Shakespeare at Key Stage 3

In spite of pressure from teachers to change the assessment of Shakespeare to coursework, at KS3, a Shakespeare play is examined by the SAT Paper 1 for May 2003. Pupils answer a question on two scenes of the selected play (from *Twelfth Night*, *Henry V* or *Macbeth*). They are required to demonstrate an understanding of the scenes on their own and to make connections between them. They may be asked to comment on character, consider how to produce the scene and explain their decisions or to demonstrate their understanding of some features of production such as 'tension' or 'humour'. They are awarded marks for writing in 'good English'. All the work on the play will obviously feed into their ability to answer the question; to do well, they also need practice in timed examinations in order to understand the need to read the question carefully, plan their answers and leave time for checking their writing.

Shakespeare at Key Stage 4

In the 2004 syllabuses, all except one examining group assess the Shakespeare play (adding up to only 5 per cent of the total marks) through coursework but prescribe the play, sometimes with a choice of two. The coursework for English may also be used for the English literature examination but, if so, it needs to meet the specific requirements of the syllabus. Usually, this involves demonstrating awareness of the historical context of the play, in addition to other reading and writing skills. The support material will give guidelines for suitable activities for assessment, such as:

1   Close study of a scene, incorporating analysis of dramatic qualities, language, development of character, reference to the social context of the play;
2   Written assignment on a character;
3   Review of a production, demonstrating the same features as for (1), including a personal interpretation of the text.

Some examination boards invite a variety of forms of assessment, such as a spoken response on tape. The new requirements for the three oral coursework marks include a drama-focused activity which may well allow for imaginative responses to a Shakespeare text.

Shakespeare at GCE A level

As for Key Stages 3 and 4, AS English literature level candidates are expected to demonstrate a close knowledge of one of the plays (e.g. *Twelfth Night, Antony and Cleopatra, The Taming of the Shrew*) through specific reference and quotation. They are expected to write in good English. In addition, there is an emphasis on interpreting the play; the need to demonstrate a more conceptual grasp of themes and characterisation and the possibility of more than one meaning in a particular passage and the play as a whole, drawing on literacy criticism in a more overt way (Assessment Objective 4) than previously. At A2 there is the possibility of studying a second Shakespeare play (*Othello, Henry the Fourth Part Two, The Merchant of Venice*) as part of the pre-1770 dramatic texts. Candidates need to show a more informed personal response together with an understanding of the historical and social context. The synoptic assessment requires candidates to make connections between texts, and the contextual influences on the writer, and plays. At English literature and language AS/A2 one Shakespeare text is studied at A2.

A final note on using productions

Taking pupils to see a play or using a video of a television or film production in the classroom can be disappointing. With any production there is a danger of 'reality referral', especially with film and television, because of their powerful illusionism. There is also a danger of embedding the sense that reading is 'work' and to be avoided,

---

**Task 11.2 Preparing to teach
Shakespeare throughout the curriculum**

This task will develop your understanding of what is common and what is specific to teaching Shakespeare at each curriculum phase. You will need to obtain copies of the following documentation for each phase.

Key Stage 3
- past SAT question papers;
- three pupils' scripts across the ability range (e.g. level 4, level 5, level 7);
- *Key Stage 3 English Tests: Mark Scheme for Levels 4–7, Paper 2* (*Paper 1 from May 2003*), QCA.

Key Stage 4
- copy of the relevant GCSE syllabus and support materials – sample questions, marking criteria.

AS/A2 Level
- Copy of the relevant AS/A2 level English literature and/or AS/A2 language and literature syllabus and support material – sample questions, marking criteria.

1   Check out Figure 11.1 against your observations of teaching Shakespeare in schools, and of the requirements for Key Stages 3 and 4 and AS/A2 Level.

2   Obtain a past Key Stage 3 question Paper 2 (Paper 1) and write an answer yourself. Use the marking criteria (QCA's *Mark Scheme*) and award yourself the appropriate level. Compare yours with actual scripts by pupils. Incidentally, you should try to write 'model' answers for your pupils at all examination levels.

3   Draw up a worksheet to support pupils in a mixed-ability class preparing for examination at Key Stage 3. You will need to identify the skills and processes being rewarded (e.g. awareness of dramatic effectiveness; character studies and personal response; good English and presentation; well-structured essay under timed conditions). You should give guidance on reading the rubric; choosing the answer; reading the questions; planning an answer using the bullet points; writing an answer. Include definitions, explanations and examples of specialist terms (e.g. 'dramatic tension').

4   Using the learning model and chart of progression in thinking above, under 'Approaches' (Figures 11.1 and 11.2), draw up a scheme of work for approaching a Shakespeare play leading to GCSE coursework. You will need to look at the relevant syllabus. Aim to use a range of strategies and resources. Discuss your scheme of work with your tutor or mentor.

---

whereas 'watching', particularly watching television, is 'pleasure'. These attitudes are undesirable because they suggest that reading cannot be pleasurable and that watching should not be analytical. In the case of video, if it is used after the text it becomes the 'carrot' – and the teacher can find herself bribing students with 'settle down; the sooner we get through the text, the sooner you can watch the film'. In addition, as Susan Leach observes,

> if the video is used after the text has been read it tends to become a realism conferring agent, to the extent that students will say things like 'I didn't know he looked like that', or 'I thought she was older than that', thereby betraying their own subjection to the expectations of realism fostered by television, infinitely powerful in its conditioning of young viewers.
>
> (Leach, 1992, p. 70)

On the other hand, watching a play or screening can enhance the reading process and develop pupils' ability to analyse critically both the text and the particular medium. To this end, Peter Reynolds recommends fracturing the perceived authority of the visual text through breaking it up:

> I would argue that to teach Shakespeare on film with the same degree of close analysis that you use in reading a printed text you have to . . . keep your finger continually on the pause button, for the whole thrust of the illusionist convention is to give the impression of continual motion, to avoid breaking up the action, and to drive the viewer inexorably forward in linear progression.
>
> (Reynolds, 1991, p. 201)

There are several very good productions of Shakespeare plays, many produced for commercial reasons, and to ask pupils to make comparisons between films can also heighten their understanding both of the original text and the visual medium. This is not so easy in a play, but can be done in the preparation for and reflection on a production.

Strategies for watching a play

Consider suitable preparation, such as:

- pupils decide on how they would produce the play – costumes; setting; actors;

- take the opening of the play and write production notes;

- pupils write their own programme – blurb; plot summary; key points; theatre history;

- show pupils two versions from different folios and they choose which to use. This puts them in the position of producers and editors and helps them to see the text as less 'fixed' or 'sacred'.

Strategies for using film and TV

Viewing should be considered as 'reading' and always be made active in preparation. Experiment with the following:

- choose a passage and ask pupils to script it using film codes – music; length of shots; background;
- use *Shakespeare Shorts* (BBC Education, 1996), or extracts from two adaptations, to illustrate that there are different interpretations and that any production is *a*, not *the*, version;
- vary the order of reading a scene, acting it out and watching the adaptation; watch two if possible to minimise 'reality referral'. While watching, pupils should be looking out for film narrative, camera manipulation of the audience and for 'differences' between book and production texts and between theirs and the producers' interpretations; this kind of considered scrutiny will enable them to become better acquainted with the text and to be critical viewers.

Resources

There are many texts designed for school use. You will have to use the ones owned by your school, but look at others for your own use or when there is the possibility of buying new ones. The Cambridge School Shakespeare editions are popular but you should compare one or two: look at the way notes, vocabulary, illustrations and scene summaries are used, for example.

There are many commercially published materials to support teaching Shakespeare. Popular ones include:

Ackroyd, J. (1998) *Book 1. English and Drama Activities for Teaching Shakespeare to 10–14 Year Olds*, London: Hodder.

Ackroyd, J. (1998) *Book 2. English and Drama Activities for Teaching Shakespeare to 14–16 Year Olds*, London: Hodder.

Ashton, P. and Bethell, A. (1997) *Macbeth*, London: English and Media Centre.

Bleiman. B. and Broadbent, S. (1999) *Twelfth Night Video Pack for KS3/KS4*, London: English and Media Centre.

Broadbent, S. (1994) *Romeo and Juliet: Classroom Material*, London: English and Media Centre.

Garfield, L. (1992) *Shakespeare: The Animated Tales*, London: BBC.

Gibson, R. (1998) *Teaching Shakespeare: A Handbook for Teachers*, Cambridge. Cambridge University Press.

Twelfth Night Teaching Materials for Teachers – English and Media Centre website: www. englishandmedia.co.uk.

Protherough, R. (2000) *Henry V*, Sheffield: National Association for the Teaching of English.

Thomas, P. (1998) *Shakespeariences*, Sheffield: National Association for the Teaching of English.

SUMMARY AND KEY POINTS

There is a sense that in the current school curriculum, the study of Shakespeare can be disproportionate to other activities. If nothing else, it takes up time which is needed for other texts and other curriculum areas. Schools often introduce a Shakespeare play in each year from Year 7 onward, even if this is providing some historical background and an overview of the plot. Teachers do have to guard against spending too much time on a Shakespeare play and rushing through other work, particularly at Key Stage 3. It is important to plan out carefully the whole scheme of work to gauge the time spent, and to remember that the Shakespeare coursework counts for only 5 per cent of the total at English GCSE. On the other hand, because the plays make demands on the pupils, they can improve their language competence which can be transferred to other curriculum areas. For example, when working on a play, pupils will be improving their skills in reading, media analysis, role-play and drama, understanding of genre, characterisation, language change, speaking and listening, writing in a variety of forms such as diaries, play scripts, posters, letters, news reports, reviews, leaflets and essays. They can develop their thinking, extend their ideas and their moral and emotional understanding. Studying Shakespeare can also develop confidence and self-esteem. Careful planning can prevent the problem of 'overkill' caused by spending too long on a play and prevent the disappointment when pupils respond to a play or film production as 'boring'.

Teachers need to understand their own and their pupils' prejudices and insecurities regarding 'Shakespeare' and find approaches which overcome the difficulty of the language differences in the plays. There are many ideas in circulation and resources available to guide pupils through the processes of learning, from preparation, reading and exploring the plays' meanings to transforming their understanding into specific purposes including examination. The most important principle is that the plays should be experienced as dramas which can be produced in more than one way. Pupils need to be actively involved in constructing meanings of the plays through taking on the roles of producers, actors and reviewers. Preparation for examination is part of this process and also requires the development of specific strategies for taking timed exams.

A Shakespeare play is studied by pupils throughout the curriculum phases; consequently, considering teaching Shakespeare texts includes considering progression and continuity through the curriculum: at KS3, for example, pupils work towards an exam but they are also being prepared for work at KS4 where assessment is by coursework. Active strategies are appropriate throughout the levels to provide the means by which pupils engage with the plays and get to know the text more closely for themselves. The principles which underlie the approaches to studying Shakespeare may be applied to many other areas of the English curriculum.

FURTHER READING

Wells, S. (ed.) (1988) *The Cambridge Companion to Shakespeare Studies*, Cambridge: Cambridge University Press. This is a collection of essays by contemporary scholars, such as Ingastina Ewbank and Harry Levin, which provides information which you feel you ought to know and are too ashamed to admit that you don't. The essays cover: Shakespeare's life, times and theatres; the language of the plays; traditions of comedy and tragedy; theatre history and critical history from 1660 to 1980. There is a section on film and television productions and on critical approaches (by Terence Hawkes), but it does not include critical theories such as cultural materialism, feminist or postcolonial criticism. It would equip readers for the demands of teaching the plays for the school curriculum.

Gibson, R. (1998) *Teaching Shakespeare*, Cambridge: Cambridge University Press. This is a principled guide to the effective classroom teaching of Shakespeare, focusing on speaking and listening, collaborative work, and language. The performance aspect takes centre stage here, with many useful practical guidelines backed up by theory.

Leach, S. (1992) *Shakespeare in the Classroom*, Buckingham: Open University Press. This is an informative and constructive discussion of teaching Shakespeare which successfully combines theory and practice. There are chapters on 'Why Shakespeare?', 'Shakespeare in the National Curriculum' (it was written before the 1995 version of *English in the National Curriculum*), 'Teachers and Shakespeare', 'Alternative Editions, Alternative Interpretations', 'Shakespeare and Video', 'Race and Gender in Shakespeare', 'Preparing for Classroom Shakespeare', 'Shakespeare in the Secondary Classroom'.

12 Possibilities with Poetry

Gabrielle Cliff Hodges

INTRODUCTION

Feelings about teaching poetry can vary a great deal. For some it is the most enjoyable aspect of teaching English; for others it is the area about which they are least confident. There are several possible reasons why poetry teaching should give rise to such diverse attitudes. Chief among them is teachers' own experiences of being taught poetry at school or university. Those who enjoy it are often people who were themselves taught by poetry enthusiasts; by teachers who were able to excite a similar enthusiasm in their pupils and to develop it through respecting their pupils' responses to poetry and by teaching critical awareness. Those who approach the teaching of poetry with some trepidation may have had less rewarding experiences, finding it difficult, when asked to read or write poetry at school, to see the pleasure or the point.

Of course, a teacher's own enthusiasm for poetry is not enough on its own to ensure that pupils will similarly appreciate it. On the contrary, if that enthusiasm is not reflected upon and tempered for the classroom it may have adverse effects. In his poem 'Them and [uz]' Tony Harrison recalls a former English teacher who would no doubt have characterised himself as a poetry enthusiast:

> 4 words only of *mi 'art aches* and . . . 'Mine's broken, you barbarian, T.W.!'
> *He* was nicely spoken. 'Can't have our glorious heritage done to death!'

> I played the Drunken Porter in *Macbeth*.
> 'Poetry's the speech of kings. You're one of those
> Shakespeare gives the comic bits to: prose!'
>
> (Harrison, 1984, p. 122)

Poetry revered as 'our glorious heritage' and 'the speech of kings' is likely to end up making many, if not all, feel excluded.

Another reason for conflicting feelings about poetry is the reading challenges it can present. Poetic language may be simple and easy to read, and poems which rhyme, which are funny, which tell a story, are often the kind of literature which children most enjoy reading in school. But the syntax, structure, imagery and allusion which some poets employ often require different kinds of reading, and until pupils know that time and effort can yield rewarding pleasures they may not want to persevere. Then their tendency is to dismiss all poetry as 'boring', especially when the challenges are exacerbated in poetry from the past with its sometimes unfamiliar vocabulary and social or cultural references which need explanation.

A third aspect of poetry that can give rise to mixed feelings about teaching is the extent to which it is remembered that poetry has its roots in the oral tradition, and is aligned closely with music, dance and drama. If this lineage is forgotten, then poetry can, for many people, be difficult to bring to life. If, however, a priority is to hear poems read or spoken aloud, its rhythms and rhymes can be appreciated differently as these dimensions are brought more clearly into play. The multi-dimensional quality of poetry is, of course, a central concern and challenge for the poet as well as for the reader. Sujata Bhatt, in her poem 'The Writer', represents it vividly:

The Writer

The best story, of course,
is the one you can't write,
you won't write.
It's something that can only live
in your heart.
not on paper.

Paper is dry, flat.
Where is the soil
for the roots, and how do I lift out
entire trees, a whole forest
from the earth of the spirit
and transplant it on paper
without disturbing the birds?

And what about the mountain
on which this forest grows?
The waterfalls
making rivers,
rivers with throngs of trees
elbowing each other aside
to have a look
at the fish.

Beneath the fish
there are clouds.
Here the sky ripples,
the river thunders.
How would things move on paper?

Now watch the way
the tigers' walking
shreds the paper.
(Bhatt, in Bhinda, 1994, p. 3)

If poetry teaching sounds somewhat daunting, remember: Tony Harrison has become a popular and widely respected poet; and Sujata Bhatt's tigers are testament to a writer's success in the struggle to create.

OBJECTIVES

By the end of this chapter you should:

- have begun to develop a rationale for teaching poetry and assessing pupils' work on it;
- have become more familiar with the range of poetry and resources for teaching poetry currently available;
- be aware of the need to justify your selection of poetry, taking into account factors such as pupils' previous reading and work on poetry, and their attitudes towards it;
- be able to explain how lessons you plan will enhance pupils' development as readers, writers and critics of poetry.

Task 12.1 Poetry memories

Discuss with a fellow student or jot down notes on:

- some of your own most vivid memories of being taught poetry in school;
- reasons why they are vivid memories;
- what the balance was between work on poetry through speaking and listening (e.g. hearing it read aloud, reciting or performing it), poetry reading and poetry writing;
- a particular teacher whom you remember teaching you poetry;
- what you think his or her views about teaching poetry were.

In school, find opportunities to:

- talk with different colleagues about teaching poetry and note how attitudes and approaches vary;
- talk with pupils about their views on poetry.

THE NEED FOR A RATIONALE

As part of the process of developing a rationale you may find it helpful to explore your own attitudes and possible prejudices concerning the teaching of poetry. One way to do this is to reflect on your experience of being taught poetry and compare it with teachers' and pupils' experiences in school today.

As student teachers embarking on the process of working out your reasons for teaching poetry you will also want to acquaint yourselves with a range of theoretical views which you can use to help you clarify your own ideas and analyse what you observe and learn in the classroom.

Speaking and listening

To start with you could try to discover when, how and why poems are read aloud or performed in class. What might be some of the pleasures and benefits to be gained by pupils who have plenty of opportunities to listen to, as well as read and write, poetry? It used to be the case that a great deal of oral work on poetry involved pupils learning poems off by heart and then reciting them aloud, together or individually, in class. Because this is not common practice nowadays, it is sometimes assumed that pupils no longer learn poetry by heart at all. It is worth finding out to what extent this is true and exploring whether they do or not and, if they do, what the purpose of doing so is.

Reading

There are different views about why and how poetry is read. For example, what views about teaching poetry, implicit or explicit, emerge from the two extracts below? How far does either of the following two pieces tie in with your own feelings and opinions?

> Clearly there are occasions when a poem needs a comfortable amount of time to be experienced, but poetry works best when it is wanted, not when the timetable decrees it. . . . The strength and relevance of the experience within it should engage the pupils' response and thus their willingness to grapple with the language. Some of the best lessons we saw were those where pupils and teacher were enjoying the exchange of opinions on points of vocabulary, attitude, atmosphere and metaphor.
>
> (DES, 1975, p. 136)

> Unless we look for them, we apprehend formal patterns subconsciously, if at all. Unless you believe that dissection murders pleasure, some explication of these tacitly apprehended features will make future apprehension more likely and effective. Poetry gives a special chance for this with its habitual re-reading. Early reading gives opportunities to induce the mechanisms; later readings give the chance to recognise them in action and enjoy the satisfactions of formal patterning.

Within current paradigms of teaching literature, mood and content in poems can look after themselves. The structures and processes which realise them need teaching. So while too much teaching and testing suggests that poems are like prose, but the sound features of poetry are well attended to, the urgent need is to foster reading of poems as single, time-free, structured experiences – like gazes at paintings.

(Stibbs, 1995, pp. 14–19)

Writing

Just as there are differing views about poetry reading, so there are various schools of thought about teaching poetry writing. It is therefore an area of your work where talking to colleagues and observing them at work in the classroom will prove extremely valuable. You may find that opinions conflict. Some teachers, for example, may view the writing of poetry as a very personal (and perhaps rather private) activity and may, as a result, be reluctant to intervene in the writing process or to assess pupils' writing with as much precision as they might a piece of non-fiction writing. Others, however, may take the view that poetry writing is an art, a craft and skill, elements of which can be taught, practised and refined. These teachers may also hold the view that if pupils' poetry is given the same kind of scrutiny and discussed in the same critical terms as published poets' work, it can enhance pupils' opinions of themselves as writers, rather than just readers of poetry. Where would you place your views within this continuum? Lavinia Greenlaw, a poet writing in the *Times Educational Supplement*, suggests that the extremes need to be balanced:

Poetry is made of a tension between sense and sensibility. Poets often seem to be those who are scalded by the acuteness of their perceptions while retaining a piece of ice in the heart. Many people find themselves writing poetry for the first time when struggling to articulate some great joy, disturbance or loss. Such poetry can offer catharsis or clarification and this has been the momentum for many great pieces of work. But, without the application of craft, this remains a therapeutic exercise, not a literary one. . . . In keeping with its image, poetry is evocative, allusive, startling and mysterious. This is achieved not only through imagination and originality but also rigour and ruthlessness. Every word should count – for its meaning as well as its music.

(Greenlaw, 1996, p. 23)

As you work through this chapter and begin the process of forming a rationale for yourself, you will become aware of the need to make your rationale explicit to others, for example, to the Year 9 class who say 'Why do we have to read poetry? Why can't we just read novels and plays?'; to English department colleagues who have to decide between spending limited resources on a class library of fiction or a class library of poetry; to the parents of a Year 10 pupil who ask, at a parents' evening, why their son should be spending time on poetry in English when his ambition is to work in a bank.

If your rationale can encompass the tension referred to by Greenlaw, it is likely to hold good in a wide range of circumstances.

PLANNING POETRY LESSONS

There are many factors that have to be taken into account when planning poetry lessons. They include:

- formulating learning objectives which are specifically to do with poetry;
- considering pupils' prior knowledge and attainment in relation to reading and writing poetry;
- differentiating between pupils in the same class if necessary;
- ensuring that your plans allow for progression in pupils' knowledge about poetry;
- drawing on your subject knowledge to select poetry and poetry-writing activities which will appeal to, interest and challenge pupils;
- drawing on your knowledge of available resources to support your chosen subject matter and approach;
- reflecting on different ways of teaching and learning which will help to achieve the aims and objectives of the lesson(s);
- considering how pupils' learning about poetry can be assessed effectively in order to inform future planning and teaching;
- relating plans to National Curriculum programmes of study or examination specification requirements.

These elements will be explored further in the sections that follow.

Poetry reading resources

Work on poetry is often one of the first things that student teachers are asked to undertake in the classroom. The class teacher may ask you to work with a group on a particular poem, or he or she may assume that you would prefer to choose a poem yourself. Explore the English department's stock of poetry texts. Allow time for some lengthy browsing. Look at:

- what sets of poetry anthologies the department has;
- what collections by individual poets they have;
- whether they keep class libraries of poetry books;
- how the department organises poetry stock (e.g. for use with different year groups);
- what else is available in other media (e.g. video, schools, television programmes, tape-recordings, CD-ROM, IT software.

A visit to the school library and resources centre will enable you to ascertain:

- how extensive the poetry stock is;
- whether it caters for all ages, tastes and abilities;
- which poetry books, according to the librarian, are most popular;
- whether they stock periodicals which review poetry publications (e.g. *The School Librarian* or *Books for Keeps*).

You could try to find out whether the school publishes pupils' own poetry. If so, are copies of school anthologies available in the library? Do pupils' poems appear on the school website?

Task 12.2 Exploring poetry resources

This task encourages you to review available poetry resources critically. Browse through some resources. Choose two with which to familiarise yourself further.

- Note one or two activities you would like to try out in the classroom, and why.
- Read introductory material to these resources and analyse what views about poetry reading and/or writing they promote.

Poetry-writing resources

Early on in your course you may also find yourself being asked to prepare a poetry-writing activity for a particular class. There are many books written about writing poetry. It is worth considering who they are written by and whom they address when deciding which, if any, to use. Many are written by teachers for teachers, or by poets for teachers. A number of websites also offer advice, often written by poets for children. You may wish to talk to your head of department or subject mentor about poetry writing in the English department. Ask:

- which texts or resources they have found most helpful when planning poetry-writing activities;
- whether there is any departmental documentation about teaching poetry writing;
- whether the department participates in writers–in–school schemes; encourages pupils to enter poetry writing events; organises workshops and poetry performances.

Selecting poems

Well-judged selection of poetry is essential to the success of poetry lessons. It is a crucial part of the planning process. You need to be able to justify your choice, to be able to say more than 'I think this would be a good poem to do with Year 7'. You need to consider:

- whether the group as a whole is likely to find the poem interesting, both in terms of its subject matter *and* the way it is written;
- how it relates to previous work they have done;
- what the poem will help to teach the group *about poetry*;
- how the poem will *reinforce* what they already know *and develop* their understanding;
- whether it will introduce the group to a familiar or a new poet;
- how your choice affects the balance of poets whose work they are reading;
- whether there are resources available to use when working on this poem (e.g. video or audio recordings; illustrations).

Task 12.3 Making an informed choice

Select a poem to study with a class you know.
  In order to see how fully you are able to justify your choice, ask yourself the above questions. Can you answer them all or do you need to find out more (e.g. about the group and what they have already done, or about available resources)?

POETRY ACROSS THE AGE RANGE

The teaching of poetry needs to be as systematic as the teaching of any other area of the English curriculum. There ought to be both differences and continuity between poetry work in, for example, Years 7, 9 and 11. But what might some of those differences be? How is that continuity to be achieved?

One possible framework for thinking about pupils' development as readers, writers and critics of poetry across the secondary age range will now be explored. It is based on a theory of reading outlined by Robert Scholes in *Textual Power* (1985). Briefly, his argument is that three interconnected and recursive elements – reading, interpretation and criticism – need to be actively in play if readers are to realise their full potential. He also argues that students need to be accorded equal status as writers and readers so that they experience their full power as both creators and re-creators of texts.

Work on young readers reading picture story books (Meek, 1988; Graham, 1990; Styles and Watson, 1996) argues that even the youngest readers not only read for pleasure but also respond to texts as interpreters and critics. So the framework is not so much linear as spiral. It is complex and multi-dimensional (Rosenblatt, 1978; Scholes, 1989). Nevertheless, there is a sense in which, with poetry especially, young people will not welcome the effort involved in interpretation and criticism unless they continue to experience the *pleasures* of reading.

EARLY KEY STAGE 3: THE PLEASURES OF POETRY

An important aim for the poetry curriculum in Year 7 might therefore be to extend pupils' enjoyment of reading, writing and performing poetry, at the same time introducing them to more challenging poems, concepts and activities through which they continue to develop their creativity and critical competence. The National Curriculum for English also states that pupils should 'read a wide range of texts independently, both for pleasure and for study'. So how might you make a start?

First find out as much as possible about the pupils whom you teach. Take every opportunity to discover what they know and what interests them. When it comes to poetry you may find yourself having to follow Polonius's advice and 'by indirections find directions out'. Pupils may not readily inform you that, for example, they are already confident readers and writers of poetry. They may know more poems off by heart than they think they do: playground rhymes and chants; song lyrics; advertising jingles; poems learned in primary school; their own made-up poems. They may have had poems displayed, read out, published in anthologies or published on the Internet. They are likely to be proud of this, but they may be reluctant to tell you about it. You must do the finding out.

While you are getting to know your pupils, you will also be extending your knowledge of what works well in the classroom. In *Continuity in Secondary English* David Jackson writes about pupils in the early years of secondary school having an 'irreverent, humorous world-view . . . a spontaneous wit' often 'revelling in word play for its own sake' (Jackson, 1982). There is certainly a great deal of poetry written and performed in schools by poets such as John Agard, Grace Nichols, Roger McGough, Michael Rosen, Ian McMillan, Jackie Kay and Valerie Bloom which seems to suggest that Jackson is right.

Reading poetry for pleasure

A poem such as 'Don' Go Ova Dere' by Valerie Bloom is a good example. Read it, and then consider the suggestions below as ways of encouraging pupils to enjoy reading poetry more widely as well as to pay close attention to how it is written.

> *Don' Go Ova Dere*
>
> Barry madda tell im
> But Barry woudn' hear,
> Barry fada warn im
> But Barry didn' care.
> 'Don' go ova dere, bwoy,
> Don' go ova dere.'
>
> Barry sista beg im
> Barry pull her hair,
> Barry brother bet im
> 'You can't go ova dere.'
> 'I can go ova dere, bwoy,
> I can go ova dere.'
>
> Barry get a big bag,
> Barry climb de gate,

Barry granny call im
But Barry couldn' wait,
Im wan' get ova dere, bwoy,
Before it get too late.

Barry see de plum tree
Im didn' see de bull,
Barry thinkin' bout de plums
'Gwine get dis big bag full.'
De bull get up an shake, bwoy,
An gi de rope a pull.

De rope slip off de pole
But Barry didn' see,
De bull begin to stretch im foot dem
Barry climb de tree.
Barry start fe eat, bwoy,
Firs' one, den two, den three.

Barry nearly full de bag
An den im hear a soun'
Barry hol' de plum limb tight
An start fe look aroun'
When im see de bull bwoy,
Im nearly tumble down.

Night a come, de bull naw move,
From unda dat plum tree,
Barry madda wonering
Whey Barry coulda be.
Barry getting tired, bwoy,
Of sittin' in dat tree.

An Barry dis realise
Him neva know before,
Sey de tree did full o' black ants
But now in know fe sure.
For some begin fe bite im, bwoy,
Den more, an more, an more.

De bull lay down fe wait it out,
Barry mek a jump,
De bag o' plum drop out de tree
An Barry hear a thump.
By early de nex' mawnin', bwoy,
Dat bull gwine have a lump.

De plum so frighten dat po' bull
Im start fe run too late,

Im gallop afta Barry
But Barry jump de gate.
De bull jus' stamp im foot, bwoy,
Im yeye dem full o' hate.

When Barry ketch a im yard,
What a state im in!
Im los' im bag, im clothes mud up,
An mud deh pon im chin.
An whey de black ants bite im
Feba bull-frog skin.

Barry fada spank im,
Im mada sey im sin,
Barry sista scold im
But Barry only grin,
For Barry brother shake im head
An sey, 'Barry, yuh win!'
(Bloom, in Styles, 1986, pp. 38–39)

Pupils will probably enjoy the humour and the narrative. They could be encouraged to browse through poetry books and seek out other humorous narrative poems as companions to this one, for example, Michael Rosen's poem, 'I share a bedroom with my brother/ and I don't like it' (Rosen, 1974, p. 67).

The style of 'Don' Go Ova Dere' provides the teacher with opportunities to study it as an artefact, not just as a narrative. It has a strong rhythm, rhyme and structure which can be reflected upon and used to discover the extent of pupils' understanding of the poet's craft and to develop that understanding more explicitly.

Because it is written in dialect and includes some dialogue, the poem has a strong sense of voice. It demands to be read aloud. You could read it. Or you could read most of it with volunteer pupils reading the dialogue of different characters. The poem would lend itself well to a group performance with different parts allocated to different voices and choric effects for lines such as 'Firs' one, den two, den three' and 'Den more, an more, an more'.

Writing poetry for pleasure

It was suggested earlier that an important aim for the poetry curriculum in Year 7 might be to extend pupils' enjoyment of writing as well as reading poetry. You may therefore wish to link pupils' poetry writing with work on this poem in several ways. One aim could be for them to experience the pleasures of writing poetry to entertain themselves and others. Another might be to use the characters and narrative of the poem as a basis for poetry writing in another form.

Writing to entertain

Pupils often want their poems to be humorous and to entertain. It is very important to take account of this and to provide opportunities for them to read their poetry aloud to one another for enjoyment and entertainment. In this case, encouraging them to talk about their own experiences of getting into scrapes like Valerie Bloom's Barry may give them plenty of material on which to base the writing of their own poems.

However, it is very hard for pupils to replicate the achievements of experienced poets, and they may need more support to help them to organise their ideas in ways which satisfy them. You might wish to focus their attention on the stanza structure, for example, and how it contributes to the humour; the division of material between stanzas and whether it adds to the humorous effect of the poem; the extent to which the rhythm and rhyme add to the way the poem entertains.

You would need to offer a differentiated structure for pupils to work within. The task, for some pupils, might be to produce a poem written in stanzas of six short lines each. Others might be able to work within the same structure but also try to achieve a regular rhythm. Others still might be able to take on all this and to try working out a rhyme scheme as well.

Transforming poetry

There will be pupils for whom the above activity may prove too demanding. They may prefer to write something shorter, more highly structured and not necessarily related structurally or stylistically to the kind of poetry they have just been reading. However, they could use the content of the poem and try transforming it, representing it in a different poetic form. Books for teachers such as *To Rhyme or not to Rhyme?: Teaching Children to Write Poetry* (Brownjohn, 1994) will provide you with various good ideas.

A favourite example of tight poetic structure is the diamante poem. Its diamond shape is determined by particular types of words being allocated to particular lines:

Noun 1

adjective   adjective

–ing   –ing   –ing

synonym 1 synonym 1: synonym 2 synonym 2

–ing   –ing   –ing

adjective   adjective

Noun 2

Although this kind of approach may seem restrictive at first it is surprising how effective the results can be. The structure lends itself well to oppositions and contrasts. Try it for yourself, and see:

Barry

carefree   fearless

daring   running   climbing

> explorer   adventurer: watcher   waiter
> stamping   snorting   running
> frightened   angry
> Bull

You can demonstrate to pupils how a diamante is composed by drafting one on the board or overhead projector with contributions from members of the group. It is a good way for them to see how in drafting you record your changing thought processes, and how poems, as with other forms of writing, may go through many versions before they are considered to be finished.

There are, furthermore, exciting possibilities for cross-curricular work here. You could talk, for example, with whoever teaches the group for music, about pupils composing pieces to accompany their diamante poems. You then have another perspective from which to discuss the sounds, rhythms and pace which pupils have built into their writing and which they can replicate in their music.

Assessing work on poetry

Whatever the activity, you need to decide how you are going to assess pupils' work. This will depend on the reasons for your assessment. If you do not know the group very well, your main purpose may be diagnostic assessment; that is, finding out what pupils know and can do in relation to poetry and what help they will need from you to rectify weaknesses.

Pupils' progress, however, is likely to be enhanced if they receive some clear, constructive feedback from you as well (formative assessment). You need to decide what form it will take. It could be by written comments from you to which the pupils may respond (e.g. in a profile or record of achievement); verbal feedback to the pupils and written notes for yourself in your mark book; or a form of assessment specified by the department. Whatever form it takes, you need to be clear about how assessment relates to learning objectives. Pupils need to be clear, too. The following example shows how that relationship might be formulated.

Linking learning and assessment

1   Learning objective:
     Pupils to develop awareness of the difference between reading poetry silently from the page and a prepared reading of it aloud to an audience.
2   Assessment objectives:
     Pupils demonstrate:

- attention to features of poetry reading such as intonation, rhythm, pace;
- ability to suggest ways of speaking different words, phrases, lines;
- ability to justify their choices;

- preparedness to contribute to group performance and to realise in practice the group's ideas.

Written comments for pupil A:

Your suggestion that your group should speed up and slow down in your reading of the poem 'Awake and Asleep' was taken up by the others because you made your reasons clear (i.e. that it would bring out the difference between the two states). Although at first you did not want to be in the group performance, you overcame your reluctance and spoke your lines clearly. Having made such a good suggestion it was a pity you did not quite have the confidence to slow down as much as you intended. It would have added to the contrasts you did achieve in terms of volume: the noisy bustle of the first part; the whispered quietness of the second. Well done!

LATER IN KEY STAGE 3: FOCUSING ON INTERPRETATION

In the preceding section we have foregrounded the importance of the pleasures of poetry. One of the ways in which those pleasures can be extended is by focusing pupils' attention more explicitly on the processes of interpretation. Interpretation has, of course, been involved in the activities described above, but it has been tacit rather than overt. We now move on to explore how developing pupils' consciousness of it might offer them greater understanding and control in their work on poetry without sacrificing the pleasure. From your growing knowledge of what appeals to and seems appropriate for Year 9 pupils, you might wish to consider whether or not you agree that this kind of activity is well suited to them at this stage in their development as readers and writers.

Choosing appropriate texts

'Interpretation', writes Scholes, 'lies on the other side of reading. Its domain is the unsaid' (Scholes, 1985). If we want pupils to engage in the interpretative process, we need to offer them texts which require it, even force it. A poem by John Mole which begins 'Someone has gone and left the swing . . .' is just such an example. If it is given to pupils without its title, as below, it will instantly generate discussion about what it may mean, and pupils will find themselves involved automatically in the process of interpretation. Some of the pleasures remembered from solving riddles will be in evidence here, but there will also be opportunities for explicit talk about metaphor. (Try guessing the title yourself before turning to the end of the chapter to find out what it is.)[1]

> Someone has gone and left the swing
> Still swinging, slowly,
> Slower, slow, and now
> It stops, and someone else
> Is coming.

Someone has gone and left the chair
Still rocking, slowly,
Slower, slow, and now
It stops, and there is silence
In the room.

(Mole, 1990, p. 13)

Exploring key concepts

Before proceeding any further, think about a concept such as metaphor which now may be so familiar to you that you take it for granted. Teaching that concept to pupils may prove tricky, so examine your own ideas first. Consider your immediate response to the question 'What is metaphor?' Have you thought how you would define the word 'metaphor' if you were asked to do so by someone, say, in Year 9?

If words such as 'simile' and 'metaphor' are taught in terms of recognising examples rather than exploring and analysing effects created by them, then the knowledge acquired is merely superficial. Pupils need to understand what metaphor can do so that they can judge for themselves its impact, both in their own and in others' poetry. They need to be able to appreciate and create what Jerome Bruner (1986, p. 22) calls the 'atmospheric change' which results from using metaphor, to understand and participate in the way in which metaphor can simultaneously grasp the familiar *and* make it strange, to 'rescue it from obviousness' (ibid., p. 24).

'Skills' by Anne Stevenson is a poem which might be used towards the end of Key Stage 3 to explore the concept of metaphor in greater depth and encourage interpretation.

Skills

Like threading a needle by computer, to align
the huge metal-plated tracks of the macadam-spreader
with two frail ramps to the plant-carrier.
Working alone on Sunday overtime,
the driver powers the wheel: forward, reverse, forward
centimetre by centimetre . . . stop!

He leaps from the cab, a carefree Humphrey Bogart,
to check both sides. The digger sits up front
facing backwards at an angle to the flat,
its diplodocus-neck chained to a steel scaffold.
Its head fits neatly in the macadam-spreader's lap.
Satisfying. All of a piece and tightly wrapped.

Before he slams himself, whistling, into his load,
he eyes all six, twelve, eighteen, twenty-four tyres.
Imagine a plane ascending. Down on the road,
this clever matchbox-toy that takes apart

grows small, now smaller still and more compact,
a crawling speck on the unfolding map.

(Stevenson, 1993, p. 23)

What follows is a series of ideas for encouraging active reading and interpretation of the poem. The ideas are intended to provide further concrete examples of some aspects of the planning process (e.g. formulating learning objectives, applying them in practice and linking them to assessment).

Progression and learning objectives

In a mixed ability Year 9 group pupils will have varying degrees of understanding of the concept of metaphor. When planning a lesson or unit of work in which the learning objective is based upon the study of metaphor, you will need to take into account (as with any topic) work they have already done and knowledge they have acquired. Your learning objectives will then be phrased in terms of how you want them to progress.

Task 12.4 Formulating learning objectives

This task is intended to help you focus on the process of formulating learning objectives in relation to poetry.

- Imagine that you are to use the poem 'Skills' with a Year 9 group you know. If possible, find out from them or from their teacher what they have learned already about metaphor.
- Then use that knowledge to help you formulate up to three learning objectives for a lesson based on 'Skills'. Remember that you are trying to articulate what pupils will *learn*. You are not, at this point in the planning, describing what they will *do*.

Class: Year 9 (mixed ability)

Length of lesson: 75 minutes

Aim: To read and study Anne Stevenson's poem 'Skills'; focusing closely on the poet's use of metaphorical language in order to develop pupils' understanding of the concept of metaphor.

Learning objectives:

1 _____
2 _____
3 _____

Ask another student teacher who has completed this task to compare their learning objectives with yours. Can you both see clearly what it is hoped that pupils will learn?

Turning learning objectives into classroom practice

'Skills' is another poem which forces interpretation particularly through the poet's use of metaphorical language. However, there are two things you want to try to avoid.

The first is simply asking pupils to spot the similes and metaphors without considering what effects and responses are being created. It is a largely pointless exercise and probably fairly devoid of pleasure as well.

The second is taking the idea of interpretation literally and asking pupils to translate the poetic language into prose. This, too, misses the point of a poetry lesson which should preferably be looking towards rather than away from the poetic.

So, what kinds of study activities invite interpretation and enable pupils to remain firmly engaged with the poem? Here are some suggestions.

DARTs

Direct Activities Related to Texts (DARTs) is an idea which arose from the *Effective Use of Reading* project directed by Lunzer and Gardner. In their report (Lunzer and Gardner, 1979) they offered a definition of 'comprehension' which they formulated as 'the pupil's ability and willingness to reflect on whatever he is reading', and a variety of activities were thus devised to bring about this ability and willingness to reflect. Two examples of DARTs are cloze procedure and sequencing. Both encourage active exploration of a text.

- *Cloze procedure.* Pupils are presented with a poem from which certain words have been deleted. They have to use their understanding of the rest of the text to suggest words to fill the gaps. Comparing the actual words used by the poet may trigger discussion about the effects he or she may have wanted to achieve.
- *Sequencing.* A poem is presented to pupils, not in its original form but divided up into fragments mixed up out of order. The pupils' task is to reconstruct the poem, trying to find the sequence of the original. For this activity pupils may need to identify formal features of the poem such as rhyme or stanza structure. If successful, they will have discovered particular organising principles of the poem for themselves.
- *Other strategies.* Tasks which make visible the processes involved in reflecting on and interpreting poetry include:
    - annotating;
    - highlighting;
    - illustrating;
    - drawing diagrams.

The following example of part of a lesson plan illustrates how some of these activities might work in the context of the particular poem, 'Skills'.

Learning objective

To enhance pupils' understanding of how metaphor works by bringing together two ideas which share similarities and differences.

Activity

- Pupils work in small groups doing a cloze procedure exercise using copies of the poem with the words computer (l. 1), Humphrey Bogart (l. 7), diplodocus (l. 10), matchbox (l. 16) deleted.
- A spokesperson from each group reports on some of their suggestions for words to fill the gaps.
- Pupils then look at the words which Anne Stevenson actually wrote and discuss the different effects and resonances created by her chosen words.
- Still in small groups, pupils explore how the metaphors used in the poem connect two ideas that are at the same time similar and different, for example, the diplodocus-neck of the digger. At this point it may help if they highlight words or phrases, annotate the text or sketch an illustration.

If you are planning to teach *poetry writing* alongside *poetry reading*, then you might like to use the work pupils do on metaphor in Anne Stevenson's poem as a starting point for them to write their own poems. In your objectives, be clear about what element of poetry writing you want them to develop. If, as here, it is their use of metaphorical language, their ability to take an element of the ordinary or mundane and 'rescue it from obviousness', then make that clear and plan your lesson accordingly. A poetry-writing activity such as 'The Furniture Game' devised by Sandy Brownjohn and described in her book *Does It Have to Rhyme?* (1980) could be used or adapted to meet your specific purposes. Requiring pupils, as it does, to think of someone known personally to them and to describe him or her in terms of a piece of furniture, for example ('she is an old, comfy armchair' or 'he is a stiff, upright, hardbacked chair'), or a time of day ('she is the early hours of a warm summer's morning' or 'he is the dark midnight hour') can produce some startling metaphors for pupils then to work into poetic forms.

ENTERING KEY STAGE 4: THE CHALLENGES OF CRITICISM

The third component of the poetry-teaching framework which has been outlined in this chapter is criticism. It is, like interpretation, a process in which most if not all readers engage intuitively from an early stage. The suggestion here, however, is that it might be timely, at Key Stage 4, to guide pupils towards a more *explicit* understanding of what the critical process involves. The challenge for teachers is to maintain the pleasure and build on the progress made in Key Stage 3 at the same time as making greater demands on pupils' knowledge, skills and understanding.

In Years 10 and 11 pupils are likely to find themselves increasingly being taught poetry with a view to being able to write about it under examination conditions.

Task 12.5 Aims and assessment objectives for poetry at Key Stage 4

- In order to familiarise yourself with the place of poetry in the curriculum for Years 10 and 11, discuss with your head of department or subject mentor where and how poetry features in the chosen GCSE specifications for English and English literature. How are the GCSE requirements translated into schemes of work by the department?
- Look at the assessment objectives and grade related criteria for poetry work in GCSE English and English literature specifications. How do they require pupils to demonstrate their achievements as readers, writers and critics of poetry? How adequate do you think they are as the means of summative assessment of pupils' poetry work?

Factors such as time pressure or the desire for pupils to achieve the highest possible grades in the examination may, in some cases, lead to what is known as 'teaching to the exam' and thus to a narrowing down of pupils' responses. To what extent do you think this might be the case in the pupil's work which follows?

Vernon Scannell's poem, 'The Fair', has been taught to a Year 10 class.

The Fair

Music and yellow steam, the fizz
Of spinning lights as roundabouts
Galloping nowhere whirl and whizz
Through fusillades of squeals and shouts;
The night sniffs rich at pungent spice,
Brandysnap and diesel oil;
The stars like scattered beads of rice
Sparsely fleck the sky's deep soil
Dulled and diminished by these trapped
Melodic meteors below
In whose feigned fever brightly lapped
The innocent excitements flow.
Pocketfuls of simple thrills
Jingle silver, purchasing
A warm and sugared fear that spills
From dizzy car and breathless swing.

So no one hears the honest shriek
From the field beyond the fair,
A single voice becoming weak,
Then dying on the ignorant air.
And not for hours will frightened love
Rise and seek her everywhere,

> Then find her, like a fallen glove,
> Soiled and crumpled, lying there.
>   (Scannell, 1971, p. 35)

Pupils have read and discussed the poem in small groups. Their attention has been drawn to some of the poetic techniques being used by the poet. Pupils have then completed the following task under test conditions:

> *Analyse the poem, commenting on subject matter, poetic techniques and your personal response.*

Here is what one pupil wrote (transcribed exactly as it was written):

> The poem is about a fair. Vernon Scannal gives us a look at one sad night at a fair. He takes us in as if we are walking towards it, first hearing the music then the lights and finally the rides. As we go around the fair we have the fair discribed to us with nice smells of the 'fast food', 'Pungent spice, brandysnap' then a very bad smell of 'diesel oil'. He then discribes the night sky with a picture for our minds to view. 'scattered beads of rice'. the rice being the stars. The fair as a whole is then discribed as being 'melodic meteors' because after we have been looking up we are up in the sky looking down on it and it would look like spinning rock dancing to the music. We now are brought back down on to the ground to feel the atmosphere of the fair. People laugh and scream with delight. Vernon Scannell discribes that the money in the people's pockets is being used to buy sweet thrills 'Pocketfulls of simple thrills, Jingle silver, purchasing a warm and sugared fear that spills. From dizzy car and breathless swing'. also this part of the poem gives us sights at the fair, and the complete look at the fair. Then the poem discribes a horrible sound a scream not a warm enjoyable scream but a 'honest shriek' a scream for real. A person has wandered from the fair and is in great distress. The scream ends. 'dying on the ignorant air'. The atmosphere now has completely reverse the fun and the frill is now cold with horror. Her friends who are at the fair will not notice that she has gone missing, but when they do they search for a long time, but when they discover her they see her lying on the ground 'And not for hours will frightened love Rise and seek her everywhere then find her, like a fallen glove, soiled and crumpled, lying there'. The rape gives us a very negative look to a night fair.

As has been noted above, pupils' *development* as critics has much to do with making the processes involved more explicit, so that they engage in critical discussion with deliberate awareness of what they are doing and why.

To be engaged in the critical process, readers need, however briefly, to take a step back from the text and to view it through others' eyes as well as their own. This is something which teachers in school are well placed to foster. After all, they are working with thirty or so individuals who may differ greatly in their outlook and beliefs. Encouraging debate, therefore, is a good way to develop the critical process.

It is important for pupils to know that criticism is not about getting the right answers or finding the correct meaning of a poem. It is about articulating their interpretation and understanding of the text and justifying it in broader terms than just their own idiosyncratic opinion.

Different perspectives from which they might read and comment on a poem could include viewing it in comparison with another poem, perhaps related in theme or structure, or viewing it from different social, cultural, historical and political standpoints. This may sound demanding but in many respects criticism is more challenging than reading and interpretation. Nevertheless, even if pupils are required to distance themselves somewhat from the text in order to be critical, the process of criticism itself can give pleasure, and the ways of achieving it need not be dry or purely academic.

Task 12.6 Developing a critical response to poetry

You may initially be slightly distracted by the writer's misspelling of the word 'describe' or by the occasional omission of a capital letter. These are points which should be addressed at an appropriate moment. But it is very important that they should not colour your judgement of the pupil's achievements in terms of completing the task set, in this case analysing and commenting on the poem.

- Using GCSE English literature grade descriptions for reading, try to decide (as far as is possible on the basis of a single piece of work) what grade best fits this pupil's work.
- If you were marking this essay, what comments would you write at the end to encourage this pupil's development in responding critically to poetry?
- How do you think the pupil has been prepared for writing this task?

By the time pupils reach Key Stage 4 there will be significant differences between those who grasp critical concepts with relative ease and those for whom they remain difficult to comprehend. Although the aim of a lesson or unit of work on poetry (e.g. to develop pupils as critics, and the poetry which is to be read) may be common to all pupils in the class, the teacher's awareness of their differing needs and her expectation of their varied levels of achievement will require the actual work to be differentiated. Here we will look at how two poems might be used to encourage a mixed-ability group of Key Stage 4 pupils to engage in the process of criticism and, perhaps, to become more consciously aware of what it means to do that.

Meeting at Night

The grey sea and the long black land;
And the yellow half-moon large and low;
And the startled little waves that leap
In fiery ringlets from their sleep,
As I gain the cove with pushing prow,

And quench its speed in the slushy sand.
Then a mile of warm sea-scented beach;
Three miles to cross till a farm appears;
A tap at the pane, the quick sharp scratch
And blue spurt of a lighted match,
And a voice less loud, thro' its joys and fears,
Than the two hearts beating each to each.
                    Robert Browning (1812–1889)

Sonnets from the Portuguese

XIV

If thou must love me, let it be for nought
Except for love's sake only. Do not say,
'I love her for her smile . . . her look . . . her way
Of speaking gently . . . for a trick of thought
That falls in well with mine, and certes brought
A sense of pleasant ease on such a day' –
For these things in themselves, Beloved, may
Be changed, or change for thee, – and love, so wrought
May be unwrought so. Neither love me for
Thine own dear pity's wiping my cheeks dry, –
A creature might forget to weep, who bore
Thy comfort long, and lose thy love thereby!
But love me for love's sake, that evermore
Thou may'st love on, through love's eternity.
                    Elizabeth Barrett Browning (1806–1861)

SUMMARY AND KEY POINTS

In order to make a successful start to your teaching of poetry in school you need to be as widely read as possible, especially in the area of contemporary poetry written for young people. There is a great deal of it and much that is of very high quality. In addition, think about writing poetry yourself to remind you of the possible challenges and satisfactions involved.

When planning for teaching poetry you need to find out what pupils enjoy, know and have studied in order to build on their achievements and offer a sense of continuity. Attention needs to be focused on what they are learning about poetry when reading, performing, writing and talking about it. Assessment of their work will enable you to judge their progress and plan ahead.

The teaching of poetry requires a clear rationale which you can begin to develop for yourself by working with pupils, observing poetry lessons, talking with colleagues in school and college, and reading what has been written on the subject, linking it with more general theories of reading.

Task 12.7 Engaging in the critical process

Look at the following list of activities which are designed to move pupils towards more explicit critical analysis of poetry. The activities are based on the two poems above.

1   (a) The teacher reads the two poems with the class without saying who they are by or when they were written. (The pronouns in line 3 of 'If thou must love me . . .' will need to be deleted before copies are handed out.). Pupils discuss in small groups how they imagine the speaker, or persona, in each poem. They refer closely to each text to justify their suggestions. Their speculations might include consideration of gender, historical period, social, cultural and moral issues.

    (b) The teacher explains who wrote them and the relationship between the two poets. Alternatively pupils could research this information for themselves. They discuss how this new information affects their rereading of the poems.

2   Pupils are challenged to write a third verse for 'Meeting at Night'. They discuss what they will need to take into account in order to complete this task (e.g. content, stanza structure, rhyme scheme, type of vocabulary).

3   Pupils imagine they are Elizabeth Barrett Browning writing a diary entry describing an incident which has taken place between herself and her lover, prompting her to write this poem. She writes about why she has chosen to communicate with him through poetry (rather than, say, writing a letter).

4   Pupils browse through poetry anthologies to find two twentieth-century love poems, one by a man and one by a woman, which they prefer to these two by the Brownings. They give reasons for their selection based on their reading of all four texts, not only the two new ones they have chosen.

   • Consider (perhaps in discussion with a colleague or fellow student) what critical processes each activity involves.

   • Decide how and why the different tasks might be suited to pupils of different abilities.

NOTE

1   The title of John Mole's poem on p. 251 is 'Youth and Age'.

FURTHER READING

Astley, N. (ed.) (2002) *Staying Alive: Real Poems for Unreal Times*, Tarset: Bloodaxe Books. If you want to extend your knowledge and understanding of poetry, this is a thought-provoking anthology with interesting commentaries and further reading suggested by the editor. It also has a useful glossary of poetic terms.

Bleiman, B. (2001) *The Poetry Book*, London: English and Media Centre. This makes an excellent resource for Key Stage 3 poetry lessons, and, along with its companion *The Poetry Book Video. The Poetry Pack* and *The Poetry Video* (1995), compiled by Barbara Bleiman and

Michael Simons and likewise published by the English and Media Centre, is a valuable resource for Key Stage 4.

Brownjohn, S. (1994) *To Rhyme or Not To Rhyme?: Teaching Children to Write Poetry*, London: Hodder and Stoughton. Sandy Brownjohn has drawn together many of her tried-and-tested ideas for teaching poetry writing in the classroom.

Heaney, S. (1995) *The Redress of Poetry*, London: Faber and Faber. These ten lectures, given by Seamus Heaney when he was Professor of Poetry at Oxford, make fascinating reading for those who want to explore ideas about poetry in greater depth.

The Poetry Society's website, *www.poetrysociety.org.uk*, is well worth visiting. It has good links to other relevant poetry websites.

13 Teaching English at 16+

GNVQ, Key Skills and GCE A Level

Peter Gilbert and Veronica Raybould

INTRODUCTION

The number of students who opt to continue their education at age 16+ has increased dramatically before and into the new millennium. To both create and respond to this demand for continuing education, new courses have been introduced, most notably vocational courses such as the General National Vocational Qualification (GNVQ). Students from widely varying academic backgrounds may be following a range of courses in the sixth-form of a secondary school, a sixth form college or college of further education. They may be retaking GCSE English or English literature or following a Key Skills course at Level 2. They may be following GNVQ at Level 2 or an AVCE, or have opted for AS or A2 level English language, English literature or English (a combination of language and literature). Post-16 courses in drama, theatre, communication and Media Studies also have an English base but demand additional specialised knowledge and skills. (See also Chapter 6.3. in Capel *et al.*, 1995.)

Because students choose to study post-16, there is a different ethos surrounding the sixth form in school and sixth form and further education colleges. Students are given new freedoms: a different dress code; free periods; a less rigid punishment system. These changes are associated with a transition from teacher dependency to independence in learning.

GNVQ AND VOCATIONAL A LEVELS

It is likely that every school with a sixth form will have a number of students following General National Vocational Qualification (GNVQ) courses at Levels 1 and 2. Many will also have students following Vocational A levels (AVCEs).

OBJECTIVES

By the end of this chapter you should have:

- considered post-16 teaching in terms of progression from GCSE English, both similarities and differences;
- have some understanding of the requirements of Key Skills and AS/A2 specifications;
- identified a range of strategies for teaching and learning at GCE AS/A2 and Key Skills;
- been introduced to resources to support teaching post-16.

WHAT IS GENERAL NATIONAL VOCATIONAL QUALIFICATION?

GNVQ courses are intended as an alternative to GCE A levels or more GCSE subjects post-16, and it is important to remember that they are equivalent qualifications to those obtainable at GCE A level and GCSE. Hence, an AVCE (Level 3) is equal to one or two A level passes obtainable at Grades A–E; an Intermediate qualification (Level 2) is equal to four GCSE passes at Grades A★–C. You will also encounter students following Foundation courses (Level 1) which cater for those likely to achieve four GCSE passes at Grades D–G.

Built into each course, in the recent past, were Key Skills in communication, application of number and IT, which students needed to pass at the appropriate level or higher to gain full certification. These Key Skills were, and still are, notated as 1, 2 and 3, rather than Foundation, Intermediate and Advanced. While you are unlikely to be asked to deliver a GNVQ or an AVCE, you may well become embroiled in the delivery of Key Skills communication.

All Key Skills are assessed by a portfolio of evidence and an externally set test (or, where applicable, a proxy qualification).

COMMUNICATION

Key Skills communication can be loosely defined as basic English language skills applied to situations appropriate to the workplace rather than to schools. It is this latter phrase which makes the teaching (and learning) of communication very different from that of GCSE English. The end result of this is that the language of GNVQs and AVCEs generally, and of communication in particular, is very different from that of a GCSE or GCE AS/A2 syllabus. They are administered by all of the awarding bodies.

The 'specifications' for communication, like all other key skills, are divided into three sections:

1   What you need to know
2   What you have to do
3   Guidance

Part 1 explains the basic skills required at each level. These vary a little from one level to another. For example, at Level 1 the main skill areas are: discussing, reading and obtaining information, and writing documents. At Level 2 giving a short talk is added and the second area becomes reading and summarising information. Level 3 replaces a short talk with a presentation and summarising is replaced by synthesising. There is nothing novel about the skills required and most of them will be automatically illustrated in any reasonable piece of work produced by the individual student.

ASSESSMENT CRITERIA

Part 2 (What you have to do) sets out what a student has to produce in the portfolio. There is also some indication of standards, although these are rather vague. It should be remembered that Level 2 is equivalent in standard to GCSE at Grade C or above and Level 3 is equivalent to AS level. As you are unlikely to meet many students in the sixth form who are operating at Level 1, the illustrations below concentrate on Levels 2 and 3.

C2.2 asks a student to present evidence that they have 'Read and summarized information from two extended documents about a straightforward subject. One of these documents should include at least one image.' The word 'straightforward' means that almost any topic will be suitable. 'Extended' requires the student to think in terms of about three sides of writing. An image, in this context, should be integral to the point of the document and not just decorative.

Task 13.1 Obtaining appropriate evidence

Working in pairs, consider what kinds of material a student following either an English language or English literature course might be able to use for this element of the portfolio. How might they be able to prove that they have produced a summary?
   The evidence for the above must show all of the following:

- selection of relevant material
- accurate identification of the main lines of reasoning from text and image
- summary of the information to suit the student's purpose.

Once again, this is not definitive in terms of standards. This is one of the great differences between the Key Skill guidance and the usual examination board syllabus: the latter has to nail down standards very tightly, while GNVQ allows a centre to make recommendations, within common-sense limits, as to what meets accepted national standards. However, the work presented should be of a quality to match that of a student following a GCSE course. If a student produces work which would earn a Grade C at English language, they are on the right course.

C3.2 is much more demanding. In fact, you will find a considerable increase in the standards for Level 3 which many students cannot reach. The national pass rates suggest that Level 2 is relatively easy to get through, but Level 3 is not. It states that a student must 'Read and synthesize two extended documents about a complex subject. One of these documents should include at least one image.' A 'complex' subject is one they encounter in their AS studies, but that is not the only difference from Level 2. At Level 2 the summaries could, and probably should, be about different topics. The synthesis demands that students use two extended documents, one including a relevant image, on the same subject. Unless they know and understand this in advance, how likely is it that they will naturally produce this kind of work for their AS course?

The evidence must show all of the following:

- selection of material that contains relevant information
- accurate identification, and comparison of, the lines of reasoning from the text and images
- synthesis into a form relevant to the student's purpose.

TESTS AND PROXY QUALIFICATIONS

The second part of the qualification is an externally set test. At Level 2 this is in the form of forty multiple-choice questions, concerned mainly with spelling and grammatical errors. If a student already has a grade C or above in GCSE English language or GCSE English literature then they do not have to take the test, but can claim a proxy qualification instead. All they then have to do is produce a suitable portfolio.

The Level 3 test is based on the interpretation of several passages with more open questions. If a student has passed a GCE at Grade E or above in English language or English literature, they do not have to take the test, but can claim a proxy qualification for that part.

Task 13.2 Tracking key skills

Given that most students will be taking four AS level courses as well as having other commitments in and out of school, propose a method of delivering communication Key Skills which is fair both to students and staff.

ORGANISATION

There are guidelines as to how centres might organise the delivery of Key Skills, but you will encounter wide variations in practice. Communication may be taught in discrete lessons on a regular basis. If this is the case, you should find that your class is aiming for the same level, even if pupils are following different AS/A2 courses. Students may be given support from a communication expert or they may just be given the paperwork and told to get on with it. Someone, however, is going to be responsible for the moderation of the portfolios.

Be careful; this is a time-consuming and complicated process.

THE FUTURE OF KEY SKILLS

The most recent pronouncement on Key Skills is that all students in post-16 education should obtain the equivalent of Level 2 in English (communication), mathematics (application of number) and ICT. They should also be working towards obtaining one Key Skill at Level 3. Many schools are keen to offer Key Skills and not just because they mean more money under the new funding arrangements for sixth forms. Key Skills carry UCAS points, and increasing numbers of students may find they are the difference between a place in higher education and a year out. They may well take over completely from the option of resitting core subjects at GCSE.

However, they are not easy to deliver and many students do not value them. It may be several years before a new shape emerges in which Key Skills sit happily in the curriculum. They may, of course, have disappeared altogether.

A LEVEL

Since September 2000, the delivery of A level has changed considerably. There is no longer the option of terminal examinations taking place only at the end of Year 13. Instead, A levels are divided into six modules, the first three of which constitute AS and need to be examined by the end of Year 12. These first three units are weighted at 50 per cent of the final A level grade, and are marked at a standard which is considered to be an intermediate step between GCSE and A level. Students *are* able to retake specific AS modules in Year 13 while following the A2 course (modules 4 – 6), although you will find that retake policies differ from school to school.

This new A level policy is still, at the time of writing, very unpopular with many teachers and students. Since English is a subject that centres on the development of analytical skills, it is felt that examining two terms into the course (and there is even a January option for module 1) does not allow students to have honed these skills enough to write confidently in the examination. A poor result in Year 12 may lead a student to drop the course altogether, especially since the AS result is part of the final result. However, the other side of the argument is that AS provides Year 12 students with a close target to work towards, rather than cruising through Year 12 doing the minimum of work. AS enables students to see how they are doing at the end of their first year, coming from an external source. It will be interesting to see whether A levels remain in their current form – change is frequent in education!

The new A level has not only forced teachers to reorganise the order in which they deliver the various components of the specification (syllabus), it is much more specific about content. Prior to 2000, A level literature syllabuses offered teachers a wide range of text choices, many of which were contemporary. The emphasis now lies very much on 'the cultural heritage'. What is more, although student responses of the 'practical criticism' kind are still highly valued, students are also expected to be well acquainted with critical readings of the texts, and with cultural theories such as feminism, new historicism and postcolonialism.

Similarly, A level English language has moved away from a central focus on personal response and personal examples, to include a greater knowledge of linguistic theory. Although analytical skills are what distinguish the A Grade candidate from the D Grade one, the knowledge base required for the A level English student is much broader than it was prior to 2000.

Teaching A level: What's the difference?

All of the above makes A level English seem like a very different subject from GCSE. However, it is important to remember that your Year 12 students were Year 11 students a few months ago and have not magically transformed themselves over the summer break. A common misconception for a student teacher is that A level will require you to teach all that you have learned about English during your degree and that students will be immediately ready to employ high-order skills such as sophisticated analysis and eloquent debate. Student and newly qualified teachers are often not given A level teaching in their first year, as if it is some kind of 'award' that you can attain only when you have taught successfully in the main school. This builds the mystique that A level is a totally different experience. Much about teaching A level follows on from teaching at Key Stages 3 and 4. You are not automatically doing anything different: many of the teaching strategies you employ at GCSE are relevant and directly transferable to A level.

Task 13.3 What is the purpose of studying A level?

It is likely that students 'stay on' or 'carry on' to sixth form or college because there is little alternative, because it is expected of them by parents or because their friends are doing so. It can be illuminating to interview some sixth-form students about their reasons for studying A level, their expectations of the courses and their ambitions when they have finished. One criticism of A level specifications is that they are too closely geared towards preparing students for higher education courses in the same subject when only a small percentage will study a single-subject course at university. In discussion with some students and/or A level teachers, try to define the purposes of A levels in English.

Bearing this in mind, there are obvious ways that A level differs from GCSE. Developing a student's own responsibility for learning is central to A level teaching. All A level specifications state that a core aim in English subjects is to reward students who show that they have developed a confident, individual voice which is analytical and perceptive. How you do this involves you achieving a balance in your teaching strategies, between providing students with knowledge of the text and allowing students to develop their own analytical skills and style independently. For example, to issue students with Toni Morrison's *Beloved* and to ask them to 'read it at home and record your reactions' would be a very daunting task for all but the most able A level student. Students need guidance on how to read the text; they will need help to see *Beloved*'s account as a rememory of the slave ships and the collective history of black America's past; they will need you to explore with them the Horsemen of the Apocalypse chapter. At the same time the novel invites close personal analysis; once you have guided students to becoming confident about how the text is working, you can begin to hand over to them the responsibility for responding to its meanings: you would not want to provide all the answers to questions such as 'Who or what is Beloved?' for them. Neither would you hand out copious quantities of critical readings of the text and expect students to be automatically able to interpret them. Your challenge is to find the balance between lecturing your students and facilitating their own ability to learn.

Thus there is, quite rightly, an academic edge to A level which your teaching and learning strategies must address. Students will need to be encouraged to approach texts much more rigorously than at GCSE, but don't assume that you will be working with all A Grade students: as with any set, you will find a remarkable range of ability in the A level classroom. Even success at GCSE does not necessarily indicate a strong A level candidate. What is more, many schools employ quite wide entrance requirements for A level, so your students' abilities are likely to be very mixed. You will need, in your teaching approaches, both to reassure students that they will be successful, providing a knowledge base from which they can grow individually, and also to forefront the importance of independence of thought.

WHICH COURSE AND WHICH SPECIFICATION?

English literature A level

As with GCSE, A level English literature specifications vary, although not as much as they used to. The eight examining boards which existed prior to 2000 were amalgamated this year (2003) into three 'awarding bodies': AQA, OCR and Edexcel. Each of these bodies has two specifications on offer (Specifications A and B). All these options have common strands. One of the three modules at AS is coursework, as is one of the three at A2, and these account for 30 per cent of the final mark. The final module, module 6, is known as the synoptic paper and will test your students' 'unseen' skills: even if your school has opted for a pre-release pack specification, students cannot discuss the material with you and will have only a weekend to look it over. The remaining four modules cover poetry, drama and novels recognised as part of our 'cultural heritage'.

Although these modules are necessarily discrete (i.e. modules 1 to 3 must be delivered first) and are therefore often taught as separate clearly defined strands, they do all link together. English literature A level aims to develop students as autonomous, critical and confident readers. In this sense, whether you are preparing students for an examination or encouraging them to read widely for individual coursework choices, your aim is always the same: to lead each student into close personal analysis of texts and to be able to consider the text in its cultural context. Your school will have considered carefully the order in which they deliver texts at AS and A2 and it is worth talking this through with your induction tutor or head of department, so that you can get a sense of the thinking behind the approach.

English language A level

Whereas with English literature the modules are determined by text, in English language the modules address categories, such as language acquisition, accent and dialect, discourse analysis and so on. Module 6 is again skills-based with pre-released/ unseen materials. As with literature, two of the modules are coursework, and should encourage students to see links between modules. The artificiality of the modular approach leads students to think that their knowledge is not transferable across modules – it is for you to show them that the spiral curriculum applies here.

A level 'English' (combined English language and literature)

The combined English language and literature A level, like English language, is relatively new. It is not, however, a straightforward combination of English literature and language A levels. It is very much a 'natural' progression from English at GCSE; thus the A level literature section of this chapter will be useful to you, the language section less so; that is, you will explore texts as in literature (although fewer), and the language element will be grounded firmly on comprehension, summary and creative skills. You will need to lead students into a greater understanding of the purposes of a wide variety of writing, and enable them to acquire analytical skills related to grammar, word choice, structure and semantics. In many ways, the underlying skills you develop are not so very different from their 'single subject' equivalents. However, the way you do this is different: there is not time to consider English language under lots of discrete thematic headings; rather, you will use your literature texts to foster close language analysis, while developing students' language skills by continuing the emphasis on 'writing for audience' that you began at GCSE.

APPROACHES TO TEACHING AT A LEVEL

As with all curriculum areas, our unconsidered approach is likely to reproduce our own experiences; with A level teaching in particular, there is a convention of a sudden change of teaching strategies which do not take into account the previous experience of the students, principles about effective learning which are considered appropriate at earlier curriculum phases and the range of abilities in the group. The comments of two A level students at the end of their first term reflect this:

'At the beginning of A levels it was like being in a different world. We came back and had a strong feeling that teachers expected us to know it all.

I did feel as if I'd be the thickest person in the class and everyone would be brainier than me, but they're not.'

(Sarah)

'I found GCSE hard but A level is even harder. You get treated so differently but I haven't changed.'

(Yin)

Task 13.4 Conventions of A level teaching

Preferably with a partner or in a group of four maximum, discuss your own experience of English at A level or equivalent. Consider the following and how these answers might affect your own teaching of A level:

- the ways you were encouraged to think independently and originally;
- the work you felt was most successful and the circumstances in which this occurred;
- occasions when you were least inspired.

Continuity and progression

English is a spiral curriculum: that is, students keep returning to familiar areas from a more sophisticated viewpoint. Therefore, what works at GCSE works at A level. Do not exclude those strategies you are using in the GCSE classroom, such as:

- display work;
- brainstorming on to sheets of sugar paper;
- sequencing/cloze activities;
- use of interactive CD-ROM or research via the Internet;
- group work (and careful planning about the group's make-up, e.g. gender mix, ability, differentiated tasks);
- 'real' work – for competitions, magazines, school publication.

The above strategies will be welcomed in the A level classroom, alongside the quieter, more self-consciously analytical seminar approach.

Organisation of the classroom

A major strategy to consider is that of seating. How you choose to position your students is very important since, as at GCSE, it will affect profoundly the kind of interaction that takes place. A level groups tend to be smaller (although some schools admit up to twenty per group) so your seating choices can be more flexible than at GCSE. Different learning objectives and teaching styles invite different seating arrangements, so do think about changing seating according to the lesson purpose. Do you want boardroom style so the group can generate opinions easily, or do you want to be the focal point of the lesson? Your decisions about seating will also need to take into account the role of note-taking, as this will be affected by your classroom layout. Students are sometimes reluctant to move once they have established their place in the classroom, so do use a variety of seating choices from the very start of the course.

Note-taking

One of the differences between a Year 11 and a Year 12 class is that Year 12 students will normally get out paper and pens in the expectation of taking notes as the teacher speaks (but not when each other speaks). If a student is absent she may 'borrow someone's notes': what does this assume about the nature of note-taking and a person's thinking: can learning be transmitted in this way? With reference to your own experiences as a student and to your observations of post-16 teaching, consider your opinion of the role of note-taking at A level. Do you expect students to note down everything you say, everything everyone says? Nothing? 'The best?' Will you guide them in their note-taking or assume that they are doing it 'right'? How will your approach to note-taking affect your classroom layout? You could interview some students about how they take notes; how confident they are about what they are doing when they make notes; what use they make of their notes. Encouraging students to buy spiral-bound A4 notebooks (one for each teacher) can really help them to organise their notes. Provide glue to attach any handouts. Too many students find loose-leaf folders unmanageable, often using one folder for all the subjects they are studying.

Task 13.5 Observation: organisation and aims

Observe A level teaching and note seating arrangements. Consider the link between the seating and the lesson purpose. Decide which kinds of seating arrangements would suit your own A level teaching if your purpose is:

- note-taking: you delivering the information;
- whole class discussion which is teacher-led;
- whole class discussion which is student-led;
- student(s) present(s) a paper to the class;
- exam practice;
- small group discussions.

Setting assignments

Although individual schools have various approaches, there are some general guidelines to setting writing activities. Again, the advice offered to you at GCSE is directly relevant here. As far as direct examination practice goes, you would use the same style of question as that on the specification's papers, although this obviously does not mean that every writing activity you set on the text needs to be styled to the examination question.

Many A level writing activities are not specifically for examination purposes but to develop further the students' skills and knowledge in a particular area of the specification. At times you may wish to set the same task for the whole group and at others to use the differentiation strategies of GCSE. Tasks which begin with 'discuss' or 'write about' are far too vague and unfocused. Although students should be encouraged to create their own essay titles at times, these will need to be negotiated with you to make sure that they are not addressing too general an issue. The key is for titles to encourage analytical exploration of something specific and the best way to formulate titles is to work closely with the specification's assessment guidelines beside you. Since 2000 these have become much more rigorous: each module has its own set of Assessment Objectives (AOs) and the percentage each one carries for the final result is broken down carefully in each module. All specifications also offer exemplar material and sample question booklets which you should receive from your school. It is well worth familiarising yourself with your specification's particular style. When setting coursework tasks, consult with your head of department who will contact the coursework moderator to confirm that your titles are in line with the AOs.

Another important way to test the success of a task is to have a go at it yourself. This is actually probably one of the best ways of testing out a writing activity's potential for success. What seems inspirational when you are planning the task can sometimes be too vague or too specific in practice. You will find out whether the task is appropriate and manageable, and it will also help you to communicate the Assessment Objectives clearly to your students.

You will need to decide how much support you are going to give students on the task once set. At A level the one-to-one tutorial is extremely useful, but it is also time-consuming. You may be able to suspend a lesson in order to see individual students; you may be able to set research topics on aspects of the social context of a text or on characters to be discussed. This would free you to speak to students individually; otherwise, your only option is to see each one in your own time. However, especially when students are working on different tasks, there will be a need to supervise writing in the classroom itself. Although the emphasis at A level is inevitably on 'the essay', other kinds of assignment will enrich your students' understanding of English at A level. A level students do have more time outside the classroom to work on your subject, but many students, especially in Year 12, will benefit if you structure this time for them.

Marking strategies

As with GCSE, it is very important to involve students in marking procedures – so they can learn from each other and become aware of what makes a 'good' essay. There are numerous ways of doing this, some of which might be as follows:

- By marking each other's work, with reference to the Assessment Objectives.
- By attempting the specification's own trial marking exercise for teachers (this usually takes place early in the spring term but there will be a copy of it in school at any time).

Task 13.6 Setting an assignment

Either on your own or with another student teacher, choose an A level text (literature) or language theme, such as language acquisition (language). For example, if you are working with the *Six Women Poets* anthology (Kinsman, 1992), your 'assignment ideas' might be:

1   Group presentations on particular aspects of the poetry: treatment of motherhood, use of everyday domestic vocabulary; the relationship of these poems to more 'traditional' poetry.
2   Dramatising a poem for radio or television such as 'Letter from a Far Country' and performing the script.
3   Working on a display for the classroom which might be collages aiming at capturing the flavour and themes of each poet.
4   Getting groups to choose a poem from the selection and to work at sympathetic choral reading.

Each of these activities can function as initial exploratory activities on the text or as revision work prior to the exam itself. They also serve to develop your students' confidence, as first they share their ideas within a small group, and then present them to a larger audience. Either on your own or with a partner, devise some similar activities on your chosen text.

- By marking Year 11 work and comparing it with their own.
- It is also essential that you are confident about which Assessment Objectives are being assessed in each module, as these will directly influence the way you choose to approach the module.

SPAG

There continues to be a close emphasis on spelling, punctuation and grammar (SPAG) at A level. The AEB Chief Examiner's Report on 1996 English language examination answers reads in much the same way as more recent ones in identifying particular areas of concern:

Quality of Language

Assessment Objective 6 requires candidates to communicate clearly the knowledge and insight appropriate to the study of language. It was of great concern therefore to find many whose control of language was such that it intruded on the communication of their ideas. Areas of particular concern were:

- gross spelling errors: *were/where, there/their, are/our*;
- spelling errors in the technical language of their own discipline: *sentance, similie, apostrophie, coma, grammer, Received Pronounciation*;

- no capital letter on English;
- the use of commas at sentence boundaries;
- weakly constructed paragraphs and essay structure;
- convoluted and rambling sentences;
- confusion about when to use *which* and *this* when using subordinate or main clauses;
- a limited range of vocabulary to articulate the effects of texts.

Needless to say such errors are more than an irritant to examiners. All specifications emphasise the importance of clarity, accuracy, fluency and articulation at A Level English. Students of language, aware of attitudes to correctness, ought to recognise how such errors and the writers of such errors are perceived and the way mechanical accuracy functions as a gate-keeping device in the educational system. You could encourage your students to carry out an investigation of how employers judge errors and their makers. Focused work in textual analysis and re-casting would help students to consider and practise the effects created by different punctuation marks and sentence constructions.

(AEB, 1996)

You will need to work with students on their SPAG skills, as well as developing with them an appropriate A level essay style (which does not mean that all students write essays following the same 'formula'). One way of raising students' awareness of writing skills is for them to read each other's work and make constructive suggestions for improving their expression, structure and style.

Task 13.7 Marking, feedback and progression

Look at the opening to a Year 12 student's A level essay (Figure 13.1). In pairs, discuss what teaching strategies you would employ to aid this student's development of writing skills. How could you adapt strategies you would use at GCSE? Would an exposure to some critical theory help – and, if it would, how would you introduce it?

PREPARING TO TEACH A LEVEL

Building on the general points raised in the previous section on approaches to A level teaching, this section looks at specific aspects of A level English literature and English language specifications.

Question: Does Gittings' anthology reveal a rich variety in Keats' poetry? ('negotiated' title)

I have studied all the various themes Keats poems have took, Keats seemed to have the ability to express his thoughts and feelings in many ways, whether it be through rhyme, humour, sonnets or long, story-like poems such as 'Hyperion'.

In Keats early poetic years he seemed to have decided on a formula for his poems. Most of them were in rhyming couplets. Although Keats early poems had a flow and imagery to them it was not until his last days that Keats put emotions and deep feelings into his work.

Keats explored many different aspects of nature and love in his poems, he seemed to be in love with the idea of being a poet and he greatly admired other poets such as Shakespeare. Keats wrote about great works of literature in his poems and gave them high praise. 'On first looking into Chapman's Homer' was one of Keats early poems, in this poem he describes the inspiration and joy he feel from reading this classic text:

> Much have I travelled in the realms of gold,
> And many goodly states and kingdoms seen.

Keats is saying how he feels he has travelled into another world through literature, he was obviously passionate about exploring the mind's imagination.

Other poems written about literary heroes of Keats include 'On sitting down to read King Lear once again'. This tells of how he is inspired by Shakespeare: 'O Golden tongued Romance, with serene lute!' he seems to want to be as well known and respected as Shakespeare.

Keats wrote many long poems, most of these told stories such as 'Endymion'. This poem was four books long and is based on a great legend"

> From jagged trunks, and overshadoweth
> Eternal whispers, glooms, the birth, life, death.

The poetry was written in rhyme and reflects on the beauty of nature and love.

I feel that when rhyming in poems Keats seems to be limited by having to find rhyming words to express himself. I can see this when 'Endymion' is compared to 'Hyperion', another of Keats long poems. This is about a Greek myth of the defeat of the Titans. In this poem I feel that Keats is far more descriptive. It is full of images and feelings: 'While his bow'd head seem'd list'ning to the earth, His ancient mother, for some comfort yet'. Keats has used a drained sound to depict fear and misery in this line.

Keats has also wrote many humorous poems, most of these in his early days of poetry such as 'On the grasshopper and cricket' which was written as a competition between Keats and a friend to write a sonnet in a set time: 'In summer luxury, – he has never done with his delights; for when tired out with fun He rests at ease beneath some pleasant weed'. Keats wrote many of these poems that seem to be very light at first but he seemed to have a respect for poetry for even in this 'joke' poem he says 'The poetry of earth is never dead'. This shows that he believes poetry comes from the natural world, poetry is found in nature.

Figure 13.1 Student's essay

Knowing the specification

As has been indicated already, you need to become familiar with the relevant documentation so that you are clear about how much you have to teach and by when; how the work is assessed: by examination (closed or open book), or coursework? How do staff mark work so that students are aware of how they are meeting the Assessment Objectives?

Task 13.8 Knowing the context

In conjunction with your induction tutor or head of department, find out the following information before you embark on planning your teaching:

1   Which awarding body and specification does the department use – and why have they chosen this particular one? Read the specification, support material, trial marking activities, latest exam papers and examiners' reports to gain a good idea of the specification's emphasis and the kinds of task set.
2   How is coursework managed?

   •   Do students make an individual coursework choice or is it teacher selected?
   •   At what point in Year 12 and Year 13 is coursework studied?
   •   Do teachers share coursework or is it the responsibility of one individual?
   •   Is coursework 'taught' differently (e.g. through tutorials, seminars, etc.)?

3   What kinds of task do the department set A level students? Do all students do the same question/do students formulate their own questions/how frequently do they get set tasks? How much time are students expected to work on English tasks outside of lessons? Do they work on them in lessons?
4   How is work marked? Schools will certainly want to alert students to each module's Assessment Objectives – but how do they do this? Do they want you to indicate an AO when it is achieved in the margin of the essay? How important is the summative comment? Individual schools have their own marking strategies and it will be useful to know these in advance.
5   What entrance requirements does the school have to the sixth form? Are some students studying only two or three AS Levels, and, if so, why? How 'mixed ability' is the group?
6   Where will you be teaching? What kind of seating is available? How is the group 'used' to being seated?

Teaching a set text

While this section focuses on teaching literature at A level, much of it transfers to English language teaching. Bear in mind all the approaches and strategies you are employing at GCSE; the main body of this chapter has already led you away from any idea that the lecture situation will be appropriate for your A level group – other than in small quantities. You should also aim to guide your students to more independence in their thinking by offering alternative ways of responding to their reading. Although the requirements of each specification differ, no examining body rewards a student who trots out a practised answer which lacks originality and does not address the question directly. Remember that one marker will see all the scripts in one group and can easily tell the 'spoon-fed' answers which will resemble each other. Awarding bodies reward fresh analysis, although this must be informed by a close knowledge of the text and critical focus in terms of genre and cultural context.

Although you are aiming to encourage your students to become more responsible for their learning, there is quite a lot of preparation you will need to do in advance, even if it does not all transform itself to the classroom in several lectures to silent note-taking students. You may be teaching a text with which you are familiar or one which is totally new to you; in either case you will need to reread and annotate the text thoroughly. You will need to engage with the critical debates surrounding a writer and the work; these should include up-to-date articles, biographies, critical works and reviews, especially if it is not a contemporary work. Good starting points are the collections of critical essays in the Macmillan *New Casebook* series. Contemporary theory can be found on the Internet and is often fascinating. Think about the kinds of teaching strategies you might employ at various points such as: 'ways in' to the text; exploration of themes and concepts during the reading; opportunities for critical debate following reading. Consider setting the students small research projects, which they can present to each other, to explore the background of the text, the literary, historical, social and cultural contexts of its production. Secondary reading is now valued at A level, as reading reviews, essays or introductions to a text are useful means of demonstrating the areas of debate about the writer and the work, and this shows that 'meaning' is not a fixed buried treasure to be unearthed but continues to be made by different kinds of readers. Setting multiple-choice questions on a passage or poem where more than one answer may be justified from the text can be a valuable way of exploring how there may be 'meanings' in any text. In addition, find out what video and tape resources exist in relation to the text, such as films, screenplays and interviews with the writer. Consider carefully how these may be used most profitably.

It is common to approach an A level group with high expectations of debate and discussion, only to find that students 'clam up' and contributions are forced in order to break a silence. As in any context, discussion needs to be structured and works best when individuals have prepared a contribution before the lesson or by working in pairs or groups before reporting back to the larger group. Although there is sometimes a need for lessons to be teacher-centred, especially at first, successful A level teaching depends upon the extent to which students assume responsibility for reading and responding to texts. On the way to becoming autonomous readers, students will benefit from opportunities to explore the text through re-creative work such as pastiche and parody, performance (poetry and drama), hotseating, writing in a scene: in fact, all those strategies suggested at GCSE. For example, if you are to be teaching Margaret Atwood's *The Handmaid's Tale*, you might:

1   Identify various gaps in the text which students could 'fill' by doing a recreative piece – the ceremony from the viewpoint of the Commander's wife or another ending after the escape scene.

2   Introduce students to interviews with Margaret Atwood, and critiques of her work (often discovered in a single chapter of a critical text devoted to contemporary women writers); delegate one article to an individual or pair who read it and report back to the whole group.

3   Show the video of the novel, concentrating on selected sequences. Explore the differences, especially the imposition of a more chronological order and its 'extra scene' at the end.

4   Give students the opportunity to re-create Atwood's style.

5   Set up hotseating of Nick, Ofred's mother, or the Commander after the game of Scrabble.

Managing the reading

There is no easy answer to managing the initial reading and close textual analysis; although it is often found to be tedious, it is still common practice to slog through a text line by line. In spite of intentions to try other methods, teachers may resort to this method as the only way of ensuring that students know the text sufficiently well because they cannot be trusted to do it for themselves. There is no doubt that students – especially the weaker ones – find such an approach reassuring. However, the new A level invites teachers to approach the text more holistically, focusing on multiple readings rather than line-by-line 'translation'. Again, strategies used at GCSE are useful, such as setting a certain number of pages to read at home and then discussing them as a whole the following lesson, and mapping or jigsaw groups working on different aspects of the text afterwards (see e.g. *Wide Sargasso Sea: Teaching a Novel at A Level*, London: English and Media Centre).

Task 13.9 Introducing a text

Along with another student teacher, plan three consecutive AS lessons of 45 minutes each on the opening chapter or scene of a text you both know. (Or you could use *The Handmaid's Tale* if you have no common ground.) Assume the students have already read through the chapter/scene once. Three lessons may seem a lot of time, but beginnings and endings are vitally important to a text; aim to get your group focusing closely on the key features of your text, including language and structure as well as central themes and concepts. Plan to set pupils a task to explore the text and find out about the context and genre of the text as well as of the writer. For example, make a bibliography of Margaret Atwood's other books; contact the Margaret Atwood Society in Canada; find out what 'dystopia' means and other books in this genre.

Synoptic module: unseen work/pre-release (literature)

Module 6 requires students to be able to cope with any literary text confidently, to demonstrate close reading skills, to be aware of literary conventions, historical and cultural developments in literature *and* to write a clearly structured essay in good English under examination conditions. The area is, in fact, so huge that it can be daunting. At the same time there can be a real opportunity to share your own enthusiasms, availability of text and photocopying rights your only limitations. You do, however, need to guard against concentrating on one genre, such as poetry, because it is your strongest. As a starting point for planning a section of Module 6 preparation, it is useful to look at the AOs, the exemplar material and your centre's own set text choices to see if there are any obvious gaps. Unseen papers do not always have extracts from literature; specifications will set non-fiction texts such as travel writing or biography, and pre-release packs include critical readings. Unseen work is easiest to approach from a genre rather than a thematic angle, because getting students to read closely around, say, Romantic poetry or Theatre of the Absurd or the sonnet across the centuries, will give them a detailed understanding of how writers use and subvert the conventions of genre. Thematic work may not be ruled out completely – one specification's final module is theme based – but if you have a Year 12 group you will need to be laying pathways towards Module 6 and the best way to do this initially is to aim at a sound grounding in the way a genre works.

If you were planning a unit of work which was genre based, you could find examples of the short story, for example; you could include sub-genres such as crime stories, folk-tales, science fiction or popular romantic fiction. When studying them with the students you would explore them in a variety of ways but finish with a question in the style of the examination board. A thematic unit of work could be a range of texts about 'War' by historical and contemporary men and women writers across genres and cultures.

Unseen work also offers the opportunity to structure students' own wider reading. Near the start of your teaching experience you could ask students to report back on a literary text they have recently read and, at the same time, feed in some of your own recommendations. A similar session could be planned for later in your experience, in order to set up an atmosphere that students will always have a book 'on the go'. They need to be answerable for their wider reading by using a 'Reading Log' so that they read different genres, genders, times and cultures.

Coursework

The 30 per cent limit on coursework means that there are two aspects to coursework assignments:

1   coursework assignments ought to develop skills for the examination;
2   students should be given the chance to shine in a way that the examination may not allow them to.

You will therefore need to address both (1) and (2) in your planning for the coursework modules. In the light of (2), awarding bodies welcome a variety of texts from your own group, especially in Year 13. As with GCSE, you are likely to approach coursework differently, the spirit of coursework being that students have more control over what they write about. It is, however, imperative that your coursework titles are checked, preferably by the external coursework moderator.

Preparing to teach a particular aspect of English language

In order to prepare for this, you will need to do some background reading. Both awarding bodies provide comprehensive reading lists within the specification infor- mation, and there is a recommended list of texts which address teaching approaches in the 'Resources' section of this chapter. Some schools may have sets of English language textbooks from which students can work. Nevertheless, English language at A level – as with English literature – is about nurturing an informed personal response. Students are rewarded for their personal engagement with the subject, shown most clearly in their wealth of personal observations and examples. Although students need to know the theory and major research, these should lead to students being able to apply them to their own experience of language in use.

Whatever area of English language you are teaching, a collection and then analysis of current examples is essential. English language A level teaching cannot take place in the classroom alone (although you should, of course, draw on examples of accent, slang, cultural and gender significance as they occur): students need to be actively encouraged to seek out the language of the shopping centre, the nursery, the common- room, the assembly. Your best preparation for teaching an area of English language will therefore be to have collected examples of your own and to have an idea of teaching strategies which will encourage students to collect theirs. For example, if you are looking at spelling, research might include:

1   Scouring each other's essays for common misspellings.
2   Looking at signs on market stalls and outside shops.
3   Considering how spelling is taught in a local school.
4   Examining the purpose of the dictionary (and its history).
5   Collecting examples of deliberate misspellings in advertising/products/news headlines.

You will need to undertake the resource hunting yourself in order to encourage your own students to do the same. In order to clarify your objectives for the research and analysis, the Assessment Objectives will provide you with very useful guidelines when both setting tasks and assessing work. It is well worth taking your students out of school, in spite of the paperwork this may involve.

English language coursework: creative writing

Although you are unlikely to be given the responsibility for this during your initial teacher training, you may be working in a school that encourages you to contribute to creative writing lessons. Creative writing is valuable even outside the coursework module, since students will be writing within an already determined genre and examining its features in relation to their own work – which will enhance their awareness of language. Ask students to collect examples of the genre they are imitating, get them to share their work, and provide the opportunity for students to employ marking procedures as suggested in this chapter. If you are keen to explore creative writing at A level, it will always be relevant and welcomed by the school, since the accompanying analysis will benefit the students in the exam itself.

Synoptic module: Unseen/pre-release work (English language)

As with literature, it is important to consult your centre's chosen specification for guidelines about what is assessed. Nevertheless, you have a free hand in choosing what texts to analyse. Since the synoptic paper could reproduce any kind of written text, you could simply analyse a different example every lesson. However, this would not create any continuity for you – or continuity and progression for the students. Far better to choose a focal point, such as 'the way women are represented in the media' or 'children's fiction: 1900 to now'. This way, students can really focus on specific examples of language use and, at the same time, develop their skills and knowledge for the final module. The six modules are inextricably linked; it is the role of the teacher to show how skills are transferable from module to module and, if you choose an embracing 'theme' for close analysis, you can combine this with an essay question on the topic, tailored to your own specification's Module 6 style.

Equipment for A level English language

Ideally, English language A level needs to be resourced with lots of dictaphones, a video camera, tape-recorders and access to television, the Internet, Powerpoint and good dictionaries. In reality this is rarely possible, but do find out what resources would be available to you and how you can book them. Build the technology available into your lesson plans. In addition, find out the textbooks which are available in your school or training institution. Recommended texts are given at the end of this chapter.

Teaching A level 'English' (combined English language and literature)

An English A level 'combines' language and literature in the same way that GCSE does. For example, a unit of work based on *I Know Why the Caged Bird Sings* would extend to an exploration of how writers of varied genres (including the media) have expressed issues of racism over the past two centuries. As with all preparation, you would need to make reference to the awarding body's specification, supporting material and AOs.

RESOURCES

There are many valuable support materials available; seek the guidance of your tutor and colleagues in school, as well as student teachers in other schools. Be on the watch for new English education programmes and screenings on television. The Internet holds a wealth of resources, and it is well worth encouraging your students to use it whenever you embark on a new text/theme. BBC education sites are particularly useful. Revision resources based on the new specifications are readily available and are worth looking at: there are too many to mention here. The following list is a selection of what is available for communication Key Skill, English literature and English language teaching. Remember that it is not the text alone which determines the level of study, but the approach and the requirements of the response.

Language

Keith, G. and Shuttleworth, J. (1997) *Living Language*, Hodder & Stoughton.
Keith, G. and Shuttleworth, J (1999) *Investigating Talk*, Hodder & Stoughton. (The above have now produced an excellent series based on the modules.)
Barker, V. and Canning, J. (eds) (n.d.) *A Level English Language Topics: Authority, Class, Gender*, Somerset Wessex Publications.
Chalkface Project Communication Key Skills. Photocopiable resources for both tests and portfolios at Levels 1, 2 and 3.
Crystal, D. (1995) *The Cambridge Encyclopaedia of the English Language*, Cambridge University Press.
Goddard, A. (1991) *English Language A Level: The Starter Pack*, Lancaster Framework Press.
Goddard, A. (1993) *Researching Language*, Lancaster Framework Press.
Kelly, B., Hunt, M. and Brooks, J. (2002) *Getting the Evidence* (Key Skills), Collins.
Wainwright, J. and Hutton, J. (1992) *In Your Own Words: Advanced Level English Language*, Walton on Thames and Edinburgh: Nelson.

Literature

Croft, S. and Cross, H. (1997) *Literature, Criticism and Style*, Oxford: Oxford University Press.
McCulloch, R. (ed.) (1994) *English Literature A Level*, Cambridge: Pearson.
Peet, M. and Robinson, D. (1992) *Leading Questions*, London and Edinburgh: Nelson.

FURTHER READING

There is a significant shortage of discussion concerning teaching post-16. The following articles are useful starting points for debating some of the current issues surrounding A level teaching.

Canwell, S. and Ogborn, J. (1994) 'Balancing the Books: Modes of Assessment in A Level English Literature', in Brindley, S. (1994), pp. 149–153.
Eaglestone, R. (2000) *Doing English*, London: Routledge.

Greenwell, B. (1994) 'Alternatives at English A Level, Again', *English and Media Magazine*, summer, pp. 11–14.

Mitchell, S. (1994) 'Argument in English Literature at A Level and Beyond', *English and Media Magazine*, summer, pp. 15–20.

The English Association has a very useful website and contains papers on the new A levels: www.le.ac.uk//engassoc

14 Teaching English: critical practice

Jon Davison and Jane Dowson

INTRODUCTION

> The vast majority of teachers reported a high level of job satisfaction. Inevitably there were some who found the job unsatisfactory. Some of these, in particular, had little capacity for self-appraisal and consequently for self-improvement. . . . Some . . . had not come to terms with the time commitment of the job. . . . New teachers who felt that they could keep abreast of the work, and who were well matched to their posts, found the job rewarding. . . . Most were able to evaluate their own work accurately and to identify strengths and weaknesses.
>
> (OFSTED, 1993, paras 2.28, 2.29)

The above quotations from an OFSTED survey of newly qualified teachers identify the tension experienced by most at the beginning of their ITE course and work as secondary teachers: teaching their subject and fulfilling the other roles of teaching can be rewarding but there is a cost in terms of time and energy. The statements also identify one key to job satisfaction: self-evaluation. The term 'critical practice' indicates the two factors which are central to successful development as a teacher: the crucial role of school experience and the ability to reflect on that experience. With English teaching it is particularly crucial to develop your own principles by which you can set targets and evaluate yourself in relation to these targets because otherwise you can find yourself driven to please others who may have conflicting criteria; it is this, often unconscious drive to please or satisfy competing demands which produces the confusion and self-doubt which are common during initial teacher education. For example, you will be wanting to meet the needs and interests of pupils, the differing expectations of parents, the varying ideals and methods of class teachers; the professional tutor in school; the requirements of an OFSTED inspection; college or university directives and guidance; criteria for assignments and the attainment of standards.

'Standards' can seem somewhat daunting when first encountered. In addition, if you are sensitive to the political issues, you will realise that school-based ITE encourages an apprenticeship model of training but expects the student teacher to operate as a professional.

Furthermore, the statements that are used as criteria for assessing student teacher progress are inadequate for a process where the requisite qualities are always emergent and interrelate. Furlong and Maynard (1995) propose five broad stages of development which student teachers undergo during school experience. These stages are: 'early idealism', 'personal survival', 'dealing with difficulties', 'hitting a plateau' and 'moving on'. Furlong and Maynard are emphatic, however, that these stages are not 'discrete or fixed; rather, they are . . . interrelated and mutable' (Furlong and Maynard, 1995, p. 73). Similarly, the writers are keen to stress that progression through these stages should not be viewed in a 'crude or simplistic way':

> We do not suggest that student teachers simply progress along a narrow linear pathway, moving smoothly from stage to stage. This is far from the case. Our research indicates that development from 'novice' to 'professional educator' is dependent on the interaction between individual students, their teacher education programme, and the school context in which they undertake practical experience.
>
> (Furlong and Maynard, 1995, p. 70)

Development as a student teacher may therefore be seen to be the product of, among other things, the complex interactions between the individual, the HEI programme and the school context. These interactions are often perceived as disconnected; it is difficult, but vital, however, that all parties understand their interdependence. Arthur *et al.* (1997) offer a useful analogy for the process of student teacher development, which they believe takes place in the same way that a photograph develops in a developing tray:

> The image does not develop uniformly from nothing: at one moment a blank sheet; the next a fully-formed, crystal-clear picture. Instead, as the image swims into view, different parts of it emerge simultaneously and independently: a highlight here; a fragment of landscape there; a detail of shadow; now a facial feature, until the complete image emerges. What emerges first and last depends on interactions between information stored in the paper and the chemicals acting upon it. Similarly, the development of the student teacher's practice, knowledge, understandings and beliefs is a synthesis of experiences.

There are then no easy answers to the questions of 'What are my goals?', 'How well am I doing?', 'Will I make a good English teacher?' What can be said is that you are not expected to demonstrate or achieve all the requirements all at once. If you are unsure about your ability to 'make it' as a teacher, what will be looked for is evidence of progress. Progress will be made, and, more significantly, measured, through a process of setting specific targets and, through reflection, identifying achievements and areas for development. According to a survey by HMI, although some newly qualified teachers looked back on their school experience as a time of testing rather than freedom for growth, many appreciated the value of being able to make mistakes and learn from them. The teachers particularly valued having a wide range of classes and an opportunity to observe experienced teachers. One teacher referred to teaching practice as a testing ground; another wrote: 'It was a vital part of training. I had to try out ideas, make mistakes, discover weaknesses in myself and start again' (OFSTED, 1993, para. 4.27).

The process of target-setting and realistic self-appraisal cannot happen in isolation; it needs to be done in conjunction with other student teachers, class teachers, the head of department, your tutor and, above all, your mentor. You need verbal and written feedback which is constructive and specific. Again, the retrospective comments of a successful NQT endorse the importance of reflection and feedback:

> The staff at my teaching practice school were very supportive – checking lesson plans, making suggestions, observing and giving advice on classroom control. My college tutor was also always available for advice.
>
> (OFSTED, 1993, para. 4.27)

In what may seem to be a sea of uncertainty, there is a stronghold of consensus that development is complex and takes time. In fearing the censorship of the many masters and mistresses to whom you are answerable, you may find that you are your own severest critic. To some extent this is how it should be; you must be self-critical but realistic and constructive as well. In order to be neither over-optimistic nor over-critical you need to identify where you are – not where you would like to be (or fear that you might be) – before you can set realistic targets and monitor your progress.

OBJECTIVES

By the end of this chapter you should:

- begin to understand the nature of reflection and the processes of teacher development;
- have an understanding of the qualities, knowledge and skills you bring to teaching;
- be aware of your needs in areas of subject knowledge;
- be aware of the kind of working relationship you wish to develop with your mentor;
- be aware of the importance of the need to develop a wider professional role in the English department and the school as a whole.

MONITORING DEVELOPMENT

Obviously, your overriding aim for the period of your initial teacher education is to develop from a person who is interested in teaching into a confident, qualified subject teacher. The difficulty is in how to measure such a development. It has to be acknowledged that 'development' is a complex process and hard to categorise, particularly in terms of a complex role such as that of the teacher; consequently, a profile of standards is bound to be inadequate to describe individual development: 'As yet we have very little detailed understanding of how students develop their own practical professional knowledge in relation to such competences' (Furlong and Maynard, 1995, p. vii).[1] However, Berliner (1994, p. 108) proposes a number of stages in the development of teacher expertise, from the novice (student and many first-year teachers) to expert teacher ('a small number' of teachers). Indeed, the Teacher Training Agency structure of accreditation for the professional development of teachers relates closely to Berliner's model. However, many are critical of Berliner's 'simplistic' description of the novice which ignores not only the diversity of entrants to teacher education courses, but also the range of knowledge, experience and expertise they bring with them (see e.g. Calderhead and Robson, 1991). As Furlong and Maynard (1995, p. 182) observe, it is 'important to recognise that no student teacher enters the classroom as a complete novice – they bring with them a vast array of skills, knowledge and understandings derived from other contexts.' Task 14.1 is intended to help you to recognise that you start off with many of the qualities needed for qualified status.

Having shared your Individual Statement with other student teachers, it will have become apparent that you all have a variety of qualities and experiences which will enhance teaching. To categorise you and your colleagues as 'novices' ignores the expertise you bring to an ITE course. Postgraduates will have followed markedly different programmes during their time studying for a first degree. No doubt you have discovered the variety of degrees your fellow student teachers have obtained: some may have studied for 'traditional' single-subject degrees in English; others may have followed modular programmes; others still may have studied English and American Studies, Media Studies, drama, English and anthropology, for example. Such diversity will enrich your discussions throughout the year. However, it will be equally clear that while you have particular knowledge, skills and qualities related to your work in the classroom, your experiences of English as a subject may mean that there are gaps in relation to National Curriculum English. You should be actively seeking opportunities not only to use your strengths but also to develop your knowledge through reading, attending poetry readings, watching documentary programmes and adaptations, seeing plays and films, and debating texts with one another and with colleagues in school.

DEVELOPING ROLES AND RELATIONSHIPS

Working with your mentor

Crucial to 'critical practice' are the relationships between the student teacher, mentor and colleagues within the English department. Most ITE programmes have a teacher

Task 14.1 Individual Statement

No doubt you have found that the student teachers in your group have had a variety of experiences before they embarked upon a teacher education course: some may be newly graduated in their early twenties, while others may have also studied for a higher degree; some may have had some teaching experience in the UK or abroad; others may have raised families or be embarking upon a second career. Whatever your and their experience may have been, it is clear that you all have different kinds of knowledge and expertise which you will bring to your teaching. Equally, it is important that you are clear in your own mind about your own reasons for teaching. Using the headings given below, write an account of yourself. This will serve as a benchmark against which you will be able to gauge your development at strategic points of your course. When you have completed it, you may wish to share its contents with another student teacher, your tutor or mentor. Keep your Individual Statement as it will be useful at any stage during the year which seeks to review your development.

Individual Statement
Write an account of yourself using the following headings:

- Stage of the course
  Note the date so that you can monitor development since an earlier point or at a later point of the course.
- Reasons for wanting to teach
  Describe why/how you have decided to become a teacher.
- Me as teacher
  What sort of teacher do you wish to become? How would you like to be seen by pupils and colleagues?
- Previous experience
  Describe any experience you feel is relevant to the course, or to your chosen career.
- Personal skills and qualities
  Describe any qualities and skills you have which you believe to be appropriate to teaching.
- Attitude to the subject
  Describe any beliefs or principles you, hold about the nature and importance of English as a school subject (see Task 2.1).
- Professional concerns
  Describe any current issues or problems you are concerned about in relation to teaching.
- Any other issues

designated as a subject mentor, but it is highly likely that you will also have the support of the head of department, or of more experienced colleagues whose classes you are teaching. It is most important that you clarify the terms of your relationship with your colleagues very early on in your school experience.

Task 14.2 Subject Review

Read Chapter 3, 'Working with the National Curriculum'. You will see that National Curriculum English requires teachers to engage with the whole range of aspects of English as a subject. While you may be particularly confident in some areas, there may be gaps in your subject knowledge which need to be filled.

Photocopy the chart in Table 14.1. Complete the boxes to identify areas of progression and 'gaps'. The 'action' column should give you goals for your own development. Discuss with your mentor and tutor strategies for developing your knowledge, understanding and experiences through relevant reading, observations in school or training courses.

Task 14.3 Expectations of student teacher and mentor

Listed below are a number of words which might describe the many roles of a mentor. In order to clarify how you perceive your needs and expectations, number the words in order of priority (or you could identify your top three):

Colleague	Role model	Critic
Mediator	Motivator	Consultant
Assessor	Counsellor	Provider of materials
Collaborator	Diagnoser	Subject guru
Reviewer	Facilitator	Source of ideas

Having done so, discuss your expectations with your mentor and ask him to discuss his own views on the mentor's role. Equally, you might invite your mentor to do this exercise separately at the same time and then compare your lists. A good starting point for beginning to discuss your needs might be the Initial Statement and Subject Review you produced earlier.

While your mentor will be a knowledgeable, experienced English teacher, who is a good source of ideas and who will engage in discussion of key issues related to the teaching of English, you should not act simply as a 'sponge' soaking up what is offered. You are expected to be proactive; to take responsibility for your own development; to set agendas; to identify targets.

Central to your relationship should be the notion of openness: an ability to ask for, and willingness to receive, advice. Such openness can be developed once you understand exactly what is the relationship between development and judgement in the work of your mentor. You need to know your mentor's expectations of you and, of course, you need to articulate what expectations you have of your mentor. This approach will enable you to engage in productive discussion of your development – your successes, needs and targets for development – during lesson debriefings and review meetings with your mentor.

Table 14.1 Subject knowledge in relation to curriculum areas			
Subject area	**Confident**	**Not confident**	**Action**
Media Studies • analysis of film, TV and journalism • media production			
Drama • conventions such as role-play, hotseating • ability to perform drama activities			
Speaking and listening • facilitate group discussion • conventions of formal activities (e.g. debates)			
Reading • literature published before 1914 (drama, poetry, novels and short stories) • twentieth-century writers (drama, poetry, novels and short stories) • text from diverse cultures • non-fiction			
Writing • creative writing (to produce or analyse) • formal purposes, e.g. reviews, reports • variety of forms Teaching English: critical practice			
ICT • word processing • using specific programs • information retrieval (e.g. library, systems, CD-ROMs)			
Language study • language varieties • language change • standard English			
Teenage fiction • class reader • wider reading			

Collaborative teaching

Much of your time in the first weeks of school experience is likely to be spent observing in an attempt to begin to understand the processes and practices of the English classroom. Some student teachers find this period frustrating. Having made the decision to embark upon a teaching career they are keen to 'do it for real': to stand alone in front of a class and 'be a real teacher'. Such feelings are understandable, particularly when a student teacher has been observing an accomplished English specialist who makes it all seem so easy. But do not be in too great a hurry. There are other ways in which you will learn as much, if not more, about teaching than from teaching alone. After all, it is sobering to think that if you enter teaching in your early twenties, you will have some forty years to teach alone – ample time to perfect the art.

Obviously, observation will take you only so far. However, focused observation in which teacher and mentor have decided on the key aspects for attention, followed by a detailed discussion of the teacher's reasons for certain decisions and actions, can enable you to learn much. Engaging in a dialogue about the mentor's reasons for choosing one course of action, for example, rather than another at a particular point, will identify the multitude of choices that a teacher makes throughout the course of a lesson. Such choices are not only made during a lesson: they will have been made at the planning, preparation and evaluation stages.

Moving on from observation you can ideally negotiate some collaborative teaching. Collaborative teaching will enable you to develop your classroom skills, knowledge and understanding progressively and coherently. By taking responsibility for parts of lessons initially, you will be able to focus upon and develop key aspects of the teaching repertoire: beginning and ending lessons; handling transitions smoothly; instruction and exposition; question and answer; story-telling; managing and working with individuals, groups and a whole class. Collaborative teaching with your mentor will help you to develop your classroom teaching skills progressively and it will also enable you to gain access to those choices in relation to all aspects of teaching.

> When a mentor and learner-teacher take joint responsibility for a lesson, plan it together, and each play different parts in the teaching, with the parts played by the learner-teacher being selected to provide focused learning experiences, very nearly ideal conditions can be achieved for practising classroom strategies . . . having to explain to one's planning partner exactly what one's purposes are and the variety of considerations that lead one to choose particular ways of pursuing these purposes can help mentors to make explicit their own planning processes.
>
> (McIntyre and Hagger, 1993, p. 33)

At the heart of collaborative teaching and, indeed, of the working relationship with your mentor, is discussion: discussion that unravels and analyses the reasons for choices made while planning, teaching and evaluating collaboratively taught lessons. It is the articulation of these reasons for choices which will present the processes and practices of teaching, and the values and beliefs about the subject which underpin English teaching.

Collaborative teaching need not necessarily be carried out only with your mentor. There is much to be gained from teaching collaboratively with another teacher or a fellow student teacher. Collaborative teaching does not have to be seen as a one-way process either; classroom teachers who can adjust to co-operative teaching often discover an interchange of ideas, approaches and resources. Again, the survey of NQTs is useful in identifying the areas where teachers learn from others and where the student teacher and NQT can contribute to the department in which they work:

> In their initial plans, the most effective teachers usually identified the structure and content of each lesson. They included the grouping of pupils, the timing of the lesson, the choice of resources and the use of non-teaching support. The survey revealed instances where some aspects of the new teachers' plans had been adapted by other teachers in the school.
>
> (OFSTED, 1993, para 3.17)

Working in the English department

In the early period of their ITE courses many student teachers relate to a model of the teacher that focuses in the main on standing in front of a class. When you listed your skills, qualities and your reasons for teaching in your Initial Statement, it is likely that you used some of the following: 'enthusiasm', 'communication', 'love of subject', 'enjoyment of subject', 'empathy with pupils'. It is precisely these reasons that bring most of us to English teaching, but such attributes focus upon the act of teaching: the teacher in a classroom working with pupils. However, once in school it is clear that your working environment goes beyond the four walls of the classroom. While most of your day may be spent engaging with pupils, you will be expected to form positive working relationships with adults, be they mentors, departmental colleagues, other student teachers, support and administrative staff and parents. It is important, therefore, that you see yourself developing professionally in three ways, not only in the classroom, but also in the English department and in the school as a whole. You need to develop your professional role not only as a classroom practitioner, but also as fellow subject professional.

You may find that when you discuss your Individual Statement with other student teachers some hold a 'cultural heritage' view of English and are interested mainly in passing on the humanistic values perceived as being located in literary texts. It may be that they see this approach to be closely linked to transmission, teacher-centred modes of teaching. Conversely, others may hold a 'cultural analysis' view of the subject and are more likely to be interested in how readings of texts are constructed, and in their teaching wish to involve pupils actively in exploring and constructing them. (For further discussion of beliefs about the nature of English as a subject, see Chapters 1 and 2.)

Equally, the same diversity of beliefs is true of experienced English teachers. While the English department in which you are placed acts as a cohesive and united team of subject specialists, it is important to recognise that in any English department there will be a wide range of beliefs about the importance of different aspects of the subject; a diversity of opinions on pedagogy; a variety of teaching styles — all of which are informed by the values and beliefs of the members of the departmental team. The shared aims and goals of the English department that are exemplified in collaboratively produced schemes of work, for example, may well be the product of a variety of values, beliefs and attitudes held by different departmental members. There is, of course, no *one* way to teach English. Indeed, when you observe experienced English teachers it is likely that you will see them employ a range of styles and approaches with different classes, or, indeed, within the same lesson.

The range of perspectives that teachers of English hold is part of the fabric of the English department. Such a range of perspectives may well be implicit in the day-to-day work of the department, but the differences are likely to be made visible in the discourse of departmental meetings. In such meetings English teachers have to respond to the variety of values, beliefs and attitudes located in the products of many educational discourses: for example, a new National Curriculum English order to be implemented; revised GCSE specifications to be planned for and taught; GNVQ initiatives; draft LEA, school and departmental policies tabled for discussion.

Departmental meetings are at the heart of a teacher's working life and are an excellent source for your own professional development. However, initially they can appear daunting occasions. To be surrounded by confident, experienced subject specialists can make you all too aware of how little you really know about teaching the subject. However, you should attempt to make a contribution to the work of the department beyond your own classroom teaching. Good relationships with your departmental colleagues also mean sharing ideas and resources. It is important, therefore, for you to take as full a part as is appropriate in departmental discussions and decision-making. Many teachers, departments and schools engage in teacher education precisely because student teachers bring a new perspective and fresh ideas. You should display confidence (but not over-confidence) in your knowledge and abilities, but also maintain a realistic awareness of your needs and the gaps in your knowledge and understanding, which are, for the most part, the result of the limited experience of teaching you have had hitherto. Above all, you will be expected to ask questions. Such involvement will develop your understandings of how a department is managed, how a school curriculum emerges, and it will highlight the fact that teaching is always a matter of choices. It will deepen your understanding of classroom practice by uncovering the complex interactions between the range of educational discourses with which an English teacher engages both inside and outside the classroom. It is important, therefore, that you discuss with your mentor not only the possibility of your attending departmental meetings but, where appropriate, parents' evenings and professional development activities at departmental and whole school levels, at which you will gain further insight into the work of an English teacher. In relation to examination work – whether or not you are actually teaching GCSE, A level or vocational groups – it will be extremely valuable to you to attend moderation meetings for two reasons. First, such meetings allow you to begin to become aware of the standards expected of pupils to achieve certain levels in the National Curriculum, or grades in public examinations. Second, discussion at such meetings explores the differences of opinion as to the relative importance of various aspects of English that are exemplified in pupils' work.

Clearly, it is important to recognise that any English department, while working as a united team, with stated aims and policies on a variety of curricular issues, is in fact the sum of a range of values and beliefs related to educational discourses. In order for you to become developed fully as a subject specialist classroom teacher, it is important to participate fully in the life and work of the English department. As Arthur *et al.* (1997, p. 144) sum up,

> subject teaching should not just be seen in terms of classroom practice; nor should further professional development only be seen in terms of a student teacher's involvement in extra curricular activities and pastoral work: both facets of school experience should be located firmly within the discourses of the subject department.

REFLECTION

Naturally, in the early days of school experience, like all student teachers, you will be most concerned by approaches to class management. Undoubtedly, one of the key targets at this point of any HEI course is the development of the basic skills of teaching. However, it is equally important to realise that the teaching of a subject is not unproblematic. As Dart and Drake (1996, p. 63) observe: 'a student must possess certain beliefs about the subject, beliefs which are acted out in the way the student teaches, manages the classroom and establishes relationships with pupils.'

Although 'a number of competing models and conceptions of the "reflective practitioner" exist, varying in the meaning which they give to the terminology they use and in the nature of the theoretical articulation of the notion which they offer' (McLaughlin, 1996, p. 30), Calderhead (1989) provides a useful overview of the definitions of reflection which have emerged in the writing related to teaching and teacher education. Reflective practice incorporates a variety of features including: problem-setting and -solving; the development of analytical skills and attitudes that facilitate reflection, such as self-awareness and self-determination; the examination of values, moral principles and ideological and institutional constraints. Such features encompass, and are the foundation of, the process, content, preconditions and product of reflection. To sum up, reflection is 'the mental process of structuring or restructuring an experience, a problem, or existing knowledge, or insights' (Korthagen and Wubbels, 1995, p. 55).

Frost (1993, p. 140) helpfully summarises the purposes of reflection and how the process enables the student teacher to:

- assess his or her own skills and to improve them;
- evaluate the chosen teaching strategies and materials in terms of their appropriateness;
- question the values embedded in those practices and proceed to challenge the aims and goals for teacher education;
- continue to examine and clarify their personal values and beliefs about society and pedagogy;
- theorise about the context of their pedagogical practice – that is, to try to develop explanations about the pupils, the interactions in the classroom and about the processes of teaching and learning;

Task 14.4 Theory and practice

The following four statements are philosophical in nature. Decide which you agree with most. Explain to your tutor or another student teacher the reasons for your choice.

1   An active involvement with literature enables pupils to share the experiences of others. They will encounter and come to understand a wide range of feelings and relationships by entering vicariously the worlds of others, and in consequence, they are likely to understand more of themselves.

(DES and Welsh Office, 1989)

2   British education is directed towards the dissemination of certain ideological values, whose preservation will ensure that the economic inequalities of British society remain unchallenged. . . . As educators, we have a duty to enable our students to understand the relations between language and society, culture and economics, knowledge and power. In other words, we must develop goals, classroom approaches and material which will transform 'English' into the study of the world and how our entire culture is produced, sustained, challenged, remade.

(Macdonald *et al.*, 1989, p. 16)

3   Teaching English at any level needs to be founded on an understanding of the nature of language and the way in which it is acquired and developed. The teacher must have a clear grasp of the range of purposes for which we need and use language. We need it for the transactions of our everyday lives. We need it for personal and social relationships. We need it for reflecting on and understanding our experiences, for responding to the world about us, and for understanding and sharing the experience and insights of others. We use it to resolve problems, to make decisions, to express attitudes. Part of the skill of the teacher is to show how the various uses of language illuminate each other: how, for example, the language resources used in a poem differ from and complement those used in a set of instructions for carrying out a process. Good teaching of English, at any level, is far more than the inculcation of skills: it is an education of the intellect and sensibility.

(DES, 1984, par. 3.2, p. 13)

4   [The future agenda for English teaching must be] a curriculum which values the whole person, where pupils are taught and learn appropriate skills and knowledge, in meaningful, relevant contexts. We need to create a situation where pupils learn to appreciate others' creativity and develop their own; to construct texts and understand how and why texts are produced; to appreciate and respond to texts. All this within a context which recognises and values cultural diversity and students' own and others' heritage. A future where students have the skills necessary to function in all aspects of their lives: at work, leisure activities and in their personal lives. Ultimately, to help students to take a full part in the local community and society at large by exercising moral values of honesty, justice, fairness and democracy.

(Shreeve, 1995, p. 1)

When you have considered the above statements, try to compose your own statement about the future agenda for English teaching.

- examine the adequacy of theories about pedagogical contexts and processes and develop a critique of them.

The purposes of reflection are much wider, then, than only the acquisition of classroom skills. Reflecting enables you to recognise the aims, values and beliefs that underpin classroom practice and the educational processes of the school. Reflection within an ITE course will enable you to develop practice in the short term, and also begin the development of habitual reflection that will subsequently enable you to continue to improve practice throughout your career. To elaborate: structured, guided reflection on, or analysis of, your own practice, in the light of required reading, or school-based investigations which are part of an ITE course, will begin to develop initial competence in the context of a particular school-experience classroom. This experience will also develop practices of reflection which, as a newly qualified teacher, you may use to facilitate further professional development.

In order to reflect, you need to have a set of terms by which to evaluate how you fulfil your role as a teacher; a commonly understood set of terms is what is understood by a 'philosophy'. It is common to hear that 'philosophy' or 'theory' are not relevant when learning skills and strategies; you do, however, need a framework of principles by which to evaluate what you are doing and to enable you to make decisions that appear to be consistent. A 'philosophy' does not have to be fixed or limiting; instead, it should be dynamic as it responds to experience. It should be developed from combining your reading and analysis of other people's theories with your own ideas and experience. When you apply for a job, your letter of application and your answers to questions in interview will be expected to reflect your personal aims as an English teacher.

SUMMARY AND KEY POINTS

Often, particularly in the early days of school experience, student teachers give little thought to their potential roles as departmental colleagues, or of at some stage being given responsibility for areas of the curriculum in a subject department. This is entirely appropriate, as the initial task on which student teachers focus is the ability to motivate and manage pupils in the classroom. However, an approach to school experience that sees it only as a basis for acquiring a set of context- and value-free skills in the English classroom is likely to lead to a relationship with a mentor which might be called an 'apprenticeship'. Such a model of school experience is insufficient. It is not the intention of ITE courses to 'clone' teachers, which would not only be undesirable, but also impossible. Such a model pays insufficient attention to the social dynamics of becoming a teacher. It undervalues the process of developing a personal philosophy that may be articulated and translated into practice through the synthesis of experiences. It does not take account of the varying experiences and skills that each student teacher brings to his or her initial teacher education.

An open working relationship with your mentor can allow you to begin to probe your own personal theories of teaching and learning – the theories and images of teaching and learning that all student teachers bring to a teacher education course

(Calderhead and Robson, 1991) and which develop and change during school experience. Griffiths and Tann (1992) propose that reflection should not be viewed as hierarchical (i.e. practical and critical modes are equally important); rather, all student teachers and teachers, who might be considered to be reflective, should engage in all levels in their careers. Therefore a student teacher, or, indeed, an experienced teacher, might engage in the form of reflective practice most appropriate to the context in which they find themselves:

> Everyone has to start somewhere, and no-one can start everywhere. It is being argued that all of the levels are an essential part of reflective practice. At any one time the focus may be on one or another of them, but it is vital that each reflective practitioner should follow all of them at some time.
>
> (Griffiths and Tann, 1992, p. 79)

Mentor and student teacher, by engaging in an articulation of personal experience, by investigating the educational discourses embedded in the descriptions of experience and practice, and by engaging in dialogue, can understand better the contexts in which they are working; in these ways they will both develop professionally.

NOTE

1   'Competences' were the forerunners of standards.

FURTHER READING

Arthur, J., Davison, J. and Moss, J. (1997) *Subject Mentoring in the Secondary School*, London: Routledge. This book looks at the nature of student teacher development in the light of the changes in teacher education since 1992. It examines tendencies in subject mentoring and proposes that 'discursive' mentoring is more likely to promote development. The book also contains case study material relating to observation and collaborative teaching in the English classroom.

Capel, S., Leask, M. and Turner, T. (2001) *Learning to Teach in the Secondary School* (3rd edn), London: Routledge. First published 1995. The companion volume to this book considers all aspects of school experience from a generic point of view. It supports student teachers whatever their subject.

Dart, L. and Drake, P. (1996) 'Subject Perspectives in Mentoring', in McIntyre, D. and Hagger, H., *Mentors in Schools: Developing the Profession of Teaching*, London: David Fulton. This chapter considers in depth aspects of subject mentoring with particular focus on the English classroom.

OFSTED (1993) *The New Teacher in School*, London: HMSO. This is a report of the third survey by HMI of newly qualified teachers, following others in 1981 and 1987. It includes reference by NQTs to their training and recommendations for improved initial teacher education.

Bibliography

Abbott, C. (1995) 'What use are the new technologies?', in Protherough, R. and King, P. *The Challenge of English in the National Curriculum*, London: Routledge.

Aers, L. and Wheale, N. (1991) *Shakespeare in the Changing Curriculum*, London: Routledge.

Alexander, P. (ed.) (1951) *William Shakespeare: The Complete Works*, London and Glasgow: Collins.

Alvardo, M. and Boyd-Barrett, O. (eds) (1992) *Media Education: An Introduction*, London: BFI/Open University Press.

Andrews, R. (ed.) (1989) *Narrative and Argument*, Buckingham: Open University Press.

Arnold, M. (1869) *Culture and Anarchy*, London: Penguin (1969 edn).

Arthur, J., Davison, J. and Moss, J. (1997) *Subject Mentoring in the Secondary School*, London: Routledge.

Arts Council (1992) *Drama in Schools: Arts Council Guidance on Drama Education*, London: Arts Council.

Bagnall, N. (ed.) (1973) *New Movements in the Study and Teaching of English*, London: Temple Smith.

Bain, E. and Bain, R. (1997) *The Grammar Book*, Sheffield: NATE.

Bain, R. (1991) *Reflections: Talking about Language*, London: Hodder & Stoughton.

Baldick, C. (1983) *The Social Mission of English Criticism*, Oxford: Oxford University Press.

Ball, S. (1985) 'English for the English', in Goodson, I. (ed.) *Social Histories of the Secondary Curriculum*, London: Falmer Press.

Barker, C. (1977) *Theatre Games*, London: Methuen.

Barker, V. and Canning, J. (eds) (n.d.) *A Level English Language Topics: Authority, Class, Gender*, Somerset: Wessex Publications.

Barnes, D. (1976) *From Communication to Curriculum*, London: Penguin.

Barnes, D., Britton, J. and Rosen, H. (1975) *Language, the Learner and the School*, Harmondsworth: Penguin.

Barrett Browning, E. (1988) *Selected Poems*, London: Chatto & Windus.

Bazalgette, C. (1989) *Media Education: An Introduction*, London: BFI.

—— (1996) 'Beyond the Province of Enthusiasts: Re-establishing Media Education', *English and Media Magazine*, 34, summer.

BBC Education (1996) *Shakespeare Shorts*, London: BBC.

Benton, P. (1996) 'Children's reading and viewing in the nineties', in Davies, C. (ed.) *What is English Teaching?*, Milton Keynes: Open University Press, pp. 76–104.

Benton, P. and Benton, S. (1991, 1990) *Inside Stories 3 and 4*, London: Hodder & Stoughton.

Berliner, D. (1994) 'Teacher Expertise', in Moon, B. and Mayes, A. S. *Teaching and Learning in the Secondary School*, London: Routledge.

Bethell, A. (1983) *Eyeopener*, 1 and 2, London: Cambridge University Press.

Bhatt, S. (1994) 'The Writer', in Bhinda, M. (ed.) *Jumping Across Worlds*, Sheffield: NATE.

Black, P. (1992) 'Introduction', in Black, P. *et al. Education: Putting the Record Straight*, Stafford: Network Educational Press.

Blatchford, R. (ed.) (1986) *The English Teacher's Handbook*, London: Hutchinson.

Bleiman, B. (1991) *Activities for A Level English*, London: Longman.

—— (1995) *The Poetry Pack*, London: English and Media Centre.

Bloom, V. (1986) 'You'll Love this Stuff!', in Styles, M. (ed.) *You'll Love this Stuff!*, Cambridge: Cambridge University Press.

Bloome, D. and Stierer, B. (1995) *Reading Words*, Sheffield: NATE.

Board of Education (BoE) (1904) *Elementary Code*, London: HMSO.

—— (1910) *Circular 753*, London: HMSO.

—— (1921) *The Teaching of English in England* (Newbolt Report), London: HMSO.

—— (1926) *Education and the Adolescent* (Hadow Report), London: HMSO.

—— (1938) *Report on Secondary Education* (Spens Report), London: HMSO.

—— (1943) *Curriculum and Examinations in Secondary Schools* (Norwood Report), London: HMSO.

Bogdanov, M. (1994) *Shakespeare on the Estate*, part of the series Bard on the Box, BBC 2 Television.

Bolton, G. (1992) *New Perspectives on Classroom Drama*, New York: Simon & Schuster.

Bowker, J. (1991) *Secondary Media Education; A Curriculum Statement*, London: British Film Institute.

Branston, R. and Stafford, R. (1996) *The Media Student's Book*, London: Routledge.

Brindley, S. (ed.) (1994) 'Part IV: Writing', *Teaching English*, London: Routledge

British Film Institute (2000) *Moving Images in the Classroom: A Secondary Teachers' Guide to Using Film and Television*, London: BFI.

Britton, J. (1970) *Language and Learning*, London: Penguin.

—— (1973) 'How we got here', in Bagnall, N. (ed.) *New Movements in the Study and Teaching of English*, London: Temple Smith.

Broadbent, S. (1994) *Romeo and Juliet: Classroom Material*, London: English and Media Centre.

—— (1995) *Key Stage 3 English Units*, London: English and Media Centre.

Brooks, G., Cato, V., Fernandes, C., Gorman, T., Kispal, A. and Orr, G. (1996) *Reading Performances at Nine*, Slough: NFER.

Browning, R. (1975) *Men and Women and Other Poems*, London: J.M. Dent.

Brownjohn, S. (1980) *Does It Have to Rhyme?*, London: Hodder & Stoughton.

—— (1994) *To Rhyme or Not To Rhyme?: Teaching Children to Write Poetry*, London: Hodder & Stoughton.

Bruner, J. (1986) *Actual Minds, Possible Worlds*, Cambridge, Mass.: Harvard University Press.

Buckingham, D. (1993) *Children Talking Television*, London: Falmer Press.

Buckingham, D. and Grahame, J. (1998) 'English and Media Teaching Ten Years On: Teachers Talking', *English and Media Magazine*, 39, autumn.

Buckingham, D., Grahame, J. and Sefton-Green, J. (1995) *Making Media: Practical Production in Media Education*, London: English and Media Centre.

Buckley, K. *et al.* (1995) *Exploring Pre-twentieth-century Fiction: A Language Approach*, Lancaster: Framework Press.

Burgess, T. (1996) 'English Teaching and its Narratives', in *Changing English*, London: Institute of Education, University of London, March, vol. 3, no. 1, pp. 57–77.

Burgess, R. and Gaudry, P. (1985) *Time for Drama*, Buckingham: Open University Press.

Burn, A. (1998) 'The Robot in the Cornfield: Media Arts Across the Curriculum', *English and Media Magazine*, 39, autumn.

Byron, K. (1986) *Drama in the English Classroom*, London: Methuen.

Calderhead, J. (1987) 'The Quality of Reflection in Student Teachers', *European Journal of Teacher Education*, 10, 3, pp. 269–278.

—— (1989) 'Reflective Teaching and Teacher Education', *Teaching and Teacher Education*, 5, 1, pp. 43–51.

Calderhead, J. and Robson, M. (1991) 'Images of Teaching: Student Teachers', *Early Conceptions of Classroom Practice, Teaching and Teacher Education*, 7,1, pp. 1–8.

Canwell, S. and Ogborn, J. (1994) 'Balancing the Books: Modes of Assessment in A Level English Literature', in Brindley, S. *Teaching English*, London: Routledge, pp. 149–153.

Capel, S., Leask, M. and Turner, T. (2001) *Learning to Teach in the Secondary School*, London: Routledge (3rd edn).

Carter, R. (ed.) (1990) *Knowledge about Language and the Curriculum: The LINC Reader*, London: Hodder & Stoughton.

Cook, H. and Styles, M. (1988) *There's a Poet behind You*, London: A. & C. Black.

Cox, B. (1991) *Cox on Cox – An English Curriculum for the 1990s*, London: Hodder & Stoughton.

—— (1995) *The Battle for the National Curriculum*, London: Hodder & Stoughton.

Crystal, D. (1987) *The Cambridge Encyclopaedia of Language*, Cambridge: Cambridge University Press.

Daiches, D. (1956) *Critical Approaches to Literature*, London: Longman.

Daly, M., Mathews, S., Middleton, D., Parker, H., Prior, J. and Waters, S. (1989) 'Different Views of the Subject: A PGCE Perspective', *The English Magazine*, 22, pp. 15–17.

Dart, L. and Drake, P. (1996) 'Subject Perspectives in Mentoring', in McIntyre, D. and Hagger, H. *Mentors in Schools: Developing the Profession of Teaching*, London: David Fulton.

Davison, J. (1990) 'Uneasy Rider', *Times Educational Supplement*, 21 October.

Davison, J. and Grahame, J. (1992) *Media Directory*, Sheffield: NATE/English and Media Centre.

Davison, J. and Moss, J. (2000) *Issues in English Teaching*, London: Routledge.

Daw, P. (1995) 'Differentiation and its Meanings', *English and Media Magazine*, 32, summer, pp. 11–15.

Dearing, R. (1996) *The New Qualifications Framework 16–19*, revised version, London: HMSO.

DES (1963) *Half our Future* (Newsom Report), London: HMSO.

—— (1975) *A Language for Life* (Bullock Report), London: HMSO.

—— (1983) *Popular TV and Schooling*, London: HMSO.

—— (1984) *English from 5 to 16*, London: HMSO.

—— (1987) *The National Curriculum 5 to 16: A Consultation Document*, London: HMSO.

—— (1988a) *The Report of the Committee of Enquiry into the Teaching of English Language* (Kingman Report), London: HMSO.

—— (1988b) *National Curriculum Task Group on Assessment and Testing: A Report* (TGAT), London: HMSO.

—— (1989) *English for Ages 5 to 16* (Cox Report), London: DES.

—— (1990) *English in the National Curriculum (No. 2)*, London: HMSO.

DES and Welsh Office (DES and WO) (1989) *English for Ages 5 to 16* (Cox Report 2), London: HMSO.

—— (1990) *The Statutory Order: English in the National Curriculum*, London: HMSO.

—— (1993a) *English 5–16 (1993)*, London: HMSO.

—— (1993b) *The Revised Order: English in the National Curriculum*, London: HMSO.

—— (1995) *English in the National Curriculum* (Dearing Report), London: HMSO.

DES/BFI (1989) *Primary Media Education: A Curriculum Statement*, London: BFI.

DFE (1993) *Boys and English*, London: HMSO.

—— (1995) *English in the National Curriculum*, London: HMSO; Cardiff, Welsh Office Education Department.

DfEE (2001) *Framework for Teaching English: Years 7, 8 and 9*, London: DfEE.

DfEE/QCA (1999a) *The National Curriculum for England: Citizenship*, London: DfEE/QCA.

—— (1999b) *The National Curriculum for England: English*, London: DfEE/QCA.

Dhondy, F. (1978) *Come to Mecca*, London: Fontana Lions.

Dickens, C. (1985) 'A Christmas Carol', in *The Christmas Books*, Vol. 1, London: Penguin Classics.

Dixon, J. (1967) *Growth Through English*, Oxford: Oxford University Press/NATE.

Dover Wilson, J. (1932) 'Introduction', in Arnold, M. *Culture and Anarchy*, London: Penguin (1969 edn).

Dutton, B. and Mundy, J. (1995) *Media Studies: An Introduction*, London: Longman.

Eagleton, T. (1983) *Literary Theory*, Oxford: Blackwell.

Elsom, J. (ed.) (1992) *Is Shakespeare Still Our Contemporary?*, London: Routledge.

English and Media Centre (1984) *Changing Stories*, Sheffield: NATE.

Evening Chronicle (1987) *Bossy Parrot*, Newcastle: Bloodaxe Books.

Foggin, J. (1992) *Teaching English in the National Curriculum: Real Writing*, London: Hodder & Stoughton.

Fraser, P. (1993) 'Chaucer with Chips: Right-wing Discourse about Popular Culture', *English and Media Magazine*, 28, p. 19.

Freire, P. (1987) *Literacy: Reading the Word and the World*, London: Routledge & Kegan Paul.

Frost, D. (1993) 'Reflective Mentoring and the New Partnership', in McIntyre, D., Hagger, H. and Wilkin, M. *Mentoring: Perspectives on School-based Teacher Education*, London: Kogan Page.

Fuller, F. and Bown, O. (1975) 'The Good Mentor', in Ryan, K. (ed.) *Teacher Education*, 74th Year Book of the National Society for the Study of Education, Chicago: University of Chicago Press.

Furlong, J. and Maynard, T. (1995) *Mentoring Student Teachers*, London: Routledge.

Garfield, L. (1992) *Shakespeare: The Animated Tales*, London: BBC.

Gibson, R. (1994) 'Teaching Shakespeare in schools', in S. Brindley (ed.) *Teaching English*, London: Routledge, pp. 140–148.

Gilmour, M. (1994) *RSA Shakespeare in Schools Project 1992–4: A Review*, London: RSA Publications.

Goddard, A. (1993) *Researching Language*, Lancaster: Framework Press.

Goodman, S. and Graddol, D. (1997) *Redesigning English: New Texts, New Identities*, London: Routledge.

Goodson, I. (ed.) (1985) *Social Histories of the Secondary Curriculum*, London: Falmer Press.

Goodwyn, A. (1992) 'English Teachers and the Cox Models', *English in Education*, 26 (3), pp. 4–10.

Gordon, L. (1984) *Virginia Woolf: A Writer's Life*, Oxford: Oxford University Press.

Gossman, L. (1981) 'Literature and Education', *New Literary History*, 13.

Graham, J. (1990) *Pictures on the Page*, Sheffield: NATE.

Grahame, J. (1990) *The English Curriculum: Media*, Sheffield: NATE/English and Media Centre.

—— (1993) *Advertising*, Sheffield: NATE/English and Media Centre.

—— (1996) *The News Pack*, London: English and Media Centre/NATE.

Greenlaw, L. (1996) 'Rhyme with Reason', *Times Educational Supplement*, 30 August, p. 23.

Greenwell, B. (1994) 'Alternatives at English A Level, Again', *English and Media Magazine*, summer, pp. 11–14.

Griffiths, M. and Tann, S. (1992) 'Using Reflective Practice to Link Personal and Public Theories', *Journal of Education for Teaching*, 18, 1, pp. 69–84.

Halliday, M.A.K. (1973) *Explorations in the Functions of Language*, London: Edward Arnold.

Hamblin, K. (1978) *Mime*, London: Lutterworth.

Harrison, T. (1984) *Selected Poems*, Harmondsworth: Penguin.

Hart, A. and Hicks, A. (2002) *Teaching Media in the English Curriculum*, Stoke-on-Trent: Trentham Books.

Hayhoe, M. and Parker S. (1988) *Words Large as Apples*, Cambridge: Cambridge University Press.

Hickman, J. (1995) 'NC English Version 3.2: Flawed but Workable', *English and Media Magazine*, 32, summer, pp. 4–7.

Hilton, M. (ed.) (1996) *Potent Fictions: Children's Literacy and the Challenge of Popular Culture*, London: Routledge.

HMI (1984a) *English from 5 to 16*, London: HMSO.

—— (1984b) *The Curriculum from 5 to 16*, London: HMSO.

—— (1986) *English from 5 to 16: The Responses to Curriculum Matters 1*, London: HMSO.

—— (1993) *The New Teacher in School*, London: HMSO.

Hodgson, J. and Richards, E. (1974) *Improvisation*, London: Methuen.

Holderness, G. (ed.) (1988) *The Shakespeare Myth*, Manchester: Manchester University Press.

Holding, P. (1992) *Romeo and Juliet*, Text and Performance Series, London: Macmillan.

Hornbrook, D. (1988) '"Go play, boy, play": Shakespeare and Educational Drama', in Holderness, G. (ed.) *The Shakespeare Myth*, Manchester: Manchester University Press, pp. 145–159.

Howe, A. (1992) *Making Talk Work*, London: Hodder & Stoughton; reprinted 1997, Sheffield: NATE.

IAAMSS (1952) *The Teaching of English*, Cambridge: Cambridge University Press.

ILEA English Centre (1984) *Changing Stories*, London: English and Media Centre/NATE.

Jackson, D. (1982) *Continuity in Secondary English*, London and New York: Methuen.

Jenkins, T. (1995) 'GNVQ Media: 1 A Beginner's Guide, 2 Work in Progress', *English and Media Magazine*, 32, summer, pp. 5–39.

—— (1996a) *GNVQ Media: Production and Communication Intermediate*, London: Longman.

—— (1996b) *GNVQ Media: Production and Communication Advanced*, London: Longman.

Johnson, J. (1992) '"Made tongue-tied by authority": The Orders for English', in Norman, K. (ed.) *Thinking Voices*, London: Hodder & Stoughton.

Jones, P. (1991) *The Shakespeare Workshop*, New South Wales: St Clair Press.

Keith, G. (1991) *Knowledge about Language*, Coventry: NCET.

Kemeny, H. (ed.) (1990) *Talking IT Through*, Coventry: NCET.

Kinsman, J. (ed.) (1992) *Six Women Poets*, Oxford: Oxford University Press.

Korthagen, F. and Wubbels, T. (1995) 'Characteristics of Reflective Practitioners: Towards an Operationalisation of the Concept of Reflection', *Teachers and Teaching: Theory and Practice*, 1,1, pp. 51–72.

Kress, G. (1992) *Learning to Write*, London and New York: Routledge.

—— (1995) *Writing the Future: English and the Making of a Culture of Innovation*, Sheffield: NATE.

Laban, R. (1948) *Modern Educational Dance*, London: Macdonald & Evans.

Lake, C. and Rose, M. (eds) (1990) *Language and Power*, London: ILEA Afro-Caribbean Language and Literacy Project in Further and Adult Education.

LATE (1995) *The Real Cost of SATs*, London: LATE.

Lankshear, C., Gee, P., Knobel, M. and Searle, C. (1997) *Changing Literacies*, Buckingham: Open University Press.

Leach, S. (1992) *Shakespeare in the Classroom*, Buckingham: Open University Press.

Leask, M. and Litchfield, D. (1999) 'Using ICT in Your Particular Subject', in Leask, M. and Pachler, N. (eds) *Learning to Teach Using ICT in the Secondary School*, London: Routledge.

Leask, M. and Williams, L. (1999) 'Whole-School Approaches: Integrating ICT across the Curriculum', in Leask, M. and Pachler, N. (eds) *Learning to Teach Using ICT in the Secondary School*, London: Routledge.

Leavis, F. R. (1948) *The Great Tradition*, London: Chatto & Windus.

Leavis, F.R. and Thompson, D. (1933) *Culture and Environment*, London: Chatto & Windus.

Lemin, K. (2001) 'Practical Production Work Within an Integrated English and Media Curriculum: Acquisition of Theory or Creative Exploration', *English in Education*, 35 (1).

LINC (1992) *Language in the National Curriculum: Materials for Professional Development*, LINC.

—— (n.d.) 'The Process of Writing' and 'The Writing Repertoire', in *Language in the National Curriculum* (unpublished).

Little, R., Redsell, P. and Wilcock, E. (1986) *Contexts*, London and Oxford: Heinemann.

London Association for the Teaching of English (1996) *The Real Cost of SATs: a Report*, London: LATE.

Longhurst, D. (1988) ' "You base football player!": Shakespeare in Contemporary Popular Culture', in Holderness, G. (ed.) *The Shakespeare Myth*, Manchester: Manchester University Press, pp. 59–73.

Lucas, P. (1991) 'Reflection, New Practices and the Need for Flexibility in Supervising Student Teachers', *Journal of Further and Higher Education*, 15 (2), pp. 84–93.

Lunzer, E. and Gardner, K. (eds) (1979) *The Effective Use of Reading*, London: Heinemann Educational Books for the Schools Council.

Lynch, W. (1991) *Planning for Language*, Coventry: NCET.

McCulloch, R. (ed.) (1994) *English Literature A Level*, Cambridge: Pearson.

Macdonald, D. *et al.* (1989) 'Different Views of the Subject: A PGCE Perspective', *English and Media Magazine*, summer, pp. 15–17.

McIntyre, D. and Hagger, H. (1996) *Mentors in Schools: Developing the Profession of Teaching*, London: David Fulton.

McIntyre, D. and Hagger, H. (1993) 'Teachers' Expertise and Models of Mentoring', in McIntyre, D., Hagger, H. and Wilkin, M. *Mentoring: Perspectives on School-based Teacher Education*, London: Kogan Page.

McLaren, P. (1988) 'Culture or Canon? Critical Pedagogy and the Politics of Literacy', *Harvard Educational Review*, 58 (2).

McLaughlin, T. (1996) *Beyond the Reflective Teacher*, unpublished paper, Cambridge University Department of Education.

Marshall, B. (2000) 'A Rough Guide to English Teachers', *English in Education* 34 (1), pp. 24–41.

Masterman, L. (1980) *Teaching About Television*, London: Macmillan.

—— (1985) *Teaching the Media*, London: Comedia.

—— (1995) *Media Studies Teachers' Guide to Studies in Depth*, Manchester: NEAB.

Mathieson, M. (1975) *The Preachers of Culture*, London: Allen & Unwin.

Maybin, J. (1996) 'An English Canon?', in Maybin, J. and Mercer, N. *Using English: From Conversation to Canon*, London: Routledge.

Maybin, J. and Mercer, N. (1996) *Using English: From Conversation to Canon*, London: Routledge.

Meek, M. (1988) *How Texts Teach What Readers Learn*, Stroud: Thimble Press.

—— (1991) *On Being Literate*, London: The Bodley Head.

Mercer, N. and Swann, J. (1997) *Learning English: Development and Diversity*, London: Routledge.

Messenger Davis, M. (1989) *Television is Good for Your Kids*, London: Hilary Shipman.

Millard, E. (1997) *Differently Literate: Boys, Girls and the Schooling of Literacy*, London: Falmer Press.

Minns, H. (1991) *Primary Practice*, Coventry: NCET.

Mitchell, S. (1994) 'Argument in English Literature at A Level and Beyond', *English and Media Magazine*, summer, pp. 15–20.

Mole, J. (1990) *Catching the Spider*, London: Blackie.

Moss, J. (2000) 'How should critical theory inform English teaching?', in Davison, J. and Moss, J. *Issues in English Teaching*, London: Routledge.

National Association for the Teaching of English (NATE) (1993) *Move Back the Desks*, Sheffield: NATE.

—— (1994) 'GCSE English: The Background to the Current Concerns', *NATE News*, spring 1994, p. 9.

National Centre for Educational Technology (NCET) (1991) *Language Learning and IT*, Coventry: NCET.

National Curriculum Council (NCC) (1990) *English Non-statutory Guidance*, London: NCC.

—— (1993) *National Curriculum in English: The Case for Revising the Order*, London: NCC.

National Oracy Project (NOP) (1991) *Teaching Talking and Learning at Key Stage 3*, London: NCC/NOP.

—— (1993) *Teaching Talking and Learning at Key Stage 4*, London: NCC/NOP.

National Writing Project (1990) *Ways of Looking: Issues from the National Writing Project*, London: Nelson.

—— (1993) *Responding to and Assessing Writing*, London: Nelson.

Neelands, J. (1984) *Making Sense of Drama*, London: Heinemann.

—— (1992) *Learning Through Imagined Experience*, London: Hodder & Stoughton.

—— (1993) *Structuring Drama Work*, London: Cambridge University Press.

Nicholls, B. (1974) *Move*, London: Heinemann.

Norman, K. (ed.) (1992) *Thinking Voices*, London: Hodder & Stoughton.

OFSTED (1993) *The New Teacher in School*, London, HMSO.

O'Neill, C. (1977) *Drama Guidelines*, London: Heinemann.

Orme, D. (1995) *Specials! Romeo and Juliet*, Dunstable: Folens.

O'Sullivan, T., Dutton, B. and Rayner, P. (1994) *Studying the Media*, London: Arnold.

Palmer, D. J. (1965) *The Rise of English Studies*, Oxford: Oxford University Press.

Patten, J. (1992) Speech to Conservative Party Conference, 7 October 1992, London: Conservative Party Press Office.

Peel, R. and Hargreaves, S. (1995) 'Beliefs about English', *English in Education*, 29 (3), pp. 38–49.

Peet, M. and Robinson, D. (1990, 1992) *Essential Articles Nos 1–4*, Carlisle: Carel Press.

—— (1992) *Leading Questions*, London and Edinburgh: Nelson.

Peim, N. (1992) 'Reading and the World of LINC', *English in Education*, 26 (3), pp. 36–39.

Pennac, D. (1994) *Reads Like a Novel*, trans. D. Gunn, London: Quartet.

Perera, K. (1987) *Understanding Language*, Sheffield: NAAE/NATE.

Powling, C. and Styles, M. (1996) *A Guide to Poetry 0–13*, Reading: Books for Keeps and The Reading and Language Information Centre.

Prain, V. (1996) 'Selves to Discover, Selves to Invent: Rethinking Autobiographical Writing in the English Classroom', in *Changing English*, vol. 3, no. 1, London: Institute of Education, University of London, March, pp. 7–19.

Price, S. (1993) *Media Studies*, London: Pitman.

Protherough, R. and King, P. (1995) *The Challenge of English in the National Curriculum*, London: Routledge.

QCA (2000) *Language for Learning*, London: QCA.

QCA (2001) 'GCSE criteria for English and English literature', in *National Criteria for GCSE*, London: QCA.

Rawlins, G. and Rich, J. (1985) *Look, Listen and Trust*, London: Macmillan Education.

Reid, J-A., Forrestal, P. and Cook, J. (1989) *Small Group Learning in the Classroom*, London: Chalkface Press/English and Media Centre.

Reynolds, P. (1991) 'Unlocking the Box: Shakespeare on Film and Video', in Aers, L. and Wheale, N. *Shakespeare in the Changing Curriculum*, London: Routledge, pp. 189–203.

Richards, I. A. (1929) *Practical Criticism: A Study of Literary Judgment*, London: Routledge & Kegan Paul.

Richmond, J. (1992) 'Unstable Materials: The LINC Story', *English and Media Magazine*, spring 1992.

Roberts, A. E. and Barter, A. (1908) *The Teaching of English*, London: Blackie.

Robson, J., Simons, J. and Sohn-Rethel, M. (1990) 'Implementing a Media Education Policy across the Curriculum', in Buckingham, D. (ed.) *Watching Media Learning*, London: Falmer Press.

Rosen, B. (1988) *And None of It Was Nonsense*, London: Mary Glasgow.

Rosen, M. (1974) *Mind Your Own Business*, London: Andre Deutsch.

Rosenblatt, L. (1978) *The Reader, the Text, the Poem*, Illinois: Southern Illinois University Press.

Rudduck, J. (1991) 'The Landscape of Consciousness and the Landscape of Action: Tensions in Teacher Education', *British Educational Research Journal*, 17, p. 4.

Sampson, G. (1921) *English for the English*, Cambridge: Cambridge University Press.

SCAA (1994) *English in the National Curriculum: Draft Proposals*, London: SCAA.

—— (1996) *A Guide to the National Curriculum*, London: HMSO.

Scannell, V. (1971) *Selected Poems*, London: Allison and Busby.

Scholes, R. (1985) *Textual Power*, Newhaven and London: Yale University Press.

—— (1989) *Protocols of Reading*, Newhaven and London: Yale University Press.

Schön, D. (1983) *The Reflective Practitioner*, London: Temple Smith.

Schools Inquiry Commission (1868) *The Taunton Report*, London: HMSO.

Sealey, A. (1991) *Language in Context*, Coventry: NCET.

Searle, C. (1998) *None But our Words: Critical Literacy in Classroom and Community*, Buckingham: Open University Press.

Self, D. (1988) *New Guidelines: Romeo and Juliet*, London: Mary Glasgow.

Shepherd, C. and White, C. (1990, 1992) *Essential Articles Nos 1–4*, Carlisle: Carel Press.

—— (1991) *Novel Ideas*, Carlisle: Carel Press.

Shreeve, A. (1995) 'The Future of English', *English in Education*, 29 (2), pp. 1–2.

Simons, M. and Plackett, P. (eds) (1990) *The English Curriculum: Reading 1 Comprehension*, London: English and Media Centre.

Stephens, *et al.* (1990) *School*, London: English and Media Centre/NATE.

Stevenson, A. (2000) *Granny Scarecrow*, Northumberland: Bloodaxe Books.

Stibbs, A. (1995) 'The Specialness of Poetry', *English in Education*, 29 (3), pp. 14–19.

Style, M. (1989) *Collaboration and Writing*, Buckingham: Open University Press.

Styles, M. and Watson, V. (1996) *Talking Pictures*, London: Hodder & Stoughton.

Times Educational Supplement (1915) 'Children and the Cinematograph', 5 January.

Trudgill, P. (1975) *Accent, Dialect and the School*, London: Edward Arnold.

—— (1983) *On Dialect*, Oxford: Blackwell.

Teacher Training Agency (1997) *Training Curriculum and Standards for New Teachers*, London: TTA.

UCLES (1996) *Report on the June 1996 Examination SR21 (UK)*, Cambridge: UCLES.

Vygotsky, L.S. (1978) *Mind in Society*, Cambridge, Mass. and London: Harvard University Press.

—— (1986) *Thought and Language*, Cambridge, Mass. and London: MIT Press.

Wainwright, J. and Hutton, J. (1992) *In Your Own Words: Advanced Level English Language*, Walton on Thames and Edinburgh: Nelson.

Wall, P. (1996) *GCSE Media Studies*, London: Collins.

Wells, S. (ed.) (1988) *The Cambridge Companion to Shakespeare Studies*, Cambridge: Cambridge University Press.

West, A. and Dickey, A. (1990) *Redbridge High School English Department Handbook*, London: Borough of Redbridge Advisory Service.

Whiting, *et al.* (1996) *Partnership in Initial Teacher Education: A Topography*, London: University of London.

Whitten, W. and Whittaker, F. (1938) *Good and Bad English*, London: Newnes.

Wilkinson, A. (ed.) (1986) *The Writing of Writing*, Buckingham: Open University Press.

Williams, R. (1961) *Culture and Society*, London: Penguin.

Williamson, J. and Woodall, C. (1996) 'A Vision for English: Rethinking the Revised National Curriculum in the Light of Contemporary Critical Theory', *English in Education*, 30 (3) pp. 4–13.

Wood, D. (1992), Teaching Talk: How Modes of Teacher Talk Affect Pupil Participation', Norman, K. (ed.) (1992) *Thinking Voices*, London: Hodder & Stoughton.

Young Observer (1987) *Words on Water*, Harmondsworth: Puffin.

Index